Experiencing the Shepherd of Hermas

Ekstasis

Religious Experience
From Antiquity to the Middle Ages

Edited by
John R. Levison

Editorial Board
David Aune, Jan Bremmer, John Collins,
Dyan Elliott, Amy Hollywood, Sarah Iles Johnston,
Gabor Klaniczay, Paulo Nogueira,
Christopher Rowland, and Elliot R. Wolfson

Volume 10

Experiencing the Shepherd of Hermas

Edited by
Angela Kim Harkins and Harry O. Maier

DE GRUYTER

ISBN 978-3-11-150244-1
e-ISBN (PDF) 978-3-11-078074-1
e-ISBN (EPUB) 978-3-11-078075-8
ISSN 1865-8792

Library of Congress Control Number: 2022931827

Bibliographic Information published by the Deutsche Nationalbibliothek
The Deutsche Nationalbibliothek lists this publication in the Deutsche Nationalbibliografie;
Detailed bibliographic data are available in the Internet at http://dnb.dnb.de.

© 2024 Walter de Gruyter GmbH, Berlin/Boston
This volume is text- and page-identical with the hardback published in 2022.

www.degruyter.com

Acknowledgements

This volume began as a session at the annual meeting of the Society of Biblical Literature (SBL) in 2018, jointly hosted by the Religious Experience in Antiquity program unit and the Inventing Christianity program unit. We are grateful to the chairs of those SBL program units—Fred Tappenden and Catherine Playoust of the Religious Experience in Antiquity, and Paul Middleton and Taylor G. Petrey of the Inventing Christianity program units—for agreeing to host this session on Experiencing the Shepherd of Hermas. We wish to also acknowledge the assistance of Sheila Boll, Hayden Cowart, and Alexander Klee for their careful work on the formatting of notes and bibliography, and to Alice Meroz and the staff at De Gruyter for their invaluable help. Finally, we are grateful to the series editor, Jack Levison, and to Albrecht Doehnert at De Gruyter for accepting this volume into the Ekstasis series.

Abbreviations

AGJU	Arbeiten zur Geschichte des antiken Judentums und des Urchristentums
AGSU	Arbeiten zur Geschichte des Spätjudentums und Urchristentums
AJEC	Ancient Judaism and Early Christianity
APF	Archiv für Papyrusforschung
ANRW	Aufstieg und Niedergang der römischen Welt
ARA	Annual Review of Anthropology
ASE	Annali di Storia dell'Esegesi
BETL	Bibliotheca Ephemeridum Theologicarum Lovaniensium
Bib	Biblica
BibInt	Biblical Interpretation
BMSSEC	Baylor-Mohr Siebeck Studies in Early Christianity
CBQ	Catholic Biblical Quarterly
ConBOT	Coniectanea Biblica: Old Testament Series
CQ	Church Quarterly
CRINT	Compendia Rerum Iudaicarum ad Novum Testamentum
ECL	Early Christianity and its Literature
ETL	Ephemerides Theologicae Lovanienses
ExpTim	Expository Times
FAT	Forschungen zum Alten Testament
FRLANT	Forschungen zur Religion und Literatur des Alten und Neuen Testaments
GCS	Die griechischen christlichen Schriftsteller der ersten [drei] Jahrhunderte
HABES	Heidelberger althistorische Beiträge und epigraphische Studien
HNT	Handbuch zum Neuen Testament
HTR	Harvard Theological Review
JBL	Journal of Biblical Literature
JCT	Jewish and Christian Texts
JECS	Journal of Early Christian Studies
JHS	Journal of Hellenic Studies
JR	Journal of Religion
JRAI	Journal of the Royal Anthropological Institute
JSJ	Journal for the Study of Judaism
JSNT	Journal for the Study of the New Testament
JSPSup	Journal for the Study of the Pseudepigrapha Supplement Series
JTS	Journal of Theological Studies
KAV	Kommentar zu den Apostolischen Vätern
LCL	Loeb Classical Library
MTSR	Method & Theory in the Study of Religion
Neot	Neotestamentica
NHC	Nag Hammadi Codices
NovTSup	Supplements to Novum Testamentum
NTOA	Novum Testamentum et Orbis Antiquus
NTS	New Testament Studies

ODCC	*Oxford Dictionary of the Christian Church*
PTS	*Patristische Texte und Studien*
RThom	*Revue thomiste*
SBL	Society of Biblical Literature
SBLEJL	Society of Biblical Literature: Early Judaism and its Literature
SBLSP	*Society of Biblical Literature Seminar Papers*
SCO	*Study classici e orientali*
SNTSMS	Society for New Testament Studies Monograph Series
ST	*Studia Theologica*
STAC	Studien und Texte zu Antike und Christentum
SVTP	Studia in Veteris Testamenti Pseudepigrapha
SymS	Society of Biblical Literature Symposium Series
TDNT	*Theological Dictionary of the New Testament.* Edited by Gerhard Kittel, Gerhard Friedrich, and Geoffrey William Bromiley. Grand Rapids, MI: W.B. Eerdmans, 1985.
TENTS	Texts and Editions for New Testament Study
ThH	Théologie historique
TU	Texte un Untersuchungen
VC	*Vigiliae Christianae*
VCSup	Supplements to Vigiliae Christianae
WUNT	Wissenschaftliche Untersuchungen zum Neuen Testament
ZAC	*Zeitschrift für antikes Christentum*
ZNW	*Zeitschrift für die neutestamentliche Wissenschaft und die Kunde der älteren Kirche*
ZPE	*Zeitschrift für Papyrologie und Epigraphik*

Foreword

Among the writings to have come down to us from Christian antiquity, the Shepherd of Hermas is by all accounts a strange and most enigmatic text—strange and enigmatic, that is, to modern scholarship, which has been poring over its pages only to find what Robert J. Hauck described as the "many puzzles in this puzzling little book."[1] Some of the greatest intellects of the early Christian Church, such as Irenaeus of Lyon or the Alexandrians Clement and Origen, as well as many others after them, read the very same book with close attention and regarded it as an important catechetical and mystagogical work of great use to God-seekers. Indeed, if there is anything puzzling about the Shepherd, it is the fact that this text never scandalized the doctrinal certainties of its contemporaries or later orthodoxy.

Perhaps our comprehension of texts such as the Shepherd is hampered by the undeniable discontinuity between the implied readers of much of early Christian literature, and the actual ones in academia. The Shepherd has high expectations of its readers, some of which are are incomprehensible, unreasonable, or impossible for scholars. When Hermas is given a booklet to read and copy, and finds that he can only decipher and copy each letter in turn, unable to make out syllables and utterly frustrated in his attempt to read and understand, his solution is the following: "Fifteen days later, after I had fasted and earnestly asked the Lord, the meaning of the writing was revealed to me" (Vis. 2.2 [6.1]); When he has difficulty making sense of the parables, he addresses the *angelus interpres*: "I do not understand nor am I able to comprehend these parables *unless you explain them to me*" (Sim. 5.3 [56.1]). Needless to say, becoming existentially involved in the text, undergoing spiritual conversion, and exercising oneself ascetically is not what the guild of Early Christian Studies is set up to do. While the Shepherd claims to bear witness to divine revelation, a scholarly approach to ancient texts is by definition one that maintains a critical distance to the text.

The study of visionary experiences is one area where the academy has shifted in the past fifty years. A distinguished expert of Jewish apocalyptic literature, such as Michael Stone, who insists, in some of his seminal essays—"Apocalyptic, Vision, or Hallucination?" (1974), "On Reading an Apocalypse" (1989), and "A

---

[1] Robert J. Hauck, "The Great Fast: Christology in the Shepherd of Hermas," *Anglican Theological Review* 75 (1993): 187–98, 187.

Reconsideration of Apocalyptic Visions" (2003)—that "a kernel of actual visionary activity or analogous religious experience" lies "behind the pseudepigraphic presentations of the religious experiences attributed to apocalyptic seers by the Jewish apocalypses of the Second Temple period," knows full well that, back in 1974, "this was not the regnant view" and that "the religious life and experience ascribed authors are rarely taken into account."[2] By the time of his 2003 essay, however, a rather blunt declaration—that these "are religious works, by religious people, and we must consider religious experience when we interpret them"—had come to carry quite a bit of weight. We are more aware today of the blind spots inherent to the project of giving scholarly accounts of texts claiming to report spiritual experiences and setting out to draw and guide their ideal readers into similar experiences by means of the very act of reading.[3]

The essays in this volume published, quite fittingly, in De Gruyter's series, *Ekstasis: Religious Experience from Antiquity to the Middle Ages*, are representative of this new and welcome strand of scholarship. They revolve around key topics of import: the Self and Subjectivity, Visions and Experiences of the Divine, and the Experience of the Shepherd as a Text.[4] Even though scholars are, *qua* scholars, not about to (pretend to) recover a misremembered pneumatic tradition of overwhelming visions and ineffable revelations, or try to experience—at their writing desk?—the necessary breakdown and refashioning of the self, or trade in their libraries for the kind of apprehension of spiritual truths that one reads about in the Shepherd, we are, it seems, more disposed to taking seriously and wrestling productively with the range of experiences described in the Shepherd of Hermas.

Bogdan G. Bucur

---

[2] Michael E. Stone, "Apocalyptic, Vision, or Hallucination?" *Milla Wa Milla* 14 (1974): 47–56; repr. in *Selected Studies in Pseudepigrapha and Apocrypha with Special Reference to the Armenian Tradition* (Leiden: E. J. Brill, 1991), 419–28; idem, "A Reconsideration of Apocalyptic Visions," *HTR* 96 (2003): 167–80; quote from 167.
[3] Bogdan G. Bucur, "Scholarship on the Old Testament Roots of Trinitarian Theology: Blind Spots and Blurred Vision," in The Bible and Early Trinitarian Theology, ed. Christopher Beeley and Mark Weedman (Washington, DC: CUA Press, 2018), 29-49.
[4] Colleen Shantz, "Opening the Black Box: New Prospects for Analyzing Religious Experience," in *Experientia, Volume 2: Linking Text and Experience*, ed. Colleen Shantz and Rodney A. Werline (Atlanta, GA: SBL Press, 2012), 1–15; and Frances Flannery with Nicolae Roddy, Colleen Shantz, and Rodney A. Werline, "Introduction: Religious Experience, Past and Present," in *Experientia, Volume 1: Inquiry Into Religious Experience in Early Judaism and Christianity*, ed. Rodney Alan Werline, Frances Flannery, and Colleen Shantz (Atlanta: SBL Press, 2008), 1–10.

Table of Contents

Introduction —— 1

I The Shepherd, the Self, and Subjectivity

Giovanni B. Bazzana
Negotiating the Experience of Possession in Hermas's Shepherd —— 9

Jung H. Choi
A True Prophet as a Mouthpiece of the Spirit? Cultivating Virtue and Control —— 31

B. Diane Lipsett
Gender, Volubility, and Transformation in the Shepherd of Hermas —— 57

Harry O. Maier
The Affect and Happy Objects of the Shepherd of Hermas —— 73

II Visions and Experiences of the Divine

Luca Arcari
Psychotropic Elements in Hermas's First Two Visions: Between Experience and Culture —— 101

Angela Kim Harkins
Entering the Narrative World of Hermas's Visions —— 117

Aldo Tagliabue
Experience through Narrative in the Shepherd of Hermas —— 137

Jason Robert Combs
Shepherd of Hermas Vision 5 and the Christian Experience of Pagan Epiphany —— 153

Brittany E. Wilson
God's Multiple Forms: Divine Fluidity in the Shepherd of Hermas —— 171

III Experiencing the Shepherd as Text

Marianne Bjelland Kartzow
The Former Slave Hermas, Lady Church and 'the Book' —— 195

Dan Batovici
Authority, Fragmentation, Dilution: Experiencing an Apocalyptic Text in Late Antiquity —— 215

Bibliography —— 235

List of Contributors —— 257

Index of Subjects —— 261

Ancient Text Index —— 265

Introduction

The Shepherd of Hermas was possibly the most widely read and popular non-canonical Christian writing from the first centuries of the Common Era. It is dated to the late first to second century CE and is the longest work in the collection known as the Apostolic Fathers. In recent years new attention has been directed toward this important work, driven in part by new questions posed from a variety of disciplinary perspectives as well as a growing interest in the study of experience in ancient religion, and facilitated by a new critical edition of the text edited by Bart Ehrman in the Loeb Classical Library.[1] It would not be an exaggeration to say that the Shepherd is enjoying a renaissance in scholarly attention and study. The essays collected in this volume began as a panel of papers delivered in a joint session of the Religious Experience in Antiquity program unit and the Inventing Christianity program unit held at the 2018 meeting of the Society of Biblical Literature Annual Meeting in Denver, Colorado. Harry O. Maier responded to the papers presented at that meeting by Giovanni Bazzana, Aldo Tagliabue, Jason Combs, and Angela Kim Harkins. These studies constitute the core of this volume, to which additional essays were invited. The volume has been organized under three thematic headings: (1) The Shepherd, the Self, and Subjectivity; (2) Visions and Experiences of the Divine; and (3) Experiencing the Shepherd as Text.

The essays in this volume represent fresh perspectives on the Shepherd of Hermas. The contributions offer new ways of thinking about the question of lived experience of religion as it relates to the Shepherd and its relationship to other ancient writings. They reflect the academy's current interest in the study of self and subjectivity, in visionary experiences and related phenomena, and in the material transmission of texts and traditions. The volume contributes to the growing body of interdisciplinary studies of early Christian texts, especially those that explore the complexity of lived experience. The authors in the collection have approached the Shepherd from diverse methodological angles: evolutionary anthropology, emotion and affect studies, linguistics and communication theories, neurohistory, phenomenological narratology, cognitive literary theory

---

[1] Bart Ehrman's translation of the Shepherd of Hermas in the *Apostolic Fathers*, vol. 2, LCL 25 (Cambridge: Harvard University Press, 2003) is the default text and translation used in this collection, unless the author has noted otherwise. This collection follows the tradititional form of citation of the text that identifies Visions, Mandates, and Similitudes, followed in parentheses by the newer convention used in Molly Whittaker's critical edition, *Der Hirt des Hermas*, 2nd ed., GCS 48 (Berlin: Akademie-Verlag, 1967).

and enactive reading, postcolonialism, history of religions, intertextuality, ritual studies, material culture studies, liturgical studies, and manuscript reception history. These represent new avenues of investigation into this ancient popular writing that move beyond traditional historical-critical approaches and theological appraisals of its place in the development of Christian doctrine.

The first group of essays fall under the topic of "The Self and Subjectivity". The contributions by Giovanni B. Bazzana, Jung H. Choi, B. Diane Lipsett, and Harry O. Maier examine the topic of the self and subjectivity in the Shepherd of Hermas using different critical approaches. The first two essays by Giovanni Bazzana and Jung Choi discuss the Shepherd in light of the phenomenon of prophecy and possession in early Christ religion. Bazzana's "Negotiating the Experience of Possession in Hermas's Shepherd," uses cross-cultural anthropological studies of spirit possession to describe the worldview in which spiritual entities regularly take up residence in persons or are under their command. Bazzana uses this model of spirit possession to analyze ethical instructions in the Mandates (the second section of the Shepherd's tripartite writing). He relates possession to Hermas's understanding of "spirits" and links it to oracular and divinatory powers the Shepherd describes. This model depends on the theoretical understanding that Hermas's self is porous—that is, subject to influence and control by external agents. Bazzana's study asks us to move beyond a modern understanding where language of spirits might be interpreted as referring to psychological states to consider Hermas's experiences of spirits as reflecting an entirely different conception of the self.

The second essay by Jung H. Choi, "A True Prophet as a Mouthpiece of the Spirit? Cultivating Virtue and Control," explores the phenomenon of oracular and divinatory experience in the Shepherd through a model of prophecy. Like Bazzana, Choi argues in favor of a porous model of the self, in which human and divine agencies are negotiated and constructed. Her study considers how prayer, fasting, and virtue function in a preparatory way for prophetic experience—an ability, some early Christians taught, that every Christ believer can attain with the right self-cultivation. This model is then compared with similar requirements for reception of oracular power that other Greek and Roman authors outline. She concludes her essay with a discussion of two of Origen's homilies. Like Hermas, Origen stresses the importance of self-cultivation in the ability to receive divine power to prophesy.

The topic of self and subjectivity continues with Diane Lipsett's essay, "Gender, Volubility, and Transformation in the Shepherd of Hermas." She investigates the construction of the gendered self in the Shepherd and the way it relates to self-cultivation and self-restraint (ἐγκράτεια). Lipsett notes that the admonishment to masculinity in Vis 1.4.3 (4.3) is in tension with Hermas's prolixity, a trait that his contemporaries would have associated with being feminine. The repetitive and copious speech of Hermas and his interlocutors offers insight into the practices of care of the self as a recurring exercise in self-scrutiny and exercise of virtue. While the redundant quality of the literary style of the Shepherd has been interpreted as the mark of its orality, Lipsett suggests that it also may be seen as an invitation to a particular kind of reading practice. The sheer amount of text presented in the Shepherd speaks to a textual resistance to "a finalization of the utterance" (quoting Bakhtin). Metanoia is time-limited and transformation is time-consuming, realized by reading and through repetitive, recursive, reiterative practices of scrutinizing the self and the church. The talkative prophet and audacious questioner point to a path toward masculinity but by means of an alternative route.

The fourth essay in this section on the self and subjectivity is Harry O. Maier's "The Affect and Happy Objects of the Shepherd of Hermas." In this study, Maier draws on affect theory, critical spatiality, and cultural anthropological notions of the partible or dividual self to analyse Hermas's vision and similitude of the tower. The anthropological concept of the partible or dividual self, in contrast to the Cartesian model, focuses on the cultural construction of the subject capable of being in several places at the same time, manifested through objects or other phenomena. Hermas is dividual. He experiences the world around him not as a bounded self, but as a porous one in relation to objects, characters, and environments. Together they form a constellation of affects. Drawing on Sara Ahmed's phenomenology of space—specifically her notion of "happy objects"—Maier considers the ways in which Hermas' orientation to objects and characters creates a dynamic, processual self, created through diverse experiences and the vital forces that absorb him.

The next five essays investigate the theme of "Visions and Experiences of the Divine" in the Shepherd. This section begins with Luca Arcari's theoretical discussion of the way Hermas's visionary experiences uses the social mechanism known as psychotrophy, namely, a wide range of cultural practices that can effect changes in the brain-body system. Included in this broad category of psychotropic experiences are the cultural experiences of enslavement in the Roman world and the larger ritual patterns that shaped that imperial culture, both of which can be seen in Vision 1 (1.1–4.3). Scribal practices of reading and copying are presented as psychotropic experiences in Arcari's discussion of Vision 2 (5.1–8.3). His study draws attention to the important consideration of the social and cultural context of Hermas and how the author's visions can themselves be understood as participating in a psychotrophic mechanism for the refashioning of prior visionary materials. Arcari thus offers a theoretical model for understanding how visions can be understood as both the product of social mechanisms and the means by which brain-body systems were changed and transformed.

The next two essays in this section by Angela Kim Harkins and Aldo Tagliabue use the cognitive literary approach known as enactive reading to analyze the experience of reading the Shepherd as narrative, with special attention to the experience of reading of Hermas's visions. Harkins's essay, "Entering the Narrative World of Hermas's Visions" applies enactive reading to Hermas's Visions 1 (1.1–4.3) and 3 (9.1–21.4). The enactive reading approach highlights the constructive process of mental imaging and is based on what is known about the cognitive process of visual perception. Seeing is not a single coherent experience like a snapshot, but one that is constructed from the viewer's past experiences of the world. Harkins's essay describes how modern scholars fill in the narrative gaps with their own experiences and expectations. In contrast to the discipline-specific questions of scholars, ordinary readers may willingly suspend their disbelief and become immersed in the narrative. Using Arcari's discussion of 'visionary *habitus*' (2020), Harkins then proposes that the immersive experience of reading can be imagined as part of the process of generating further visions from first-person visionary reports. Following Harkins's essay, Aldo Tagliabue's essay, "Experience through Narrative in Shepherd of Hermas" discusses Hermas's encounter with the beast in Vision 4 (22.1–24.7). Hermas's experiences are described in a way that expresses his sensory perceptions of the events as they take place. He presents it as an immersive narrative in which the reader and hearer experience a changed perception of time. Tagliabue argues that this can be understood as an experience of timelessness, in effect, "a glimpse of the divine nature of the spiritual church."

The next two essays in this section are by Jason Combs and Brittany Wilson, both of which examine the experience of the divine in the Shepherd. Jason Combs's essay, "Shepherd of Hermas, Vision 5 and the Christian Experience of Pagan Epiphany," looks at the phenomenon of angelic encounter, as it appears in Vision 5 (25.1–7) and in other ancient comparanda. Combs argues that the encounter between Hermas and the shepherd in Vision 5 can be understood as an "early Christian polemic against pagan epiphanies." The encounter is analyzed as a 'dream-text', a retelling that follows the cultural patterns and norms of its time. Combs argues that Hermas's vision of the shepherd resembles that of pagan epiphanies. Especially important for his analysis is the hesitation that Hermas shows toward the shepherd, one that differs strikingly from Hermas's previous encounters with divine beings in the Book of Visions, all of whom he regards positively. Combs reads the reference to the shepherd in the Fifth Vision together with the information that appears later in the work, that the figure of the shepherd is an evil angel, found in the Sim. 6.1.5–6.2.2 (61.4–62.2). The association of the shepherd with a diabolical being is then placed alongside multiple comparanda in which a shepherd is an epiphany of a pagan deity or hero. Combs's essay is followed by Brittany Wilson's essay "God's Multiple Forms: Divine Fluidity in the Shepherd of Hermas," which offers a different account of the multiple ways the divine is described in the Shepherd of Hermas. Using studies of Israel's God by Benjamin Sommer 2009, Wilson argues that these depictions are concretely described and reflect an experiential knowing of the divine—not simply symbolic and abstract references to a bodiless God. According to Wilson, these multiple references to the divine in the Shepherd point to the phenomenon of divine fluidity, one that can still be understood within the context of monotheism.

The volume concludes with two essays that examine the theme of "Experiencing the Shepherd as Text." These studies consider questions of the cultural representation of texts and the transmission of the Shepherd through time. In "The Former Slave Hermas, Lady Church and 'the Book': Rethinking the Visions with Intersectionality and Book History," Marianne Bjelland Kartzow considers references to 'the book' in the Shepherd. In the first two visions Hermas has several experiences with books: the Lady reads to him or reads from one; he is told to read another; he borrows and copies a book because of his poor memory; he is told to add to the copy he is producing; books are sent to different places. Kartzow discusses book reading, production, copying, adding, editing, and circulating by non-elites, women, and (manumitted) slaves in the period contemporary with the Shepherd. Using an intersectional analysis, she considers the ways gender and social status were at work in complex ways in ancient book production. Her essay explores the relationship between the Divine Lady and Hermas by looking at what role 'the book' plays as an artifact, as a container of meaning, a symbolic tool, a mediator, and as a means of power.

The final essay in the collection is Dan Batovici's "Authority, Fragmentation, Dilution: Experiencing an Apocalyptic Text in Late Antiquity." He moves beyond the usual questions about the canonical status of the Shepherd in the early church to consider its popularity and its production even after the content of the canon was largely settled. Batovici proposes an evaluation of the Shepherd's authority in view of its use in early and late antique Christianity. He draws attention, one the one hand, to the remarkable variety of its material reception contexts, and on the other to the interplay between the genre of the Shepherd and the ways in which the writing was taken an authoritative text in ancient testimonies. Batovici moves from experiences that are described *within* the Shepherd to the experience that later readers had of the text, its transmission and its circulation in its many afterlives.

The editors hope that the essays in *Experiencing the Shepherd of Hermas* will stimulate new questions that go beyond and complement the usual historical and theological approaches to this text. The methodological approaches represented in this volume reflect the diverse interests of contemporary scholars who bring new voices and perspectives to the study of the Shepherd and the ancient world.

Angela Kim Harkins
Harry O. Maier

I The Shepherd, the Self, and Subjectivity

Giovanni B. Bazzana
Negotiating the Experience of Possession in Hermas's Shepherd

The Shepherd of Hermas is unquestionably one of the most important writings stemming from the early Christ movement. It is also a text that has suffered from a massive scholarly neglect both for its being relegated in the artificial category of the so-called "Apostolic Fathers" and for the frankly idiosyncratic nature of many features and themes included in it.[1] Thankfully, in recent years the study of the Shepherd seems to be experiencing a real renaissance, which has involved important issues such as the reevaluation of its dating and of its christology among other things.[2]

As attested by some of the contributions collected in the present volume, an aspect of Hermas's work that is attracting significant scholarly interest is the way in which this author represents the religious experience of himself and of his group.[3] Not surprisingly for the Shepherd, such a representation is quite peculiar, with features that equally puzzle and fascinate scholars because they are tempted by the opportunity of finally getting reliable information on the life of early Christ believers and at the same time are frustrated by the many oddities encountered in the writing of Hermas. The present contribution is an attempt to participate in such a conversation by trying at the same time to elucidate a few ideas included in the Shepherd and to place them within the overall context of the early Christ movement. It goes without saying that even this task, limited as it is, is too broad for the space at my disposal here. Thus, this essay should be taken as a sketch in need of further exploration and deepening.

---

[1] On the artificial nature of the "Apostolic Fathers" collection and its modern construction, see now David Lincicum, "The Paratextual Invention of the Term 'Apostolic Fathers'," *JTS* 66 (2015): 139–48, and Clare K. Rothschild, *New Essays on the Apostolic Fathers*, WUNT 375 (Tübingen: Mohr-Siebeck 2017), 7–33.

[2] On christology, see Bogdan G. Bucur, "The Son of God and the Angelomorphic Holy Spirit: A Rereading of the Shepherd's Christology," *ZNW* 98 (2007): 121–43, and, on the dating, Andrew Gregory, "Disturbing Trajectories: *1 Clement*, the *Shepherd of Hermas*, and the Development of Early Roman Christianity," in *Rome in the Bible and the Early Church*, ed. Peter Oakes (Carlisle: Paternoster, 2002), 142–66.

[3] See also Jörg Rüpke, "Fighting for Differences: Forms and Limits of Religious Individuality in the 'Shepherd of Hermas'," in *The Individual in the Religions of the Ancient Mediterranean*, ed. Jörg Rüpke (Oxford: Oxford University Press, 2013), 315–40.

https://doi.org/10.1515/9783110780741-005

Throughout this contribution (and as indicated in the title), one will refer to the religious experience described by Hermas as *possession*. One major claim presented here is that *possession* constitutes a crucial element in the construction and conceptualization of religious experience in the Shepherd, even though obviously the category does not cover all the multifaceted and rich experience of the relationship between divine and human worlds that one encounters in the work of Hermas. It goes without saying that the label *possession* is in large part a modern construction. As such, several scholars have already explored its genealogy, rooted in the early encounter between European colonizers and ethnographers on one side and non-European religious traditions and cultures on the other.[4] This encounter happened at the very moment when European philosophers were busy building the early modern understanding of a *buffered* self, endowed with autonomous moral agency and free from external influences that could destabilize it. At the same time, pointing at *possession* phenomena within non-European cultures was a way to deny the indigenous peoples' capability to "own" themselves—a view that ultimately served to justify their colonization and enslavement. The critical apprehension of such a genealogy should give pause to any facile use of the terminology of *possession* even in the field of early Christian studies, given how deeply implicated Christian traditions have been in the entire process.[5] In the present analysis *possession* terminology will be retained for two main reasons. First, it is well established in the parlance of early Christian scholarship and thus changing it would render even more difficult an already complicated task. Second (and arguably more importantly from an intellectual standpoint), in more recent times, as noted by Christopher Johnson as well, the language of *possession* and *alienation* has been successfully employed in some philosophical traditions as a powerful critical tool against European modernist projects.[6] There is no space here for a full treatment of such an important theme, but it is this author's hope that the present essay may serve as a building block for this conversation.

Of course, in its constructedness, *possession* is no different from many other categories that one uses all the time in the study of religion. To employ any cat-

---

[4] For a compelling critical exploration of this genealogy, see Paul C. Johnson, "Toward an Atlantic Genealogy of 'Spirit Possession'," in *Spirited Things: The Work of "Possession" in Afro-Atlantic Religions*, ed. Paul C. Johnson (Chicago: University of Chicago, 2014), 23–45.
[5] See the balanced rejoinder to Johnson in Michael Lambek, "Afterword," *ibidem*, 261–62, with his call to anthropologists to work *through* and not *around* the problematic genealogy of "possession."
[6] See Karl Marx, *Scritti sull'alienazione. Per la critica della società capitalistica*, ed. Marcello Musto (Donzelli: Rome, 2018).

egory is after all an exercise in comparison. According to a well-known *dictum* of Jonathan Z. Smith, comparison itself is the recourse to a disciplined exaggeration and distortion of some features within our sources in order to illuminate aspects that one deems interesting and important.[7] In the case of *possession*, the present goal is that of highlighting some aspects of the religious experience of the Shepherd (and of other early Christ texts, for that matter) that are otherwise obscured when they are looked at through the prism provided by our familiarity with modern western ontological and epistemological categories.

In this perspective, *possession* will be defined here broadly as any situation in which an entity stronger than a human being exerts a hold on him or her.[8] While there are numerous instances of this phenomenon in the writings belonging to the early Christ movement, it is important to keep in mind that possession will be looked at here in light of the innovative work done on it in recent years by anthropologists and ethnographers.[9] The modern genealogy of possession, fueled both by Christian theology[10] and the modern subjectification described above, has often cast the phenomenon as totally negative, implying a complete subjection of the human 'hosts' to their 'spirits.' However, a number of recent ethnographic studies of possession, conducted in the most diverse cultural contexts, have called into question these traditional assumptions. For one thing, anthropologists have noted that possession cannot be cast only as a form of reaction to the pressure experienced by individuals in the face of social or political marginalization and oppression.[11] While the socio-political dimensions of possession should not be discarded out of hand either, the phenomenon of possession performs also an unequivocally *positive* work in many cultures. Ethnograph-

---

[7] Literally, "comparison is a disciplined exaggeration in the service of knowledge," in Jonathan Z. Smith, "Re: Corinthians," in *Redescribing Paul and the Corinthians*, ed. Ron Cameron and Merrill P. Miller, ECL 5 (Atlanta: SBL Press, 2011), 17–33, here 27.
[8] I am borrowing an anthropological definition, offered initially by Janice Boddy, "Spirit Possession Revisited: Beyond Instrumentality," *ARA* 23 (1994): 407–34, here 407.
[9] Besides the already-mentioned Boddy and Lambek, see also the works of Diana Espírito Santo, "Imagination, Sensation, and the Education of Attention among Cuban Spirit Mediums," *Ethnos* 77 (2012): 252–71, and Adeline Masquelier, "From Hostage to Host: Confessions of a Spirit Medium in Niger," *Ethos* 30 (2002): 49–76.
[10] On the complex nature of the Christian tradition outside theological systematization, even in modern times, see Moshe Sluhovsky, *Believe Not Every Spirit. Possession, Mysticism, and Discernment in Early Modern Catholicism* (Chicago: University of Chicago, 2007).
[11] This is the substance of Boddy's call to move beyond the 'instrumentality' of earlier (and very influential to this day, for instance in New Testament studies) analyses, such as the one provided in Ioan M. Lewis, *Ecstatic Religion. A Study of Shamanism and Spirit Possession*, 3rd ed. (London: Routledge 2003).

ic study and writing have showed that through possession human beings can be in contact with the Other, can re-actualize past experiences of their groups and can even ground their selves as moral agents and ethical subjects. It goes without saying that the writings belonging to the early Christ movement do display a number of cases of possession that have a different character. These can be qualified as *negative* and thus in need of exorcism. But it is equally clear that the Christ groups knew also a more *positive* type of possession, which was crucial in giving shape to their religious experience and in grounding their communal life.[12] The latter, in particular, is another aspect of possession that has been illuminated by recent ethnographic works. Possession is never a cultural phenomenon that is limited to the experience of disjointed individuals. On the contrary, possession is defined by a constantly shifting negotiation along the three sides of a triangle that is formed through the interaction of the human *host*, the possessing *spirit*, and their larger audiences.[13]

The present analysis of possession within Hermas's work will focus on these two aspects that have been just presented. On the one hand, one will attend to the *positive* (and not merely reactionary) work performed by possession in the patterns of Hermas's religious experience and, on the other hand, to the communal negotiation that constituted the authentication of the effectiveness and reality of possession.

Before moving on to this, however, a few quick words of introduction to the Shepherd are in order to declare the assumptions on which the present examination is built. As noted above, this writing is experiencing a significant resurgence of scholarly interest in recent years. Among the aspects of Hermas's work that are being revised and rediscussed, one should certainly count the unity and the dating of the writing. As far as the first aspect is concerned, the present treatment will focus predominantly on the Mandates, leaving aside, for the time being, the Visions and the Similitudes. In particular, the first section of the Shepherd (the Visions) does not seem to present an understanding of possession similar to the one seen in the remaining two. This might be counted as an argument in favor of the hypothesis that the Mandates and the Similitudes were composed earlier and independently from the rest of the work. There are other, more compelling pieces of evidence supporting such a hypothesis particularly in

---

[12] For a more thorough treatment of this point, with examples drawn from mainly New Testament texts, see Giovanni B. Bazzana, *Having the Spirit of Christ: Spirit Possession and Exorcism in the Early Christ Groups* (New Haven: Yale University Press, 2020).

[13] For a good treatment, see Kristina Wirtz, *Ritual, Discourse, and Community in Cuban Santería: Speaking a Sacred World* (Gainesville, FL: University of Florida Press, 2007).

regard to the peculiar textual tradition of the Shepherd,[14] but reaching a definite solution on this specific aspect is largely irrelevant with respect to the main focus of the present contribution. Similarly, it appears that the traditional dating of Hermas's work should be revised in light of new critical observations and discoveries.[15] With respect to the present contribution—again—the determination of a precise dating for the Shepherd is largely not an issue. However, it is worth stressing that the following observations tend to envisage a similar conceptualization of possession phenomena in Hermas and in other very early texts belonging to the Christ movement (and in the so-called 'authentic' letters of Paul, in particular). On these grounds, one might be led to suggest that the traditional dating of (at least parts of) the Shepherd should be revised, moving tentatively the composition of at least the Mandates section towards the end of the first or the beginning of the second century.

The present essay will have two main sections of unequal length. The first one will illustrate how the theme of possession occurs in the doctrine of the "spirits" developed by Hermas in his Mandates. There, the experience of possession does not serve merely the purpose of representing what we would call psychological states but goes well beyond that in constituting the readers of the Shepherd as moral agents and subjects. This is analogous to what one can see for the Christ possession that appears as a foundational building block in Paul's 'authentic' letters.[16] The final section of the paper will come briefly to the facet of possession that is most often singled out as the hallmark of the phenomenon particularly in early Christian studies: oracular and divinatory activity.[17] The Shepherd addresses this issue in the eleventh Mandate, which constitutes one of the clearest ancient descriptions of the trilateral negotiation that constitutes possession as a legitimate and *real* phenomenon. Another document belonging to the early Christ movement that reports about the same negotiation is obviously 1 Cor 12–14 and the paper will conclude with a comparison and contrast between the ritual negotiation described by Paul and the one described by Hermas.

---

14 Antonio Carlini, "P. Michigan 130 (inv. 44–H) e il problema dell'unicità di redazione del Pastore di Erma," *La parola del passato* 208 (1983): 29–37.
15 Antonio Carlini, "Testimone e testo: il problema della datazione di PIand I 4 e il Pastore di Erma," *SCO* 42 (1992): 17–30. Interestingly, Carlini's paleographic observations would call for an earlier dating of the Mandates in particular.
16 As already noted in the seminal study by Adolf Deissmann, *Die Neutestamentliche Formel "in Christo Jesu"* (Marburg: Elwert, 1892). For an updated reconsideration of the same themes, see John Ashton, *The Religion of Paul the Apostle* (New Haven, CT: Yale University Press, 2000).
17 See, on this, the very influential contribution of David E. Aune, *Prophecy in Early Christianity and in the Ancient Mediterranean* (Grand Rapids, MI: Eerdmans, 1983).

"Possession" in the Mandates

Mandate 5 (33-34)

In Mandate 5 (33-34) Hermas is exhorted by the Shepherd to be 'patient' (μακρόθυμος) as a way to avoid being taken over by 'irascibility' (ὀξυχολία).[18] This description of the two contrasting impulses can be understood in psychological terms, but that reading would miss a significant part of the story. In fact, the language as well as some of the concepts employed here have roots both in Stoic moral teachings and—as shown recently and thoroughly by Clare Rothschild—in medical writing of the second century CE.[19] Rothschild identifies a Galenic background for the notion of ὀξυχολία employed by Hermas in Mandate 5 (33-34). This background, in turn, implies that having recourse to a modern idea of psychological states would be reductionistic, since the very medical context calls for a more integrated understanding of the relationship between body and mind/soul.

Rothschild's observations, while undeniably correct and foundational, can be extended. At first, it is worth noting that the mechanics of the opposition sketched by Hermas in Mandate 5 (33-34) present some features that would not sit well either in a Stoic or a medical context. For one thing, both 'patience' and 'irascibility' are introduced with the terminology and the actions that are characteristic of 'spirits' (πνεύματα).[20] Most importantly, it appears that for Hermas both these impulses literally 'occupy' a human being. In this perspective, one could argue (and it has been often argued in scholarship on Hermas) that the Shepherd is simply recasting in metaphorical and imaginative terms some *regular* psychological phenomena. However, one must consider that such an understanding of Hermas's exposition might be biased by modern and Western notions of the *regular* mechanics of human psychology. Indeed, Rothschild

---

[18] For this translation, see the careful lexical discussion in Rothschild, *New Essays*, 233–34, n. 32.
[19] Rothschild, *New Essays*, 227–44.
[20] Rothschild calls for a translation of πνεῦμα as 'breath' in line with her overall physiological and medical reading of 'irascibility' and Mandate 5 (33-34) more in general (*New Essays*, 244). But 'breath' would not fit well with the use of πνεῦμα or analogous phrases in the following Mandate, which will be examined shortly. It is likely that Hermas is playing with the multiple nuances of a term like πνεῦμα in a way not different from the one adopted by other Greek writers in antiquity (for an example contiguous in terms of chronology and socio-religious location, see the Gospel of John).

has shown—as noted above—that the medical and, more in general, scientific sophistication of Mandate 5 (33-34) is quite significant, when one takes into due consideration its antiquity.²¹

For the purposes of the present treatment, it is noteworthy that the behavior of these two 'spirits' seems altogether non-metaphorical. For instance, in Mand. 5.2.4–5 (34.4–5), this is how the Shepherd describes to Hermas the cohabitation of the two 'spirits' within the same human being:

> Ἡ δὲ ὀξοχυλία πρῶτον μὲν μωρά ἐστιν, ἐλαφρά τε καὶ ἄφρων. Ἔιτα ἐκ τῆς ἀφροσύνης γίνεται πικρία, ἐκ δὲ τῆς πικρίας θυμός, ἐκ δὲ τοῦ θυμοῦ ὀργή, ἐκ δὲ τῆς ὀργῆς μῆνις. Ἔιτα ἡ μῆνις αὕτη ἐκ τοσούτων κακῶν συνισταμένη γίνεται ἁμαρτία μεγάλη καὶ ἀνίατος. 5. Ὅταν γὰρ ταῦτα τὰ πνεύματα ἐν ἑνὶ ἀγγείῳ κατοικῇ, οὗ καὶ τὸ πνεῦμα τὸ ἅγιον κατοικεῖ, οὐ χωρεῖ τὸ ἄγγος ἐκεῖνο, ἀλλ' ὑπερπλεονάζει.

> At the outset irascibility is insipid, insubstantial, and imperceptible.²² And then, from out of nowhere comes bitterness, from bitterness anger, from anger wrath, and from wrath rage. Then this rage, which is compounded of such evil things, becomes a great and incurable sin. 5. For when these spirits dwell in one and the same vessel with the holy spirit, the vessel no longer has sufficient space but overflows.

These many 'spirits' have personalities and preferences: in particular, they cannot coexist within the same 'vessel.'²³ Such a description of psychological states and dynamics is the complete opposite of what one can find at the foundation of modern western anthropological paradigms. That being said, it is important to stress that such a difference does not depend on Hermas's inadequate or metaphoric understanding of *true* human psychology. On the contrary, one may claim that the representation is so divergent because it relies on an ontological and anthropological paradigm that is the complete opposite of the one hegemonic within western modernity. Instead of conceiving of the self as an autonomous and 'buffered' monad whose feelings and modifications have all an internal origin,²⁴

---

21 Obviously, this refutes Brox's judgment that Hermas is "banalizing" or "popularizing" here, for which see Norbert Brox, *Der Hirt des Hermas*, KAV 7 (Göttingen: Vandenhoeck & Ruprecht, 1991), 221.
22 Rothschild's translation of this sentence is much more consistent and precise (*New Essays*, 240).
23 On the complexity of this terminological choice (which has different counterparts in the Greek of Hermas), see below.
24 The phrase 'buffered self' and the general idea used to describe hegemonic modern conceptions is taken from the influential analysis of Charles Taylor, *A Secular Age* (Cambridge, MA: Harvard University Press, 2007), 3–6

Hermas (like almost all other ancient authors) conceives of it as fundamentally porous and susceptible to be influenced and controlled by external agents.[25]

The anthropological paradigm grounded on 'porousness' is at the root of possession as well. Several ethnographies of possession (produced by scholars whose field of expertise ranges from shamanism in Central Asia to Cuban *Santerìa* or to the African *zar* cults, just to name a few[26]) have recently emphasized this aspect of the phenomenon. These studies show compellingly that, in order to achieve a more adequate understanding of other cultures as well as of ancient texts (such as the Shepherd), one needs to abandon or at the very least sideline modern western ontologies.[27]

In this perspective, it is worth considering how pervasive is the possession-related terminology employed by Hermas in the passage quoted above. The most evident feature is certainly the designation of the states (which we would call 'emotions') as πνεύματα with the accompanying emphasis put on their personality and autonomy from their human 'host.' To this observation it can be added that the very terminology of 'inhabiting' (κατοικεῖν literally in the passage quoted above) is widely used in describing possession in ancient documents as well as in modern ethnographic accounts. The same can be said with respect to the designation of the human host, here as a 'vessel' (αγγεῖον).[28] Other writings belonging to the early Christ movement make an analogous reference. For instance, this happens in the well-known saying of "binding the strong man," which is consistently associated in the synoptic tradition with the infamous ac-

---

[25] For this notion, see also Denise K. Buell, "The Microbes and Pneuma That Therefore I Am," in *Divinanimality: Animal Theory, Creaturely Theology*, ed. Stephen D. Moore (New York, NY: Fordham University, 2014), 63–87.

[26] Besides the studies mentioned earlier, see also Janice Boddy, *Wombs and Alien Spirits: Women, Men, and the Zâr Cults of Northern Sudan* (Madison, WI: University of Wisconsin Press, 1989); Michael Lambek, "How to Make Up One's Mind: Reason, Passion, and Ethics in Spirit Possession," *University of Toronto Quarterly* 70 (2010): 720–41, and Ana M. Bacigalupo, *Thunder Shaman: Making History with Mapuche Spirits in Chile and Patagonia* (Austin: University of Texas Press, 2016).

[27] For an exemplary methodological analysis at the crossroads between ancient texts and ethnographies of possession in the all-important case of India, see Fredrick M. Smith, *The Self Possessed: Deity and Spirit Possession in South Asian Literature and Civilization* (New York City: Columbia University Press, 2006).

[28] Rothschild (*New Essays*, 240n69) wants to render the Greek term as 'cavity' (indicating a specific space within the human body and in line with the general medical tenor of the passage), but it is worth noting that Hermas uses elsewhere σκεῦος, which cannot be but a 'vessel.' It seems that Hermas is using the medical terminology to make sense and express the experience of possession.

cusation that Jesus might perform exorcisms in league with Beelzebul.[29] Thus, the "strong man" of the saying is identified as Satan and it is significant that the property that is then taken away from him is designated again as 'vessels.' Even though there the Greek is σκεύη (which is, however, used in the Shepherd with the same meaning[30]), the referent is the same: human beings who are possessed by an evil spirit. In Hermas as in the Gospel passages, the choice of such a terminology objectifies human hosts in a way that is not surprising when one pays attention to the widespread cultural understanding of possession. Again, ethnographic accounts confirm that similarly unbalanced power relationships are often used cross-culturally to conceptualize the phenomenon. Thus, it is very common to encounter descriptions of the relationship between a 'spirit' and its 'host' in terms of the relationship between husband and wife or between masters and their slaves.[31] I will come back on this crucial feature later in the essay, but one needs to delve a little more in the rest of the Mandates to show that the language and idea of possession does not appear only in Mandate 5 (33-34).

Mandate 12 (44-49)

In Mandate 12 (44-49), the Shepherd sets up for Hermas another ethical binary, which is fundamentally similar to the one just encountered in Mandate 5 (33-34). This time, however, the opposition is not between two contrasting 'spirits,' but between two 'desires' (ἐπιθυμίαι), one evil and one good. Also, the moral fault that is produced by the bad side of the binary is different in Mandate 12 (44-49): while in Mandate 5 (33-34) the instruction was about avoiding irascibility and ultimately rage, in this case the exhortation is to avoid excess in material appetites related to sexuality and food. But, does the use of the language of 'desire' here mean that this Mandate is closer to the modern understanding of psy-

---

29 "But no one is able to enter a strong one's house and steal his vessels (σκεύη), unless he first binds the strong one; then he will thoroughly plunder his house" (Mark 3:27//Matt 12:29//Luke 11:21–22). For a more sustained analysis of this passage in relationship to the Beelzebul pericope, see Bazzana, *Having the Spirit of Christ*, 45–51.
30 Indeed, Hermas does it right before the passage quoted above, but still within Mand. 5.1.2 (33.2).
31 See, for instance, J. Lorand Matory, "Government by Seduction: History and Tropes of 'Mounting' in the Oyo-Yoruba," in *Modernity and Its Malcontents: Ritual and Power in Postcolonial Africa*, ed. Jean Comaroff, John L. Comaroff (Chicago: University of Chicago Press, 1993), 58–85.

chological states? Let us take a look at how the issue is described, for instance, in Mand. 12.1.1–2 (44.1–2):

> Ἄρον ἀπὸ σεαυτοῦ πᾶσαν ἐπιθυμίαν πονηράν, ἔνδυσαι δὲ τὴν ἐπιθυμίαν τὴν ἀγαθὴν καὶ σεμνήν. Ἐνδεδυμένος γὰρ τὴν ἐπιθυμίαν ταύτην μισήσεις τὴν πονηρὰν ἐπιθυμίαν καὶ χαλιναγωγήσεις αὐτὴν καθὼς βούλει. 2. [...] Δαπανᾷ δὲ τοὺς τοιούτους τοὺς μὴ ἔχοντας ἔνδυμα τῆς ἐπιθυμίας τῆς ἀγαθῆς, ἀλλὰ ἐμπεφυρμένους τῷ αἰῶνι τούτῳ. Τούτους οὖν παραδίδωσιν εἰς θάνατον.

> Remove from yourself every evil desire, but clothe yourself with the desire that is good and reverent. For when you clothe yourself with this desire you will hate the evil desire and put a bridle on it as you wish. 2. [...] (The evil desire) exhausts all who are not clothed with good desire but are enmeshed in this age. People like this it delivers over to death.

Instead of the 'inhabitation' of Mandate 5 (33-34), Mandate 12 (44-49) has chosen the imagery of 'clothing' and it is worth noting that it too is often used cross-culturally to indicate possession. Among the Christ movement writings, an interesting parallel is offered by Paul, who can speak about "putting on Christ" (but the Greek verb is the same ἐνδύω) in Gal 3:27 to indicate the initiation that introduces people to be part of the Christ possession cult.[32] In a recent but illuminating incursion into the Shepherd, Ishay Rosen-Zvi has pointed exactly at Mandate 12 (44-49) as a text very close to the conception of the Hebrew *yetzer* as a 'demonic desire' that he sees in several other Jewish texts of the Second Temple period.[33] This demonization of the biblical *yetzer* is definitely consistent with the ontology that one has sketched also behind Mandate 5 (33-34), understood as a case of possession.[34] Thus, the 'desire' of Mandate 12 (44-49) should not be taken too hastily as a mystification of internal psychological states, but an additional variation of the possession terminology that permeates this section of the Shepherd.

---

[32] "As many of you as were baptized into Christ have clothed yourselves with Christ"; for the Pauline groups as possession cults, see Christopher Mount, "1 Corinthians 11:3–16: Spirit Possession and Authority in a Non-Pauline Interpolation," *JBL* 124 (2005): 313–40, and Bazzana, *Having the Spirit of Christ*, 102–205.
[33] Ishay Rosen-Zvi, *Demonic Desires: Yetzer Hara and the Problem of Evil in Late Antiquity* (Philadelphia: University of Pennsylvania Press, 2011), 55–58.
[34] It seems right to suggest that ἐπιθυμία could also be translated as "compulsion" (*Trieb*) or "passion" (*Leidenschaft*) in Mandate 12, as done by Brox, *Hirt*, 272.

Mandate 6 (35-36)

Such a conclusion is easily confirmed when one looks at Mandate 6 (35-36), which offers an additional version of the same motif. In Mandate 6 (35-36) the Shepherd speaks at first of ethical choices by adopting the trope—very widespread in antiquity—of the choice between two paths, one straight (ὀρθὴ ὁδός) and one crooked (στρεβλὴ ὁδός). When Hermas asks for more precise instruction, however, the exhortation devolves once more into a binary that contrasts this time not two 'spirits' or 'desires,' but two 'angels' (ἄγγελοι). Despite such a change in terminology though, the mechanics of the interaction between these entities and their human hosts remain fairly similar, as attested by Mand. 6.2.3–4 (36.3–4):

> Ὁ μὲν τῆς δικαιοσύνης ἄγγελος τρυφερός ἐστιν καὶ αἰσχυντηρὸς καὶ πραὺς καὶ ἡσύχιος. Ὅταν οὖν οὗτος ἐπὶ τὴν καρδίαν σου ἀναβῇ, εὐθέως λαλεῖ μετὰ σοῦ περὶ δικαιοσύνης, περὶ ἁγνείας, περὶ σεμνότητος καὶ περὶ αὐταρκείας καὶ περὶ παντὸς ἔργου δικαίου καὶ περὶ πάσης ἀρετῆς ἐνδόξου. [...] 4. Ὅρα νῦν καὶ τοῦ ἀγγέλου τῆς πονηρίας τὰ ἔργα. Πρῶτον πάντων ὀξύχολός ἐστιν, καὶ πικρὸς καὶ ἄφρων, καὶ τὰ ἔργα αὐτοῦ πονηρά, καταστρέφοντα τοὺς δούλους τοῦ θεοῦ.

> The angel of righteousness is sensitive, modest, meek, and mild. And so, when he mounts in your heart, he immediately speaks with you about righteousness, purity, reverence, contentment, every upright deed, and every glorious virtue. [...] 4. See now also the works of the angel of wickedness. First of all, he is irascible, bitter, senseless, and his works are wicked, bringing ruin on the slaves of God.

It may appear at first sight that this new variation in Hermas's terminology might lead us away from possession. However, in a recent and brilliant reexamination of the pneumatology of the Shepherd, Bogdan Bucur has observed—following an original suggestion of the great Jean Daniélou—that when Hermas speaks of 'angels' he is again repeating a widespread move in Second Temple Jewish literature.[35] According to Bucur, Jewish authors referring to 'angels' are simply adopting a specifically biblical terminology that serves to indicate what other Greek writers of the same time call πνεύματα, meaning "beings with distinct personality who occupy an ontologically intermediate position between humans and God."[36] If that is the case (and there is no reason to doubt that on the basis of

---

[35] Bogdan G. Bucur, "The Son of God and the Angelomorphic Holy Spirit: A Rereading of the Shepherd's Christology," *ZNW* 98 (2007): 121–43, but see also idem, *Angelomorphic Pneumatology: Clement of Alexandria and Other Early Christian Witnesses*, VCSup 95 (Leiden: Brill, 2009).
[36] "The word angel connotes a supernatural being manifesting himself. The nature of this supernatural being is not determined by the expression, but by the context. 'Angel' is the old-fash-

the text), then there is very little difference between the reasoning developed in Mandates 5 (33-34) and 6 (35-36). Hermas switches terminology from one Mandate to the other either because he is using different sources or because he has a rhetorical interest in taking advantage of the weight carried also by other intellectual traditions than the Jewish one (in this case, the medical or the Stoic ones in particular).

A preliminary conclusion after this textual analysis is that Hermas is building the ethical instruction enshrined in the Mandates on the basis of the religious experience of possession. Readers of the Shepherd are exhorted to cultivate the presence within them of a good 'spirit' (or 'angel,' or 'desire') and to avoid the inhabitation of a bad one. It is important to stress here that being controlled by the 'holy spirit' (or by the 'angel of righteousness,' or by the 'good desire') should still be designated as possession, even though the moral result for the human host is positive in contrast with the outcome of possession by an 'evil spirit' (or the 'angel of wickedness,' or the 'evil desire'). As observed above, ethnographic studies are helpful at this juncture because they establish very clearly that possession phenomena are not only harmful experiences in need of exorcism. Possession manifests itself in many forms and several among them produce positive outcomes, often in the form of healings, divinations, or other cultural benefits both for the possessed individuals and their groups. In this perspective, a major positive element is certainly the capability that possession has of constructing the human being as moral agent.[37] This is what is envisaged in the Mandates reviewed above: Hermas conceives the experience of possession as a negotiation between the 'spirit' and its human 'host' through which the host can reach a satisfactory and productive balance as an ethical subject.

Summary

A model of subjectification, grounded in an ontological frame that is very different from the modern western one, ends up also being very different from the internalized and autonomous conception of the subject or self that we are used to expect in our cultural context. The model developed by Hermas sees the moral subject as emerging from a contrast and a negotiation with an external and overwhelming force. This is nowhere more evident than in the phrase employed by

---

ioned equivalent of 'person'," in the words of Jean Daniélou, *The Theology of Jewish Christianity* (London: Darton, Longman & Todd, 1964), 118.

37 This aspect of possession has been highlighted in particular by Michael Lambek, "The Continuous and Discontinuous Person: Two Dimensions of Ethical Life," *JRAI* 19 (2013): 837–58.

these Mandates to talk about what we call 'Christ believers.'[38] It is well known that Hermas never refers to his addressees as 'Christians,' but it is less often observed that the designation that occurs more often in the section at hand is actually 'slaves of God' (οἱ δοῦλοι τοῦ θεοῦ, in Mand. 5.2.1 [34.1]; 6.2.6 [36.6]; 12.1.2 [44.2]).[39] Scholars have been more than willing to speculate whether Hermas's proclivity for the usage of such a terminology might have reflected his social location as a freedman.[40] To evaluate such proposals is beyond the scope of the present intervention. Instead, it seems more important to note for the sake of the current discussion that, despite being quite a widespread way for ancient authors to refer to religious allegiance, the language of slavery is very common cross-culturally as a means to speak about possession as well.[41] One has already observed above that in Mandate 5 (33-34) the Shepherd indicates the human hosts of the 'spirits' as 'vessels,' another element that—together with 'slavery'—signifies quite clearly their subordination in the relationship of possession.

One might object to this reasoning by pointing to Mandate 12 (44-49) and the language of "putting on a desire," which has been reviewed above. Does not this language indicate a situation in which the host is not subject to the 'spirit,' but can actually exert control on it (by *putting* it on or *taking* it off at will)? This scenario seems to be at first sight contradictory with respect to the preceding observations and closer to the modern western understanding of the buffered self as autonomous moral agent.

The situation, however, is a little more complicated than that. First of all, it is not clear that the ancient cultural understanding of clothing matched perfectly the modern (and fundamentally consumeristic) conception of dress as an external accoutrement of our individual bodies that can be easily changed at will. It is entirely possible (if not likely) that in other cultures a specific dress may be con-

---

38 While one should also keep in mind that even such a phrase is largely inappropriate for Hermas, since there is no mention of 'Christ' in the Shepherd.
39 On the potential impact of the use of such a phrase on an ancient reader, see Martin Leutzsch, *Die Wahrnehmung zozialer Wirklichkeit im "Hirten des Hermas"*, FRLANT 150 (Göttingen: Vandenhoeck & Ruprecht, 1989), 151–53, but now also the more thorough examination in Marianne B. Kartzow, *The Slave Metaphor and Gendered Enslavement in Early Christian Discourse: Double Trouble Embodied* (New York: Routledge, 2018), 105–24.
40 See the handy summary (with balanced assessment of the speculative nature of such proposals) in Rothschild, *New Essays*, 229–30.
41 To this effect it is also worth noting that other authors belonging to the early Christ movement do use the phrase, and in particular Paul who makes a very liberal use of it in reference to himself.

ceived as a constitutive and essential part of personal identity.⁴² Thus, changing clothes entailed more effort than what we are used to imagine, perhaps in a way similar to the effort that we tend to associate with changing one's bodily features. To use an oversimplified analogy, Hermas's employment of the imagery of "putting on a desire" might be reminiscent of the controlled (and compulsory) change of seasonal military uniforms more than the swapping off of a formal suit for gym gear at the end of a long day at the office.

That being said, the problem with the modernizing interpretation of "putting on a desire" in Mandate 12 (44-49) has also a more textual dimension. For instance, in Mandate 5 (33-34) as well the Shepherd has recourse to the image of clothing in exhorting Hermas to "clothe yourself with patience and resist irascibility and bitterness" (5.2.8 [34.8]: ἔνδυσαι δὲ τὴν μακροθυμίαν καὶ ἀντίστα τῇ ὀξοχυλίᾳ καὶ τῇ πικρίᾳ). Likewise, Mandate 12.2.4 (45.4) instructs Hermas thus:

> Σὺ οὖν ἔνδυσαι τὴν ἐπιθυμίαν τῆς δικαιοσύνης, καὶ καθοπλισάμενος τὸν φόβον τοῦ κυρίου ἀντίστηθι αὐταῖς. Ὁ γὰρ φόβος τοῦ θεοῦ κατοικεῖ ἐν τῇ ἐπιθυμίᾳ τῇ ἀγαθῇ. Ἡ ἐπιθυμία ἡ πονηρὰ ἐὰν ἴδῃ σε καθωπλισμένον τῷ φόβῳ τοῦ θεοῦ καὶ ἀνθεστηκότα αὐτῇ, φεύξεται ἀπὸ σοῦ μακράν, καὶ οὐκέτι σοι ὀφθήσεται φοβουμένη τὰ ὅπλα σου.

> You should be clothed with the desire of righteousness and resist these [other desires] by being armed with the fear of the lord. For the fear of God dwells in good desire. If evil desire should see you armed with the fear of God and resisting it, it will flee far away from you and no longer appear before you for fear of your weapons.

The repeated employment of various forms of the verb ἀνθίστημι in these contexts seem to emphasize autonomy and independence for the individual human self. Indeed, the verb is used mainly in military references, which is also consistent with the echoes of images encountered in other writings belonging to the early Christ movement, such as Ephesians and James.⁴³ In these metaphorical applications, it seems that the verb ἀνθίστημι denotes a 'resistance' entailing at least the psychological setting up of one's mind to withstand the assault of an evil and harmful enemy.⁴⁴

That being said, it appears that other passages are moving in an opposite direction. A particularly striking instance occurs in Mandate 6 (35-36), this

---

42 On this point, see the illuminating contributions collected in *Dressing Judeans and Christians in Antiquity*, ed. Kristi Upson-Saia, Carly Daniel-Hughes, Alicia J. Batten (Farnham: Ashgate, 2014).
43 As noted by Brox, *Hirt*, 274.
44 See, for instance, the many passages from classical Greek authors listed in LSJ, *sub voce* ἀνθίστημι.

time speaking of what a human can do to 'resist' the influence of the two contrasting 'angels' (6.2.7–8 [36.7–8]):

> Ἐὰν γὰρ ᾖ τις πιστότατος ἀνήρ, καὶ ἡ ἐνθύμησις τοῦ ἀγγέλου τούτου ἀναβῇ ἐπὶ τὴν καρδίαν αὐτοῦ, δεῖ τὸν ἄνδρα ἐκεῖνον ἢ τὴν γυναῖκα ἐξαμαρτῆσαί τι. 8. Ἐὰν δὲ πάλιν πονηρότατός τις ᾖ ἀνὴρ ἢ γυνή, καὶ ἀναβῇ ἐπὶ τὴν καρδίαν αὐτοῦ τὰ ἔργα τοῦ ἀγγέλου τῆς δικαιοσύνης, ἐξ ἀνάγκης δεῖ αὐτὸν ἀγαθόν τι ποιῆσαι.

> If a man is completely loyal, but the thought from this angel [of wickedness] should overcome his heart, that man or that woman must commit sin. 8. But again, if there is a most wicked man or woman, but the works of the angel of righteousness should overcome their heart, that one must necessarily do something good.

This scenario appears to move in a completely different direction from the one identified behind the previous quote. Norbert Brox is not wrong in remarking that the passage envisages the 'angels' as exerting "a constricting compulsiveness of a demonic kind" (*eine zwingende Triebhaftigkeit dämonischer Art*).[45] This is true in as much as one conceptualizes demons as they have been systematized in centuries of Christian theological reflection as malevolent and controlling agents (it goes without saying that the conceptualization before Christianity —and including the very early Christ movement—was different, understanding demons as more ambiguous entities).[46] In Mandate 6 (35-36) the activity of the 'angels' is absolutely independent from the internal disposition of their human 'hosts' and these 'spirits' seem to exert total control on human fates.

Indeed, following immediately the statement quoted before from Mandate 12.2.4 (45.4), the Shepherd goes on to say (12.2.5 [45.5]):

> Σὺ οὖν νῖκος λαβὼν καὶ στεφανωθεὶς κατ' αὐτῆς ἐλθὲ πρὸς τὴν ἐπιθυμίαν τῆς δικαιοσύνης, καὶ παραδοὺς αὐτῇ τὸ νῖκος ὃ ἔλαβες. Δούλευσον αὐτῇ καθὼς αὐτὴ βούλεται. Ἐὰν δουλεύσῃς τῇ ἐπιθυμίᾳ τῇ ἀγαθῇ καὶ ὑποταγῇς αὐτῇ, δυνήσῃ τῆς ἐπιθυμίας τῆς πονηρᾶς κατακυριεῦσαι καὶ ὑποτάξαι αὐτὴν καθὼς βούλει.

> And so, when you have achieved victory [against the evil desire] and have been crowned, come to the desire of righteousness, and hand over to it the victory you achieved; serve as its slave, as it wishes. If you are enslaved to the good desire and submit to it, you can lord over evil desire and submit it, just as you wish.

Hermas is certainly not well known for his systematicity, but it seems that the ambiguity characterizing the above-mentioned passages is not due to his faulty thinking. On the basis of the ethnographic literature presented before, one is led

---

45 Brox, *Hirt*, 227–28.
46 For a more detailed discussion, see Bazzana, *Having the Spirit of Christ*, 24–59.

to conclude that such inconsistencies are inherent to the very experience of possession. Accounts produced by ethnographers are again helpful here inasmuch as anthropologists have noted that possession can scarcely be reduced to a single event or even to a succession of manifestations of a spirit in human mediums. Instead, possession is more adequately conceptualized as a relationship between two beings who inhabit the same body and negotiate such a state of affairs over a long arc of time in a way that is subject to almost constant reconfigurations as any other personal relationship.[47] Thus, Adeline Masquelier can describe the trajectory of a Nigerien medium, Zeinabou, who moves—over the course of her years of acquaintance with the overbearing spirit Rankasso—from being a mere 'hostage' (entirely subject to the whims and wills of Rankasso) to becoming a host. In the process, the case of Zeinabou enables us to understand possession—in Masquelier's words—"as a system of communication that mystifies agency, authority, and accountability at the same time that it provides a means to relocate one's selfhood within a concrete and enduring web of mythical, moral, and material relations."[48]

I would claim that a similar trajectory is behind the images developed in the Shepherd's Mandates. At the point of its emergence, Hermas envisages the experience of possession (by a spirit, or a desire, or an angel) as subjection and submission of the human host to an external will. In the process of time, humans can try to exercise some form of control on the 'spirit,' by 'resisting' bad possession or striving to 'put on' good possession (to use Hermas's own language). It is important to stress that these images do not convey the idea of a modern western independent and autonomous subject. Instead, they reflect a negotiation with an overpowering external force, in which an ethical subject is built through enslavement to a good and beneficial possessing spirit. Ultimately, this scenario goes a long way to explain why the worst moral trait for Hermas is διψυχία (often imperfectly translated as 'double-mindedness'). The latter translation is far too narrowly focused on cognicentric elements, such as 'mind' or even 'loyalty' and 'allegiance.'[49] Building on the results of the present analysis, however, one can see that διψυχία does not envisage a moral fault related to intellectual

---

[47] See the insightful description of a case in Michael Lambek, "Rheumatic Irony: Questions of Agency and Self-Deception as Refracted Through the Art of Living with Spirits," in *Illness and Irony: On the Ambiguity of Suffering in Culture*, ed. Michael Lambek and Paul Antze (New York: Berghahn, 2004), 40–59.
[48] Masquelier, "Host," 71.
[49] The earlier cognicentric approach had already been critiqued by Oscar J. F. Seitz, "Relationship of the *Shepherd* of Hermas to the Epistle of James," *JBL* 63 (1944): 131–40, followed by a series of additional studies.

doubt or hesitancy, but—more consistently with the general ethical instruction of the Shepherd—the failure to submit one's entire self to a single, good controlling power.

As noted at the beginning, Hermas is not alone among early Christ followers in relying in this way on possession as a cornerstone to ground and conceptualize religious experience. With significant differences, Paul offers an interesting analogy. As noted by a long tradition of scholarship stretching from Deissmann and Schweitzer all the way to John Ashton and Christopher Mount, Paul uses the phrase 'being in Christ' to express possession by the 'spirit' (πνεῦμα) that is Christ and such a situation becomes the foundation of his religious experience.[50] In a manner similar to Hermas, also Paul envisages this relationship as enslavement to Christ, a negotiation through which the human hosts who have been "bought at great price" can build themselves as moral subjects by letting Christ live fully in them.[51]

Communal Negotiation in Mandate 11 (43)

The sections of the Mandate that have been analyzed so far have focused on negotiating the experience of possession between the possessing spirit and the human host. However, I have noted above that ethnographic accounts of possession indicate that no phenomenon of this type really takes place outside a more complex, triangular negotiation including, alongside the two participants mentioned above, also the community of which the medium is a member. In such a context, the medium has the responsibility of meeting the cultural expectations of her audience. Indeed, adequately fulfilling the 'script' is the only means to make the ritual effective and possession *real*.[52] But this negotiation extends well beyond the moment of the actual 'manifestation' of the spirit

---

[50] The passages indicating the understanding of Christ as πνεῦμα in the so-called authentic Paul are well-known and much-discussed (Rom 1:3–4; 1 Cor 15:45; Rom 8:9–11; 2 Cor 3:17) as are those indicating the active presence of this Christ "spirit" in Paul (chiefly Gal 2:19–20 and 2 Cor 4:7–15). For a more detailed analysis of these themes and texts, see now Bazzana, *Having the Spirit of Christ*, 102–166.
[51] The point is illustrated most clearly in 1 Cor 6:12–20, for which see the insightful reading offered by Halvor Moxnes, "Asceticism and Christian Identity in Antiquity: A Dialogue with Foucault and Paul," *JSNT* 26 (2003): 3–29.
[52] In order to emphasize this aspect of possession phenomena, Lambek designates mediums as *artists* (obviously without implying that their performances are 'fake' or 'make-believe'); on this theme, see also several of the essays collected in *The Problem of Ritual Efficacy*, ed. William Sturman Sax, Johannes Quack, Jan Weinhold (Oxford: Oxford University Press, 2010).

in the medium. Ethnographies illustrate quite clearly that one cannot speak about *performance* as a narrowly-defined event. On the contrary, performance includes all the conversations, debates, and negotiations that precede and follow the actual moment of manifest possession.[53]

As far as the early Christ movement is concerned, there are several documents that give us a glimpse on how these conversations might have developed within groups.[54] In this perspective, one should almost expect Hermas to include this type of discussion as well. And indeed, Mandate 11 (43) deals precisely with this issue of effectiveness in a possession ritual. This Mandate is too often treated as an extraneous body that just happened to be dropped by clumsy Hermas within the sequence, but its role is far more coherent and even crucial.

The Mandate opens up again with a vision offered to Hermas by the Shepherd portraying an instance of oracular divination that is offered by an individual designated as 'false prophet' (ψευδοπροφήτης). Immediately after this scene, the Shepherd describes to Hermas the conditions needed for the opposite case to come true, that is for the manifestation of real 'prophecy.' Besides the obvious binary pattern and the overall terminology that associate this Mandate to the others reviewed above, it is also the way in which the Shepherd describes true prophetic inspiration that reveals how this is again possession (11.9 [43.9]):

> Ὅταν οὖν ἔλθῃ ὁ ἄνθρωπος ὁ ἔχων τὸ πνεῦμα τὸ θεῖον εἰς συναγωγὴν ἀνδρῶν δικαίων τῶν ἐχόντων πίστιν θείου πνεύματος, καὶ ἔντευξις γένηται πρὸς τὸν θεὸν τῆς συναγωγῆς τῶν ἀνδρῶν ἐκείνων, τότε ὁ ἄγγελος τοῦ πνεύματος τοῦ προφητικοῦ ὁ κείμενος ἐπ' αὐτῷ πληροῖ τὸν ἄνθρωπον καὶ πλησθεὶς ὁ ἄνθρωπος ἐκεῖνος τῷ πνεύματι τῷ ἁγίῳ λαλεῖ εἰς τὸ πλῆθος καθὼς ὁ κύριος βούλεται.

> When, then, the person who has the divine spirit comes into a gathering of just men who have the loyalty of the divine spirit, and a petition of the just men gathered together comes to God, then the angel of the prophetic spirit lying upon that person fills him; and once he is filled, that one speaks through the holy spirit to the crowd, just as the Lord wishes.

First of all, Mandate 11 (43) combines together the various terminologies encountered in 5 (33-34) and 6 (35-36) to form the unusual phrase "angel of the prophetic spirit." Despite the unusual label, however, this angel or spirit takes possession of the human host in the same way in which one has seen 'spirits' and 'angels'

---

[53] For a particularly insightful analysis of this point, see Sarah Goldingay, "To Perform Possession and to Be Possessed in Performance: The Actor, the Medium, and the Other," in *Spirit Possession and Trance: New Interdisciplinary Perspectives*, ed. Bettina E. Schmidt and Lucy Huskinson (London: Continuum, 2010), 205–22.

[54] Besides the case of Hermas, the other major instance occurs in 1 Cor 12–14, for which see now Bazzana, *Having the Spirit of Christ*, 167–205.

acting in the other Mandates. If we agree—as noted above, following Bucur and Daniélou—that 'angel' is an alternative Second-Temple way to speak about 'spirits,' the present formulation loses quite a bit of its oddity.

Moreover, it is worth noting that the Shepherd is not portraying a one-time or random event: the manifestation of the 'angel' might be unpredictable, but the text tells us clearly that—even when it seems absent—the 'angel' is always 'lying upon' its host. This is clearly a relationship that has developed along a protracted and continuous arc of time, as noted in several ethnographies of possession. On the opposite side, the false prophet is acted upon in the same way as the 'true' one, but he speaks on the impulse of a bad kind of possession, as stated clearly in 11.3 (43.3) ("the devil fills him with his own spirit, to see if he can break a just one"[55]).

The passage quoted above stresses also the importance of the communal aspect in constituting possession events and rituals. Even though 11.8 (43.8) states that "the holy spirit does not speak when a person wants it to speak, but when God wants it to speak,"[56] it appears that such a manifestation is conditioned by the presence of a group (συναγωγή) requiring it. It would be difficult to find a more explicit expression of the triangular negotiation that has been mentioned above. Conversely, the instance of false prophecy as well is brought about by the presence of a group of people who are δίψυχοι (in 11.4 [43.4]).[57]

Possession events are ultimately performances, so much so that a very influential anthropologist of possession, Michael Lambek, often calls the mediums with which he works, *artists*. As such, the effectiveness of a performance of possession depends in large measure from the precise match between the skill of mediums and the cultural expectations of their audience. Thus, as noted before, it cannot be surprising to see that a good deal of ethnographies of possession highlight the intense discussions and negotiations focused on establishing if and when a case of possession might be *real* or failed and if any given medium can be considered skilled enough. These are other crucial negotiations that accompany the internal one sketched in the preceding section and truly give to possession its decidedly ritual character.

---

55 Ὁ γὰρ διάβολος πληροῖ αὐτὸν τῷ αὐτοῦ πνεύματι, εἴ τινα δυνήσεται ῥῆξαι τῶν δικαίων, *Apostolic Fathers*, vol. 2 (Ehrman, LCL), 284.
56 Οὐδὲ ὅταν θέλῃ ἄνθρωπος λαλεῖν, λαλεῖ τὸ πνεῦμα τὸ ἅγιον, ἀλλὰ τότε λαλεῖ, ὅταν θελήσῃ αὐτὸν ὁ θεὸς λαλῆσαι, *Apostolic Fathers*, vol. 2 (Ehrman, LCL), 286.
57 "But all those who are double-souled and are constantly repenting (μετανοοῦσι), they consult a prophet as even the outsiders consult an oracle (μαντεύονται ὡς καὶ τὰ ἔθνη) and they bring a greater sin upon themselves by thus committing idolatry."

Accordingly, Mandate 11 (43) is mostly focused on the task of establish how one can discern the difference between a true and a false case of oracular possession. The path taken by Hermas in regard to this is quite similar to the one often observed cross-culturally in analogous circumstances. The validation and effectiveness of possession is guaranteed by the fact that mediums are not (or show that they are not) in control when they are possessed. In earlier ethnographic literature this is usually equated with a loss of consciousness and being in a state of trance.[58] The focus on states of consciousness has led several anthropologists to concentrate their attention almost exclusively on the analysis of the neurophysiological traits of possessed mediums. In contrast to such a trend, Lambek wittily notes that possession provides a cultural context for trance as marriage provides a context for sex. Accordingly, anthropologists, who are naturally more interested in marriage than in sex, should also find culturally more fruitful to focus on possession than on trance.[59]

Thus, it is interesting to evaluate how the Shepherd describes the conditions for *valid* possession to Hermas. The crux of the argument is that the true prophet does not speak upon request and does not turn prophetic activity into an opportunity for personal gain (as we have just seen in 11.9 [43.9]). It goes without saying that the depiction of the false prophet is entirely the opposite: the latter accepts queries from clients and is actually intent on earning material profit from his service (11.12 [43.12]).[60]

There is not enough space for developing this comparison in full here, but it is worth mentioning at least in passing that Hermas's concern for a communal negotiation of possession emerges also elsewhere in writings belonging to the Christ movement. A representative instance is obviously the long discussion of *charismata* in 1 Cor 12–14. There too, Paul deals with the task of establishing criteria that might help assessing the validity and effectiveness of possession (which is designated there too as 'prophecy' as it happens in Mandate 11 [43]). That being said, it is noteworthy that the line of reasoning chosen by Paul is very different (one could even say, opposite) from the one embraced by

---

[58] A classic structuralist study written in this vein is Erika Bourguignon, *Religion, Altered States of Consciousness, and Social Change* (Columbus: Ohio State University Press, 1973).
[59] Michael Lambek, "From Disease to Discourse: Remarks on the Conceptualization of Trance and Spirit Possession," in *Altered States of Consciousness and Mental Health: A Cross-Cultural Perspective*, ed. Colleen A. Ward (London: Sage, 1989), 36–61, here 45–46.
[60] First the people who appear to have this spirit [the earthly and empty one] exalt themselves and wish to be given pride of place. [...] Moreover, they receive wages for their prophecy—without them, they do not prophesy. But can the divine spirit receive wages for its prophecies? The prophet of God cannot do this, but the spirit of those other prophets is earthly."

Hermas. An evaluation of the contents of prophecies does not play any role in Mandate 11. Such a choice is not surprising, since an emphasis on that aspect would have been difficult to square with the principle that there should be no human control on the manifestations of the spirit. On the contrary, Paul puts the contents of revelation and divination at the center of discussion from the very first verses of 1 Cor 12.[61] Then Paul continues his treatment in a direction that is quite the opposite of Hermas's: for the apostle, the crucial point is the control of possession (in particular, under the form of glossolalia) on the part of its human practitioners, so that it may better serve the ultimate goal of edifying the group.[62]

Conclusions

The present paper has examined the religious experiences described in Hermas's Mandates by putting them under the label of possession. The introduction of this category highlights that only a change of ontological and psychological paradigms can yield a more adequate understanding of Hermas's discourse. In the Mandates the Shepherd describes the subjectification of Christ followers as the result of a negotiation between humans and possessing spirits that exert a hold on them. In due course this negotiation, articulated as enslavement to the good spirit, can produce a morally sound subject according to Hermas. Hermas's conceptualization of possession has also a communal side, evidenced in Mandate 11 (43) and in which the validity and effectiveness of possession phenomena are assessed through a triangular discussion involving spirits, mediums, and their audiences. Hermas's ideas on possession can be compared and contrasted with similar conceptions occurring in other writings belonging to the early Christ movement and with Paul's letters, in particular.

---

61 "Therefore I want you to understand that no one speaking by a spirit of God ever says 'Let Jesus be cursed!' and no one can say 'Jesus is Lord' except by a holy spirit" (1 Cor 12:3); for a perceptive reading of these verse, see Clint Tibbs, *Religious Experience of the Pneuma: Communication with the Spirit World in 1 Corinthians 12 and 14*, WUNT 2/230 (Tübingen: Mohr-Siebeck, 2007), 170–74. More generally, on divination in Paul against the Greco-Roman background, see now the seminal study of Jennifer Eyl, *Signs, Wonders, and Gifts: Divination in the Letters of Paul* (New York: Oxford University Press, 2019).
62 See the rhetorical reading of this section of the letter in Margaret M. Mitchell, *Paul and the Rhetoric of Reconciliation: An Exegetical Investigation of the Language and Composition of 1 Corinthians* (Tübingen: Mohr-Siebeck, 1991), 266–83, and a more extensive analysis in Bazzana, *Having the Spirit of Christ*, 167–205.

Jung H. Choi
A True Prophet as a Mouthpiece of the Spirit? Cultivating Virtue and Control

Prophetic experiences were ubiquitous in the ancient Mediterranean world. The Shepherd of Hermas,[1] among the most popular and widely read works in early Christianity,[2] is one of the most extensive sources of information on prophecy and possession in early Christian writings.[3] Prophecy is the prime locus where human and divine agencies are negotiated and constructed. In this work, we see that there are diverse voices about human and divine agency and that a stringent distinction between human-divine agencies is problematic.[4]

In the Shepherd of Hermas, two interlocking themes about the performance of prophecy emerge. First, the Shepherd of Hermas presents (true) prophecy as a passive and involuntary experience, incorporating a trope that a prophet functions as a sort of mouthpiece for God. The concept of prophecy as a passive phenomenon is also demonstrated by its use of images of vessels. Second, there is a strong suggestion that certain cultivation is required in order to be the right vessel for the Spirit to indwell. It is necessary to cultivate and perform self-control to be a proper self to receive the Holy Spirit. Whereas Hermas emphasizes the cultivation of self-control as preparation for prophecy, the tenor has shifted at the moment of prophecy. At the moment of prophecy, a lack of self-control is the hallmark of true prophecy.

---

[1] English translations follow but sometimes modify *Apostolic Fathers*, vol. 2 (Ehrman, LCL). In this essay, I assume the consensus is correct that the provenance of the Shepherd is Rome and its date of production is the early or mid-second century.

[2] Carolyn Osiek, *The Shepherd of Hermas*, Hermeneia (Minneapolis: Fortress, 1999). "From the papyri [Epistula Iacobi Apocrypha], it appears that Hermas, with his full description of prophetic activity within the church communities (Mand XI) belonged to the most popular reading of early Christian Egypt," 39. Jacques van der Vliet, "Spirit and Prophecy in the Epistula Iacobi Apocrypha (NHC i.2)," *VC* 44 (1990): 25–53.

[3] Giovanni B. Bazzana, *Having the Spirit of Christ: Spirit Possession and Exorcism in the Early Christ Groups* (New Haven: Yale University Press, 2020), 126.

[4] On helpful discussions on agency, see Saba Mahmood, "Feminist Theory, Embodiment, and the Docile Agent: Some Reflections on the Egyptian Islamic Revival," *Cultural Anthropology* 16 (2001): 202–36; Michael Lambek, "How to Make Up One's Mind: Reason, Passion, and Ethics in Spirit Possession," *University of Toronto Quarterly* 79 (2010): 720–41. For a discussion of the differences between pre-modern and modern ideas of subjectivity, see Angela Kim Harkins, "The Pro-social Role of Grief in Ezra's Penitential Prayer," *BibInt* 24 (2016): 466–91, esp. 470–79.

https://doi.org/10.1515/9783110780741-006

Our investigation of the phenomenon of prophecy in the Shepherd of Hermas will include a comparison with Origen's writings, which can shed light on what is at stake in the discussions on prophecy.[5] While the notion that prophecy and the prophet are distinctively moral pervades the Shepherd of Hermas and Origen's writings, they offer different arguments. The Shepherd of Hermas considers one of the hallmarks of true prophecy to be its involuntary and passive nature, a view consistent with a popular and longstanding ancient discourse on prophecy as characterized by loss of human control. By contrast, Origen takes a different view. The second part of this essay engages Origen's alternative perspective as found in *Contra Celsum* Book 7 and Balaam's story in his *Homilies on Numbers* 14–17 in order to see how Origen deploys rhetorical constructions of prophecy. These discussions on prophecy intertwine with the theme of control and the loss of control, and draw attention to the gender of the prophet as well. In engaging these issues, Origen attempts to persuade the readers and hearers to develop a self that is differentiated from pagan prophets and other Christian prophets.

Mandate 11 (43)

With an extended discussion of prophecy and related phenomena, Mandate 11 (43) of the Shepherd of Hermas concerns the central theme of discerning true prophecy and false prophecy. Mandate 11 presents a singular instance regarding prophecy: in discussing several criteria of a true prophet, this work asserts that passivity, loss of control, or involuntariness is one of the major markers of true prophecy.[6] While the false prophet is the one who, having no power of the divine

---

5 The comparison between the Shepherd of Hermas and Origen's works concerning prophecy is warranted, even if he never engages the text implicitly in his discussion of prophecy past and present gifts, by the fact that Origen's works reveal his familiarity with the *Shepherd of Hermas* through frequent citation (for example, *de Principiis* 3.2 and *Homilies on Numbers* 8). In his *Commentary on Romans* 10:31, Origen claims that the Hermas of Rom 16:14 is the same Hermas of the Shepherd. Scheck argues that although Origen does not view the Shepherd of Hermas as canonical, he considers the work to be immensely useful and even "divinely inspired" (Thomas P. Scheck and Christopher A. Hall, *Homilies on Numbers* [Downers Grove: IVP Press, 2013], 33). Origen refers to the Shepherd of Hermas, for example, in order to support his own argument about two spirits that work in a human being.
6 It is widely recognized that in antiquity prophecy, oracles, dreams, and visions were all closely related. Patricia Cox Miller notes, "According to Hermas, the revelatory visions were dreams [....] The term used by Hermas to characterize his fine visions, *horaeseis*, was a metaphor of seeing, like the Latin *visio*, that constituted part of the technical vocabulary of oneiric description in

spirit in himself/herself, speaks with them in light of the requests and evil desires they have, and s/he fills their souls as they themselves wish (Mand. 11.2 [43.2]).[7] The true prophet is the one who follows the cue of the Holy Spirit.

> καὶ οὐδενὶ οὐδὲν ἀποκρίνεται ἐπερωτώμενος, οὐδὲ καταμόνας λαλεῖ, οὐδὲ ὅταν θέλῃ ἄνθρωπος λαλεῖν, λαλεῖ τὸ πνεῦμα <τὸ> ἅγιον, ἀλλὰ τότε λαλεῖ, ὅταν θελήσῃ αὐτὸν ὁ θεὸς λαλῆσαι.
>
> [A true prophet] never gives an answer to anyone when asked, nor does s/he speak in private. The Holy Spirit does not speak when the person wants to speak, but when God wants him/her to speak. (Mand. 11.8 [43.8])[8]

This statement that a true prophet speaks, not when she or he wants to speak, but when God wills her or him to speak is embedded within the important discussion around experiences such as prophecy, divination, possession, or dreams that highlight the nuanced relationship between human agency and divine agency. In this passage, true prophecy lies where human beings relinquish their agency to the Spirit. As Carolyn Osiek comments, "the application to the functioning of prophecy is that all prophetic communication from the divine spirit comes not through human questioning or prompting, but directly and unplanned from the power of God."[9] The Spirit from God takes over the human will, for "Every spirit given by God is not questioned, but since it has the divine spirit, it says everything *on its own accord* because it is from above, from the power of the divine speech" (Mand. 11.5 [43.5]).

The rhetorical strategy of the Shepherd of Hermas is to argue that a true prophet is passive or involuntarily prophesies, for he or she is "never consulted

---

antiquity." Patricia Cox Miller, "'A Dubious Twilight': Reflections on Dreams in Patristic Literature," *Church History* 55 (1986): 133. See also Eric Robertson Dodds, *The Greeks and the Irrational* (Boston: Beacon Press, 1957), 105; Peter Brown, *The Making of Late Antiquity* (Cambridge, MA: Harvard University Press, 1976), 65; Giovanni Bazzana, "'Il corpo della carne di Gesù Cristo' (P. Oxy. I.5): conflitti ecclesiologici nel cristianesimo del II secolo," *Adamantius* 10 (2004): 100–22. Luca Arcari, "P.Oxy. 1.5 and the Codex Sangermanensis as 'Visionary Living Texts': Visionary *habitus* and Processes of 'Textualization' and/or 'Scripturalization' in Late Antiquity," *Lived Religion in the Ancient Mediterranean World: Approaching Religious Transformations from Archaeology, History and Classics*, ed. Valentino Gasparini et al. (Berlin: De Gruyter, 2020), 469–91.
7 οὗτοι οὖν οἱ δίψυχοι ὡς ἐπὶ μάντιν ἔρχονται καὶ ἐπερωτῶσιν αὐτόν, τί ἄρα ἔσται αὐτοῖς· κἀκεῖνος ὁ ψευδοπροφήτης, μηδεμίαν ἔχων ἐν ἑαυτῷ δύναμιν πνεύματος θείου, λαλεῖ μετ' αὐτῶν κατὰ τὰ ἐπερωτήματα αὐτῶν καὶ κατὰ τὰς ἐπιθυμίας τῆς πονηρίας αὐτῶν, καὶ πληροῖ τὰς ψυχὰς αὐτῶν καθὼς αὐτοὶ βούλονται.
8 I have slightly modified Ehrman's translation.
9 Osiek, *Hermas*, 143.

(οὐκ ἐπερωτᾶται)" (Mand. 11.5 [43.5]), nor does the prophet speak on her/his own.[10] The argument that a prophet speaks when God wants him/her to speak instead of speaking on his or her own expresses Hermas's view that a prophet functions as a sort of mouthpiece for God which is shown in Greek literature and Jewish literature alike. For example, an oracle attributed to Montanus by Epiphanius reflects this tradition: "For Montanus says, for instance: 'Behold, man is like a lyre, and I flit about like a plectron; man sleeps, and I awaken him; behold, it is the Lord who changes the hearts of men [sic] and gives men a heart.'"[11]

While one influential marker of a true prophet is a lack of control over herself/himself and over the content of the prophecy,[12] a false prophet controls the content of the prophecy that he/she utters. A false prophet chooses what to speak according to the desires of the people who ask him/her questions.

> οὗτοι οὖν οἱ δίψυχοι ὡς ἐπὶ μάντιν ἔρχονται καὶ ἐπερωτῶσιν αὐτόν, τί ἄρα ἔσται αὐτοῖς· κἀκεῖνος ὁ ψευδοπροφήτης, μηδεμίαν ἔχων ἐν ἑαυτῷ δύναμιν πνεύματος θείου, λαλεῖ μετ' αὐτῶν κατὰ τὰ ἐπερωτήματα αὐτῶν καὶ κατὰ τὰς ἐπιθυμίας τῆς πονηρίας αὐτῶν, καὶ πληροῖ τὰς ψυχὰς αὐτῶν καθὼς αὐτοὶ βούλονται.

> And so, these double-minded people (οἱ δίψυχοι) come to him/her [a false prophet] as if s/he were a diviner (soothsayer) (ὡς ἐπὶ μάντιν), and ask him/her what will happen. And that false prophet, having no power of the divine spirit in himself/herself, speaks with them in light of the requests and evil desires they have, and s/he fills their souls as they themselves wish. (Mand. 11.2 [43.2])

With the same intensity with which the Shepherd of Hermas criticizes the false prophet—likened to a μάντις (a diviner or soothsayer)—it also pillories those who associate with the false prophet by asking him questions.

---

10 Mand. 11.5 (43.5), "For no spirit given by God is consulted, but having divine power it speaks all things from its own authority, because it comes from above, from the power of the divine spirit." In order to contextualize this discussion, it is helpful to examine the work of Epictetus. For example, in the *Handbook: Guides to Stoic Living*, Epictetus discusses the meaning of diviner and divination, noting, "therefore, do not bring desire and aversion to the diviner (for, if you do, you will be fearful of what you may hear), but go with the understanding that everything that happens will be indifferent and of no concern to you, for whatever it may be it is in your power to make good use of it, and that no one can hinder you in this," cited by Keith Seddon, *Epictetus's Handbook and the Tablet of Cebes: Guides to Stoic Living* (London: Routledge, 2005), 124.
11 Ronald E. Heine, *The Montanist Oracles and Testimonia* (Leuven: Peeters, 1989), 3.
12 Cf. Bazzana, "'Il corpo," 111. "A decisive factor is likely able to be identified in the role that Paul claims for control of the oracles and the intelligibility (*nous*) of those who exercise the prophetic charism."

ὅσοι δὲ δίψυχοί εἰσι καὶ πυκνῶς μετανοοῦσι, μαντεύονται ὡς καὶ τὰ ἔθνη, καὶ ἑαυτοῖς μείζονα ἁμαρτίαν ἐπιφέρουσιν εἰδωλολατροῦντες· ὁ γὰρ ἐπερωτῶν ψευδοπροφήτην περὶ πράξεώς τινος εἰδωλολάτρης ἐστὶ καὶ κενὸς ἀπὸ τῆς ἀληθείας καὶ ἄφρων.

All those who are double-minded and who are constantly changing their minds, consult the oracle (μαντεύονται) as do even the gentiles. And they bring a greater sin upon themselves by committing idolatry this way. For the one who asks (ἐπερωτῶν) a false prophet about any matter is an idolater, devoid of the truth, and foolish. (Mand. 11.4 [43.4])

Why does the Shepherd of Hermas takes pains to contest the practice of consulting an oracle, and asking questions (ἐπερωτάω) which, as Robin Lane Fox puts it, was a "'neutral technology' of prophecy" in antiquity?[13] One of the answers would be the polemical tendency to criticize the other—be they non-Christian or internecine Christian—prophetic experiences. A representative example from non-Christian culture would be the Delphic oracle: After people bring their questions, the Pythia delivers answers from Apollo.[14] As we shall see later, the polemics are set forth in multiple ways. While Hermas would have criticized those who came to ask questions for Pythia, he would not have criticized Pythia's possession as a mode of her prophecy.

The Shepherd of Hermas emphasizes that a spirit invades and fills human beings in the moment of prophecy. In Mandates 11 (43) and 5.1.1–5.2.8 (33–34), Hermas states that both the Holy Spirit and the evil spirit invade and penetrate certain kinds of people. We can see several interesting features here in these passages. First, like attracts like. That is, the Holy Spirit occupies virtuous people, while the evil spirit invades empty people. Mandate 11 (43) states: "The devil (ὁ διάβολος) fills (πληροῖ) a false prophet with his own spirit so that he may be able to break down some of the righteous people" (Mand. 11.3 [43.3]).[15] In contrast, "the angel of the prophetic spirit lying on (κείμενος) that person fills him/her, and once the person is filled, she/he speaks in the Holy Spirit to the congregation, just as the Lord desires" (Mand. 11.9 [43.9]).[16] Mandate 11.6 (43.6) also criticizes the spirit that works in the false prophet.

---

13 Robin Lane Fox, *Pagans and Christians* (London: Penguin, 2006), 389.
14 For this practice, see Sarah Iles Johnston, "The Divine Experience: Delphi and Dodona," in *Ancient Greek Divination* (Oxford: Wiley Blackwell, 2008), 33–75.
15 αὐτὸς γὰρ κενὸς ὢν κενὰ καὶ ἀποκρίνεται κενοῖς· ὃ γὰρ ἐὰν ἐπερωτηθῇ, πρὸς τὸ κένωμα τοῦ ἀνθρώπου ἀποκρίνεται. τινὰ δὲ καὶ ῥήματα ἀληθῆ λαλεῖ· ὁ γὰρ διάβολος πληροῖ αὐτὸν τῷ αὑτοῦ πνεύματι, εἴ τινα δυνήσεται ῥῆξαι τῶν δικαίων.
16 ὅταν οὖν ἔλθῃ ὁ ἄνθρωπος ὁ ἔχων τὸ πνεῦμα τὸ θεῖον εἰς συναγωγὴν ἀνδρῶν δικαίων τῶν ἐχόντων πίστιν θείου πνεύματος, καὶ ἔντευξις γένηται πρὸς τὸν θεὸν τῆς συναγωγῆς τῶν ἀνδρῶν ἐκείνων, τότε ὁ ἄγγελος τοῦ πνεύματος τοῦ προφητικοῦ ὁ κείμενος ἐπ' αὐτῷ πληροῖ

τὸ δὲ πνεῦμα τὸ ἐπερωτώμενον καὶ λαλοῦν κατὰ τὰς ἐπιθυμίας τῶν ἀνθρώπων ἐπίγειόν ἐστι καὶ ἐλαφρόν, δύναμιν μὴ ἔχον· καὶ ὅλως οὐ λαλεῖ ἐὰν μὴ ἐπερωτηθῇ.

But the spirit (τό πνεῦμα) that, when consulted, speaks in light of human desires is earthly and insubstantial, having no power. And it does not speak at all unless it is consulted.

The phenomenon of *Geisterfüllung*[17] is also discussed in Mand. 5.1.1–4 (33.1–4):

Μακρόθυμος, φησί, γίνου καὶ συνετός, καὶ πάντων τῶν πονηρῶν ἔργων κατακυριεύσεις καὶ ἐργάσῃ πᾶσαν δικαιοσύνην. ἐὰν γὰρ μακρόθυμος ἔσῃ, τὸ πνεῦμα τὸ ἅγιον τὸ κατοικοῦν ἐν σοὶ καθαρὸν ἔσται, μὴ ἐπισκοτούμενον ὑπὸ ἑτέρου πονηροῦ πνεύματος, ἀλλ' ἐν εὐρυχώρῳ κατοικοῦν ἀγαλλιάσεται καὶ εὐφρανθήσεται μετὰ τοῦ σκεύους ἐν ᾧ κατοικεῖ, καὶ λειτουργήσει τῷ θεῷ ἐν ἱλαρότητι πολλῇ, ἔχον τὴν εὐθηνίαν ἐν ἑαυτῷ. ἐὰν δὲ ὀξυχολία τις προσέλθῃ, εὐθὺς τὸ πνεῦμα τὸ ἅγιον, τρυφερὸν ὄν, στενοχωρεῖται, μὴ ἔχον τὸν τόπον καθαρόν, καὶ ζητεῖ ἀποστῆναι ἐκ τοῦ τόπου· πνίγεται γὰρ ὑπὸ τοῦ πονηροῦ πνεύματος, μὴ ἔχον τόπον λειτουργῆσαι τῷ κυρίῳ καθὼς βούλεται, μιαινόμενον ὑπὸ τῆς ὀξυχολίας. ἐν γὰρ τῇ μακροθυμίᾳ ὁ κύριος κατοικεῖ, ἐν δὲ τῇ ὀξυχολίᾳ ὁ διάβολος. ἀμφότερα οὖν τὰ πνεύματα ἐπὶ τὸ αὐτὸ κατοικοῦντα, ἀσύμφορόν ἐστιν καὶ πονηρὸν τῷ ἀνθρώπῳ ἐκείνῳ ἐν ᾧ κατοικοῦσιν.

"Be patient (Μακρόθυμος)," he said, "and have understanding and you will have power over all evil deeds and do everything that is righteous. If you are patient, the Holy Spirit that dwells (κατοικοῦν) in you will be pure, not overshadowed by another, evil spirit, but living openly, it will rejoice and be happy along with the vessel (σκεύους) in which it dwells (κατοικοῦν), and it will serve God in great joy, having within it a sense of well-being. But if any bad temper enters it, immediately the Holy Spirit, which is sensitive,[18] feels suffocated; and not having a pure place it seeks to leave (ἀποστῆναι). For it is suffocated (πνίγεται) by the evil spirit, not having a place to serve the Lord as it wishes, being polluted by the bad temper. For the Lord dwells in patience, but the devil in bad temper. And so, when both spirits dwell in the same place, it is unprofitable and evil for that person in whom they dwell."

Both Mandates 5 (33–34) and 11 (43) presuppose that the human can be possessed by a spirit, even if the technical terms ἔκστασις or the noun form of κατέχω that are usually used to denote possession or trance do not appear in the text. Osiek argues that the terms ἀποστῆναι ("leave") and πνίγεται ("feel suffocated") in Mand. 5.1.3 (33.3) suggest a possession. Mandate 5.2.2 (34.2) has an-

---

τὸν ἄνθρωπον καὶ πλησθεὶς ὁ ἄνθρωπος ἐκεῖνος τῷ πνεύματι τῷ ἁγίῳ λαλεῖ εἰς τὸ πλῆθος καθὼς ὁ κύριος βούλεται.

17 One example of "spirit-filling" in a Greek source is Pollux, *Onomasticon* 1.15, which describes how a prophetic spirit flows into a human being. Jannes Reiling, *Hermas and Christian Prophecy* (Leiden: E. J. Brill, 1973), 114.

18 Regarding the sensitive and delicate spirit, J. E. Morgan-Wynne, "The 'Delicacy' of the Spirit in the *Shepherd of Hermas* and in Tertullian," *Studia Patristica* 21 (1989): 154–57.

other example of possession, according to Osiek, in its assertion that a bad temper, which is frequently described as an attribute of the evil spirit, sees "those who are empty and of two minds" at rest, "it barges in violently (παρεμβάλλει) itself into their hearts."[19] In contrast, the Shepherd of Hermas does not use such a violent and forceful image for the Holy Spirit, which is portrayed as gentle. One also sees this idea in other passages. For example, in Sim. 5.6.5–6 (59.5–6), Hermas states:

> God made the Holy Spirit dwell in the flesh that he [or: it] desired, even though it preexisted and created all things. This flesh, then, in which the Holy Spirit dwelled, served well as the spirit's slave, for it conducted itself in reverence and purity, not defiling the Spirit at all. Since it lived in a good and pure way, cooperating with the Spirit and working with it in everything it did, behaving in a strong and manly way, God chose it to be partner with the Holy Spirit. For the conduct of this flesh was pleasing, because it was not defiled on earth while bearing the Holy Spirit.

Here we see two conceptual ideals. First, God's agency is privileged. God chooses. Secondly, human beings cooperate with the Holy Spirit. There are also preexisting requirements for the human beings to be chosen (or worthy to be chosen) by the Spirit.[20]

The Shepherd of Hermas's concept of prophecy as a passive phenomenon is also demonstrated by its use of images of vessels or containers (σκευή) in Mand. 11.13 (43.13), also in Mand. 5.2.6 (34.6).[21] In contemporaneous literature, σκευή is sometimes used to denote a human being.[22] With respect to prophecy, this image reflects the understanding that a human being harbors a spirit (either good or evil) as the source of prophecy. The image of a jar (κέραμος) in Mand. 11.15 (43.15) is also used in a similar vein. These images undergird the idea of an occupation by a spirit and are used to emphasize the passivity of a prophet in the sense of the loss of control over oneself. One may interpret both passages to mean that being a prophet or a diviner is not like a radio transmitter that

---

[19] Osiek, *Hermas*, 119–20; see Mand. 5.2.2 (34.2). ὅταν γὰρ ἴδῃ τοὺς τοιούτους ἀνθρώπους εὐσταθοῦντας, παρεμβάλλει ἑαυτὴν εἰς τὴν καρδίαν τοῦ ἀνθρώπου ἐκείνου. To see a larger context of the Shepherd of Hermas: while he was "praising God's creations, how great and powerful they are," Hermas "went into a sleep," which is a common expression for trance, at which point he was "seized by the spirit/Spirit, which 'lifted him beyond rough country to a level plain'" (Vis. 1.1.3–1.2.2 [1.3–2.2]). Fox, *Pagans and Christians*, 382.

[20] The Shepherd does not provide a clear distinction "between the holy spirit dwelling in Jesus and the holy spirit that dwells in others." Osiek, *Shepherd of Hermas*, 180-81n43.

[21] In the entirety of the Mandates, σκευή appears only in these two places.

[22] C. Maurer, "σκευή," *TDNT* 7: 1039.

just passively receives the revelation of the divine. Rather, they argue that philosophical exercises (ἀσκήσεις), such as self-control, lead to prophecy.

Cultivating Passivity to Become an Appropriate Vessel

We have seen that the Shepherd of Hermas privileges the passive nature of prophecy and involuntariness of the prophet as the norm of prophecy. At the same time, this text reflects a couple of conditions through which one becomes virtuous. Since the Holy Spirit occupies virtuous people and an evil spirit invades empty people, it is crucial for the Shepherd of Hermas that one cultivate oneself to be virtuous in order to attract the Holy Spirit. Put differently, it is important to create an adequate *condition* for becoming a vessel in which the divine can dwell.[23] For example, Mand. 11.7b–8 (43.7b–8) discusses the way in which one can discern a true prophet. An important criterion is their (way of) life:

> ἀπὸ τῆς ζωῆς δοκίμαζε τὸν ἄνθρωπον τὸν ἔχοντα τὸ πνεῦμα τὸ θεῖον. 8. πρῶτον μὲν ὁ ἔχων τὸ πνεῦμα τὸ ἄνωθεν πραΰς ἐστι καὶ ἡσύχιος καὶ ταπεινόφρων καὶ ἀπεχόμενος ἀπὸ πάσης πονηρίας καὶ ἐπιθυμίας ματαίας τοῦ αἰῶνος τούτου καὶ ἑαυτὸν ἐνδεέστερον ποιεῖ πάντων τῶν ἀνθρώπων.

> You must discern the person with the divine spirit[24] by his/her way of life. First, the one who has the spirit that comes from above is meek (πραΰς), mild or gentle (ἡσύχιος), and humble; s/he abstains from all evil and the vain desire of this age; s/he makes herself/himself more lowly than all others.

The same terms used in Mand. 11.8 (43.8)—meek, mild or gentle—are deployed in the next passage:

> For when these spirits dwell in one and the same vessel with the Holy Spirit, the vessel no longer has sufficient space but is stuffed to the brim. And so the sensitive spirit, which is

---

23 The text itself does not describe the exact *method* of cultivating the properly prophetic self. The technical term ἄσκησις (philosophical exercise) and its cognate appear only once in Mand. 8.10 (38.10), when the Shepherd exhorts the readers to cultivate an ethical stance and to "train in righteousness (δικαιοσύνην ἀσκεῖν)." However, despite the absence of the technical term ἄσκησις, which is greatly developed in ascetic practices in various forms, we can infer similar practices.

24 In the passage above, "the person with the divine spirit" is discussed in the context of discerning a prophet, and thus the text seems to equate the prophet and "the person with the divine spirit."

not accustomed to dwelling with an evil spirit nor with bad temper, leaves the person and *seeks to live with meekness and mildness.* (Mand. 5.2.5–6 [34.5–6], with emphasis added)

The Holy Spirit searches for those who are meek and mild in order to dwell with them. Read together, both Mandates 11.8 (43.8) and 5.2.5–6 (34.5–6) not only describe, but also implicitly *prescribe*, the characteristics of a (true) prophet. The prophet is meek and mild. This ethical condition is crucial so that she may *invite* the Holy Spirit to dwell in her and so that she, vessel-like, may contain the Holy Spirit. If they are neither meek nor mild, the Spirit will not dwell in them. If they are no longer virtuous, the Spirit will leave them.[25]

How then does this text conceive of making oneself virtuous so that the Holy Spirit can dwell within a person? The foremost ethical condition is created through controlling desire (ἐπιθυμία).[26] As B. Diane Lipsett cogently argues in her *Desiring Conversion: Hermas, Thecla, Aseneth*, the terms ἐγκράτεια and ἐπιθυμία[27] are "workhorse words within this text's register of virtue language. Though in later Christian texts ἐγκράτεια becomes a technical term for celibacy, the use here is broader."[28] The Shepherd of Hermas thus evinces its own philo-

---

25 This view that connects prophecy to morality is prevalent in many writings. For example, see Alan Cooper, "Imagining Prophecy," in *Poetry and Prophecy: The Beginnings of a Literary Tradition*, ed. James L. Kugel (Ithaca: Cornell University Press, 1990), 26–44; he writes, "The typical Jewish view, inherited from the rabbis, is that prophets were supposed to be 'wise, strong and wealthy'" (35); citing here B.Shabbat 92a; B.Nedarim 38a.

26 A concordance of Hermas's usage reveals an important aspect of prophecy in connection with ἐπιθυμία. The significance of this term, ἐπιθυμία, and its cognates, is shown by its many uses (twenty-eight) in the Mandates. Of these twenty-eight occurrences in the Mandates, it is noteworthy that twenty-five uses occur in Mandates 11 (43) and 12.1–6 (44–49); particularly, four in Mandate 11 (43) and twenty-one in 12.1–6 (44–49), where discussions of prophecy are centered. Two in 6.2.5 (36.5); once in 8.1.5 (38.5). See J. David Thompson and J. Arthur Baird, *A Critical Concordance to the Shepherd of Hermas—The Mandates* (Wooster, OH Biblical Research Associates, 1998), 94–95. Compared to the Mandates, there are smaller occurrences of ἐπιθυμία and its cognates in the Similitudes (seventeen times) and in the Visions (seven times). See idem, *A Critical Concordance to the Shepherd of Hermas—The Parables*, 182; idem, *A Critical Concordance to the Shepherd of Hermas—The Visions*, 93.

27 Osiek discusses both Stoic and Jewish-Christian influence in the discussion of desire (ἐπιθυμία), when she says, "desire is usually understood negatively, especially under Stoic influence [...] But in the Jewish-Christian context, Hermas realizes that not all desire is bad. This dualism of desires could well correspond to the good and bad desire of Jewish two-ways moral teaching." *Hermas*, 148n1. However, her division between Stoic and Jewish-Christian influences oversimplifies the situation.

28 Diane Lipsett also draws on Foucault's description of the term's general usage in the moral philosophical tradition. "Enkrateia, with its opposite, akrasia, is located on the axis of struggle, resistance, and combat; it is self-control, tension, 'continence'; enkrateia rules over pleasures

sophical concerns over desire, a concept highlighted in the Greco-Roman schools of moral philosophy in controlling passions.[29] For example, Epictetus highlights "desires and aversions,"—passions that are, "inappropriate emotions caused by errors of judgment, in particular desire (*epithumia*), fear (*phobos*), intense pleasure (*hedone*), and grief (*lupe*)."[30] Mandate 10.2 (41.2), for example, shows a discussion of how grief (λύπη) impacts the Holy Spirit: "So listen, you foolish one, he said, to how grief (λύπη) wears out the Holy Spirit and then again saves it [....] Both double-mindedness and irascibility, therefore, grieve the Holy Spirit." It is important to have a control over one's emotions, such as grief, in order for the good spirit to keep dwelling within the person.[31]

Mandates 9–11 (39–43) also emphasize the importance of the discerning of spirits and actively intertwine such discernment with judging false and true prophecy. The point of the struggle or discernment is this: the person is responsible for which kind of spirit predominates in him. Mandate 6.1–2 (35–36), in particular, is devoted to the topic of discernment of Spirits, based on a two-way parenetic theology found in both Greek and Jewish moral traditions.[32] When Hermas asked about how to recognize which spirit is the right one, the Shepherd says,

> When bad temper or bitterness overcomes you, you know it is in you; then come desire for doing more business, for extravagant food and drink reveling, varied and unnecessary delicacies, lust for women, avarice, arrogance, pride, and whatever else goes along with them. So when these things enter your heart, you know that the angel of evil is in you. (Mand. 6.1.5 [35.5])

After discerning the proper spirit, it is also significant to practice purity in order to invite the good spirit. For example, Hermas fasts before he receives visions:

---

and desires, but has to struggle to maintain control." B. Diane Lipsett, *Desiring Conversion: Hermas, Thecla, Aseneth* (New York: Oxford University Press, 2011), 21–22; Michel Foucault, *The Use of Pleasure*, trans. Robert Hurley, *The History of Sexuality*, vol. 2 (New York: Vintage Books, 1990), 65.
29 Or "extirpation of passions." See Martha Nussbaum, "The Stoics on the Extirpation of the Passions," *Apeiron* 20 (1987): 122–77.
30 Lipsett, *Desiring Conversion*, 11; A. A. Long, "Epictetus on Emotions," in *From Epicurus to Epictetus: Studies in Hellenistic and Roman Philosophy* (Oxford: Clarendon Press, 2006), 381.
31 Bad desires need to be resisted and controlled, whereas people need to succumb to and submit (υποτάσσειν) to good desires. This is succinctly stated in Mand. 12.1–2 [44–45]. "He said to me: 'Get rid of all evil desire from yourself, and put on the desire that is good and reverent, for if you are clothed with that desire, you will despise the evil desire and bridle it as you wish.'" Here lies the tension between controlling/bridling evil desire and putting on the good desire.
32 Osiek, *Hermas*, 123.

"After fifteen days of fasting and many prayers to the Lord, the knowledge of the writing was revealed to me" (Vis. 2.2.1 [6.1] and 3.1.2 [9.2]). For the Shepherd of Hermas, fasting engenders "the humility of spirit": "Every request requires humility of spirit. And so fast, and you will receive from the Lord what you ask" (Vis. 3.10.6b [18.6b]). Fasting is understood as a way to foster purity in one's life. For example, in *Exhortation to Chastity* 10:5, Tertullian discusses purity of life coupled with prophecy. "'For purification produces harmony,' she [the holy prophetess Prisca] says, 'and they see visions, and when they turn their faces downward, they also hear salutary voices, as clear as they are secret.'"[33] Indeed, Robin Lane Fox, in his *Pagans and Christians,* says: "In the pagan world, fasting was deliberately practiced at cults and oracles to elicit significant dreams and 'receive' the gods' inspiration."[34] For example, in Cicero's discussion of natural divination in *de Divinatione*, John R. Levison notes that Quintus is concerned to "dispute the inference that a few false dreams invalidate the entire enterprise," and he argues that "untrustworthy dreams come to ill-prepared people, and those unskilled interpreters misconstrue the meaning of dreams and oracles" (1.29.60).[35] Cicero's argument drew on the long-held philosophical tradition from Plato as well as Pythagoras. He says, "Then Pythagoras and Plato, who are most respectable authorities, bid us, if we would have trustworthy dreams, to *prepare* (*praeparatos*) for sleep by *following a prescribed course in conduct and in eating*" (2.58.119, emphasis added).[36] Although Cicero criticizes those who participate in these practices, these passages are a potent example of how the preparation for dreams, ecstasy, divination, and prophecy is a prevalent topic in the ancient Mediterranean.

The third/fourth century Syrian neoplatonic philosopher Iamblichus discusses rituals of preparation for prophecy at shrines such as Delphi and Claros. Iamblichus explicates rituals as mechanisms that help the souls of the diviners to become more receptive to divine inspiration. Regarding the oracle at Colophon, Iamblichus writes:

καὶ πρὸ τοῦ πίνειν δὲ οὕτως ἀσιτεῖ τὴν ἡμέραν ὅλην καὶ νύκτα, καὶ ἐν ἱεροῖς τισιν ἀβάτοις τῷ πλήθει καθ' ἑαυτὸν ἀνακεχώρηκεν ἀρχόμενος ἐνθουσιᾶν, καὶ διὰ τῆς ἀποστάσεως καὶ ἀπαλλαγῆς τῶν ἀνθρωπίνων πραγμάτων ἄχραντον ἑαυτὸν εἰς ὑποδοχὴν τοῦ θεοῦ

---

33 See Peter Brown, *The Body and Society: Men, Women, and Sexual Renunciation in Early Christianity* (New York: Columbia University Press, 2008), 65–82; Bazzana, "Il corpo," 122.
34 Robin Lane Fox, *Pagans and Christians*, 396.
35 John R. Levison, *The Spirit in First Century Judaism*, AGJU 29 (Leiden: Brill, 1997), 9.
36 "Iam Pythagoras et Plato, locupletissimi auctores, quo in somnis certiora videamus, praeparatos quodam culta atque victu proficisci ad dormiendum iubent" (*Div.* 2.58.119). Marcus Tullius Cicero, *On Old Age. On Friendship. On Divination* (W. A. Falconer, LCL), 505.

> παρασκευάζει· ἐξ ὧν δὴ εἰς καθαρὰν ἕδραν τῆς ἑαυτοῦ ψυχῆς ἐλλάμπουσαν ἔχει τὴν τοῦ θεοῦ ἐπίπνοιαν, ἀκώλυτόν τε αὐτῇ παρέχει τὴν κατοκωχὴν καὶ τὴν παρουσίαν τελείαν ἀνεμπόδιστον.

> Even before drinking, he fasts the whole day and night, and after becoming divinely inspired, he withdraws by himself to sacred, inaccessible places, and by this withdrawal and separation from human affairs, he *prepares for the reception of the god by making himself undefiled*; and through these means, he has the inspiration of god illuminating the pure sanctuary of his own soul, and providing for it an unhindered divine possession, and a perfect and unimpeded presence. (*Myst.* 3.11)

Emma Clarke and John Dillon translate the middle part of this passage ἄχραντον ἑαυτὸν εἰς ὑποδοχὴν τοῦ θεοῦ παρασκευάζει as "he purifies himself for receiving the god." But my rendering—"he *prepares* for the reception of the god by making himself undefiled"—follows the Greek text more closely. The water that the prophet drinks provides him with "the receptivity and purification of the luminous spirit in us, through which we are able to receive the god" (μὲν ἐπιτηδειότητα μόνον καὶ ἀποκάθαρσιν τοῦ ἐν ἡμῖν αὐγοειδοῦς πνεύματος ἐμποιεῖ, δι' ἣν δυνατοὶ γιγνόμεθα χωρεῖν τὸν θεόν) (*Myst.* 3.11). The word "to prepare" appears again in the same passage, when Iamblichus discusses the oracle at Branchidai.

> Καὶ μὴν ἥ γε ἐν Βραγχίδαις γυνὴ χρησμῳδός, εἴτε ῥάβδον ἔχουσα τὴν πρώτως ὑπὸ θεοῦ τινος παραδοθεῖσαν πληροῦται τῆς θείας αὐγῆς, εἴτε ἐπὶ ἄξονος καθημένη προλέγει τὸ μέλλον, εἴτε τοὺς πόδας ἢ κράσπεδόν τι τέγγουσα τῷ ὕδατι ἢ ἐκ τοῦ ὕδατος ἀτμιζομένη δέχεται τὸν θεόν, ἐξ ἁπάντων τούτων ἐπιτηδεία παρασκευαζομένη πρὸς τὴν ὑποδοχὴν ἔξωθεν αὐτοῦ μεταλαμβάνει. Δηλοῖ δὲ καὶ τὸ τῶν θυσιῶν πλῆθος καὶ ὁ θεσμὸς τῆς ὅλης ἁγιστείας καὶ ὅσα ἄλλα δρᾶται πρὸ τῆς χρησμῳδίας θεοπρεπῶς, τά τε λουτρὰ τῆς προφήτιδος καὶ ἡ τριῶν ὅλων ἡμερῶν ἀσιτία καὶ ἡ ἐν ἀδύτοις αὐτῆς διατριβὴ καὶ ἐχομένης ἤδη τῷ φωτὶ καὶ τερπομένης ἐν πολλῷ χρόνῳ.

> And as for the woman at Branchidai who gives oracles, it is either by holding the staff first given by a certain god that she is filled by the divine radiance; or else when sitting on the axle she predicts the future; or whether dipping her feet or skirt in the water, or inhaling vapor from the water, at any rate, she receives the god: *prepared and made ready by any or all of these preliminaries for his reception from without, she partakes of the god*. This is what is shown by the abundance of sacrifices, the established custom of the custom of the whole ritual, and everything that is performed with due piety *prior to divination*: also the baths of the prophetess, her *fasting for three whole days*, abiding in the innermost sanctuaries, already possessed by light, and rejoicing in it for a long time. (*Myst.* 3.11)[37]

---

[37] English translation follows John M. Dillon, Jackson P. Hershbell, and Emma C. Clarke, *Iamblichus: De mysteriis* (Leiden: Brill, 2003) with my modification.

The ritual preparation includes practices such as fasting (ἀσιτία, associated with the oracle at Branchidai), withdrawal into a sacred, inaccessible place and abiding there (at the oracle at Colophon). The end goal of these ritual preparations is, Iamblichus suggest, for prophets and diviners to "partake of God."

Is Everyone a Potential Prophet?: Inculcating a Worthy Self

As we have seen, the Shepherd of Hermas exhorts the audiences to cultivate a particular way of life so that they may both *invite* the Holy Spirit to dwell in them and *contain* the Holy Spirit. As Reiling maintains, "*charismata* for Hermas are not extraordinary endowments, but moral qualities [and] virtues."[38] Since the particular way of life, that is, moral formation, that the Shepherd emphasizes is related to the general cultivation of a particular self that is worthy to receive the spirit, this call is not aimed at selected people, but rather at the wider community. In this way, I suggest that Shepherd is in the tradition that anyone can *potentially* become a prophet, as long as the divine spirit dwells in her. Scholars have discussed whether the prophet is a "specialist in mediating divine revelation" or an "ordinary member of the church" in early Christianity.[39]

The Shepherd reflects the tradition that anyone is a potential prophet in Vis. 2.3.4 (7.4), "The Lord is near unto them that turn to Him, as it is written in Eldad and Medad, who prophesied to the people in the wilderness." When Joshua wanted to stop Eldad and Medad prophesying upon whom the Spirit rested, Moses maintained, "Are you jealous for my sake? Would that all the Lord's people were prophets, that the Lord would put his spirit on them?" (Num 11:29).

Hermas himself also reflects this tradition. He is an unworthy and unheroic prophet who struggles with ἐπιθυμία. Hermas is also a porous self with a passive and involuntary experience, which his slave subjectivity intensifies. At the same time, he also participates in the cultivation of moral qualities and virtues that

---

[38] Reiling, *Hermas and Christian Prophecy*, 146.
[39] Scholars have discussed whether the prophet is a "specialist in mediating divine revelation" or an "ordinary member of the church." See David Aune, *Prophecy in Early Christianity and the Ancient Mediterranean* (Grands Rapids, MI: Eerdmans, 1981), 198; Aune, 73–4; Reiling, *Hermas*, 97. Aune discusses the theme that in early Christianity all believers were "potential, if not actual prophets" in a theological, not a historical sense (195). He also discusses how the theme that all people are potential prophets is reflected in Plutarch (*De sera numinis* 566c; *De def. orac.* 413e–432b; *De gen. Socr.* 588d–e, 589b–c), and also in Philostratus (*Vita Apoll.* iii. 42), cited by Aune, 349n13; see also, Reiling, *Hermas*, 124–25, 135–36, 146.

would make him a right vessel for the Spirit to dwell. For example, Hermas fasts before he receives visions: "After fifteen days of fasting and many prayers to the Lord, the knowledge of the writing was revealed to me" (Vis. 2.2.1 [6.1] and 3.1.2 [9.2]). For the Shepherd, fasting engenders "the humility of spirit": "Every request needs humility of spirit. Fast, then, and you will receive from the Lord what you ask" (Vis. 3.10.6 [18.6]). As the visions unfold, Hermas gradually controls his ἐπιθυμία.

In this way, the text implicitly tries to shape readers so that they will adopt a prophet's way of life, and thus influences early Christian readers regardless of whether they would ever attain the status of prophet. The Shepherd of Hermas engages with the themes of virtue and control as criteria of a true prophet and encourages the audience to cultivate a self that can harbor the Holy Spirit. As Bazzana cogently argues, the Shepherd considers the "Holy Spirit" as "son of God,"[40] and so it is integral for the audience to participate in the practice of forming a self that is worthy to receive the Holy Spirit, that is, the spirit of Christ.

The Shepherd was a crucial catechetical text in early Christianity, and we can understand how it would have appealed to the elite Christian readers well versed with spiritual practices connected to formations of the self.[41] Recent studies in various fields have employed Hadot's "spiritual exercises" as a useful tool for explaining disciplines and training.[42] For instance, some scholars have explored how the self is disciplined in stories of martyrdom. Nicole Kelley in particular provides an innovative way of studying early Christian martyr acts, suggesting that we read them as "instrument(s) of discipline," by which ancient audiences are exhorted to train themselves as potential martyrs. She cogently argues that, regardless of whether such Christians really became martyrs or not, they were encouraged to adopt a particular lifestyle to prepare themselves to become such. Drawing on Hadot's scholarship as well as Kelley's insights, I contend that discourses on prophecy in early Christianity call for training in a par-

---

40 Bazzana, *Having the Spirit of Christ*, 128–29.
41 Malcom Choat and Rachel Yuen-Collingridge, "The Egyptian Hermas: The Shepherd in Egypt before Constantine," in *Early Christian Manuscripts: Examples of Applied Method and Approach*, ed. Thomas J. Kraus and Tobias Nicklas (Leiden: Brill, 2010), 191–212.
42 Elizabeth A. Castelli, *Martyrdom and Memory: Early Christian Culture Making* (New York: Columbia University Press, 2004), 86; Nicole Kelley, "Philosophy as Training for Death: Reading the Ancient Christian Martyr Acts as Spiritual Exercises," *Church History* 75 (2006): 723–47; Karen King, "Martyrdom and its Discontents in the Tchacos Codex" in *Proceedings of the International Congress on the Tchacos Codex Held at Rice University, Houston Texas, March 13–16, 2008* (Leiden: Brill, 2010); Mikael Haxby, "The First Apocalypse of James: Martyrdom and Sexual Difference" (Ph.D. diss., Harvard University, 2013).

ticular way of living, and thus could be influential to early Christians regardless of whether they would ever attain the status of prophet or not.

Reading the Shepherd along with Origen's Works

We have seen that, in the Shepherd of Hermas, two connected themes emerge: first, (true) prophecy is presented as a passive experience (in the sense that the prophet is the mouthpiece of God) and second, there is a strong suggestion that a certain cultivation is required, in order to be a right vessel for the spirit to indwell. It is necessary to cultivate self-control (ἐγκράτεια) to be a proper self to receive the Holy Spirit. However, at the moment of prophecy, the tenor has shifted: now a lack of self-control is the hallmark of true prophecy.

In the next section, we will compare the Shepherd of Hermas with select works by Origen (*Contra Celsum* Book 7 and the *Homilies on Numbers* 14-17), for these writings can serve as potent instantiation of a Christian counterpart that holds a different idea about true prophecy as a lack of control, and yet which has similar rhetorical strategies.

Contra Celsum Book 7: The Wrong Form of Prophecy

In *Contra Celsum* 7[43] and in his treatment of Balaam's story in the *Homilies on Numbers* 14–17,[44] Origen deploys the same themes of virtue and control as the criteria of the true and worthy prophet. On the surface, Origen's discussions differ from the Shepherd of Hermas. While the Shepherd of Hermas emphasizes the

---

[43] Celsus claims that Christianity is a religion of false prophecy. Jesus is the Magus, who fails to understand divine wisdom. According to Celsus, Jesus is merely possessed by the daemons who reside in the lower realm. Against Celsus, Origen claims that Christianity is a religion with true prophets. Furthermore, he deflects Celsus's criticism against Christianity by arguing that Celsus's attack does not apply to Christianity; it is applied to the "heretical" groups that Origen opposes. So, according to him, genuine Christianity is comprised of the true prophets, whereas the so-called heretical groups are full of false prophets. Dale Martin, *Inventing Superstition: From the Hippocratics to the Christians* (Cambridge, MA: Harvard University Press, 2004), 140–43.
[44] The original Greek of Origen's *Homilies on Numbers* is lost, but it survives in Latin. The "Book of Balaam" (which is the traditional rabbinic name for the material) is an extended narrative couched in the book of Numbers. R. W. L. Moberly, *Prophecy and Discernment* (Cambridge: Cambridge University Press, 2006), 138.

lack of control as a marker of true prophecy, Origen refutes this idea. Yet Origen is fundamentally in agreement with the Shepherd of Hermas, since both exhort the audience to inculcate certain virtues, just as the prophets did.

Origen emphasizes the importance of worthiness, morality, and virtue as necessary qualities of the prophet. He also has another key emphasis in his understanding of prophecy: a distrust of losing control of one's consciousness during prophecy. Origen emphasizes that the will of God initiates prophecy, but he equally emphasizes the will and control of the prophet during prophecy. He defies the notion that the moment of prophecy is involuntary and involves losing control of one's consciousness.

In *Contra Celsum*, the theme of the moral character of a prophet is emphasized in several places (*Cels*. 2.51; 4.95; 5.42; 7.3).[45] In addition, over against Pythia, Origen emphasizes "those of the prophets in Judea"—who are "our" prophets—as the champions of virtues, such as strength, courage, and a holy life, which makes them "worthy of" (ἄξιος) God's spirit":[46]

> Διόπερ ἐν οὐδενὶ μὲν τιθέμεθα λόγῳ τὰ ὑπὸ τῆς Πυθίας ἢ Δωδωνίδων ἢ Κλαρίου ἢ ἐν Βραγχίδαις ἢ ἐν Ἄμμωνος ἢ ὑπὸ μυρίων ἄλλων λεγομένων θεοπρόπων προειρημένα· τὰ δ' ὑπὸ τῶν ἐν Ἰουδαίᾳ προφητευσάντων τεθήπαμεν, ὁρῶντες ὅτι ἄξιος ἦν αὐτῶν ὁ ἐρρωμένος καὶ εὔτονος καὶ σεμνὸς βίος πνεύματος θεοῦ, τρόπῳ προφητεύοντος καινῷ καὶ οὐδὲν ἔχοντι παραπλήσιον ταῖς ἀπὸ δαιμόνων μαντείαις.

> That is the reason why we reckon of no account the predictions uttered by the Pythian priestess, or by the priestesses of Dodona, or by the oracle of Apollo at Claros, or at Branchiade, or at the shrine of Zeus Ammon, or by countless other alleged prophets; whereas we admire *those of the prophets in Judaea*, seeing that their strong, courageous, and holy life *was worthy of* God's Spirit, whose prophecy was imparted in a new way which had nothing in common with the divination inspired by daemons. (*Cels*. 7.7, emphasis added)

Origen's emphasis on "being worthy of" the Holy Spirit[47] (or seeking "to deserve/earn" the Spirit[48]) recurs throughout his works such as *Commentary on Romans*

---

45 Origen, *Contra Celsum*, trans. Henry Chadwick (Cambridge: Cambridge University Press, 1953); Origen, *Contre Celse*, ed. Marcel Borret, 5 vols, Sources chrétiennes 132, 136, 147, 150, 227 (Paris: Cerf, 1967–76). English translation follows Chadwick, unless otherwise noted.
46 It is all the more significant to consider that Origen, along with other early Christian writers, takes great pains to distinguish between the Jews and the Christians. See Susanna Drake, *Slandering the Jew: Sexuality and Difference in Early Christian Texts* (Philadelphia: University of Pennsylvania Press, 2013).
47 For Origen, the Holy Spirit, God's spirit, and the divine spirit are equivalent. See Pablo Argarate, "The Holy Spirit in Prin I. 3," *Origeniana Nona: Origen and the Religious Practice of his Time*, ed. G. Heidl and R. Somos (Leuven: Peeters, 2009), 25–48.

and *de Principiis*. Origen highlights that the Holy Spirit chooses prophets "on account of the quality of their lives" (*Cels.* 7.7). In a later passage, Origen reiterates that the prophets "received the divine Spirit because of purity of life" (*Cels.* 7.18).⁴⁹

This Jewish and Christian prophetic purity stands in contrast to the Pythia. In *Contra Celsum* 7, Origen constructs Christian prophecy over against the so-called pagan prophecy and mantic practices, with the Pythia as the target of his polemic. He employs the Pythia as the epitome of pagan mantic practices more generally, and thus through the invective against Pythia, Origen essentially polemicizes "pagan" prophecy as something fundamentally different from Christian prophecy.

Origen's polemic against Pythia is two-fold: first, according to Origen, the Pythia lacks virtue and morality necessary for prophets, as we have seen above. Second, the Pythia loses control. Origen develops a sexualized polemic against Pythia, in saying,

> Ἱστόρηται τοίνυν περὶ τῆς Πυθίας, ὅπερ δοκεῖ τῶν ἄλλων μαντείων λαμπρότερον τυγχάνειν, ὅτι περικαθεζομένη τὸ τῆς Κασταλίας στόμιον ἡ τοῦ Ἀπόλλωνος προφῆτις δέχεται πνεῦμα διὰ τῶν γυναικείων κόλπων·

> Indeed, of the Pythian priestess—the oracle that seems to be more distinguished than the others—it is related that while the prophetess of Apollo is sitting at the mouth of the Castalian cave she receives a spirit through her womb. (*Cels.* 7.3.25)

Origen's sexualized invective against the Pythia is grounded in a physiological understanding commonly found in Greco-Roman discourses on prophecy. Plutarch, in his *On the Obsolescence of Oracles*, for example, famously narrates "the dangers of prophecy," discussing how prophecy is popularly understood as the loss of control, and even penetration and divine rape enacted by a male god on a female seer:⁵⁰

---

48 Greek (ἄξιος) is mostly translated as "worthy of." Latin (*mereo*), which is probably used to translate Greek (ἄξιος) in Origen's works, has wider linguistic parameters such as "deserve," "earn," "merit," and "be worthy of.", see *TDNT*, s.v. ἄξιος.
49 According to Origen, "the prophets, according to the will of God, said without any obscurity whatever could be at once understood as beneficial to their hearers and helpful towards attaining moral reformation" (*Cels.* 7.10).
50 Dale Martin, *The Corinthian Body* (New Haven: Yale University Press, 1995), 239–42. Plutarch, in *Moralia* 437 D, explicitly discusses that the issue of the control by God and the prophets' loss of control is ingrained in the discourses on prophecy.

πολλαὶ μὲν γὰρ αἰσθομένης πλείονες δ' ἄδηλοι τό τε σῶμα καταλαμβάνουσι καὶ τὴν ψυχὴν ὑπορρέουσι δυσχέρειαι καὶ κινήσεις· ὧν ἀναπιμπλαμένην οὐκ ἄμεινον ἐκεῖ βαδίζειν οὐδὲ παρέχειν ἑαυτὴν τῷ θεῷ μὴ παντάπασι καθαρὰν οὖσαν ὥσπερ ὄργανον ἐξηρτυμένον καὶ εὐηχές, ἀλλ' ἐμπαθῆ καὶ ἀκατάστατον.

For many annoyances and disturbances of which she is conscious, and many more unperceived, lay hold upon her body and filter into her soul; and whenever she is replete with these, it is better than she should not go there and *surrender herself to the control of the god*, when she is not completely clean (as if she were a musical instrument, well strung and well-tuned), but in a state of emotion and instability (*Def. orac.* 437 D, emphasis added).

Plutarch participates in a broader understanding of *pneuma* as "a physical entity that enters the body and produces a condition free of mental restraint—enthusiasm."[51] In *On the Obsolescence of Oracles* (405 C), he posits a more explicitly sexualized understanding of prophecy when he says, "a pure, virgin soul, becomes the associate of (σύνειμι) the god." As Dale Martin points out, the better translation of σύνειμι might be "to have sexual intercourse."[52]

In maligning Pythia, Origen thus draws on the sexual invective which is a mode of constructing and denigrating the "Other." Furthermore, Origen has a particular spin on the sexual polemic that she "loses control" in arguing that Pythia loses control by *consciousness*. As Jennifer Knust succinctly sums up, "sexualized invective serves several purposes at once: outsiders are pushed further away, insiders are policed, and morality is both constituted and defined as 'Christian'."[53] Through sexualized polemic against Pythia, Origen depicts the Pythia and her prophecy as an outsider to the pure practices of "the prophets in Judaea," who are treated as proto-Christian. Contrary to Pythia, "the one who is inspired by the divine spirit," argues Origen, "ought to possess the clearest vision at the very time when the deity is in communion with him (*Cels.* 7.3)."

Origen levels criticism against Pythia and her ecstasy, claiming that the Pythia is an "alleged prophetess (τὴν δῆθεν προφητεύουσαν)" in order to devalue her as a prophetess. The fact that Origen uses "prophet" to refer to Pythia, instead of another term such as "diviner," I would suggest, means that he directly juxtaposes "pagan" with "Christian" prophecy:

---

51 Levison, *Inspired: The Holy Spirit and the Mind of Faith* (Grand Rapids, MI: Eerdmans, 2013), 92. For a helpful discussion on this topic, see idem, *Filled with the Spirit* (Grand Rapids, MI: Eerdmans, 2009), 178–201.
52 Martin, *Body*, 240.
53 Jennifer Wright Knust, *Abandoned to Lust: Sexual Slander and Ancient Christianity* (New York: Columbia University Press, 2006). Susanna Drake, *Slandering the Jew*, 10.

Ἀλλὰ καὶ τὸ εἰς ἔκστασιν καὶ μανικὴν ἄγειν κατάστασιν τὴν δῆθεν προφητεύουσαν, ὡς μηδαμῶς αὐτὴν ἑαυτῇ παρακολουθεῖν, οὐ θείου πνεύματος ἔργον ἐστίν· ἐχρῆν γὰρ τὸν κάτοχον τῷ θείῳ πνεύματι πολλῷ πρότερον παντὸς οὑτινοσοῦν τοῦ ἀπὸ τῶν χρησμῶν διδασκομένου τὸ συμβαλλόμενον εἰς τὸν μέσον καὶ κατὰ φύσιν βίον ἢ πρὸς τὸ λυσιτελὲς ἢ πρὸς τὸ συμφέρον ὠφεληθῆναι καὶ διορατικώτερον παρ' ἐκεῖνο μάλιστα καιροῦ τυγχάνειν, ὅτε σύνεστιν αὐτῷ τὸ θεῖον.

It is not the work of divine spirit to lead the alleged prophetess into a state of ecstasy and frenzy so that she loses possession of her consciousness. The person inspired by the divine spirit ought to have derived from it far more benefit than anyone who may be instructed by the oracles to do that which helps towards living a life which is moderate and according to nature, or towards that which is of advantage or which is expedient. And *for that reason he ought to possess the clearest vision at the very time when the deity is in communion with him.* (Cels. 7.3, emphasis added)

In doing so, Origen drives a wedge between prophets who lose consciousness and prophets who keep clear vision in the moment of communication with the divine. Origen opines, "Because of the touch, as it were, of what is called the Holy Spirit upon their soul they possessed clear mental vision and became more radiant in their soul, and even in body, which no longer offered any opposition to the life lived according to virtue (κατ' ἀρετὴν)" (Cels. 7.4).[54] Again, Origen tightly connects virtue to possessing clear mental vision in the moment of prophecy, crafting a particular way of prophecy as the right form of prophecy.

Furthermore, Origen questions, "If the Pythian priestess is out of her senses and has *no control of* her faculties when she prophesies, what sort of spirit must we think it which poured darkness upon her mind and rational thinking?" (Cels. 7.4, emphasis added).[55] Origen tightly connects the loss of control of consciousness with the loss of bodily control. Put differently, for Origen, Pythia is sexually vulnerable both in physical body and mind.[56]

---

[54] καὶ διὰ τῆς πρὸς τὴν ψυχὴν αὐτῶν, ἵν' οὕτως ὀνομάσω, ἁφῆς τοῦ καλουμένου ἁγίου πνεύματος διορατικώτεροί τε τὸν νοῦν ἐγίνοντο καὶ τὴν ψυχὴν λαμπρότεροι ἀλλὰ καὶ τὸ σῶμα, οὐδαμῶς ἔτι ἀντιπρᾶττον τῷ κατ' ἀρετὴν βίῳ.
[55] Εἰ δ' ἐξίσταται καὶ οὐκ ἐν ἑαυτῇ ἐστιν ἡ Πυθία, ὅτε μαντεύεται, ποδαπὸν νομιστέον πνεῦμα, τὸ σκότον καταχέαν μαντεύεται, ποδαπὸν νομιστέον πνεῦμα, τὸ σκότον καταχέαν τοῦ νοῦ καὶ τῶν λογισμῶν.
[56] In analyzing the gendered imageries in Greek tragedies in the classical Greek period, Padel claims, "The mind—like a woman in society, like female sexuality in relation to male—is acted upon, invaded, a victim of the outside world (especially of divinity)." Ruth Padel, *In and Out of the Mind: Greek Images of the Tragic Self* (Princeton: Princeton University Press, 1992), 111.

Balaam, An Unworthy Prophet: The *Homilies on Numbers* 14–17[57]

Origen mobilizes the Pythia to represent prophetic practices of "the Other," and begins to construct a portrait of prophetic practices for Christians and Jews based on their scriptures. Contrary to the Pythia, the Hebrew prophets are virtuous and do not lose control of their consciousness in the moment of divine communication via prophecy. But what if one of "our Hebrew prophets" does not have the necessary ethical qualities? Or worse, what if he seems to lose control in the moment of prophecy?

Balaam in the Book of Numbers is such an unheroic prophet. Just as Hermas is an unheroic and unworthy prophet, who experiences many visions, so is Balaam. If Hermas has a problem in regulating his desires, Balaam has a problem of greed, for he prophesies for money. While Origen defends Balaam as a prophet because his story is in the Bible, he takes pains to solve the problem of prophecy he finds in this instance. His solution was to read allegorically and interpret Balaam as someone undergoing training and making progress and thus to utilize Balaam as a *pedagogical* example for Christian audiences.

In his interpretation of Balaam's story in the *Homilies on Numbers* 14–17, Origen deploys the same themes of virtue and control as the criteria of the true and worthy prophet that we see in the Shepherd of Hermas. On the surface, Origen's discussions might differ from the Shepherd of Hermas. While the Shepherd emphasizes the lack of control as a marker of true prophecy, Origen refutes this idea. Yet Origen ultimately is in agreement with the Shepherd, since both exhort the audience to inculcate certain virtues, just as the prophets did.

The prophet Balaam enjoys a spectacular narrative in Num 22–24. With his ability to curse and bless as well as tell the future, he eventually saves Israel and follows YHWH's command to bless Israel. He received contrasting evaluations by Jewish and Christian writers in antiquity: some considered him either as a villain, a diviner, or a magician who is a herald of the Magi, or as a hero who prophesies about Christ.[58] Furthermore, Balaam's "foreign" identity compound-

---

[57] The "Book of Balaam" (which is the traditional rabbinic name for the material) is an extended narrative couched in the book of Numbers. R. W. L. Moberly, "Elisha and Balaam," in *Prophecy and Discernment* (Cambridge: Cambridge University Press, 2006), 138.

[58] Judith Reesa Baskin, "Origen on Balaam: The Dilemma of the Unworthy Prophet," *Vigiliae Christianae* 37 (1983): 22–35; Robert M. Berchman, "Arcana mundi between Balaam and Hecate: prophecy, divination, and magic in later Platonism," *SBLSP* 28 (1989):107–83; Catherine Chin, "Who is the Ascetic Exegete? Angels, Enchantments, and Transformative Food in Origen's Homilies on Joshua," in *Asceticism and Exegesis in Early Christianity: The Reception of New Testament*

ed his characterization. As for Origen, Balaam is an unequivocally problematic and unheroic prophet.

Given that Origen considers virtue and morality to be essential to a prophet, his puzzlement over Balaam is understandable. What is more problematic for Origen is that Balaam's portrayal in Numbers does not fit into Origen's understanding of prophecy as an active and controlled phenomenon. With his emphasis on human free will,[59] Origen's focus on the mind as the locus of prophecy and on the active mind in the moment of prophecy is crucial. Origen struggles to fit the troubling figure of Balaam into his theological landscape, and his grappling with the story in Numbers allows us to shed a different light on Origen's understanding of prophecy.

In *Contra Celsum* 7, as we saw, Origen emphasizes "those of the prophets in Judea"—who are "our" prophets—as the champion of virtues, such as strength, courage, and a holy life, which make them "worthy of" (ἄξιος) God's spirit. In describing Balaam, Origen concedes that Balaam is not worthy (*dignus*) to receive prophecy.[60] Yet he does not pillory Balaam for his unworthiness, as he criticized the Pythia. Instead, he emphasizes that "God put God's words into his [Balaam's] mouth," although his heart was "not 'yet able to have room for the word of God" (*Hom. Num.* 15.2.2).[61] Paying attention to the scriptural phrase that God "put a word into his mouth" (Num 23:16), Origen notes:

> Si dignus fuisset Balaam, uerbum suum Deus non in 'ore eius', sed in corde posuisset. Nunc autem quoniam in corde eius desiderium mercedis erat et cupidus pecuniae, uerbum Dei non in corde, sed in ore eius ponitur.

Texts in Ancient Ascetic Discourses, ed. Hans Ulrich Weidemann (Göttingen: Vandenhoeck & Ruprecht, 2013), 203–18.

59 The main theme of book 3 of *de Principiis* is the intricate correlation between God's providence (*pronoia/providentia*) and human will (*propositum* or *pro arbitrii sui libertate*). Providence is fundamental to Origen's understanding of human engagement with God. Origen makes claims about the goodness of God and emphasizes human free will and human responsibility. Origen delves into a fairly sustained discussion of prophecy in 3.3, for prophecy is the focal site for thinking about human beings and the human-divine relationship, however, the soul, the locus of prophecy, is open to both daemonic and divine powers. The human being, with her own free will, chooses which influence will be a governing power for her soul. As Henry Chadwick sums up, Origen is concerned that "human beings are not automata, deterred from acts only by some external cause or consideration." Henry Chadwick, "Philosophical Tradition and the Self," in *Late Antiquity: A Guide to the Postclassical World*, ed. G. W. Bowersock, Peter Brown, and Oleg Grabar (Cambridge, MA: Belknap Press of Harvard University Press, 1999), 76.
60 Karl A. E. Enenkel and Walter Melion, eds., *Meditation-Refashioning the Self: Theory and Practice in Late Medieval* (Leiden: Brill, 2010), 391.
61 Unless otherwise noted, I follow the translation of Scheck and Hall, *Homilies on Numbers*.

> If Balaam had been *worthy* (*dignus*), God would not have put his word in his mouth, but into his heart. But now, since the desire for reward was in his heart (*cor*) and he was greedy for money, the word of God was put not in his heart, but in his mouth. (*Hom. Num.* 14.3.2, emphasis added)

While explicating five prophecies that Balaam uttered in Numbers 22, Origen keeps juxtaposing "God's words in Balaam's mouth" and "Balaam's heart." This repetition is significant, for Origen understands that the heart (or mind) is the locus where prophecy occurs. I posit that Origen's contrast between mouth and heart/mind (*cor*) in the *Homilies on Numbers* draws on the *topos* of the prophet as the mouthpiece of God—the topos that Origen problematizes.

Some other ancient readers of the Balaam story pick up this imagery in their interpretation of Balaam's story. Philo, for example, in his *Life of Moses* (1.273–74),[62] tries to solve the conundrum of how Balaam, a villain, was able to prophesy by suggesting that he essentially becomes a mouthpiece of God.[63]

---

[62] Philo, *De vita Mosis*, I. (273–74); John R. Levison, "The Prophetic Spirit as an Angel According to Philo," *HTR* 88 (1995): 189–207, 191; idem, *Filled with the Spirit*, esp. 154–77; idem, "The Debut of the Divine Spirit in Josephus' Antiquities," *HTR* 87 (1994): 123–38.

[63] Philo portrays Moses as the ultimate masculine prophet, who participates in the ascetic practices associated with prophecy. William Loader analyzes how Moses was engaged with "constant self-discipline and temporary abstinence." Loader continues, "Philo is not in favor of people simply rushing off into the wilderness to engage in contemplation before they have developed the necessary self-discipline within the context of a socially and politically active life." William Loader, *Philo, Josephus, and the Testaments on Sexuality* (Grand Rapids, MI: Eerdmans, 2011), 100. As Philo writes:

> Moses also represents Balaam, who is the symbol of a vain people, stripped of his arms, as a runaway and deserter, well knowing the war which it becomes the soul to carry on for the sake of knowledge; for he says to his ass, who is here a symbol of the irrational designs of life which every foolish man entertains, that "If I had had a sword, I should ere now have slain Thee." And great thanks are due to the Maker of all things, because he, knowing the struggles and resistance of folly, did not give to it the power of language, which would have been like giving a sword to a madman, in order that it might have no power to work great and iniquitous destruction among all whom it should meet with. *But the reproaches which Balaam utters are in some degree expressed by all those who are not purified, but are always talking foolishly, devoting themselves to the life of a merchant, or of a farmer, or to some other business, the object of which is to provide the things necessary for life.* As long, indeed, as everything goes on prosperously with respect to each individual, he mounts his animal joyfully and rides on cheerfully, and holding the reins firmly he will by no means consent to [....]

(*De Cherubim* 32–3, emphasis added). English translation follows that of C. D. Yonge, *A Treatise on the Cherubim in the Works of Philo: Complete and Unabridged* (Peabody, MA: Hendricken, 1993).

Philo states that Balaam loses his consciousness when the spirit of God possesses him, albeit briefly, and speaks through him. As John Levison explains Philo's reading, the angel spirit "made Balaam's mind inoperative"[64] and this angel "directs his vocal organs, guides the reins of speech, and employs his tongue actually accomplished this when it reappeared, identified as the prophetic spirit."[65] Josephus, a half century later, also repeatedly states the fact that Balaam was "not in himself" (*Ant.* 4.118), "unconscious" (*Ant.* 4.119), and that he lost the possession of his "mental faculties" (*Ant.* 4.121).[66] This description of Balaam by Josephus is similar to Origen's polemical portrayal of Pythia, who loses control —literally, who was not in herself—and loses consciousness in the moment of prophecy.

Within an interpretation of the story of Balaam, Origen expounds his view of prophecy in his *Homilies on Numbers*. J. R. Baskin argues, "Origen's view of prophecy is clear. The true prophet collaborates in the delivery of the divine message; he speaks with his heart, and is perforce a righteous man. Yet, to bring all people to righteousness, unworthy men may occasionally serve as vessels for the divine message, though they will always speak with their mouths, not with their hearts."[67] As Baskin interprets it, Origen divorces the *content* of Balaam's prophecy from the *person* of the prophet. Thus, Origen tries to solve the problem that Balaam was chosen to prophesy.

Yet Origen's *Homilies on Numbers* 14–17 add another component to the complex matter of Balaam and prophecy that Baskin does not notice: Balaam is now interpreted allegorically,[68] Origen portrays him as participating in "the journey to

---

In *De Cherubim* 32, Philo juxtaposes Moses and Balaam by portraying Balaam as the antithesis of Moses. While Moses is the culmination of control and poise, which are the important traits of masculinity, Balaam is the opposite with his lack of control. See Colleen Conway, "Gender and Divine Relativity in Philo of Alexandria," *JSJ* (2003): 471–91. I am thankful to Olivia Stewart, who provided me with this idea in our private conversation. Origen, however, interestingly does not portray Balaam as effeminate. I suggest that Origen views the Hebrew Bible as a Christian prerogative, and thus Origen rather tries to utilize Balaam as a model for the Christian audience instead.

64 Levison, "The Prophetic Spirit," 192.
65 Ibid., 191.
66 John R. Levison, *Of Two Minds: Ecstasy and Inspired Interpretation in the New Testament World* (Texas: Bible Press, 1999), 19.
67 Baskin, "Origen on Balaam," 30.
68 The literature for allegory in Origen's works is vast. See K. J. Torjesen, *Hermeneutical Procedure and Theological Method in Origen's Exegesis* (Berlin: de Gruyter, 1986); J. Whitman, *Allegory: The Dynamics of an Ancient and Medieval Technique* (Cambridge, MA: Harvard University Press, 1987); Peter W. Martens, "Revisiting the Allegory/Typology Distinction: The Case of Ori-

the wisdom of God" (*Hom. Num.* 17.4.4). Origen allegorizes the problematic prophet Balaam, whose name means "vain people" (*populous uanus*):[69] he can be understood as a person who gradually learns to be engaged with God. In the *Homilies on Numbers* 27, a section which is proximate to his description of Balaam, Origen explains that these stories are understood to be an allegory of the soul's advancement:

> He [God] posits two journeys of the soul. 'One is the means of *training the soul in virtues* through the Law of God when it is placed in flesh; and by ascending through certain steps it makes progress as we have said, *from virtue to virtue*, and uses these progressions as stages." The other is a journey by which the soul gradually ascends to the heavens after the resurrection. It does not reach the highest point "unreasonably, but ... is led throughout many stations. In them it is enlightened...illumined at each stage by the light of Wisdom, until it arrives at the Father of Lights Himself. (*Hom. Num.* 27, emphasis added)

Commenting on Num 24:1–3,[70] Origen allegorically interprets the verse that Balaam "sees that it is good in the sight of the Lord to bless Israel." He notes that "those people who are now a vain people, and those teachers who detain that people in vanity by not believing in Christ, will one day see, namely, 'in the last days.'" Origen continues to posit that Balaam's eyes "have been opened," and that "it is as if those eyes, [which] were closed up to this point, will now be opened through the spirit of God 'who came on him' when the veil was removed" (*Hom. Num.* 17.3.1).[71] Thus Balaam, who first has only prophecy "on his mouth," not "in his heart," now has progressed to "see" God. I suggest that Origen portrays Balaam as increasing in maturity and holiness. The gradual development of Balaam's character can be observed in the text, which serves rhetorically as a good exemplar of moral progress to the audience.

While discussing Balaam's story in the *Homilies on Numbers* 14–19, Origen emphasizes Balaam's gradual "pursuit of wisdom and knowledge" (*Hom. Num.* 17.3.5). Balaam now becomes a model for a person who always "strives

---

gen," *JECS* 16 (2008): 283–96; idem, *Origen and Scripture: The Contours of the Exegetical Life* (Oxford: Oxford University Press, 2014)

69 *Hom. Num.* 14.4.1.

70 Num 24:1–3: "And Balaam, seeing that it is good in the sight of the Lord to bless Israel, did not go out according to custom to meet the auspices, but turned his face toward the desert. And Balaam, lifting up his eyes, observes that Israel had set up their camps by tribes; and the Spirit of God came to him. And he took up his parable and spoke."

71 Sed videamus jam quae sint quae in tertia prophetia proloquatur Balaam. "Dixit, inquit, Balaam filius Beor, homo vere videns, dixit, audiens verba fortis, qui visum Dei vidit in somnis, revelati oculi ejus." Mirum profecto est quomodo tantae laudis dignus habeatur Balaam, qui accepta parabola sua, haec de semetipso pronuntiat.

for what is ahead" (*Hom. Num.* 17.4.4).[72] As Moberly succinctly maintains, for Origen, "moral failure induces spiritual blindness."[73] For Origen's Balaam, then, regaining morality is the key to regaining spiritual vision. In his attempt to make sense of the biblical story of the enigmatically unworthy prophet Balaam, Origen shifts the focus of the story to one of his central theological themes: even an unworthy person can have a hope of salvation and, more importantly, everyone is expected to participate in the journey to God.

As the Shepherd of Hermas does, Origen draws on the theme of virtue as the pre-requisite of a prophet. Balaam, who was known for his lack of virtue, is transformed, representing a journey of *the soul* in virtue by participating in moral progress. In this way, Balaam's story has an edifying value for Christian readers and audience, encouraging them to participate in moral formation as well. In another homily, Origen enjoins the audience, "thus let all of us, as far as our ability allows, strive for the prophetic life" (*Hom. Jer.* 14.5). In *Contra Celsum* 7, which we just saw, "the prophets, according to the will of God, said without any obscurity whatever could be at once understood as beneficial to their hearers and helpful towards attaining moral reformation" (*Cels.* 7.10). Even Balaam's story in Numbers can educate, showing a soul that has the power to strive for perfection and sanctity, and thus benefitting all by this story.

Conclusion

By reading the Shepherd of Hermas along with two comparanda from Origen (*Cels.* 7 and *Hom. Num.* 14–17), this essay has examined the way in which prophecy and prophet are contested categories. The Shepherd of Hermas and Origen's two works deploy similar discussions and use similar rhetorical strategies with similar targeted (Christian) audiences, implicitly seeking to persuade their readers and hearers to cultivate a particular kind of self.

The first part of this essay focused on the way in which the Shepherd of Hermas emphasizes virtue and other ethical qualities of a prophet as well as the cultivation necessary to be a prophet through moral formation. In modeling its own view of a true prophet and true prophecy, the text shows the centrality of cultivation in becoming a true prophet. These are similar strategies to Origen's. However, in the moment of prophecy, the Shepherd of Hermas subscribes to the discourse of prophecy that favors the loss of control, a discourse with which Ori-

---

72 Moberly, *Prophecy and Discernment*, 131–49.
73 Ibid., 147.

gen would disagree. In *Contra Celsum* 7, drawing upon this discourse on prophecy, the loss of control, Origen uses a sexualized invective against Pythia whose female physiology ("receiving a spirit through her womb") is negatively portrayed. From this concrete context, the importance of virtue and morality emerges as the qualification for a true prophet, which in turn serves to circumscribe the Christian prophecy against "the Other." Likewise, Origen's *Hom. Num.* 14–17 consistently sustains the same notion of prophecy that one should not lose control while prophesying. In order not to dismiss, but to defend, the existence of the troubling prophet Balaam in the divinely-inspired Scripture, Origen offers an allegorical interpretation of this story, utilizing him as a pedagogical example for the Christian audience.

In modeling their own views of a true prophet and true prophecy, these texts show the centrality of cultivation in becoming a true prophet. The works of both the Shepherd of Hermas and Origen are not manuals on how to become a prophet, but rather serve to educate and thus influence the (Christian) audience in a particular way.[74]

---

[74] This chapter contains elements from "Gender, Race, and Normalization of Prophecy in Early Christianity," in Mitzi J. Smith and Jin Young Choi, eds., *Minoritized Women Reading Race-Ethnicity: Intersectional Approaches and Early Christian* (Con)Texts (London: Lexington Books, 2020). I am grateful to Lexington for its permission to include materials in this chapter.

B. Diane Lipsett
Gender, Volubility, and Transformation in the Shepherd of Hermas

The religious transformation or *metanoia* summoned by the Shepherd of Hermas is construed in some ways as gendered. "Be a man [Ἀνδρίζου],"[1] Hermas is urged, as visionary figures address problems of desire, household order, and the vigor, stability, purity and interdependent social relations of the second-century Roman church. The text also celebrates ἐγκράτεια, self-restraint, as a core virtue, and at moments conventionally assumes restrained speech to be a masculine trait, a marker of the composed masculine self, unlike the fluid, feminine tendency to garrulousness. Yet Hermas is a prolific talker, as are his visionary interlocutors, from the elder woman who represents the church to the male Shepherd, the angel of *metanoia*. They at times chastise his persistent questions as shameless (ἀναιδής), cunning or crafty (πανοῦργος), and presumptuous (αὐθάδης), but the revealers, too, are loquacious. A narrative popular in antiquity, the Shepherd is dominated by dialogue over plot—or rather, speech and talk *are* the action. The uttering of the words is the performance of the action.[2] The prolix text both manifests and resists what M. M. Bakhtin in a discussion of "speech genres" terms a "finalization of the utterance,"[3] and may carry implications for how religious and ethical transformation is envisioned. Moreover, the additive, aggregative, prolonged quality of the Shepherd of Hermas may hint at imitable social practices of self-scrutiny, reading and interpretation, and communal dialogue.

---

[1] Throughout I rely on the *Apostolic Fathers*, vol. 2 (Ehrman, LCL 25) for the Greek text and offer my own translations.
[2] A characterization of performative language drawn from J. L. Austin, *How to Do Things with Words*, ed., J. O. Urmson (Cambridge: Harvard University Press, 1962), 8.
[3] Mikhail M. Bakhtin, "The Problem of Speech Genres," in *Speech Genres & Other Late Essays*, transl. Vern W. McGee, ed., Caryl Emerson and Michael Holquist (Austin: University of Texas Press, 1986), 60–102, 76.

Gender, Self-Restraint, and Transformation

Gender matters in The Shepherd of Hermas; the achievement of masculinity is one key trope for virtue and transformation.[4] As the first Vision urges, "Be a man, Hermas" (Vis. 1.4.3 [4.3]), so the final Parable exhorts, "Conduct yourself manfully [*viriliter*] in this ministry" (Sim. 10.4.1 [114.1]).[5] As *pater familias*, Hermas holds the responsibility of admonishing his household, is chastised for his neglect, and suffers for his children's deeds even after they repent (Vis. 1.3.1 [3.1]; 2.2.2 [6.2]; Sim. 7.2 [66.2]). As one who desires to "live to God," he must discern the paradoxical danger of evil desire or lawlessness rising up within an "upright man" (Vis. 1.1.8 [1.8]; Mand. 4.1.3 [29.3]) and, conversely, the spiritual power of a gathered assembly of "upright men" [ἀνδρῶν δικαίων] (Mand. 11.9, 13, 14 [43.9, 13, 14]; Sim. 9.15.4 [92.4]). Rejuvenation of the spirit that results from receiving revelation is envisioned as *becoming manly* [ἀνδρίζεται] (Vis. 3.12.2 [20.2]). Parabolic characters add theological weight to the gendered social and ethical values. Similitude 5, in a turn surprising to readers expecting more conventional Christology, describes a worthy slave who is adopted as Son and partner to the Holy Spirit in part because the flesh of the slave manifested holy, cooperative, strong, and *manly* or brave [ἀνδρείως] conduct (Sim. 5.6.6 [59.6]). Memorably, in both Vision 3 and Similitude 9, feminine personifications of theological virtues also represent gendered values. In Vision 3, seven symbolic women support a tower that stands for the church under construction. Each has a name, and the first two have prominence. The first is called Faith, "Then the other who is belted and acting like a man [ἀνδριζομένη], is called Self-restraint ['Εγκράτεια]" (Vis. 3.8.4 [16.4]). One appreciative ancient reader, Clement of Alexandria, commented, "'The virtue, then, that encloses the Church in its grasp,' as the Shepherd says, 'is Faith, by which the elect of God are saved; and that which acts the

---

[4] Studies of masculinity and gender construction in antiquity are extensive. See, for instance, Maud W. Gleason, *Making Men: Sophists and Self-Presentation in Ancient Rome* (Princeton: Princeton University Press, 1995); Ralph M. Rosen and Ineke Sluiter, *Andreia: Studies in Manliness and Courage in Classical Antiquity* (Leiden: Brill, 2003); Judith Hallett and Marilyn B. Skinner, eds., *Roman Sexualities* (Princeton: Princeton University Press, 1997); Brittany E. Wilson, *Unmanly Men: Refigurations of Masculinity in Luke-Acts* (New York: Oxford University Press, 2015); L. Stephanie Cobb, *Dying to be Men: Gender and Language in Early Christian Martyr Texts* (New York: Columbia University Press, 2008).
[5] See analyses by Steve Young, "Being a Man: The Pursuit of Manliness in *The Shepherd of Hermas*," *JECS* 2 (1994): 237–55; B. Diane Lipsett, *Desiring Conversion: Hermas, Thecla, Aseneth* (New York: Oxford University Press, 2011), 34–36.

man is Self-Restraint'."⁶ As the tower/church image is elaborated in Similitude 9 (78-110), more female figures appear: twelve women in black (personifications of vice) carry stones away from the tower, and twelve virgins (personifications of virtue), dressed in belted linen tunics, bring stones in. Hermas expresses some confusion about the virgins because "even though they were delicate, they stood like men [ἀνδρείως] as though they were about to bear the whole of the heavens" (Sim. 9.2.5 [79.5]). When the Shepherd later reveals the virgins' names, the first two again are Faith [Πίστις] and Self-Restraint [Ἐγκράτεια]. Like some other ancient representations of virgins, these symbolic characters exhibit a kind of "dynamic androgyny"⁷ that makes gender a complex cipher for virtue and godliness, with masculine self-control a worthy achievement for both male and female figures.⁸

While some ancient moral philosophers drew distinctions among ἐγκράτεια, σωφροσύνη, and related terms,⁹ in the Shepherd, ἐγκράτεια is the central, recurrent term for moderation, control, and self-governance, here characteristically associated with faith or the heart rather than with reason.¹⁰ Despite this lack

---

6 Clement of Alexandria, *Strom* 12.2, transl., Alexander Roberts & James Donaldson.
7 See, for instance, the discussion of virginity and androgyny in Eleanor Irwin, "The Invention of Virginity on Olympus," in *Virginity Revisited: Configurations of the Unpossessed Body*, ed. Bonnie MacLachlan and Judith Fletcher (Toronto: University of Toronto Press, 2007), 13–23.
8 Vivid narrative depictions of other female characters also contribute to the gender dynamics– Hermas's former owner Rhoda speaks authoritatively, elevated to heaven as she chastises Hermas for the unrecognized consequences of his admiration for her. A literate woman Grapte has instructional authority to disseminate revelation and admonish widows and orphans (Vis. 2.4.3 [8.3]). A female revealer who personifies the Church serves as Hermas's first authoritative guide to *metanoia* and revelation. For varied analyses of female figures in Hermas see, for instance, Carolyn Osiek, *The Shepherd of Hermas: A Commentary*, Hermeneia (Minneapolis: Fortress Press), 16–18; Lora Walsh, "The Lady as Elder in the Shepherd of Hermas," JECS 27 (2019): 517–47; Mark Grundeken, *Community Building in the Shepherd of Hermas: A Critical Study of Some Key Aspects* (Boston: Brill, 2015), 98–109; Edith Humphrey, *The Ladies and the Cities: Transformations and Apocalyptic Identity in Joseph and Aseneth, 4 Ezra, the Apocalypse and the Shepherd of Hermas*, JSPSup 17, (Sheffield: Sheffield Academic Press, 1995), 119–26.
9 See, for instance, Christopher Gill, *The Structured Self in Hellenistic and Roman Thought* (Oxford: Oxford University Press, 2006), 95–96; Helen North, *Sophrosyne: Self-Knowledge and Self-Restraint in Greek Literature* (Ithaca: Cornell University Press, 1966), 197–203; 227–28. Michel Foucault summarizes North's distinctions in *The Use of Pleasure*, Vol 2 of *The History of Sexuality*, trans. Robert Hurley (New York: Vintage Books, 1990), 65.
10 In contrast to some other ancient Jewish and Christian texts. See, for instance, David E. Aune, "Mastery of the Passions: Philo, 4 Maccabees and Earliest Christianity," in *Hellenization Revisited: Shaping a Christian Response within the Greco-Roman World*, ed. Wendy E. Helleman (Lanham, Md.: University Press of America, 1994), 125–58. *Enkrateia* and masculinity in 4 Mac-

of differentiation, Michel Foucault's description of ἐγκράτεια seems as apt for the Shepherd as for the moral philosophic tradition: "*Enkrateia*, with its opposite, *akrasia*, is located on the axis of struggle, resistance, and combat; it is self-control, tension, 'continence'; *enkrateia* rules over pleasures and desires, but has to struggle to maintain control."[11] In the text's opening Vision, Hermas, already being rebuked for unrecognized evil desire, is also addressed as "Hermas, the Self-Restrained" (ὁ ἐγκρατής) (Vis. 1.2.4 [2.4]).

Manly Restraint of Speech

Such restraint, then, should also pertain to speech—so said ancient norms. The worthy man must rule over his tongue as well as pleasures and desires. In certain respects, the speech ethics of the Shepherd of Hermas are conventional. Those who would "live to God" must "Love truth" and speak it exclusively (Mand. 3.1 [28.1]), refraining from hypocritical speech, boasting, blasphemy, and false witness (Mand. 8.3–5 [38.3–5]). Other ancient moralists agree. The *Sentences of Sextus* (second or third century CE) urges: "Love the truth. Treat lying like poison.... It is better to be defeated while speaking the truth than to overcome with deceit. The one who conquers with deceit is conquered in character.... Deceive no one, especially one in need of advice" (*Sent Sextus* 158–159, 165a–b, f).[12] The Shepherd warns Hermas sharply against either speaking or listening to slander or evil speech (καταλαλιά), calling it "an agitated demon, never at peace, always in dissension" (Mand. 2.2 [27.2], cf. Sim. 9.16.3 [93.3]). On this point the text resembles the roughly contemporaneous *1 Clement*, insisting that ἐγκράτεια necessitates "keeping ourselves far from all gossip and slander" (1 Clem 30:3).

Restraint, however, pertains not merely to what kind of speech, but how much. For many ancient moral writers, garrulousness marks a breach of the controlled, virtuous self. Luke T. Johnson observes: "The ancient world agreed that the wise person was also taciturn. Silence was generally better, and always safer, than speech. Brevity in speech was preferred to loquacity."[13] Tersely, Sirach

---

cabees are discussed by Stephen D. Moore and Janice Capel Anderson, "Taking It Like A Man: Masculinity in 4 Maccabees," *JBL* 117 (1998): 249–73.
11 Michel Foucault, *The Use of Pleasure*, 65.
12 Walter T. Wilson, *The* Sentences *of Sextus* (Atlanta: SBL Press, 2012), 177–89. Sirach advises, "A lie is an ugly blot on a person; it is continually on the lips of the ignorant" (Sir 20:24 NRSV). Maxims about truth and lying abound, of course, among moralists.
13 Luke T. Johnson, *Brother of Jesus, Friend of God: Studies in the Letter of James* (Grand Rapids, MI: Eerdmans, 2004), 155–56. Johnson includes extensive ancient examples. See also the anal-

notes, "Whoever talks too much is detested" (Sir 20:8a NRSV). In a study of Ignatius on the silence of bishops, Harry Maier traces the ancient cultural connection between men's restraint of speech and their capacity to advance civic life: "The cultivation of temperance in speech and the checking of inclinations toward talkativeness were central to the task of 'making men' in antiquity. In the oral culture of the period much attention was given to speech as a means of training the self in virtues and disciplines conducive to good civil order."[14] For Philo, as others, unchecked speech runs to evil and irrelevance: "But the greater part of [the] employment [of the wicked] consists in saying what they ought not; for having opened their mouth and leaving it unbridled, like an unrestrained torrent, they allow their speech to run on indiscriminately, as the poets say, dragging on thousands of profitless sayings" (*De somniis* 2.275).[15] According to Theophrastus, "Loquacity (λαλιά), should you wish to define it, would seem to be an incontinence (ἀκρασία) of speech" (*Char* 7.1).[16] How, then, was verbal excess to be further diagnosed or remedied? In his comic caricatures of both Garrulousness (ἀδολεσχίας) and Loquacity (λαλιά), Theophrastus sketches characters identifiable as much by the irrelevance and social misdirection of their speech as by quantity (*Char* 3, 7).[17] The garrulous man indulges in comically disconnected speech addressed to strangers (*Char* 3.1–2). The chatterer heedlessly disrupts civic life—the education of children, work of juries, enjoyment of plays, and more (*Char* 7.5–9). Both types outrageously lack awareness that speech is to be addressed, responsive, and socially productive.[18] With a focus on remedies, Plutarch insists in his essay on talkativeness or garrulousness (ἀδολεσχίας), that ungoverned speech must be controlled through repeated disciplinary practices (19, 511E), exercises in habituation that include admiring terse and pithy speakers, practicing "the solemn, holy, mysterious character of silence" (17, 510E), and cultivating vigilant habits of reflection (23, 514E–F).[19]

At moments, the Shepherd endorses restrained speech. Hermas is warned, for example, that a false prophet will be impetuous, shameless (ἀναιδής), and

---

ysis of the relations between speech and thought in the Hebrew Bible, mostly Psalms and wisdom literature, by Yael Avrahami, *The Senses of Scripture* (Sheffield: T&T Clark, 2012), 84–93.
14 Harry O. Maier, "The Politics of the Silent Bishop: Silence and Persuasion in Ignatius of Antioch," *JTS* 55 (2004): 503–19, 508.
15 Philo, *De Somniis* (C. D. Yonge, LCL).
16 Theophrastus, *The Characters*, III and VII (J. M. Edmonds, LCL).
17 Robert G. Ussher points out the misdirection of audience in the chatterer. *The Characters of Theophrastus* (London: MacMillian & Co, 1960), 51–54, 82–88.
18 See discussion below of "addressivity" in Bakhtin, *Speech Genres*, 63.
19 Plutarch, *De Garr, Moralia*, (William C. Helmbold, LCL).

chattering or loquacious (πολύλαλος) (Mand. 11.12 [43.12]). The text gestures toward the conventional view that garrulousness is a feminized vice. Whereas the masculine self is closed, composed, and boundaried, including in speech, the female self, more porous, raises worries about speech that surface, as we know, from Aristotle to the pastoral epistles.[20] Plutarch assumes the gender stereotype in an anecdote about a senator whose wife presses him to tell her a state secret. She is, "a woman prudent in other respects, but yet a woman." Predictably, she spills the secret, but wisely, her husband has told her a harmless lie, knowing even a prudent woman to be "a leaky vessel" (*Mor* 507–508.11). With similar assumptions at play, Hermas is commanded to rebuke his wife for her unrestrained speech, though she, it seems, is capable of change: "[your wife] does not restrain her tongue, by which she is committing evil. But when she hears these words, she will restrain it and she will have mercy" (Vis. 2.2.3 [6.3]). Nevertheless, in the Shepherd, such expressions of conventional speech ethics do not yield a taciturn hero, communicating more by action than speech. For that matter, the parade of heavenly revealers, female and male, are hardly models of brevity. Do the copiousness of the text and its extended, sometimes unpredictable dialogues then pull against its expressed value of masculine self-restraint?

Expansive Speech / Expansive Text

The expansiveness of the Shepherd has, of course, been explored from other angles than gendered speech ethics. Its length, repetitiveness, and loose organization bear on composition history, leading some scholars to theories of multiple authors, though recently most conclude the text is the work of a single hand, some arguing for stages of composition over time, others for a shorter period given its message of urgency.[21] Its relatively simple Greek style, with paratactic syntax and organization, is sometimes explained by the author's level of literacy

---

20 For discussion of ancient norms relating to women, see Susan E. Hylen, "Speech and Silence," *Women in the New Testament World* (New York: Oxford University Press, 2019), 131–59.
21 Osiek surveys a range of views, *The Shepherd*, 8–10. See, for instance, Stanislas Giet, *Hermas et les Pasteurs: Les trois auteurs du Pasteur d'Hermas* (Paris: Presses universitaires du France, 1963); William Coleborne, "A Linguistic Approach to the Problem of Structure and Composition of the Shepherd of Hermas," *Colloquium* 3 (1967): 133–42. For arguments of single authorship, see Philippe Henne, *L'Unité du Pasteur: Tradition et Rédaction*. Paris: J. Gabalda, 1992; Harry O. Maier, *The Social Setting of the Ministry as Reflected in the Writings of Hermas, Clement and Ignatius* (Waterloo, ON: Wilfrid Laurier Press, 1991), 57.

or education.[22] Yet even given a non-elite author, the text's aggregate quality does not seem inadvertent, but an explicit narrative emphasis. All of the visionary revealers remark on repetition and addition as characteristic of their dialogues with Hermas. "But you will not stop asking for revelations, for you are shameless (ἀναιδής)," says the woman-church, exasperated (Vis. 3.3.2 [11.2]). But shortly afterward, "Then, when I stopped asking her about all these things, she said to me, 'Do you want to see something else?'" (Vis. 3.8.1 [16.1]).

Carolyn Osiek has argued, perceptively, that the Shepherd's narrative and speech forms reflect the "orality" of the text, "close to oral thought patterns." In her exposition of key markers of orality, Osiek further suggests that the long text arose from its spoken use and oral proclamation in Christian groups.[23] The inference seems plausible as the Shepherd repeatedly depicts the interplay of speech, writing, and reading in processes of oral communication, dictation, interpretation and performance. Hermas listens to a mysterious reading (Vis. 1.3.3–4 [3.3–4]), copies books with or without comprehension (Vis. 2.1.3–4 [5.3–4]; 2.4.3 [8.3]),[24] and transcribes for further reading and interpretation the oral messages he has received through repetitive, extended dialogue, not mere dictation (Vis. 5.5–7 [25.5–7]; Sim. 10.1.1 [111.1]). Moreover, the dialogue repeatedly highlights what Bakhtin terms "addressivity."[25] That is, Hermas is oriented toward other speakers, and in two directions: he listens and responds to his divine revealers *and* is repeatedly commissioned to pass on speech he is receiving to his family and to the church, who need to "hear these words"

---

[22] Grundeken notes: "the work is relatively long, there are various sorts of repetitions and inconsistencies and the passages are connected in an associative and additive way on the basis of a variety of themes. All this, however, does not necessarily imply multiple authorship; it merely indicates that the author, just like many other early Christian authors, was not a very skilled writer." Grundeken, *Community Building*, 14. Or see the wry comment on Hermas's intellectual ability in Henry Chadwick, review of *Der Hirt Des Hermas*, by Norbert Brox, *Journal of Ecclesiastical History* 47 (1996): 119.

[23] Carolyn Osiek, "The Oral World of Early Christianity in Rome: The Case of Hermas," in *Judaism and Christianity in First-Century Rome*, ed. Karl P. Donfried and Peter Richardson (Grand Rapids, MI: Eerdmans, 1998), 151–74.

[24] See discussion of Christian scribal practice in Kim Haines-Eitzen, *Guardians of Letters: Literacy, Power, and the Transmitters of Early Christian Literature* (Oxford University Press, 2000), 40.

[25] Bakhtin, "Speech Genres," 63. Bakhtin analyzes the forms of everyday spoken utterances that literary language presupposes. As Michael Holquist notes in the "Introduction," Bakhtin explores the differences between literary and everyday language "as graduated rather than as absolute," xv–xvii.

(e.g., Vis. 2.2.3 [6.3], 3.8.11 [16.11], Sim. 5.5.1 [58.1]).[26] Repetition can be divinely commissioned. Unlike Theophrastus' heedless men chattering randomly to anyone and no-one, all speakers in the Shepherd, however prolix, convey a sense of socially purposeful, indeed urgent, salvific address.

Verbal Disciplines and the Changed Self

The very copiousness and repetitiveness of speech forms in the Shepherd of Hermas seem related to the goal of bringing about change in the protagonist, his household, and the church: to resolve doublemindedness (διψυχία), remedy problems of desire (ἐπιθυμία), and revitalize social relations and interdependence between rich and poor in Christian groups. Here as in other ancient moral texts, didactic instruction and the techniques necessary to scrutinize and improve the self are understood to be iterative–not accomplished once for all or quickly. The woman church provides a simile for didactic, even percussive, repetition: "For as the coppersmith hammering his work prevails over the object as he desires, so also the righteous word spoken daily prevails over all evil. Do not therefore break off admonishing your children. For I know that if they will repent from their whole hearts, they will be inscribed in the books of life with the holy ones" (Vis. 1.3.2 [3.2]).

Particularly in the Mandates, moral instruction can be plain and conventional, sometimes proverbial, as various sins and communal shortcomings are exposed. Yet repetitive didactic instruction[27] is also marked by responsiveness–a quality of the utterance Bakhtin says characterizes both the listener and the speaker: "[W]hen the listener perceives and understands the meaning ... of speech, he simultaneously takes an active, responsive attitude toward it. He either agrees or disagrees with it (completely or partially), augments it, applies it, prepares for its execution, and so on."[28] Not just the listener, but the speaker is oriented toward an actively responsive understanding: "He does not expect passive understanding that, so to speak, only duplicates his own idea in someone else's mind. Rather, he expects response, agreement, sympathy, objection, exe-

---

[26] Jannes Reiling has observed, the "words [of the divine revealers] are, so to speak, passing right through Hermas without becoming his words." *Hermas and Christian Prophecy: A Study of the Eleventh Mandate* (Leiden: E. J. Brill, 1973), 164.
[27] S. Giet remarks, with a wry tone, "...l'auteur est un moraliste dont la manie didactique brave la monotonie et la fatigue..." *Hermas et les Pasteurs*, 155.
[28] Bakhtin, "Speech Genres," 68–69.

cution, and so forth...."[29] To take one example, in Mandate 3 (28), when the Shepherd issues the conventional directive to "Love truth" and warns against repudiating or defrauding the Lord, Hermas's response is abject. Paraenesis yields to dramatic dialogue and the need to decipher more precisely moral instruction and the self:

> When I heard these things, I wept excessively.
> Seeing me weeping he said, "Why do you weep?"
> Because Lord," I said, "I do not know whether I can be saved."
> "Why?" he said.
> "Because, Lord," I said, never in my life have I spoken a true word, but I have always lived cunningly with everyone, and represented my falsehood as truth to everyone; and no-one has ever countered me, but believed my word. How then, Lord," I said, "can I live having done these things?"
> "You are thinking well and truly," he said. "For you must conduct yourself in truth as a slave of God, and a wicked conscience must not dwell with the spirit of truth, nor bring grief to the reverent and true spirit."
> "Never, Lord," I said, "have I heard such words so precisely." (Mand. 3.3–4 [28.3–4])

The Shepherd reassures Hermas that he can now be saved, as can others who will hear the commandment through him, because his former falsehoods in business (or daily life) may now be found truthful—though the practical sense of how falsity becomes truthful is not particularly clear (Mand. 3.5 [28.5]). The revealers' responses can also veer in surprising directions. As the Mandates near their conclusion, the Shepherd responds harshly to Hermas: "You are senseless, man." (Mand. 10.1.2 [40.2]); "Listen, therefore, foolish one" (Mand. 10.2.1 [41.1]). By the 12th Mandate, the Shepherd grows frighteningly angry, then relents: "But when he saw me so confused and confounded, he began speaking to me more moderately and cheerfully, 'You senseless, foolish, double-minded man!'" (12.4.1–2 [47.1–2]). Hardly moderate or cheerful, the address also does not seem ironic; the scolding mirrors Hermas's own fluctuating self-descriptions. The two-way talk—the revealers' lengthy explanations and Hermas's incessant questions—may contribute to how Hermas and his household stand in for the church. The reader sees in Hermas the mix of humility and brazenness that the Roman church is to have with God: desperately slow learners, they must ask and ask again.

Such disciplinary exchanges in some ways resemble the practices of acute and reiterated self-scrutiny advised by more elite ethical writers of the period —attention of the self upon the self. Moral philosophers urge repeated exercises

---

[29] Bakhtin, "Speech Genres," 69.

including meditations, listening, and reading to foster continuous vigilance about the state of one's self.[30] Some exercises were to build character in advance, while others were "applied in retrospect after an emotional provocation has occurred."[31] Seneca, for instance, urges nightly self-interrogation of any ills done and faults remedied.[32] For this moralist, the soul is disciplined by examination of one's own thoughts, undertakings, and companions, accompanied by the assistance of friendship.[33] Plutarch too speaks of techniques for making progress in virtue: examination of one's thoughts, actions, and dreams, one's level of comfort around good people, one's tendencies to excuse personal errors.[34] Marcus Aurelius models meditation, reading, and writing as therapeutic exercises, disciplining himself not to shirk public or familial duty and deliberately contemplating the prospect of death.[35] The techniques are analogous to those depicted by Hermas, though he obviously diverges from elite philosophic writers in style, genre, and oral speech patterns. Furthermore, for Hermas, transformation comes not through internalized techniques but in dialogue with divine revealers. Yet the Shepherd shares an emphasis on repetitive prolonged disciplines of transformation, here fused with revelation.

Revelation and the Changing Church

While a distinction between didactic and revelatory utterances is fluid in the Shepherd, revelatory exchanges typically begin with a visual disclosure. Hermas is a visionary, repeatedly asking to see.[36] Questions follow, with rejoinders from the divine revealers that range from anger to laughter, from reassurance to cas-

---

[30] Pierre Hadot, *Philosophy as a Way of Life: Spiritual Exercises from Socrates to Foucault*, trans., Michael Chase (Oxford: Blackwell, 1995), 81–83.
[31] Richard Sorabji, *Emotion and Peace of Mind: From Stoic Agitation to Christian Temptation*, The Gifford Lectures (Oxford University Press, 2000), 161.
[32] Seneca, "On Anger," III.36.1–3, in *Moral Essays* (John W. Basore, LCL), 1.339–41.
[33] Seneca, "On Tranquility of Mind," in *Moral Essays*, 2.215–37.
[34] Plutarch, "On Being Aware of Moral Progress," 12–17, *Moralia* I (LCL).
[35] Marcus Aurelius, *Meditations*, for examples, II.17; III.4,7; IV.45; V.30; IX.35.
[36] Similar verbal patterns occur, of course, in other apocalyptic or revelatory literature. In 4 Ezra, for instance, Ezra questions over and over the justice of God (3:4–36), is rebuked by an angel (4:1–25), but then instructed about the future (4:26–5:12). The back-and-forth only ends when the angel tells the prophet that if he really wants to understand the deeper things, he should fast and pray and return in a week for the next installment (5:13). See discussion of Jewish pseudepigrapha in Graydon F. Synder, *The Shepherd of Hermas, The Apostolic Fathers 6* (London: Thomas Nelson & Sons, 1968).

tigation, from frightening displays of divine distance to intimate touches on the breast. Throughout, as already noted, Hermas is charged with being a speaking transmitter of the revelation he receives. Hermas's volubility, then, implies an expansive divine choice to open divine reality to scrutiny in the interest of promoting the stability of the church. And revelation resists finality, even when a final statement seems to be offered.

Consider, for example, Vision 3, marked by particular variety in how the revealer responds to Hermas's desire to interpret revelation. The elderly woman shows Hermas a great tower being built in an extremely complicated way (Vis. 3.2.4–9 [10.4–9]). She then wants "to depart hurriedly," but Hermas detains her, insisting that visions without explanation are no good (Vis. 3.3.1 [11.1]). Throughout the ensuing dialogue, the woman calls Hermas crafty (πανοῦργος) and "shameless" (ἀναιδής) for his ceaseless requests, and he admits his own shamelessness (Vis. 3.3.1–2 [11.1–2]; 3.7.5 [15.5]). She can erupt harshly, "How long will you be foolish and senseless, asking everything and understanding nothing?" (Vis. 3.6.5 [14.5]), and "Senseless person!" (Vis. 3.8.9 [16.9]), yet also urge him to "keep seeking..." and "speak all these words in the ears of the holy ones" (Vis. 3.3.5 [11.5]; 3.8.11 [16.11]. Osiek points out that the scoldings function as literary-rhetorical devices to underscore the importance of the teaching that follows.[37] Such variable responses also convey that the experience of revelation and interpretation is uneven, unpredictable, mixed with deterrents as well as incentives. Vision Three concludes with a momentary sense of finalization: "Now you have the revelation complete (ὁλοτελῶς). No longer ask anything about revelation; if anything is necessary, it shall be revealed to you" (Vis. 3.13.4 [21.4]). Yet, this seemingly final utterance invites a response,[38] and Vision Four has Hermas again asking for more: "While walking alone I was asking the Lord to complete the revelations and visions which he showed me through his holy church, so that he might make me strong and grant repentance to his slaves who had stumbled..." (Vis. 4.1.3 [22.3]). So the story accumulates episodes.

In the lengthy parables, visionary images and interpretations proliferate. As Patricia Cox Miller observes, "a rich variety of images is offered to the reader to 'try on' in terms of his or her own ethical condition."[39] Often, one repeated symbol—twigs or sticks, stones or mountains—is described in widely varying states,

---

37 Osiek, *The Shepherd*. See, for instance, commentary at 73, 78, 85.
38 So, Bakhtin observes of oral forms: "The first and foremost criterion for the finalization of the utterance is *the possibility of responding to it* or, more precisely and broadly, of assuming a responsive attitude toward it...." *Speech Genres*, 76.
39 Patricia Cox Miller, "Hermas and the Shepherd," in *Dreams in Late Antiquity: Studies in the Imagination of a Culture* (Princeton: Princeton University Press, 1994), 145.

all inviting investigation. In Similitude 9, for example, stones are tested for their fitness to be used in building the tower-church, and every conceivable aspect of stones becomes significant: their colors, shape, strength, brightness or dullness, weight-bearing capacity, soundness or presence of cracks or brokenness—all such features bear meaning (Sim. 9.5–9 [82–86]). Stones, then, are susceptible to change in multiple ways: they can be cleaned, hewn, transformed by the one who carries or places them, filled, or thrown aside (Sim. 9.7 [84]). Stones go through more than one inspection by a divinely appointed figure (Sim. 9.7–9 [84–86]); the process is iterative, until an idealized vision is briefly possible—the church resembling a monolith, unified and flawless because of *metanoia* (Sim. 9.9.7 [86.7]).[40] In a more economical text, some such categories could surely be combined. In Hermas, however, multiplication of distinctions and interpretations seems the point. Miller observes these images are "mobile, many-faceted, metaphoric, and, like parable, they shatter the kind of literal-minded consciousness that would ask for a single meaning."[41] Similarly, Philippe Henne characterizes the figurative technique of the Shepherd overall: what appears awkward or confusing is in fact an elaborate interpretive technique—an "allegorical polysemy" that nevertheless reaches internal coherence at the level of explanation.[42] Understanding revelation or building up the church —such tasks merit ongoing sifting, revelation, interpretation—and talk.

Metanoia and Manliness

The extensive dialogue between Hermas and the visionary revealers aims at *metanoia*—as topic, goal, and process. *Metanoia* in Hermas has broad reference, from renewal of soul, heart, mind, disposition, and morality, including regret for past actions and acts of penitence, to a gendered transformation toward manliness, to restoration of social dimensions of community life, including right relations and interdependence between rich and poor.[43] As Grundeken notes,

---

40 See discussions by Martin Dibelius, *Der Hirt des Hermas. Die Apostolischen Väter.* Vol. 4. (Tübingen: J. C. B. Mohr [Paul Siebeck], 1923), 615; Norbert Brox, *Der Hirt des Hermas.* (Gottingen: Vandenhoeck & Ruprecht, 1991), 404.
41 Miller, "Hermas and the Shepherd," 142.
42 P. Henne, "La polysémie allégorique dans le *Pasteur* d'Hermas," *Ephemerides Theologicae Lovanienses* 65 (1989): 131–35; here 135.
43 See the recent analysis in Mark Grundeken, *Community Building*, 133–40. Grundeken draws attention to an insightful summary by Joseph Paramelle and Pierre Adnès. "Hermas (Pasteur D'), 2ᵉ siècle," *Dictionnaire de spiritualité. Ascétique et mystique. Doctrine et histoire,* vol.7, ed. A. Der-

"Hermas sees the church as a *corpus mixtum* where good and bad coexist until the last day."[44] Those who have sinned since baptism therefore urgently need *metanoia* and a new beginning,[45] a "changed consciousness," as Miller glosses it,[46] which Hermas works to comprehend. "Does it not seem to you," [the Shepherd] said, "that repentance is itself understanding. Repentance is great understanding...." "This is the reason, Lord," I said, "why I inquire so precisely about everything from you..." (Mand. 4.2.2–3 [30.2–3]). At times the revealers assert limits to the time or availability of *metanoia*: "... *metanoia* for the righteous has a limit (*telos*). The days for the repentance of all the holy ones have been completed. But for the outsiders, repentance extends until the last day" (Vis. 2.2.5 [6.5]). At another juncture, the Shepherd warns, "If after that great and reverend calling, anyone being tempted by the devil sins, that person has one repentance" (Mand. 4.3.6 [31.6]). Yet as Osiek and others remark, such limitations work more to communicate urgency than to institute rules of church discipline.[47] Furthermore, the copiousness of the narrative and dialogue conveys that *metanoia*, even if time-limited, is also time-consuming, ongoing, and discursive.

How, then, do the talkative narrative and the voluble Hermas affect the text's construction of what it means to become manly, or to conduct oneself manfully in ministry (Vis. 1.4.3 [4.3]; Sim. 10.4.1 [114.1])? How is *metanoia* represented as gendered transformation? Clearly, in crucial ways, the Shepherd does *not* conform to a taut set of elite Greco-Roman social hierarchies, categories, or gendered markers.[48] Hermas offers a non-elite Christian revaluation of gendered virtue through a freedman whose struggle for *metanoia* is launched by an encounter with his former mistress, yet who is entrusted with weighty communal responsibilities and an authoritative message. The talkative prophet of self-restraint disrupts at least some ancient gender norms. In particular, Hermas departs from typical elite representation of the idealized male as closed and boundaried, dig-

---

ville et al. (Paris: Beauchesne, 1969), 316–34, here 328: 'La *metanoia* que prêche le *Pasteur*, est un sentiment, une attitude, une activité complexe qui renferme en soi, avec le regret du passé et le ferme propos pour l'avenir, un changement d'âme, un renouvellment moral, une transformation de toute la vie. En un mot, c'est une vraie conversion ....' in Grundeken, 134n26.
44 Grundeken, *Community Building*, 82.
45 Brox, *Der Hirt des Hermas*, 235, 484.
46 Miller, *Hermas and the Shepherd*, 146.
47 Osiek, *The Shepherd*, 115. See also Henne, *L'unité*, who comments on the emphasis on divine mercy, extended to all sinners, 139.
48 Similarly, Brent Shaw argues fourth Maccabees and other Christian writings show a "loosening of rigid gender categories from their anchoring in the social hierarchies of the polis." "Body / Power / Identity: Passions of the Martyrs," *JECS* 4 (1996): 269–312, here 287.

nified and composed, self-sufficient and impenetrable.⁴⁹ Whereas women and those lacking self-restraint were often deemed deficient because porous, the body and self of the noble, dignified elite man were idealized as sealed. Hermas, in contrast, is open in speech, labile in emotions, and penetrable by the holy spirit and by visions. Those very qualities, however, are presented as admirable and imitable. Gendered values are here re-imagined.

Others of Hermas's qualities seem more conventionally masculine in the text's ancient context: he shows courage and daring, strength and the capacity for strenuous work. Yet in the Shepherd, these too are inflected by the communal horizon of the church and oriented toward speech rather than embodied action. Courage and daring, for instance, are manifested not in physical valor but verbal audacity. Hermas presses for interpretation, is chastised for presumption, then persists. Similitude Five (54-60) provides one of many examples:

> I begged him repeatedly (πολλὰ) to make clear to me the parable of the field... He answered me saying, "You are extremely presumptuous (αὐθάδης) in your questions. You should ask nothing at all, for if it needs to be made clear to you, it will be made clear." I said to him, "Lord, whatever you show me and do not make clear, I will have seen pointlessly, not understanding what it is. Similarly, if you speak parables to me and do not explain them to me, my hearing them from you will be pointless." (Sim. 5.4.1–2 [57.1–2])

Hermas is tenacious, undeterred by unpredictable responses. He frequently endures frank criticism of varying intensities, as moral philosophers recommend men do.⁵⁰ A strong-but-not-silent type, Hermas's strength shows in praying and seeing visions. Whereas "those who are feeble (βληχροί) and lazy (ἀργοί) in prayer hesitate to ask anything from the Lord. (Sim. 5.4.3 [57.3]), Hermas, empowered, asks with persistence (παράμονος) and industriousness (πανοῦργος)⁵¹ (Sim. 5.5.1 [58.1]). Renewed strength enables him to see angels and visions: "For since you were weaker in the flesh, it was not revealed to you through an angel. When you were strengthened by the spirit and made stronger in your own strength, so that you could see an angel, then the building of the tower was revealed to you through the church; you saw everything in a noble and worthy way" (Sim. 9.1.2 [78.2]). The masculine capacity for strenuous work, then, is con-

---

49 Tim Whitmarsh reflects succinctly on the ancient masculine ideal and its relation to desire and self-control. *Ancient Greek Literature* (Malden, MA: Polity Press, 2004), 197–99.
50 Philodemus, *Of Frank Criticism (Peri Parrēsias)*; Plutarch, *On Being Aware of Moral Progress*; see discussion in Sorabji, *Emotion and Peace of Mind*, 217–18.
51 The Bauer-Danker lexicon says in Christian literature πανοῦργος always carries some negative connotation, suggesting translations of crafty, clever, or sly (754), yet other lexica point to usages such as industrious, active, shrewd, prudent.

strued as precision and acuteness in interpretation. The repeated verb ἐξακριβάζομαι, to see more accurately, requires power rather than fear: "But you must see everything more accurately through me. For this reason I was given by the illustrious angel to dwell in your house, that you might see all things powerfully, not fearing anything as you did before" (Sim. 9.1.3 [78.3]). The verb occurs, as Henne points out, whenever there is a new discovery, a new deepening of revelation.[52] In all divisions of the Shepherd, self-restraint, ἐγκράτεια, is a key value associated with masculinity. Yet Hermas is instructed, "Self-restraint (ἐγκράτεια) is also dual. For you must restrain yourself from some things, but you must not from others" (Mand. 8.1 [38.1]). In this diffuse narrative, speech and talk exploring repentance and revelation seem among those entities not subject to restraint.

Attention to the speech ethics and speech acts of the Shepherd of Hermas suggests how the form, content, and function of this ancient Christian narrative are inter-related—how this tale with its extended, extensive dialogue and decipherment invites participation in the process of transformation that it also explicitly urges. The text inscribes an ongoing, albeit precarious, process of acute self-examination and relentless seeking of revelation and experiences of the spirit, in dialogue with the series of visionary revealers. Throughout the Shepherd, ἀνδρεία is demonstrated not in civic arenas and fields of action but through spoken words in and for the church: "Conduct yourself manfully in this ministry, proclaiming the Lord's mighty acts to everyone, and you will find favor in this ministry" (Sim. 10.4.1 [114.1]). In the text's own grammar of gender, manliness is marked not only by rule of one's self, household, and community, but by openness to revelation, persistence in interpretation, scrutiny of the self and the church, and the proclamation and pursuit of *metanoia*. Manliness must continually be "reasserted and revived."[53] Hermas's prayers, questions, confessions, commitments to repeat oral instruction, and rejoinders "bear great responsibilities for maintaining the communities in which they circulate."[54] As Hermas talks—as he seeks and receives repeated revelation, scrutinizes himself and his community, and commits himself to proclaiming what he has received—the measure of effective speech is less "Are the words true?" or "Are there too many words?" than "Are the words working?" Are these speech-acts having their intended effect? Are they felicitous or successful, changing Hermas

---

52 Philippe Henne, "La pénitence dans le *Pasteur* d'Hermas," *Revue Biblique* 98 (1991): 358–97, 373.
53 Whitmarsh, *Ancient Greek Literature*, 91, discussing Gleason, *Making Men*.
54 Sandy Petrey, *Speech Acts and Literary Theory* (New York: Routledge, 1990), 37.

on the way to transforming the church?[55] *Metanoia* is the end, both urgent and prolonged, to which the narrative aims, the content and intended effect of its visions, mandates, and parables.

---

[55] Austin, *How To Do Things with Words*, 14–15, 83.

Harry O. Maier
The Affect and Happy Objects of the Shepherd of Hermas

This essay deploys affect theory, critical spatiality, and cultural anthropological notions of the partible or dividual self to investigate Hermas's third vision (9 – 21) and ninth parable (78 – 110) of the tower and the ways they relate to experience.[1] In each instance, revelatory guides lead Hermas to visions of a tower under construction, which he learns are representations of the church made up of stones that represent various kinds of Jesus followers. As the revelations unfold, they reveal various kinds of orientations followers have to one another and to the world around them. Crucially for this discussion, Hermas's visions blur the lines dividing objects, places, and people so that each of these items is not a container unto itself but spills over into the others in ways that are porous and processual. Vision 3 (9-21) and Similitude 9 (78-110) offer an excellent set of data for an interdisciplinary and experimental exploration the aim of which is to observe, survey, and consider a landscape of objects, characters, and places that together form a constellation of affects in the Shepherd of Hermas. Through examination of the vivid affects found in and created by the narrative, the essay contributes to the overall objectives of this collection, which is to depart from traditional disciplinary boundaries and preoccupations in order to read the Shepherd with new lenses and to promote a reappraisal of a text that has seen a resurgence of scholarly interest in recent years.

At the outset it is necessary to introduce the term "affect" to orient the more general approach to Hermas and experience developed here. I will take up application of spatial theory and the anthropology of the partible self later in the essay. The terms "affect" and "affect theory" represent a vast theoretical literature with multiple definitions and conceptualizations whose modern roots can be traced back to the philosophical theorization of Baruch Spinoza (1632–1677), but whose tendrils reach further back into ancient notions of the self as a porous entity in dynamic relationship with both physical and metaphysical

---

[1] The theoretical orientation complements the perspectives advanced by Giovanni Bazzana in this volume. Like him, I draw on cultural anthropology to help recognize aspects of the text that are otherwise passed over through more traditional methods of biblical interpretation.

forces, places, beings, and objects.² The biblical scholar Maia Costrosits offers a simple definition when she writes, "'affect' means being *affected*; it suggests being touched, moved. It implies less some kind of internal, personal experience than relationality, physicality, and susceptibility."³ Gregory Seigworth and Melissa Gregg expand further: "Affect at its most anthropomorphic, is the name we give to those forces—visceral forces beneath, alongside, or generally *other than* conscious knowing vital forces existing beyond emotion—that can serve to drive us toward movement, toward thought and extension...." They go on to state, "Affect is in many ways synonymous with *force* or *forces of* encounter" (emphasis original). Force need not be "forceful" but rather indicates that "affect more often transpires within and across the subtlest of shuttling intensities: all the miniscule or molecular events of the unnoticed. The ordinary and its extra–. Affect is born in the *in-between-ness* and resides as accumulative *beside-ness*."⁴ Affect, they continue, extends beyond bodies

> both into and out of the interstices of the inorganic and non-living, the intracellular divulgences of sinew, tissue, and gut economies, and the vaporous evanescences of the incorporeal (events, atmospheres, feeling-tones). At once intimate and impersonal, affect *accumulates* across both relatedness and interruptions in relatedness, becoming a palimpsest of force-encounters traversing the ebbs and swells of intensities that pass between 'bodies' (bodies defined not by an outer skin-envelope or other surface boundary but by their potential to reciprocate or co-participate in the passages of affect). Bindings and unbindings, becomings and un-becomings, jarring disorientations and rhythmic attunements. Affect marks a body's *belonging* to a world of encounters or: a world's belonging to a body of encounters but also in non-belonging through all those far sadder (de) compositions of mutual in-compossibilities.⁵

A consideration of the Shepherd of Hermas from the perspective of affect identifies the "*force* or *forces of encounter*" that Hermas describes and which absorb him. It focuses on the vital forces existing within and beyond emotion and the ways Hermas belongs to the world of encounters the text creates for him, that traverse and inhabit him, which bind to him and which are unbound from him.

---

2 Baruch Spinoza, "On the Origins and Nature of the Emotions," *Ethics*, Part 3, ed. Matthew J. Kisner (Cambridge: Cambridge University Press, 2018), 93–156; Moira Gatens and Genevieve Lloyd, *Collective Imaginings: Spinoza, Past and Present* (London: Routledge, 1999), 14–19.
3 Maia Kostrosits, *Rethinking Early Christian Identity: Affect, Violence, and Belonging* (Minneapolis: Fortress, 2015), 4.
4 Gregory J. Seigworth and Melissa Gregg, "An Inventory of Shimmers," in *The Affect Theory Reader*, ed. Gregory J. Seigworth and Melissa Gregg (Durham, NC: Duke University Press, 2010), 1–28 at 1.
5 Seigworth and Gregg, "Inventory," 2.

Seigworth and Gregg usefully describe two ways of conceptualizing affect, one that analyses it from the inside-of-a-person-out and the other from the outside-in.[6] The inside-out perspective draws on human biology, cognitive science, and study of the autonomic nervous system. It describes affect as a physiological response to stimuli prior to cognition and emotion.[7] Affects are innate biological states that belong to the evolution of the species and as such are acultural and transhistorical. The classical treatment of affect in this sense is by the psychologist Silvan Solomon Tomkins (1911–1991) who identified nine biologically based affects of which Fear-Terror was one, namely a reaction to danger with an impulse to run or hide, accompanied by a frozen stare, a pale face, coldness, sweat, and erect hair.[8] An excellent example from the Shepherd of this inside-out perspective appears at the start of the third vision (Vis. 3.1.5 [9.5]) where Hermas goes to a field, sees an ivory couch with a linen pillow and a linen cloth on top, and has a powerful reaction: "When I saw these things laid out with no one there, I was astounded and seized with trembling and my hair stood on end—terrified, because I was alone [ἰδὼν ταῦτα κείμενα καὶ μηδένα ὄντα ἐν τῷ τόπῳ ἔκθαμβος ἐγενόμην, καὶ ὡσεὶ τρόμος με ἔλαβεν, καὶ αἱ τρίχες μου ὀρθαί· καὶ ὡσεὶ φρίκη μοι προσῆλθεν, μόνου μου ὄντος]." A similar description appears earlier in Vis. 1.2.1 [2.1] (the first vision in which he sees the church as an elderly woman) where, after seeing the skies shut, Hermas "was trembling all over and upset [πεφρικὼς καὶ λυπούμενος]." Douglas Cairns argues that in Homeric literature onward, the term φρίκη "can be the name of an emotion, but its primary significance lies in its reference to a physical symptom that is common to a range of emotional and non-emotional events." It often appears in descriptions of human responses to divine epiphanies.[9] The middle passive verb λυπούμενος, which Erhman translates too blandly as "upset," denotes a powerful reaction of distress which in ancient medical discourse was related to various physiological disturbances.[10] Thus Galen, for example, describes λύπη as synonymous

---

6 Seigworth and Gregg, "Inventory," 6.
7 Brian Massumi, *Parables for the Virtual: Movement, Affect, Sensation. Post–Contemporary Interventions* (Durham: Duke University Press, 2002), represents an authoritative treatment.
8 Silvan S. Tomkins, "Fear and its Socialization," in *Affect Imagery Consciousness: The Complete Edition, Two Volumes. Book Two, Volume III: The Negative Affects: Anger and Fear* (New York: Springer, 2008), 931–76.
9 Douglas Cairns, "A Short History of Shudders," in *Unveiling Emotions II—Emotions in Greece and Rome: Texts, Images, Material Culture*, ed. Angelos Chaniotis and Pierre Ducrey, HABES 55 (Stuttgart: Franz Steiner Verlag, 2013), 85–107, for epiphanies, 88–91.
10 Daniel King, "Galen and Grief: The Construction of Grief in Galen's Clinical Work," in *Unveiling Emotions II*, ed. Chaniotis and Ducrey, 251–73; Daniel King, *Experiencing Pain in Imperial Greek Culture*, Oxford Classical Monographs (Oxford: Oxford University Press, 2018); also,

with suffering from a "distressed, vexed, pained, disturbed or burdened perception" that is also accompanied by various physical states.[11] Galen's description is of course a part of ancient medical discourse and physiological theorization that cannot be imported into the modern conceptualization of affect, but his account points to dimensions that are relevant to modern studies of affect. From the perspective of contemporary biological study, these passages describe preconscious bodily responses (Seigworth and Gregg's, "*force* or *forces of encounters*") generated by the autonomic nervous system that are only subsequently given meaning when brought to awareness and interpreted according to cultural scripts.

Tomkins is not only interested in physiology, he also observes the relationship between affect and culture and society, and the ways affect makes its way into cultural symbolization and the social generation of meaning (as for example in Galen's medical treatises). In the case of the Shepherd, for example, following his physiological reaction to seeing the linen-coloured chair in Vis. 3.1.5 (9.5), Hermas states, "[W]hen I came to myself, I remembered the glory of God and took courage [ἐν ἐμαυτῷ οὖν γενόμενος καὶ μνησθεὶς τῆς δόξης τοῦ θεοῦ καὶ λαβὼν θάρσος]." In other words, an autonomic nervous system response gains meaning through being interpreted through reference to a system of religious belief. What Tomkins describes as the fear-terror-belief nexus combination plays an important role in channeling a preconscious reaction in the service of Hermas's revelations and overall goals of communicating them. This is the one passage where affect appears unambiguously in the *Shepherd*, but analysis could be expanded to include joy and a fuller treatment of sadness, the two recurring states (from an affect perspective) to which Hermas returns repeatedly.[12]

Clare Rothschild, *New Essays on the Apostolic Fathers*, WUNT 375 (Tübingen: Mohr Siebeck, 2017), 227–44 at 241, where she analyzes λύπη and its relation to ὀξυχολία in Mand. 10.2 (41.2) with reference to Galen's physiological theories. Bazzana's essay in this volume offers a different account though consideration of λύπη /ὀξυχολία from a comparative anthropological perspective. My own view is to offer an account that utilizes both kinds of interpretations.
11 Galen, *Causes of Symptoms* 7.117–118K. King, "Galen," discusses ways in which Galen links grief with fever and links it with the theory of the humors. For example, "biting vapours and humours when they move through sensing bodies generates rigors and shivering" (Galen, *On Therapeutic Method* 10.679K, cited by King, 262). It is notable that Hermas's representation of φρίκη and λυπούμενος includes τρόμος. This does not imply that Hermas is deploying a medical model of grief, only that the experience of grief is associated with observable bodily states that Galen theorizes physiologically.
12 Tomkins, "Enjoyment–Joy and the Smiling Response: Developments, Physiological and Comparative Aspects," 205–72; "Distress—Anguish and the Crying Response," 289–350; Hermas's recurring reference to shame also invites use of Tomkins's discussions of the "Shame—Humiliation" affect, 351–602.

The other approach to the study of affect, the one that this essay develops, focuses on the outside-in. It considers the ways in which complex assemblages of the human and non-human create what Seigworth and Gregg describe as "an entire vital, and modulating field of myriad becomings across human and non-human."[13] This is the account Gilles Deleuze (again building on Spinoza) theorized.[14] The Deleuzian framework points beyond the idea of affect as resting on physiological states prior to cognition, and toward the ways in which the human and nonhuman are affected through relations, experiences, encounters, environments, atmospheres, and so on. On this account, affect describes states of being "in the midst of things and relations ... and, then, in the complex assemblages that come to compose bodies and worlds simultaneously."[15] In the Deleuzian theorization, affect describes a processual or non-static world of forces, flows, and influences. For Deleuze (together with Félix Guattari) the focus is on the ways in which bodies affect and are affected through assemblages of material and nonmaterial things and the ways they are held together through a kind of expression or set of values and codes.[16] Deleuze furnishes the theoretical point of departure where, commenting on Spinoza's *Ethics*, he writes: "When a body 'encounters' another body, or an idea another idea, it happens that the two relations sometimes combine to form a more powerful whole, and sometimes one decomposes the other, destroying the cohesion of its parts ...We experience *joy* when a body encounters ours and enters into composition with it, and *sadness* when, on the contrary, a body or an idea threatens our own coherence."[17] The insight this statement represents for a study of experience in the Shepherd will become clear as the discussion proceeds. But here it is worth pausing to notice that of the emotions that appear in the Shepherd, joy and sadness dominate,[18] and further that they are both internal and external states that flow into, out of, beside and between entities. As we will see, the Shepherd con-

---

13 Seigworth and Gregg, "Inventory," 6.
14 What follows is similarly influenced by my reading of Manuel DeLanda, *Assemblage Theory* (Edinburgh: Edinburgh University Press, 2016) and Bruno Latour, *Reassembling the Social: An Introduction to Actor Network Theory*, Clarendon Lectures in Management Studies (Oxford: Oxford University Press, 2007) both of whom also develop Deleuze's (and Guatarri's) theorization.
15 Seigworth and Gregg, "Inventory," 6.
16 Gilles Deleuze and Félix Guatarri, *A Thousand Plateaus: Capitalism and Schizophrenia*, trans. Brian Massumi (Minneapolis: University of Minnesota Press, 1987).
17 Gilles Deleuze, *Spinoza: Practical Philosophy* (San Francisco: City Lights Books, 1988), 19.
18 Λύπη and cognates appear 39 times in the Shepherd; ἱλαρός appears 38 times; μακάριος, 16 times; χαρά and cognates, 7 times; γελάω, 2 times. In the Latin text of Sim. 10 (111-114): in/felix, gaudium, affabiles, libenter.

tains "sad" and "happy" objects and powers (entities that draw Hermas in varying ways toward them) that penetrate and thereby render selves not heavily bounded, impenetrable, indivisible agents but dividual and partible (see below), parsed amongst things and states. They show us that in the affective field of the Shepherd entities coalesce with each other through "bindings and unbindings, becomings and un-becomings, jarring disorientations and rhythmic attunements."[19] To build on a famous concept of Charles Taylor, in the "enchanted world" of the Shepherd, selves (and we may add, objects, including living things and geographies) are not buffered as they are in modernity but are porous.[20]

This essay describes the ways in which Hermas is affected through his location in and responses to the multiple characters, settings, objects, and events that comprise Vision 3 (9-21) and Similitude 9 (78-110) and the ways in which they work together to mutually influence one another. My thesis is that Hermas and his audiences are not static, but, located amongst a dynamic set of phenomena, they are actants amongst other characters, places, animals, plants, and objects that express a creative set of flows and forces that are greater than sum of their parts.[21] Hermas delivers his apocalypse in a vivid way to awaken the audiences' participation in his revelations and thereby to persuade listeners by engulfing them in the affects his narratives generate.

Hermas as Assemblage

Hermas fascinates scholars.[22] Was he an historical person?[23] Is he a pure fiction?[24] Is he a composite allegorical figure constructed from Greek and Roman

---

19 Seigworth and Gregg, *Affect*, 2.
20 Charles Taylor, *A Secular Age* (Cambridge, MA: Belknap, 2007), 31–43, where he contrasts the enchanted world of premodernity with that of modernity.
21 I borrow the term "actant" from Latour's Actor Network Theory in *Reassembling*, 54–56, which theorizes that human and non–human actors (including objects, places, animals, and so on) form a network of relations that assemble with and mutually influence one another.
22 For an overview of theories about the identity and literary persona of Hermas, see the excellent summaries of scholarship by Norbert Brox, *Hirt des Hermas*, Kommentar zu den Apostolischen Väter 7 (Göttingen: Vandenhoeck & Ruprecht, 1991), 15–22; Mark Grundeken, *Community Building in the Shepherd of Hermas: A Critical Study of Some Key Aspects*, VCSup 131 (Leiden: Brill, 2015), 16–17.
23 Martin Leutzsch, *Die Wahrnehmung zozialer Wirklichkeit im „Hirten des Hermas"*, FRLANT 150 (Göttingen: Vandenhoeck & Ruprecht, 1989), 20–50.

literature?²⁵ Is he a skilled weaver of intertestamental apocalyptic texts and traditions woven together to form an elaborate intertextual product?²⁶ These are some of the questions that have produced many hours of study amongst Hermas scholars. But perhaps no topic fascinates researchers more than a desire to trace the psychological roots of his visions. As Peter Brown confesses, "Few figures in the Early Church are as delightful or open-hearted as Hermas.... He carried conviction because he so transparently described the tensions of his own heart."²⁷ "One of the oddest subtexts of Hermas's book," notes Wayne Meeks, "is a kind of subtext of sexual allusions that run throughout, but which is never developed."²⁸ Interpreters have jumped into the breach. Åke von Ström argues that his bad conscience about seeing Rhoda bathing in the nude and his dissatisfaction with his family generated his revelations.²⁹ This echoes Jung's understanding that Hermas's visions were the result of repressed erotic fantasy about his former master sublimated into dreams of her as a chaste church and compensated for through admonitions to his community to adhere to ideals of purity and loyalty to the worshiping assembly.³⁰ Pamela Cox Miller discovers in Hermas a man who struggled "with affairs of conscience" and that the Shepherd depicts

---

24 R. Joly, *Hermas le Pasteur*, Sources chrétiennes 53 bis, 2nd ed. (Paris: Les Editions du Cerf, 1968), 17–21; E. Peterson, "Kritische Analyse der V. Vision des Hermas," *Historisches Jahrbuch* 77 (1958), 362–69.
25 Martin Dibelius, *Der Hirt des Hermas*, HNT 4 (Tübingen: J. C. B. Mohr [Paul Siebeck], 1923), 419–20, 445–46.
26 Angelo P. O'Hagan, *Material Recreation in the Apostolic Fathers*, TU 100 (Berlin: Akademie Verlag, 1968), 111–32.
27 Peter Brown, *The Body and Society* (New York: Columbia University Press, 1988), 69.
28 Wayne Meeks, *The Origins of Christian Morality: The First Two Centuries* (New Haven: Yale University Press, 1993), 148.
29 Åke von Ström, *Der Hirt des Hermas. Allegorie oder Wirklichkeit?* Arbeiten und Mitteilungen aus dem neutestamentalichen Seminar zu Uppsala (Leipzig: A. Lorenz, 1936), 3–7. See similarly, K. W. Clark, "The Sins of Hermas," in *Early Christian Origins: Studies in Honor of H. R. Willoughby*, ed. A. Wikgren (Chicago: Quadrangle Books, 1961), 102–19 at 118, where he argues that Hermas personally struggled with sin and repentance.
30 C. G. Jung, *Psychological Types* in *The Collected Works of C.G. Jung*, Vol. 6, ed. Gerhard Adler et al. (Princeton: Princeton University Press, 2014), 224–31 at 224. Jung similarly explains the vision of a threatened tribulation in Vis. 4 (22–24) as the consequence of repressed desire unconsciously transmogrified into a warning against sin, *Mysterium Coniunctionis: An Inquiry into the Separation and Synthesis of Psychic Opposites in Alchemy* in *The Collected Works of C. G. Jung*, Volume 14, ed. Gerhard Adler et al. (Princeton: Princeton University Press, 2014), 226–28. For fuller discussion and critique, see R. Joly, "Philologie et psychanalyse: C. G. Jung et le 'Pasteur' d'Hermas," *L'Antiquité classique* 22 (1953): 422–28.

his dreams "in autobiographical terms as an angelic therapy of consciousness."[31] Psychological reconnaissance of this kind reveals that Hermas contained a complex emotional topography. Simon Tugwell discovers a more featureless landscape. Hermas is

> one of those inoffensive religious people who preserve their good humour by keeping themselves to themselves, even if this does mean abandoning their responsibilities rather lightly. They are genuinely moral, but with little moral sensitivity. They find it easy to confess their sins, they are rather helpless in face of the much worse behaviour of other people. Their very harmlessness makes them unlikely to be victims of persecution. There is little to stop them getting through their whole lives in benign ineffectiveness.[32]

Hermas was not as fascinating as he was anodyne. In accounts such as these, the focus is on Hermas's interior life.

Such perspectives, however, ignore that the bulk of the Shepherd orients the gaze of its main character outward and that the outside and the inside of Hermas flow in and out of each other as the narrative proceeds. The outward orientation points to a long list of items: objects (stones, towers, couches, chairs, water, food, wealth); places (the Tiber, the Via Campania, vineyards, fields, mountains, Arcadia, the sea, the city); characters (Rhoda, *kyriai/oi*, household members, the rich and poor, elders, a shepherd, angels, the devil, slaves, old and young women, men, virgins, spirits, widows, orphans, and so on); and plants and animals (trees, branches, vines, apocalyptic beasts, reptiles, and sheep). It is true that the Shepherd invites us into Hermas's inner world, but those internal workings are never in isolation from the settings and the objects, places, plants, and animals that together create the media by which Hermas's revelations unfold. We encounter Hermas *in situ*. To put it differently, Hermas *takes place*—literally in particular places, but also amidst a constellation of both animate beings and "inanimate" objects. As he does so, he makes spaces for his audience to *occupy* themselves with during the time they listen to his revelations. Indeed, they reveal that members of his audience are *preoccupied* with things, especially the pursuit of wealth ("fields, dwellings, and many other possessions [ἀγροὺς καὶ οἰκήσεις καὶ ἑτέρας ὑπάρξεις πολλάς]," Sim. 1.4 [50.4]; "riches and business affairs [πλοῦτον αὐτῶν καὶ ... τὰς πραγματείας]," Vis. 3.6.5 [14.5]; also Vis. 1.1.8 [1.8]; Mand. 3.5 [28.5]; 5.2.2 [34.2]; 10.1.4 [40.4]; Sim. 4.5 [53.5]; 8.8.1 [74.1]; 9.20.1–2 [97.1–2]). More importantly, as we will see below, Hermas and his audience

---

[31] Pamela Cox Miller, *Dreams in Late Antiquity: Studies in the Imagination of a Culture* (Princeton: Princeton University Press, 1994), 131.
[32] Simon Tugwell, *The Apostolic Fathers* (London: Geoffrey Chapman, 1989), 48.

are *occupied* by various entities, whether they be spiritual powers that inhabit them or the objects they desire and pursue. Whatever Hermas's interior life may be, his narratives bring his audience on a number of journeys to different kinds of spaces populated by various characters, settings and things. Hermas and his audience discover themselves to be an assemblage of these items: spiritual powers, desires, objects such as towers and stones and mountains, animals and plants such as sheep and willow branches are simultaneously things and representations of people and groups that overlap and interpenetrate one another.

Building on the observation of Deleuze cited above, that joy and sadness arise from when two or more relations combine and form a more powerful whole or threaten to decompose an assembly, we may say that in the Shepherd, Hermas is more than an inner life and exterior objects are more than simply inanimate things. Indeed, the term "inanimate" is misleading in a discussion of the Shepherd and imports a modern understanding of the physical world onto the past. It is true that various objects (stones or mountains for example) function allegorically, but they are more than allegories, or metaphors, they are entities in Hermas's visions that have characteristic lives that the apocalyptic explanations describe. Political theorist and philosopher Jane Bennett uses the phrase "vibrant materiality" to describe the ways in which material formations become operators on account of their particular location in an assemblage and as such are generative of life and affect.[33] Bennett's work focuses on our contemporary world, but she offers an insight to which we will return in the last section of our discussion when we use anthropological theory of partibility and dividuality to consider the vision and parable of the tower as a network of human and non-human spiritual and material actants. The point here is that in Hermas's visions, objects such as stones and mountains join together with beings to create an assemblage that creates an *animated* constellation greater than the sum of its parts. The Shepherd unfolds in an ecology of characters, places, objects, and animals.

More notable still is the way in which the boundaries between beings and objects shift and modulate as Hermas receives his revelations. There is a two-way flow between branches, sheep, mountains, and stones and people and more than human creatures. Fields and vines are the poor (Sim. 1.6 [50.6]; 2.1–9 [51.1–9]); trees are people (Sim. 3–4 [52–53]; Sim. 8 [67–77]); various people are different kinds of stones (Sim 9.6–9, 16–31 [83–86, 93–108]). Virtues and vices are spiritual powers (Man 3.1–3 [28.1–2]; Man 5.2.2–4, 5–8 [34.2–4,

---

[33] Jane Bennett, *Vibrant Matter: A Political Ecology of Things* (Durham: Duke University Press, 2010), 8–9.

5–8]; Man 10.2 [41.2]; Man. 11.2–21 [43.2–21]; Sim 9.13.2–7 [90.2–7]; 9.16.1–5 [93.1–5]). Dress and self flow into each other (Sim. 9.2.4 [79.4]; 9.9.5 [86.5]; 9.13.8 [90.8]. Variegated mountain topographies have characteristics and lives that represent varieties of Jesus followers (for example, Sim 9.20.1 [97.1]). As modulations unfold, objects, places, and beings take on affects. They are charged with emotional meanings and they, in turn, interact with Hermas to produce states within him, surrounded by peoples, places, and things that affect his various moods, even as those states shape the perceptions of and attitudes toward things around him. Hermas as literary character unfolds in the middle of people and things in ways that are not heavily bounded but are permeable. Attention to the dynamic and living assemblages of Hermas's work shows that it is not sufficient to use the Shepherd to explore the inner life of its main characters and that we must always consider the experiences and reactions of Hermas together with and amongst the situations, environments, objects, places, and entities in which he finds himself.[34]

---

34 Preoccupation with internal states remains a shortcoming of traditional studies concerning emotion and affect in the Shepherd; see for example, Petra von Gemünden, *Affekt und Glaube: Studien zur historischen Psychologie des Frühjudentums und Urchristentums*, NTOA 73 (Göttingen: Vandenhoeck & Ruprecht, 2009), 309–28, where she works with the anthropological theorization of August Nitschke to consider three dynamic formations of affect in Hermas: "Auto, Hetero–, und Transformationsdynamik," which she names "Tiefendynamik" and Hermas as dedicated to "Affektkontrolle", (310). I do not doubt that affects are internal to Hermas or that he is called upon to control them, but I would prefer to speak of "Zwischendynamik" or even "Verflechtungsdynamik" in order to preserve the notion of dynamic, shifting assemblage outlined here. Von Gemünden comes closer to the position advanced here in her discussion of "heterodynamische Affektkontrolle" but she does not consider the agency of powers within the assemblages the Shepherd represents. This is also the tendency of Andrew Crislip, "The Shepherd of Hermas and Early Christian Emotional Formation," *Studia Patristica* 9 (2017): 231–40, who treats Hermas's references to λύπη and ἱλαρότης as the poles of "two emotional communities" (238) διψυχία represents and which μετάνοια overcomes. Crislip describes "double-souledness as emotionally implicated, and connected to Hermas's concerns with being trapped between two worlds or a liminal state"—namely "the Church and the present age" which are "experienced through conflicting expectations of emotions," 239. (Similarly, Mark Grundeken, *Community Building in the Shepherd of Hermas: A Critical Study of Some Key Concepts*, VCSup 131 [Leiden: Brill, 2015], 76–82; also, too simplistically binary, Benjamin H. Dunning, *Aliens and Sojourners: Self as Other in Early Christianity* [Philadelphia: University of Pennsylvania Press, 2009], 78–90). But it is overly reductionist to state that Hermas is trapped between two worlds or that he is a liminal character as though he is neither one thing nor the other. On the contrary, he is a figure constituted by a dynamic multiverse of actants that present multiple visible and invisible worlds that together create assemblages in which he is a part. Brox, *Hermas*, 549–53 captures the dynamism of Hermas's treatment of emotions through analysis of the Shepherd's descriptions of powers dwelling within Hermas and/or his household and the relationship of such residence to *dispychia*; also, Osiek, *Hermas*, 31, 33–34.

It is self and place, objects, and living things that work together in Hermas to create a vivid set of descriptions of emotions geographically and spatially located.

Further, as is typical of ancient apocalypses, these assemblages of characters and things occur within revelatory journeys that not only furnish a vibrant materiality but also a vivid spatiality that form a vital part of the assemblages Hermas finds himself a part of.[35] Even as objects are charged with emotional valences, settings take on affects through the atmospheres they create. In Similitude 9.1.4 (78.4) Hermas brings his audience to a wide-open plain at Arcadia, a place that is evocative of the pastoral, a place that the first listeners of his revelation must have noticed was in striking contrast with over-crowded, impoverished tenements and warren of alleys and passage ways of the imperial capital where they were living.[36] As such, his apocalypse functions the way others examples of its genre do, namely to lift his listeners out of the everyday into another set of places. As is typical of the genre, Hermas narratively seeks to *replace* his audience. Through vivid autobiography and lively descriptions of what he sees, the questions he asks, and the answers he receives from his various revelators, he wishes to reorient the listeners of his revelations from one set of spatial coordinates to another, to embed them in a world of characters and objects that flow in and out of one another and take on multiple meanings as they do. One of Hermas's main concerns is that his audience's wealthier members are more concerned with their business prospects than with caring for the poor. As a consequence, Hermas's revelations aim to lift his listeners out of the daily practices of their everyday commercial lives and to resituate them in a new set of transactional coordinates in which differing kinds of stones quarried from various mountains become incorporated into a tower that is at once living and inanimate and are selected by their angelic masons as building material. Through these revelations Hermas takes his audience out of their quotidian spaces in order to orient them to new real and imagined places. Thus, Hermas is on the way to his fields and business interests when he comes upon his former master bathing which then opens up to a whole new set of coordinates that comprise the first four visions of the work. He learns that his orientations and those of his audience have all been wrong: there has been too much attention to gaining wealth and not enough to caring for the poor.

---

35 For vivid spatial journeys in apocalyptic roughly contemporary with the Shepherd, Kelley Coblentz Bautch, "Spatiality and Apocalyptic Literature," *Hebrew Bible and Ancient Israel* 3 (2016): 273–88.

36 "Romans Watching Romans: Jesus Religion in Close Urban Quarters and Neighbourhood Transformations" in *Religion of Quarters*, ed. Harry O. Maier and Emiliano Urciuoli, *Journal of Religion in the Roman Empire* 6 (2020): 106–21.

Happy Objects

This essay's title draws its inspiration from Sara Ahmed's phenomenological study of space and states of being.[37] She uses the phrase "happy objects" to describe the ways in which selves and environments create wholes that produce existential orientations in which spaces, objects, and selves interact with one another positively and negatively. Hermas was obviously not a postmodern phenomenologist, but Ahmed's notion of happy objects invites a way of offering an angle of investigation of Hermas's visions that might otherwise be ignored, namely the ways in which objects and environments affect Hermas and how he interacts with them. Ahmed refers to "sticky objects" as things that are seen as the cause of happiness or unhappiness. "Groups cohere around a shared orientation toward some things as being good, treating some things and not others as the cause of delight. If the same objects make us happy—or if we invest in the same objects as being what should make us happy—then we would be oriented or directed in the same way."[38] She describes "happy objects" as those things that "are passed around, accumulating positive affective value as social goods."[39] Building on the work of Silvan Tomkins and others she conceptualizes affects as contagious, phenomena that we catch and take hold of us and in turn result in us affecting others. As contagion, "affects pass between bodies, affecting bodily surfaces or even how bodies surface."[40] Further, bodies are situated within affective fields that influence and shape them according to the environments in which they exist. Ahmed notes, for example, that if we walk into a room we can "catch" a feeling of tension or anxiety; the affective state a person is in can in turn affect impressions of a space. Happy objects are those objects that align with one's feeling of pleasure whereas sad ones appear when one is out of line with them and alienation arises when one is outside an affective community and there is a gap between a consensus about the affective value of an object and how one experiences it. This means that there is always a possibility of a range of affects in which we attribute meaning to objects and objects carry signification that in turn relate to us and occupy us in certain ways.

Hermas's visions unfold amidst a circulation of "sticky objects" to which a series of affects are attached. His aim in his apocalypse is to make those affects contagious, to make his audience "catch" them and by doing so to situate them

---

37 Sara Ahmed, "Happy Objects," in Seigworth and Gregg, *Reader*, 29–51.
38 Ahmed, "Happy Objects," 35.
39 Ahmed, "Happy Objects," 35.
40 Ahmed, "Happy Objects," 36.

in a world of objects and desires that he hopes to shape. The sticky objects he sees and describes are instruments for channeling affect. As they unfold, they work cumulatively as a kind of paedagogy for shaping emotions, moods, and orientations. As is typical of apocalypses generally, Hermas uses ekphrastic description to place his listeners on the scene of visionary accounts; we see this for example in Sim. 9.6.1 (83.1), captured well by Ehrman's translation, where Hermas speaks directly to the audience before the vision unfolds: "And look! After a short while I saw…. [Καὶ ἰδοὺ μετὰ μικρὸν βλέπω]." According to rhetorical theory contemporary with Hermas, the function of vivid, detailed description was to persuade listeners by fostering emotional participation amongst listeners in the topics declaimed upon.[41] Modern scholars have complained that the Shepherd is a monotonous, repetitive, and a one-dimensional text.[42] But for Hermas's first listeners, detailed accounts of his revelations caught them up in his visions and in the emotional valences of his descriptions. As such they reveal their cultural location in an oral culture.[43]

Hermas amplifies the persuasive power of his revelation by couching them in a first-person narrative that invites listeners into emotional responses to what he sees. This has the effect of drawing listeners into the world of the implied author through on-site reporting. As Angela Kim Harkins has argued, detailed narrative and commentary has a cognitive function of increasing the suspense of the receiving audience by forcing it to depend upon the visionary's reports for narrative resolution.[44] The extended allegories that scholars experi-

---

[41] Ruth Webb, *Ekphrasis, Imagination, and Persuasion in Ancient Rhetorical Theory and Practice* (Surrey: Ashgate Publishing, 2009).
[42] Thus Theodor Zahn, *Der Hirt des Hermas* (Gotha: Friedrich Andreas Perthes, 1868), 486: Hermas's style "ist von Anfang bis zu Ende von einer ermüdenden Monotonie." For citations of other similar complaints, Brox, *Hermas*, 43–45.
[43] For the Shepherd as a product of oral culture, Osiek, 13–16: "Characteristics of oral style include: additive rather than subordinative structure; use of repeated traditional and circumlocutionary formulas; redundancy; traditionalism; practicality of examples; and situational, present-oriented consciousness and mode of delivery," p. 15.
[44] See the discussion of spatiality and apocalypses in Angela Kim Harkins, "Immersing Oneself in the Narrative World of Second Temple Apocalyptic Visions," in *Re-Imagining Apocalypticism: Apocalypses, Apocalyptic Literature, and the Dead Sea Scrolls*, ed. Lorenzo DiTommaso and Matthew J. Goff, SBLEJL (Atlanta: SBL Press, 2022). For a discussion of how Hermas's first-person reporting to the implied audience simulate a living experience of the detailed experiences of the spaces in the third vision of the tower see, Angela Kim Harkins, "Experiencing the Journey: Spaces in the *Book of Visions* of the *Shepherd of Hermas*," unpublished paper presented to the Boston Area Patristics Group, Harvard Divinity School, January 24, 2019; revised as chapter 4 in Angela Kim Harkins, *Re-reading the Visions in the Shepherd of Hermas*, Studies in Ancient Religion and Culture (Sheffield: Equinox, 2023). I am grateful to Professor Harkins for granting

ence as monotonous had the opposite effect on their first audiences; by enveloping audiences they became three-dimensional accounts. However, labored the text is to modern sensibilities, judging by the widespread geographical distribution of the text across the Roman Empire, Hermas's narratives captured the imagination of ancient Christian audiences.

First person ekphrasis also has the effect of creating moods and orientations to the topics treated. A range of emotions and moods accompany Hermas's visions. Hermas is regularly sad, happy, perplexed, curious, marveling, weeping, laughing, terrified, and upset. This repeated attention to Hermas's emotions draws the listener into his visions and shapes the experiences of the listeners watching them unfold. The implied audience sees and hears what Hermas perceives and thereby increases its participation in his experiences. As his revelations unfold, the personal failings he learns of improperly governing his family (Vis. 1.3.1–2 [3.1–2]; 2.2.2–3 [6.2–3]; 2.3.1 [7.1]; 3.1.6 [9.6]; Mand. 2.7 [27.7]; 5.1.7 [33.7]; 7.5, 7 [37.5, 7]), giving too much attention to his business interests (Vis. 2.3.1 [7.1]; Mand. 3.5 [28.5]; Sim. 4.5 [53.5]), and most damning of all, being double-minded (Vis. 1.1.8 [1.8]; 3.3.4 [11.4]; 3.10.9 [18.9]; 4.1.4 [22.4]; Mand. 9.1 [39.1]; 12.4.2 [47.2]; Sim. 6.1.2 [61.2]), focus the eyes of the listeners on their own failings. The objects comprising the worlds of Hermas's audiences become "sticky" in the sense that Hermas reveals the affects that are attached to them. Hermas has mistaken one set of happy objects for another and his apocalypse furnishes him and his listeners a means toward a reorientation. This change of direction unfolds powerfully at the start of the third vision. Hermas choses "a beautiful spot that was secluded" (Vis. 3.1.3 [9.3]) to meet the *kyria* for a further revelation. When he sees an ivory couch (συμψέλιον) "with no one at the place [μηδένα ὄντα ἐν τῷ τόπῳ ||]," the affects of astonishment [ἔκθαμβος] and trembling (τρόμος) seize him and he "shuddered in panic [φρίκη μοι προσῆλθεν] ... because I was alone [μόνου μου ὄντος]" (Vis. 3.1.4 [9.4]). With the threefold mention of being alone, the atmosphere Hermas creates is one of isolation compounded by terror. Panic gives way to sadness (λυπούμενος) when Hermas learns from the *kyria* that he cannot sit on the right side of the

---

me access to these papers prior to their publication. Also eadem, "Looking at the *Shepherd of Hermas* through the Experience of Lived Religion," in *Lived Religion in the Ancient Mediterranean World: Approaching Religious Transformations from Archaeology, History and Classics*. Edited by Valentino Gasparini, Maik Patzelt, Rubina Raja, Anna-Katharina Rieger, Jörg Rüpke, Emiliano Urciuoli (Berlin: De Gruyter, 2020), 49–70. Another good example of this is the Book of Revelation, for which see Harry O. Maier, *Apocalypse Recalled: The Book of Revelation after Christendom* (Minneapolis: Fortress, 2002), 64–122, where components of oral culture and their role in creating experience of revelations are discussed with respect to the Apocalypse.

couch which is reserved for "only those who have already pleased God and suffered on behalf of the name" (Vis. 3.1.9 [9.9]). She instructs him: "Many things must happen to you before you can sit with them. But continue in your simplicity, as you are doing, and you will sit with them, as will everyone who does what they have and endures what they have endured" (σοὶ δὲ πολλὰ λείπει ἵνα μετ' αὐτῶν καθίσῃς· ἀλλ' ὡς ἐμμένεις τῇ ἁπλότητί σου, μεῖνον, καὶ καθιῇ μετ' αὐτῶν, καὶ ὅσοι ἐὰν ἐργάσωνται τὰ ἐκείνων ἔργα καὶ ὑπενέγκωσιν ἃ καὶ ἐκεῖνοι ὑπήνεγκαν, Vis. 3.1.9 [9.9]). The συμψέλιον is a sticky object in an atmosphere of isolation that first creates an affect of terror and then awakens desire which in turn becomes contagious amongst the listeners who see and experience the vision through Hermas's vivid description. It will become a happy object if his apocalypse is successful.

The συμψέλιον and atmospheric isolation form an excellent example of the way affect and emotion circulate amongst objects, characters, places in the Shepherd. The Visions and Similitudes expand this circulation in drawn out ways. Three Similitudes are instructive. In the third Similitude of the trees (Sim. 3–4 [52–53]), the sixth of the shepherd and the sheep (6.1–6.5 [61–65]), and the eighth of the willow branches (8.1–11 [67–77]), Hermas's revelations bring different moods to various places, trees, sheep, branches, shepherds, and angels. Atmosphere dominates when Hermas sees wintry withered trees and blossoming spring ones (Sim. 3.1–3 [52.1–3]; 4.1–3 [53.1–3]) to represent "the coming age [αἰὼν ὁ ἐρχόμενος]" that is "a summer for the upright, but a winter for sinners [θερεία ἐστὶ τοῖς δικαίοις, τοῖς δὲ ἁμαρτωλοῖς χειμών]" (Sim. 4.2 [53.2]). Parable six strikes an evocative mood when Hermas beholds a "large wild looking shepherd" [ποιμένα μέγαν ὡσεὶ ἄγριον τῇ ἰδέα] clothed in a white goatskin, with a knotty staff and a great whip. "He had an extremely bitter look about him. I was afraid of him, he had such a look "τὸ βλέμμα εἶχε περίπικρον, ὥστε φοβηθῆναί με αὐτόν· τοιοῦτον εἶχε τὸ βλέμμα" (Sim. 6.2.5 [62.5]). He drives "frisky and luxuriously fed" sheep into a steep area where they entangle themselves in thorns and thistles and are "extremely sorrowful from being beaten by him [λίαν ἐταλαιπώρουν δαιρόμενα ὑπ' αὐτοῦ]" (Sim. 6.2.7 [62.7]). Hermas states that when he saw them "flogged like this and made so miserable [οὕτω μαστιγούμενα καὶ ταλαιπωροῦντα ἐλυπούμην ἐπ' αὐτοῖς]" (Sim. 6.3.1 [63.1]), he grieved for them [ἐλυπούμην ἐπ' αὐτοῖς] and learned that the landscape of thorns and thistles represents "financial losses, deprivations, various diseases, or every kind of disruption, or being abused by miscreants, and ... many other kinds of suffering financial losses [τιμωροῦνται γὰρ οἱ μὲν ζημίαις, οἱ δὲ ὑστερήσεσιν, οἱ δὲ ἀσθενείαις ποικίλαις, οἱ δὲ πάσῃ ἀκαταστασίᾳ, οἱ δὲ ὑβριζόμενοι ὑπὸ ἀναξίων καὶ ἑτέραις πολλαῖς πράξεσι πάσχοντες]" (Sim. 6.3.4 [63.4]). Again, in the parable of the willow branches, Hermas provokes a different mood when he sees a great and healthy willow tree "that spread its shade out over plains and mountains; and all those who have been called by the name of the Lord came under the shadow of the willow" (Sim. 8.1.1 [67.1]). Its branches in various states (moth eaten, withered, green) or combinations of them are pruned by a tall and "glorious angel of the Lord" and given "to the people who were in its shade" (Sim. 8.1.2 [67.2]); the angel examines them and is "extremely happy [ἐχάρη λίαν]" when he sees the majority of the branches are green (Sim. 8.1.16 [67.16]); those who hand him budding branches bearing fruit are "extremely cheerful [λίαν ἱλαροί]"; the shepherd is "extremely cheerful [λίαν ἱλαροί]" and the angel rejoices [ἠγαλλιᾶτο] over them (Sim. 8.1.18 [67.18]). They receive budding crowns made of palm leaves, are given white clothing and proceed into the tower (Sim. 8.2.1–4 [68.1–4]). The shepherd plants all the other branches and waters them to see if they will live (Sim. 8.2.6–9 [68.6–9]), "for the one who created this tree wishes all those who received branches from it to live" and he hopes "that the vast majority of these branches... will live" (Sim. 8.2.9 [68.9]).

Scholars have given much attention to the elaborate allegories that follow or are embedded in each of these parables, but they have passed over the vivid emotional valences and dynamic relationships of the places, objects, animals, plants, and characters of them. These entities become sticky objects that are either sad or happy through the ekphrastic descriptions Hermas lavishes upon them. This results in their becoming more than a set of abstract teachings on conversion and repentance which scholars have mined and sought to locate in an unfolding history of Christian doctrine and certainly not the "tiresome monotony" that Theodor Zahn once impugned them as possessing. They are living entities that aim at persuasion by evoking various moods and directing the emotions of listeners. As they do this, assemblages of items emerge as seasons, trees, sheep, branches and landscapes of various kinds, as well as the tower, the shepherds, and the angel combine together to create a whole that is more than any single part and to express a vibrant materiality delivered through recreated visionary experiences.

Assembling the Tower

The most extended example this ekphrastic assemblage of elements into "a sticky object" appears in Hermas's vision and parable of the tower (Vis. 3.1–3.13 [9–21]; Sim. 9.1–9.33 [78–110]). Hermas seeks to awaken amongst his listeners a desire for incorporation into the tower by aligning them with ideal objects and charging those entities with various emotional properties. Hermas seeks to make such desire urgent by holding forth a limited time offer of a speedy second repentance (Vis. 3.7.5 [15.5]; Sim. 9.19.1–3 [96.1–3]; 9.20.4 [97.4]; 9.21 [98.4]; 9.26.6 [103.6]; 9.33.1 [110.1]) and incorporation into the tower under rapid construction (Vis. 3.8.9 [16.9]; Sim. 9.3.1–2 [80.1–2]; 9.5.1–2 [82.1–2]; 10.4.4 [114.4]). Place is central: we have seen that in the third vision, Hermas is in a beautiful, secluded spot; in the parable, Hermas is taken to Arcadia, to the peak of a breast-shaped (μαστῶδες) mountain, where he sees a great plain surrounded by twelve mountains (Sim. 9.1.4–10 [78.4–10]) representing the "tribes that inhabit the whole earth... and they are diverse in thought and mind" (Sim. 9.17.2 [94.2]). Elaborate theories have been attached to the reference to Arcadia, including that Hermas was a native of the Peloponnese.[45] Of significance for our discussion here is that the landscape establishes an immediate mood: it is home to both Pan and Hermes and is arguably evocative of a bucolic setting of natural harmony between humans and nature.[46] This is the backdrop for Hermas's detailed description of the mountains whose resources he describes as belonging to and or finding no place in the tower, an object that is at home in its Arcadian setting. The first six mountains he sees contain resources that do not fit: for example, the black mountain (Sim. 9.19 [96]); another with thorns and briars (Sim. 9.20 [97]); a further one that is rugged (Sim. 9.22 [99]), the sixth with large and small rifts and withered plants (Sim. 9.23 [100]); the ninth mountain is "desolate, which had on it reptiles, and wild beasts that destroy people" (Sim. 9.26.1 [103.1]). The rest of the mountains, namely the ones that are filled with things that bring life, do belong in Arcadia: resting, well fed sheep inhabit the tenth mountain; fruit trees filled with various kinds of fruit cover the eleventh one. Hermas describes the seventh mountain as a place "where vegetation was green and blooming and the whole mountain was thriving and cattle of every kind and birds of the sky were feeding on the vegetation on that mountain, and the vegetation on which they fed became all the more luxuriant" (Sim. 9.24.1 [101.1]). More striking still is its living affect: it has "happy plants [βοτάνας ἱλαράς] and the whole

---

45 See J. Rendel Harris, "Hermas in Arcadia," *Journal of the Society of Biblical Literature and Exegesis* 7 (1887): 69–83. See Brox, *Hermas*, 382–86 and Snyder, *Hermas*, 128–130 for reviews of various treatments. Wolfgang P. Schmid, "Eine frühchristliche Arkadienvorstellung," in *Ausgewählte philologische Schriften*, ed. Harmut Erbse and Jochem Küppers (Berlin: De Gruyter, 1984), 510–18 considers Arcadia as indicative of a place of divine revelation because of its association with Hermes.
46 For its ancient associations, Bruno Snell, "Arkadien, die Entdeckung einer geistigen Landschaft," in *Antike und Abendland* 1 (1945): 26–41 and the critique of Snell in Ernst A. Schmidt, "Arkadien: Abendland und Antike." in *Antike und Abendland* 21 (1975): 36–57; for discussion of theories concerning pagan influences and Hermas's appropriation, Brox, *Hirt*, 384–85 who is unduly skeptical of idyllic associations.

mountain was thriving [ὅλον τὸ ὄρος εὐθηνοῦν ἦν]" (Sim. 9.1.8 [78.8]). Similarly, the twelfth mountain "is of an exceedingly cheerful appearance [καὶ ἡ πρόσοψις αὐτοῦ ἱλαρὰ λίαν]" (Sim. 9.1.10 [78.10]).[47]

None of these mountains, whether negative or positively portrayed, is a lifeless object. Not only are they inhabited by various living things, Hermas lavishes ekphrastic description on these mountains and turns them into vibrant entities whose life or death he magnifies by allegories exegeting them as typifying different kinds of Jesus followers. Even as the mountains are alive, so is the tower.[48] It is a cheerful entity: after a day of construction "the virgins took brooms and sprinkled water around, the area of the tower became cheerful and beautiful [καὶ ἐγένετο ὁ τόπος ἱλαρὸς καὶ εὐπρεπέστατος τοῦ πύργου]" (Sim. 9.10.3 [87.3], modifying Ehrman's translation which improperly renders ἱλαρός, "bright," thereby removing the valence of emotion from the object). The mountains and the tower are sticky objects that embody negative and positive affects.

The happy objects fit the affect of the characters involved with the construction of the tower. The twelve virgins in linen tunics are "exceedingly cheerful and eager [λίαν γὰρ ἱλαραὶ ἦσαν καὶ πρόθυμοι]" to participate in the construction of the tower (Sim. 9.2.4 [79.4]). Hermas reports upon spending a night with them in prayer that "they were very cheerful and treated me well [ἱλαρώτεραι καὶ πρὸς ἐμὲ εὖ εἶχον]" (Sim. 9.10.7 [87.7]). The twelve "wild [ἄγριαι]" women dressed in black and belted, with loose hair and bare shoulders (Sim. 9.9.5 [86.5]) "cheerfully [ἱλαραὶ ἦραν]" take away the stones discarded form the tower (Sim. 9.9.6 [86.6]). Affect is contagious: Hermas himself is cheered by what he sees (Sim. 9.10.1 [87.1]) even as he "feels happy [ἱλαρὸς ἤμην]" to be with the virgins with whom he spent the night and feels as though he is young again as they kiss him, and he plays with them (Sim. 9.11.5 [88.5]). He tells the shepherd when asked about his evening in their company: "I was glad to stay with them [εὐφράνθην μετ᾽ αὐτῶν μείνας]" (Sim. 9.11.8 [88.8]). Upon its completion "the lord of the tower" (Sim. 9.6.1 [83.1]) examines the stones and some of those found wanting the shepherd cleanses, hews, and reincorporates into the building (Sim. 9.8.3–9.9.4 [85.3–86.4]). There follows another emotion laden response

---

[47] Ehrman's and Holmes' English translations render the adjective ἱλαρός in Sim. 9.1.8, 10 (78.8, 10) as "blooming" and "bright"; Brox reads "entzückend" ("delightful"); Snyder has "bright vegetation" and "very bright"; Lake translates "vigorous herbage" and "joyful." Greek has a perfectly good word for "bright": λαμπρός; "blooming" and "vigorous" are incorrect. Osiek reads "joyful plants" and "full of joy."

[48] For discussion of the dynamic quality and solidity of the stones of the tower in the third Vision, see Harkins, "Looking at the *Shepherd of Hermas* through the Experience of Lived Religion," 63–64.

by both Hermas and him: "When the shepherd saw that the tower was beautifully built, he was extremely cheerful [ἰδὼν δὲ ὁ ποιμὴν τὸν πύργον εὐπρεπῆ ὄντα τῇ οἰκοδομῇ, λίαν ἱλαρὸς ἦν]" (Sim. 9.9.7 [86.7]). "As I walked with him I was cheerful, seeing such good things [Κἀγὼ περιπατῶν μετ0 αὐτοῦ ἱλαρὸς ἤμην τοιαῦτα ἀγαθὰ βλέπων]" (Sim. 9.10.1 [87.1]). Through this assemblage of happy objects Hermas creates a circuitry of affect that flows through him, other than human characters, and objects like.

All of this construction and testing unfolds with a good deal of activity, magnifying the currents of affect flowing through the network of characters and objects. Angela Kim Harkins has noted the ways audience participation is increased through the kinesthetic elements of his revelations. In an evocative description she refers to the "scaffolding of perceptual experience" in Vision 3: "The Tower is not inert but possesses qualities of lived experience as the mind [of the implied reader/audience] carefully contemplates handling, rotating, inspecting each stone for cracks and flaws. Feeling the dust and hearing the noise of the construction become additional aspects of the enactive perception that can be supplied by the readers' and hearers' imagination."[49] Indeed, Hermas and the characters around him are continually on the move in the Shepherd. This is especially true in the parable of the tower in which Hermas devotes a good deal of attention to the actions associated with its construction and Hermas's participation in it. This creates a mood of urgency. After Hermas sees the twelve mountains, he sees six men commanded to build a tower: "There was great disturbance amongst those who had come to build the tower, as they were running back and forth around the gate [ἦν δὲ μέγας θόρυβος τῶν ἀνδρῶν ἐκείνων τῶν ἐληλυθότων οἰκοδομεῖν τὸν πύργον, ὧδε κἀκεῖσε περιτρεχόντων κύκλῳ τῆς πύλης]" (Sim. 9.3.1 [80.1]). The virgins standing around the tower "tell the men to hurry [ἔλεγον τοῖς ἀνδράσι σπεύδειν] and build the tower" (Sim. 9.3.2 [80.2]). Detailed instructions follow the movements that accompany the stones through the gate and onto the building site (Sim. 9.3.4–5 [80.4–5]), accompanied with vivid description of the course of construction (9.3.1–8 [80.1–8]).

Whereas the earlier mood is one of urgency, the atmosphere now changes through slow motion investigation. Upon the arrival of its inspector, the lord of the tower, the virgins "ran up and kissed him, and they started walking near him around the tower [προσδραμοῦσαι κατεφίλησαν αὐτόν, καὶ ἤρξαντο ἐγγὺς αὐτοῦ περιπατεῖν κύκλῳ τοῦ πύργου]" (Sim. 9.6.2 [83.2]), whereupon he "examined the building carefully, touching each stone, one by one [τὴν οἰκοδομὴν ἀκριβῶς, ὥστε αὐτὸν καθ0 ἕνα λίθον ψηλαφᾶν]" (Sim. 9.6.3 [83.3]). As the vision

---

49 Harkins, "Looking at the *Shepherd of Hermas* through the Experience of Lived Religion," 63.

continues, the stones are cleaned, trimmed, replaced, and re-examined, lime is brought to fill the cracks in the tower, it is swept and sprinkled with water (Sim. 9.8 – 9.9 [85 – 87]).

The mood shifts again when Hermas spends an evening with the virgins. During the night, their leader "began to kiss me and hold me in her arms" together with the others (Sim. 9.11.4 [88.4]) and as though young again he plays with them: "For some of them were prancing, others dancing, and still others singing But I was keeping silent, walking around the tower with them feeling happy to be with them [αἱ μὲν γὰρ ἐχόρευον, αἱ δὲ ὠρχοῦντο, αἱ δὲ ᾖδον· ἐγὼ δὲ σιγὴν ἔχων μετ' αὐτῶν κύκλῳ τοῦ πύργου περιεπάτουν, καὶ ἱλαρὸς ἤμην μετ' αὐτῶν]" (Sim. 9.11.5 [88.5]). Hermas not only sees but feels. In Sim. 9.10.1 (87.1), Hermas reports: "As I walked with him [the shepherd] I was cheerful, seeing such good things [Κἀγὼ περιπατῶν μετ' αὐτοῦ ἱλαρὸς ἤμην τοιαῦτα ἀγαθὰ βλέπων].

Affect is dynamic in the Shepherd. Hermas's happy objects express a shifting set of relations between characters and entities. Taken together these sticky objects ask us to recall Deleuze's observation that joy (Hermas would call it 'cheerfulness') arises when one enters into composition with another body and sadness when one's coherence is threatened. Sticky objects create and reveal affects and in doing so prompt the audience to enter into the Shepherd's atmospheric affects of the various mountains, as well as the urgency of the tower's construction, the lord's careful examination of the tower, and Hermas's amazing night with the virgins. In orchestrating these affects, he wants to promote the possession of cheerfulness in his audience and to exorcize the sadness that has taken up residence within them. The role of Hermas's visions is to reveal to the audience the affects that they house and in doing so to threaten his listeners' coherence and to re/construct them through happier compositions.

Dividual Selves and Partible Objects and Places

We have spoken of possession, exorcism, and residences. What does it mean when Hermas says that his listeners furnish various kinds of residence for spirits or that spaces like mountains and an object like a tower possess cheerfulness? These concepts do not fit into a modern Cartesian mindset which grants humans preeminent agency and sees other living things as separate from the human and objects, places, and geographical formations as inert and lifeless. The ancient world did not make the distinction between lifeless and living objects and humans, animals, and places that modernity does. In Roman religion, for example, numina or divine powers inhabited objects, people, animals, places, and natural phenomena that were alive in differing ways and belonged to a shared ecology with their own kinds of agency.⁵⁰ Greg Anderson writes evocatively of the "many real worlds of the past" to capture the idea that antiquity was closer in its epistemologies to other premodern cultures around the world—both past and present—than it is to modernity. It conceived animals, objects, places, and people, each with their own properties of agency, as joining together to form the world, an idea that confounds modern western epistemologies.⁵¹ When Hermas sees a cheerful place with a tower with renovated or discarded stones he interprets the construction materials allegorically as personified qualities he desires his implied audience to possess. But those personifications also arise out of a worldview where entities have living qualities. Hermas's accounts are at home in Hebrew Bible and Second Temple Jewish literature which regularly describe a variety of non-human entities such as mountains, trees, the land, the sea and so on as having agency.⁵² This is especially the case in Jewish apocalyptic literature.⁵³ A good example is 1 Enoch 24–36, which some scholars have argued is the source of Hermas's vision of the twelve mountains of Arcadia.⁵⁴ In the vision Enoch is taken for a tour through the four points of the compass where he sees seven mountains, smells fragrant trees, beholds a valley of judgment, a wilderness, huge beasts, stars, and the gates to heaven. Even if the connection with the Shepherd is forced, the chapters from Enoch share with Hermas's revelation a vivid description of natural phenomena with their own forms of agency. These

---

50 See Greg Anderson, *The Realness of Things Past: Ancient Greece and Ontological History* (Oxford: Oxford University Press, 2018), 71–88 for a sustained consideration of this insight for the task of historiography of the ancient world, a set of insights that apply equally to investigation of apocalypses like the Shepherd of Hermas.
51 Anderson, *Realness*, 68–128.
52 For an extended account of the Hebrew Bible with the help of anthropological theory of animism and agencies of other than human entities, Mari Joerstad, *The Hebrew Bible and Environmental Ethics: Humans, Nonhumans, and the Living Landscape* (Cambridge: Cambridge University Press 2019); at 39 she exegetes Is 55:12 ("The mountains and the hills will burst into jubilation before you, and all the trees of the field will clap their hands") as exemplary of nonhuman agents (my own preference would be to refer to actants to avoid anthropocentrism) that are more than metaphorical representations; also, William P. Brown, *The Seven Pillars of Creation: The Bible, Science, and the Ecology of Wonder* (Oxford: Oxford University Press, 2010).
53 For example, Jub. 2:2 refers to "the angels of the spirits of cold and of heat, and of winter and spring and of all the spirits of God's creatures which are in the heavens and on earth"; in Rev 12:16 the earth comes to the help of the woman pursued by the serpent; in Sib. Or. 5.514–530 the stars of the Zodiac battle against one another; in 4 Ezra 4:13–21 the forest and the sea battle one another; in 2 Bar. 29.1–8, Behemoth and Leviathan as well as the fruit of the earth feed the hungry.
54 Harris, "Hermas in Arcadia," 69–83; picked up later in Snyder, *Hermas*, 129.

are living entities at home in the premodern worldview that Hermas and the authors of the Enochic literature shared.⁵⁵

The Shepherd of Hermas belongs to a world where spirits inhabit people and take possession of them or live alongside them in their households and fill them with their presence (for example, Mand. 4.2.1 [30.1]; Sim. 7.1 [66.1]; 9.11.3 [88.3]; 10.4.1–5 [114.1–5]). Hermas's favourite word, double-mindedness (διψυχία) and cognates—a term that appears 55 times in the Shepherd—expresses (as Giovanni Bazzana's essay in this volume argues) possession by more than one inimical power and expresses much more than being divided by conflicting allegiances.⁵⁶ Bazzana also insightfully relates this to Hermas's notion of being possessed by spirits as the putting on clothing where dress expresses the presence of a non-human entity or power (Vis. 3.12.2 [20.2]; 4.1.8 [22.8]; Mand. 1.2 [26.2]; 5.2.8 [34.8]; 9.7 [39.7]; 12.1.2 [44.2]; 12.2.4 [45.4]; Sim. 6.1.2 [61.2]; 8.2.3 [68.3]; 9.13.2, 5, 7, 8 [90.2, 5, 7, 8]; 9.15.3 [92.3]; 9.32.3–4 [109.3–4]). Hermas learns that nobody can enter the tower unless they "are clothed in the virgin's garments" (Sim. 9.13.3 [90.3]; cf. 9.13.2 [90.2]) who assist in the building's construction. He describes these as "holy spirits [ἄγια πνεύματά]" and "powers of the Son of God [δυνάμεις ... τοῦ υἱοῦ τοῦ θεοῦ]" (Sim. 9.13.2 [90.2]) and the necessity of bearing their names (Sim. 9.13.3 [90.3]). Later he learns the names of their powers Hermas is to wear/bear: a series of twelve titles that includes cheerfulness ('ιλαρότης; Sim. 9.15.2 [92.2]). Likewise, the women with black garments have twelve names amongst which is sorrow (λύπη; Sim. 9.15.3 [92.3]). These are powers that take up residence inside members and/or their households and orient

---

55 See also, 1 En. 60:15–22; 61:10; 80:1–8; 82:4–20; 85—90; 2 En. 4:1–2; 19:1–6.
56 Most of the scholarship that takes up διψυχία in the Shepherd focuses on internal states (see note 34 for representative accounts); also, Anna Nürnberger, *Zweifelskonzepte im Frühchristentum. Dispychia und Oligopistia im Rahmen menschlicher Dissonanz– und Einheitsvorstellungen in der Antike*, NOTA 122 (Göttingen: Vandenhoeck & Ruprecht, 2019); for discussion of the Shepherd with a review of literature: 26–34. As we will see, the notion of partibility offers a strikingly different approach to διψυχία that places Hermas amidst the world of objects and entities that populate his narratives. Further, such a situated reading of Shepherd departs radically from a purely lexicographical or etymological approach to διψυχία that seeks to exegete the term through reference to its literal meaning and semantic origins (thus, Oscar J. F. Seitz, "Antecedents and Signification of the Term δίψυχος," *JBL* 66 (1947): 211–19; "Afterthoughts on the term δίψυχος," *NTS* 4 (1958): 327–34; further problematic is the idea that διψυχία refers to a kind of internal vacillation and indecision, a purely modern psychological account: Calum Gilmour, "Religious Vascillation and Indecision: Doublemindedness as the Opposite of Faith: A Study of *Dispychos* and Its Cognates in the *Shepherd of Hermas* and Other Early Christian Literature," *Prudentia* 16 (1984): 13–42.

them toward or away from God.⁵⁷ In keeping with Hermas's vibrant ecology of things, they also can reside in places such as mountains, the tower, animals, and plants. Thus a mountain can be cheerful because an entity Hermas can describe as cheerfulness inhabits it.

If mountains and places can be possessed in such a manner, so can other places and objects in Hermas's world. Preeminent amongst these are the businesses that Hermas admonishes his wealthier members for pursuing. Hermas sees commercial interests as possessing agency: those entangled by many affairs are "distracted" and "choked" by them a go astray (Sim. 4.5 [53.5]; 9.20.1 [97.1]). "[E]ntangled in business affairs and wealth and friendships with outsiders and many other concerns with the world" they do not understand the shepherd's parables "because they are darkened by these matters and are ruined and become barren" (Mand. 10.1.4 [40.4]). The "angel of wickedness" creates "desire for much business, and extravagant kinds of food and drink, and much drunkenness, and various kinds of unnecessary luxuries, and the desire for women, and greed, and arrogance and pretentiousness, and whatever else resembles or is similar to these things" (Mand. 6.2.5 [36.5]). In Sim. 1.8 (50.8), the "angel of repentance" instructs Hermas not to purchase fields but "souls that have been afflicted... and take care of widows and orphans...; spend your wealth and all your furnishing for such fields and houses as you have received from God." This instruction when placed within the context of Hermas's larger ecology speaks to a dynamic world where the material and human are porous and penetrated by active actants that situate and orient Hermas's world, give rise to various affects, and prompt various actions.

Sticky happy and sad objects reflect a world in which people and things are not bounded but penetrate one another and where space is not an inert backdrop for human behaviours but actants in the spacetime life of its residents.⁵⁸ The anthropological notion of partibility and dividuality pioneered by Mary Strathern in her study of Melanesian culture furnishes a useful conceptual tool for western scholars shaped by a Cartesian modernist mindset to enter into this world.⁵⁹ She deploys the term dividuation as a reference to persons "fre-

---

57 Brox, *Hermas*, 549–50 distinguishes too sharply between the language of residence in the self and in one's household; I interpret the household language more porously.
58 For spatiality and the Shepherd see Harry O. Maier, "From Material Place to Imagined Space: Emergent Christian Community as Thirdspace in the *Shepherd of Hermas*" in *Christian Communities in the Second Century: Between Ideal and Reality*, ed. Joseph Verheyden and Mark Grundeken (Tübingen: Mohr Siebeck, 2015), 66–89.
59 Marilyn Strathern, *The Gender of the Gift: Problems with Women and Problems with Society in Melanesia* (Berkeley: University of California Press, 1988).

quently constructed as the plural and composite site of relationships that produce them."[60] The dividual is both single agent and cause of effects, but is also multiple. "The singular must also be seen with respect to the two forms out of which unity is composed—the multiple or composite person and the dividual. Here what is taken for granted are the multiple external relations in which a person is embedded...."[61] This means that when a person acts as an in/dividual s/he also is acting as a plurality: "a person in the form of a dividual, is potentially one of a pair [in taken-for-granted relationships], or may know him or herself as a composite microcosm, potentially bounded as a unit."[62] This concept of dividuality is particularly useful for a study of the self in Hermas as partitive, or a composite of social relations, supernatural powers, spaces, and material objects.

In the same way that selves are dividual, so are things and places, with the result that different qualities of spaces and lifeworlds can agglomerate into shifting constellations of people, objects, and so on. Objects and places are never inert in Hermas but have agency even as spiritual powers do. These are useful categories for understanding the object world of Hermas where affects circulate and identities intermingle amongst resident powers as well as orientations to places and things. This is especially seen in the case of gifts where the gift of another joins the two together and makes them larger than their sum total.[63] When Hermas exhorts business owners not to be "darkened by" the possession of their material goods, the desire for luxuries, and associations with outsiders, but rather to expend their wealth to care for widows and orphans, he is revealing a particular kind of dividuality or partibility, an identity that expresses both the residence of spiritual powers and selves as conglomerates created through material gift giving. Hermas's visions make some objects stickier than others. Widows and orphans become happy "objects" joined together with the wealthier to create an assemblage of affects. They express the potencies of the resident spiritual powers Hermas says must live inside members/households to be included in the tower. Instead of assembling the self with fields and possessions, Hermas's wealthier listeners are to join with widows and orphans, which also has a reverse flow of the poor being assembled with the rich. The picture is one of flows and counterflows, forces, rather than what we might say when we affirm that "we can identify with" somebody or something. Recalling Seigworth and Gregg's orientation to affect theory, such unions "mark a body's *belonging* to a

---

60 Strathern, *Gift*, 13.
61 Strathern, *Gift*, 275.
62 Strathern, *Gift*, 275.
63 Strathern, *Gift*, 171–224 where she analyses partibility in gift exchange.

world of encounters" to "bindings and unbindings, becomings and un-becomings, jarring disorientations and rhythmic attunements," where "an outer skin-envelope or other surface boundary" does not define bodies," but rather "the potential to reciprocate or co-participate in the passage of affect" does.[64]

Conclusions

This experiment in the use of affect theory in the interpretation of the Shepherd of Hermas ends with a number of conclusions. First, affect theory moves us beyond a two-dimensional reading of the Shepherd as a rambling text with simplistic moral teachings or a moment in the history of an unfolding theology of penance. Instead, it promotes a three-dimensional reading that interprets the text as a vivid piece of literature designed to awaken a set of responses in its implied audience by situating it a world of sticky and happy/sad objects. Second, it promotes an understanding of Hermas's world in which the self is not a discrete, heavily bounded phenomenon but a part of a series dynamic entities that circulate amongst assemblages of different kinds of phenomena that include spiritual powers, material goods, experiences, spaces, and other humans. These assemblages together form a porous ecology that is more than the sum of its parts and where entities interpenetrate one another and join up together in kaleidoscopic combinations. Third, it locates Hermas in a non-Cartesian ontology and recommends that scholars step away from modern psychological tools to plumb the depths of the Shepherd's inner workings and rather to understand the implied author as belonging to a world unrecognizable to modern western of knowing. Perhaps the best way to enter into that world is with the help of the tools of cross-cultural anthropology of non-western and premodern societies. Fourth, it encourages a step away from studies of double-mindedness and repentance/conversion that focus on the inner world of Hermas as though it were a universe contained unto itself, to consider διψυχία and its opposite as embedded in a world of material and non-material assemblages wherein double-mindedness is a dynamic flow of affect circulating among people, places, objects, and other than human persons. Finally, it encourages expansion of an ecological study of affect in the interpretation of other apocalypses where new avenues of investigation will lead to discoveries otherwise passed over by traditional historical-critical and philological exploration.

---

64 Seigworth and Gregg, "Inventory," 2.

II Visions and Experiences of the Divine

Luca Arcari
Psychotropic Elements in Hermas's First Two Visions: Between Experience and Culture

Introduction to Neurohistory and Psychotropy

Daniel L. Smail's work[1] stands prominently in the complex approach known as 'neurohistory,' in which understandings of the embodied mind are brought into conversation with history.[2] A key concept in Smail's approach is the 'neurochemical mechanism' of the human brain, by which the human species has learned "how to assess our status and our standing in the group largely through chemical clues [—from pheromones and hormones to an addiction to gossip]."[3] Humans have come to rely on these signals "as markers of our self-esteem and our sense of belonging."[4] Neurochemical mechanisms of human brains underlie and shape much human behavior in ways now recognized to be more important than language—and they do so in predictable ways: "Their existence means that [the] predispositions and behavioral patterns [of humans] have a universal biological substrate that simply cannot be ignored"[5] by historians.

In Smail's approach, culture emerges as a biological phenomenon. Founded on neurophysiology and emerging in the dress of neural networks and receptors, "culture can operate in a relatively mechanistic, quasi-biological fashion."[6] Culture, in other words, is made possible by the plasticity of human neurophysiology. With this new vision, historians are now in a position to finally dispense

---
1 See Daniel L. Smail, *On Deep History and the Brain* (Berkeley: University of California Press, 2008); idem, "Psychotropy and the Patterns of Power in Human History," in *Environment, Culture, and the Brain: New Explorations in Neurohistory*, ed. Edmund Russell, *Rachel Carson Center Perspectives* 6 (2012): 43–8. See also *Deep History: The Architecture of Past and Present*, ed. Andrew Shryock, Daniel L. Smail, and Timothy Earle (Berkeley: University of California Press, 2011) and Luther H. Martin, *Deep History, Secular Theory. Historical and Scientific Studies of Religion*, Religion and Reason 54 (Berlin: De Gruyter, 2014), 240–71.
2 See Jeremy T. Burman, "Bringing the Brain Into History: Behind Hunt's and Smail's Appeals to Neurohistory," in *Psychology and History. Interdisciplinary Explorations*, ed. Cristian Tileagă and Jovan Byford (Cambridge: Cambridge University Press, 2014), 64–82.
3 *On Deep History*, 176.
4 *On Deep History*, 163.
5 Ibid., 114.
6 Ibid., 154.

with the idea that biology gave way to culture with the advent of civilization. Nevertheless, civilization did not bring biology to an end, but rather has come to enable important elements of human biology. The historical changes in Paleolithic and Neolithic eras have created a new neurophysiological ecosystem, "a field of evolutionary adaptation in which the sorts of customs and habits that generate new neural configurations or alter brain-body states could evolve in unpredictable ways."[7]

Particularly interesting examples of this are provided by the mechanisms which Smail calls psychotropic, i.e. human cultural practices that alter or affect brain-body chemistry. Whereas "moods, emotions, and predispositions inherited from the ancestral past... form a [panhuman] structural backdrop for many things we do and have done,"[8] human emotional effects are never universals but are contextual to a given culture and/or society, as well as to single individuals. If, for example, fear is a human universal, the stimuli that elicit fear can be local. "Such contingent stimuli are interesting to the historian for how they violate, manipulate, or modulate panhuman proclivities. Such practices as sports, education, novel reading, pornography, recreational sex, gossip, military training, or religious rituals all reinforce or inhibit synapses and receptors and stimulate, beyond baseline levels, the production or reuptake of various neurochemicals."[9]

Smail speaks of 'brain-body system' which is "a chemical sounding board that is highly responsive to inputs of all sorts, among them drugs,"[10] but not only them. If the most common stimuli to such a system are drugs, they arise from everyday phenotypic experiences—that is, things that individuals do with their own bodies. Listening to pleasing music leads to higher dopamine levels in synapses; seeing a scenographic spectacle can produce oxytocin and serotonin; playing an active part in a public ceremony elevates levels of endorphins and enkephalins—a condition which can lead to a euphoric state not unlike that produced by opiates.

Smail also identifies a taxonomy of the psychotropic practices. He differentiates the use of psychotropics into two types: the first is autotropic practices, whereby the body chemistry of the self is influenced, and the second is teletropic practices, whereby the body chemistry of others is influenced. The first one influences the body chemistry of the self, such as the chemicals or foods people ingest for their mind-bending effects, typically by causing a cascading set of

---

7 Ibid., 155.
8 Ibid., 117.
9 Martin, *Deep History*, 257.
10 "Psychotropy and the Patterns of Power," 43.

changes that ultimately generates higher levels of dopamine in synapses, albeit temporarily. Another category of autotropic mechanisms consists of the behaviors people practice that stimulate the production of their own chemical messengers, i.e. a vast array of leisure activities, including sports, music, novel-reading, movies, sex, and pornography, all affecting the body in similar ways. Teletropic practices include a category of psychotropy embracing the various devices used in human societies to create mood changes in other people—across space, as it were (hence, "tele"). The case of political dominance hierarchies offers an example of the evolution of psychotropic mechanisms that affect the body states of other people.

Like any taxonomy, Smail's system is primarily classificatory. Beyond all of this, all psychotropic mechanisms are ensured by a direct interplay between 'supply' and 'demand.' Like a microeconomic model of price determination, Smail's approach seems to postulate that dominant classes often provide teletropic practices, which are assumed by other people as autotropic elements; in so doing, people are conditioned to make choices in a very complex 'psychotropic market.'

Psychotropy, Visionary Experiences and Visionary Texts in the Roman Empire

Religious practices of the Roman Imperial world provide a clear example from the history of religions of the employment of teletropic practices and their acceptance at the expense of other practices, as autotropic mechanisms by particular individuals. Based on the surviving material and literary evidence,[11] we can conclude that cults and practices of the Roman Empire were specifically constructed to alter the body chemistry of people. Affiliation with early Christian groups, for example, included collective rituals and initiatory practices that made use of symbolic elements through which the lives of the adepts were deeply modified. Another element frequently associated with such an in-group dimension was the awareness characterized by the density of associations. Forms of public or private reading or meditation of authoritative scriptures and traditions favored concentration, including experiences reinterpreted as direct contact with the other world. Such experiences had significant cognitive ef-

---

11 In general, see *Senses of the Empire: Multisensory Approaches to Roman Culture*, ed. Eleanor Betts (New York: Routledge, 2017). For early Christian groups, see Risto Uro, *Ritual and Christian Beginnings: A Socio-Cognitive Analysis* (Oxford: Oxford University Press, 2016).

fects and were at least in part responsible for the tendency of some individuals to think they were seeing 'higher' realities in an unmediated way.

A clear example of the connections between psychotropic (i.e. ritual) inputs and visionary outputs (i.e., first-person descriptions of the otherworld) is found in an account concerning a Montanist sister as it is reported in Tertullian's *De Anima*. Tertullian states:

> We have now among us a sister whose lot it has been to be favored with sundry gifts of revelation, which she experiences in the Spirit by ecstatic vision amidst the sacred rites of the Lord's day in the church: she converses with angels, and sometimes even with the Lord; she both sees and hears mysterious communications; some people's hearts she understands, and to them who are in need she distributes remedies. Whether it be in the reading of Scriptures, or in the chanting of psalms, or in the preaching of sermons, or in the offering up of prayers, in all these religious services matter and opportunity are afforded to her of seeing visions. It may possibly have happened to us, while this sister of ours was rapt in the Spirit, that we had discoursed in some ineffable way about the soul. After the people are dismissed at the conclusion of the sacred services, she is in the regular habit of reporting to us whatever things she may have seen in vision (for all her communications are examined with the most scrupulous care, in order that their truth may be probed).[12]

Psychotropy participates in the shared heritage of ancient religions and this emerges in various forms according to the different cultural contexts in which it is attested. Tertullian's account casts light on the different levels called into question by first-person experiences and their subsequent written forms in early Christianity. Psychotropic inputs occur in the context of public and/or semi-public rituals and the prophetess's reaction emerges as a response to a very psychotropic (i.e. ritual) input. After the experience, which is available to both the prophetess and her audience only as it has been filtered through her memory, people are able to access her religious experience only through a chain of textual transmission, i.e. a visionary account according to which she declares to have directly seen the 'higher' realities.

While no-one would ever connect directly Tertullian's description with what is found in the Shepherd of Hermas, this essay aims to show how some visionary descriptions we read in the latter text re-convert some well-known psychotropic mechanisms, transforming them from autotropic to teletropic inputs. Like the Montanist sister, Hermas—a well-defined individual—claims to have a direct ac-

---

[12] Tertullian, *An*. 9.4; English translation by Peter Holmes, in *Ante-Nicene Fathers. Vol. 3: Latin Christianity: Its Founder, Tertullian; I. Apologetic; II. Anti-Marcion; III. Ethics*, repr. ed. (Grand Rapids, MI: Eerdmans, 1986), 188, slightly modified.

cess to a different, 'higher,' reality. After having lived some psychotropic experiences, he puts them down in writing, offering to his audience a psychotropic platform for other processes of inner chemical mutations. This process thereby explains the re-appropriation by Hermas (and by his audience) of psychotropic elements in order to fabricate a competitive psychotropic 'market.' One of the most important features of psychotropic mechanisms is that they induce or incorporate changes to behavior. This is the essence of power, whether it is the conventional understanding of it (one individual or group exerting control over another) or the more complex idea of 'bio-power,' whereby individuals, in effect, unconsciously discipline their own manners or behaviors through the internalization of norms and rules.

In the case of the Shepherd of Hermas, we are looking at one text (thus, at a cultural product), which explicitly presents itself as an account originating from direct experiences of contact with the otherworld. While it was not explicitly entitled as an 'apocalypse', this text refers to various revelatory dynamics clearly enough, with an emphasis on the process of transmission from which the writing claims to have originated.

The tension between visionary experience and revelatory writing in the Shepherd of Hermas confronts us with a direct-contact experience with the otherworld which is strongly characterized by language that operates on a double level, both ritual and literary. Generally speaking, visions of the other-world follow psychotropic procedures according to which the staging of the experience is structured and divided into two phases: in the first, the prevailing characteristic is the description of the material and physical effects of the psychotropic experience; in the second, the act of writing reinforces what Hermas himself seems to have actually experienced, offering a kind of transformation of what was an autotropic experience into a teletropic one. Experience of first-person contact with the otherworld belongs to the shared heritage of ancient cultures and/or religions (and it emerges in various forms according to the different cultural contexts in which it is attested), and Hermas's account casts light on the different levels called into question by first-person experiences and their subsequent written forms in Roman Empire. Religious experience occurs in the context of culture and cognition. Hermas's previous knowledge shapes the experience from the beginning, probably even before it reaches his consciousness. After the experience, this is available to both Hermas and his audience only as it is filtered through the author's memory (an author who may or may not be Hermas himself). Finally, we have access to descriptions of Hermas's visionary experience only through a chain of textual transmission, i.e. the Shepherd of Hermas in its *longue durée* existence.

Psychotropic Elements and Their Literary Re-configurations in Hermas's first *horasis* (Vis. 1.1.1 – 4 [1.1 – 4])

Especially in the first five visions (*horasis* or *apokalypsis*) of the Shepherd of Hermas, we find many psychotropic elements by which it is possible to reconstruct the process of transformation of autotropy in teletropy involved in Hermas's literary construction.

The introduction to the first vision is emblematic in this respect:

Ὁ θρέψας με πέπρακέν με Ῥόδῃ τινὶ εἰς Ῥώμην· μετὰ πολλὰ ἔτη ταύτην ἀνεγνωρισάμην καὶ ἠρξάμην αὐτὴν ἀγαπᾶν ὡς ἀδελφήν. μετὰ χρόνον τινὰ λουομένην εἰς τὸν ποταμὸν τὸν Τίβεριν εἶδον καὶ ἐπέδωκα αὐτῇ τὴν χεῖρα καὶ ἐξήγαγον αὐτὴν ἐκ τοῦ ποταμοῦ. ταύτης οὖν ἰδὼν τὸ κάλλος διελογιζόμην ἐν τῇ καρδίᾳ μου λέγων· Μακάριος ἤμην εἰ τοιαύτην γυναῖκα εἶχον καὶ τῷ κάλλει καὶ τῷ τρόπῳ. μόνον τοῦτο ἐβουλευσάμην, ἕτερον δὲ οὐδέν. μετὰ χρόνον τινὰ πορευομένου μου εἰς κώμας καὶ δοξάζοντος τὰς κτίσεις τοῦ θεοῦ, ὡς μεγάλαι καὶ ἐκπρεπεῖς καὶ δυναταί εἰσιν, περιπατῶν ἀφύπνωσα. καὶ πνεῦμά με ἔλαβεν καὶ ἀπήνεγκέν με δι' ἀνοδίας τινός, δι' ἧς ἄνθρωπος οὐκ ἐδύνατο ὁδεῦσαι· ἦν δὲ ὁ τόπος κρημνώδης καὶ ἀπερρηγὼς ἀπὸ τῶν ὑδάτων. διαβὰς οὖν τὸν ποταμὸν ἐκεῖνον ἦλθον εἰς τὰ ὁμαλά, καὶ τιθῶ τὰ γόνατα καὶ ἠρξάμην προσεύχεσθαι τῷ κυρίῳ καὶ ἐξομολογεῖσθαί μου τὰς ἁμαρτίας. προσευχομένου δέ μου ἠνοίγη ὁ οὐρανός, καὶ βλέπω τὴν γυναῖκα ἐκείνην ἣν ἐπεθύμησα ἀσπαζομένην με ἐκ τοῦ οὐρανοῦ, λέγουσαν· Ἑρμᾶ, χαῖρε.[13]

The one who raised me sold me to a certain Rhoda at Rome. Many years later, I became reacquainted with her and began to love her as a sister. After some time, as she was bathing in the river Tiber, I saw her, gave her my hand, and brought her out of the river. Seeing her beauty, I thought in my heart: "How happy I would be if I had such a wife, both in regard to beauty and manner." I wanted only this, nothing more. After some time, as I was on my way into the countryside and glorying in the greatness, splendor, and power of God's creatures, I became drowsy as I walked along. A spirit took hold of me and brought me through a place off the road, humanly impassable. It was very steep and eroded by running water. When I had crossed that stream I came to level ground and kneeling, I began to pray to the Lord and confess my sins. As I was praying, heaven opened, and I saw that woman upon whom I had set my heart, greeting me from heaven with: "Hello, Hermas!" (Vis. 1.1.1 – 4 [1.1 – 4]).[14]

---

[13] For the Greek text of the Shepherd, *Apostolic Fathers*, vol. 2 (Ehrman, LCL 25), 174 – 6.

[14] Engl. translation is from Carolyn Osiek, *The Shepherd of Hermas:* On the exordium of the Shepherd, see the recent study by Emanuele Castelli, "Gli esordi alternativi del Pastore di Erma," *Adamantius* 26 (2020): 551-75. Castelli underlines that the exordium attested by the Codex Sinaiticus cannot be considered as genuine. Therefore, in order to reconstruct the original beginning of the Shepherd, Castelli pays attention to the exordium of an ancient Latin version of

The opening line offers autobiographical information about Hermas. He tells (or at least presupposes) a history of slavery and manumission;[15] he was sold to Rhoda and then later gained the status of freedman. Nevertheless, Hermas's description still seems to imply a close patron-client relationship that persisted upon manumission.[16]

In the Roman Empire, slaves were constantly exposed to punishment—they were merely *instrumenta vocalia* ("tools with a voice")—, and this–as Jörg Rüpke has recently remarked–implied that "Reflection on, and in individual cases experiences of, such contrasts gave rise to notions of a body separate from the soul or the 'self'."[17] The presence of freedmen—i.e. individuals who were *previously* slaves–reminds us that these people, in their cultural agencies, would be able to use communicative techniques which were peculiar to the hierarchical social relationship that would have been customary between former slaves and slave-owners. This suggests also a hypothesis whereby "power accrued as states gradually isolated and controlled bottlenecks in the circulation of psychotropic mechanisms."[18]

Hermas's account in Vis. 1.1.1–4 (1.1–4) offers a means to evaluate just how responsive a social order can be to the emotional lives of its members. William M. Reddy's book *Navigation of Feeling* assumes that there are social scientific ways to assess emotion in different cultures.[19] At the core of Reddy's analysis is the concept of 'emotional suffering'. When viewed historically, it is the intensification or alleviation of this experience of suffering that is a channel through which it is possible to evaluate cultural constructions. Cultures construct contexts for the experience of feelings, and Reddy's definition of suffering intends it to be a conflict between primary life goals. A chief illustration of this can be

---

the work (the so-called Vulgata), in which it is said that an anonymous *puella* was sold in Rome. *A Commentary*, Hermeneia (Minneapolis: Fortress Press, 1999), 42.
15 On both slavery and enslavement metaphors in early Christian discourses, see Marianne Bjelland Kartzow, *The Slave Metaphor and Gendered Enslavement in Early Christian Discourse: Double Trouble Embodied*, Routledge Studies in the Early Christian World (New York: Routledge, 2018). On how various early Jewish and early Christian authors used, abused and silenced enslaved characters to articulate their own social, political, and theological visions, see Ronald Charles, *The Silencing of Slaves in Early Jewish and Christian Texts*, Routledge Studies in the Early Christian World (New York: Routledge, 2019).
16 Osiek, *The Shepherd of Hermas*, 42.
17 *Pantheon. A New History of the Roman Religion*, transl. David M. B. Richardson (Princeton: Princeton University Press, 2018), 214.
18 Smail, "Psychotropy and the Patterns of Power in Human Society," 46.
19 William M. Reddy, *The Navigation of Feeling. A Framework for the History of Emotions* (Cambridge: Cambridge University Press, 2008).

the slavery conditions during the Roman imperial period. The primary goals brought into conflict by patrons are respect for the status quo and the embodied forms of legitimation of the social order. A former slave, by constructing for him or her self a new life as a freedman, is always faced with a double horizon, i.e., "what I was" and "what I am."

Hermas is able to manifest his 'new' life in the report that immediately follows his encounter with Rhoda of his journey εἰς κώμας (esp. Vis. 1.1.3 [1.3]).[20] Although with due differences, we are in the presence of a travel account and description of everyday life,[21] a journey which seems to be indicative of a new social atmosphere of 'universal mobility' in the period, that was typical of the social status of freedmen under a variety of circumstances.[22] A veritable 'travelling mania' seemed to take hold of new classes of population. Travel was deeply woven into the fabric of the ancient world, involving many aspects of the experiences associated with it (especially for the lower and middle classes, being in another territory whilst trying to arrive at one's destination, unreliable transport, robbery and even abduction. For all people experiencing travel themselves, travel looks different from the perspective of individuals and for this, further distinctions are made by both ancient sources and modern scholars between individual, personally motivated religious journeys and travel undertaken on behalf of a community).

---

[20] It is known that the lectio εἰς κώμας is attested in Greek manuscripts as well as in the Ethiopic translation; in the so-called *translatio Latina vetus* (third century CE) we find *cum his cogitationibus*, while in the so-called *translatio Latina palatina* (fifth century CE) we have *apud civitatem Ostiorum*. The same phrase is attested in the second vision (Vis. 1.2.1 [2.1]), where εἰς κώμας is found always in Greek manuscripts, while the *palatina versio* has *apud regionem Cumarorum*. Many editors have preferred to restore the geographic notation of the Latin version, and for this they have read εἰς Κούμας in both the passages where the Greek has εἰς κώμας. Other editors (e.g., Ehrman), on the contrary, accept the phrase as we read it in the Greek manuscripts: see Antonio Carlini, "Le passaggiate di Erma verso Cuma (su due luoghi controversi del Pastore)," in *Studi in onore di Edda Bresciani*, ed. Sandro Filippo Bondì, S. Pernigotti, F. Serra, and A. Vivian (Pisa: Giardini, 1985), 105–9; Manlio Simonetti, "Il Pastore di Erma," in *Seguendo Gesù. Testi cristiani delle origini*, vol. 2, ed. Emanuela Prinzivalli and Manlio Simonetti, Scrittori Greci e Latini. Fondazione Lorenzo Valla (Milan: Mondadori, 2015), esp. 550. On this topic, see also the recent study by Enrico Norelli, "Due viaggi di Erma: verso villaggi o verso Cuma?" *Adamantius* 26 (2020): 537-50.

[21] On travel descriptions in other sections of the Shepherd (for example Hermas's journey in Arcadia, Sim. 9.1.4 [78.4]), see also Jörg Rüpke, *From Jupiter to Christ. On the History of Religion in the Roman Imperial Period* (Oxford: Oxford University Press, 2014), esp. 57, 71, 75, 78.

[22] Roger Chartier, "Reading and Reading Practices," in *Encyclopedia of the Enlightenment*, ed. Alan C. Kors, 4 vols. (Oxford: Oxford University Press, 2003), 3:399–404 (esp. 399). See also Smail, *On Deep History and the Brain*, 181.

If slaves represent a group of individuals whose travel can be read as a mirror of Roman economic and political power, and if it is an obvious fact that they likely represent the largest group of economic travelers, it is also true that a central principle of slavery is the abnegation of basic elements of human agency. About this, it has to be said that there are no references to the behest of his owner in Hermas's allusion to his journey.[23]

An intriguing element emerges in the first vision, during which Hermas manages to obtain a special contact with the otherworld. We read: "After some time, as I was on my way into the countryside and glorying in the greatness, splendor, and power of God's creatures, I became drowsy as I walked along. A spirit took hold of me (καὶ πνεῦμά με ἔλαβεν) and brought me through a place off the road, humanly impassable" (ἀπήνεγκέν με δι' ἀνοδίας τινός, δι' ἧς ἄνθρωπος οὐκ ἐδύνατο ὁδεῦσαι. See also Vis. 2.1.1–2 [5.1–2] and 4.1.2–3 [22.2–3]). Ancient sources show that both religious and healing travels helped to articulate the contours of Roman hegemony in a (partially) global world, governing and maintaining a geographically, culturally, and ethnically diverse territory.[24] Travelling rituals of élites like *profectio* (departure) and *adventus* (arrival) played a key role in making a journey manifest to a wider public. Both *adventus* and *profectio* rituals were highly choreographed, representing transactional performances between the governing and the governed: "through ritual practice the conceptual geography of the Roman world was temporarily inverted: the center was invited to imagine travel to the periphery, and the periphery was made into a temporary center."[25] Like many typical traits of Roman worship, rites of arrival and departure had their origins in the Roman republic and persisted into the imperial period, but the use of rituals to demarcate movement was, despite everything, part of a much wider Mediterranean ritual pattern. Similar actions were also an important feature of Jewish visits to the Temple of Jerusalem[26] as well as of the

---

23 Cf. Keith Bradley, "Animalizing the Slave: The Truth of Fiction," *Journal of Roman Studies* 90 (2000): 110–25 (esp. 118).
24 See Robert L. Cioffi, "Travel in the Roman World," in *Oxford Handbooks Online*, 2016, DOI: 10.1093/oxfordhb/9780199935390.013.110 (*l.a.* 02/03/2020).
25 Ibid.
26 See Samuel Safrai, *Relations between the Diaspora and the Land of Israel*, in *The Jewish People in the First Century: Historical Geography, Political History, Social, Cultural and Religious Life and Institutions*, ed. idem., Menahem Stern, David Flusser and Willem C. van Unnik, CRINT 1/1 (Assen: Van Gorcum, 1974), 184–215; Martin Goodman, "The Pilgrimage Economy of Jerusalem in the Second Temple Period," in *Judaism in the Roman World: Collected Essays*, AJEC 66 (Leiden: Brill, 2007), 59–67.

healing journeys of the lower and middle classes of the Roman provinces.²⁷ In posing direct access to the otherworld during a journey experience, Hermas seems to reconvert the complex social, cultural, and religious negotiations presupposed or explicitly recalled in ancient Mediterranean rituals of arrival and/or departure²⁸—and it is not by chance that the language of 'visiting' (ἐπιδημία) and 'presence' (παρουσία) is frequently used in Greek inscriptions to describe imperial visits as well as both religious and healing travels of the various types of people.²⁹ In the case of Hermas' first vision, however, the seer is alone, and the vision is conducted in "a place off the road, humanly impassable." He specifies also that it "was very steep and eroded by running water." Upon crossing that stream, coming to level ground and kneeling, he begins to pray to the Lord and to confess his sins. When understood through the ritual framework of religious travels, the isolation of Hermas may be read as a particularly elaborate version of ritual movements in Greco-Roman world. Hermas moves away from the urban context (see also Vis. 2.1.1–2 [5.1–2]; 4.1.1–3 [22.1–3]) and only after such a psychotropic experience he is able to communicate to a wider group of people (3.1.1 [9.1]; 3.9.1–2 [17.1–2]), claiming to achieve a direct contact with the other-world also in his own home (5.1 [25.1]).

Hermas's account is not based on *sui generis* experiences. It must have been ritually reproduced in light of the various reactions to travelling that are present in his real-life context, which are individually interpreted by him, as was the case with the journey experiences of an ex-slave. If that ritually reproduced experience represents a mutation from baseline neurocognitive activity, its identifica-

---

27 See Ghislaine van der Ploeg, *The Impact of the Roman Empire on the Cult of Asclepius*, Impact of Empire 30 (Leiden: Brill, 2018), esp. 6–45 and 166–262.
28 This pattern can also be observed in John's journey in Rev 1:9.
29 More generally, see Alexia Petsalis-Diomidis, "The Body in Space: Visual Dynamics in Graeco-Roman Healing Pilgrimage," in *Pilgrimage in Graeco-Roman and Early Christian Antiquity: Seeing the Gods*, ed. Jaś Elsner and Ian Rutherford (Oxford: Oxford University Press, 2005), 183–218. On the association between travelling monarchs and divinities, see Ludwig Koenen, "The Ptolemaic King as a Religious Figure," in *Images and Ideologies: Self-Definition in the Hellenistic World*, ed. Anthony Bulloch, Erich S. Gruen, A. A. Long and Andrew Stewart (Berkeley: University of California Press, 1993), 25–115, esp. 65; Walter Burkert, "Epiphanies and Signs of Power: Minoan Suggestions and Comparative Evidence" *Illinois Classical Studies* 29 (2004): 1–23, esp. 16 (repr. in idem., *Kleine Schriften VI: Mythica, ritualia, religiosa 3: Kulte und Feste*, ed. E. Krummen [Göttingen: Vandenhoeck & Ruprecht, 2011], 156–76); Verity Platt, *Facing the Gods: Epiphany and Representation in Graeco-Roman Art, Literature, and Religion* (Cambridge: Cambridge University Press, 2011), esp. 142–3. On religious travelling as a typical élite *habitus* in the Roman Empire, see Marco Galli, "Pilgrimage as Elite *Habitus*: Educated Pilgrims in Sacred Landscape During the Second Sophistic," in *Pilgrimage in Graeco-Roman and Early Christian Antiquity*, 253–90.

tion as a 'new' religious experience shows a culturally contingent individual approach, which is able to reformulate and/or re-orientate a well-known psychotropic activity in order to offer a new narrative that can in turn stand as a psychotropic generator of ever-changing psychotropic responses by a subsequent and wider audience.

Reading and Writing as Psychotropic Experiences in Hermas's Second *horasis* (Vis. 2.1.1 – 2.2.1 [5.1 – 6.1])

A passage included in Hermas's second vision shows a very intriguing process of change as regards a well-established psychotropic activity, that is the reading/writing practice. This seems to clarify the fact that in the case of the Shepherd, we are in the presence of a cultural shift in which psychotropy assumes a pivotal role.

> Πορευομένου μου εἰς κώμας κατὰ τὸν καιρὸν ὃν καὶ πέρυσι, περιπατῶν ἀνεμνήσθην τῆς περυσινῆς ὁράσεως, καὶ πάλιν με αἴρει πνεῦμα καὶ ἀποφέρει εἰς τὸν αὐτὸν τόπον ὅπου καὶ πέρυσι. ἐλθὼν οὖν εἰς τὸν τόπον τιθῶ τὰ γόνατα καὶ ἠρξάμην προσεύχεσθαι τῷ κυρίῳ καὶ δοξάζειν αὐτοῦ τὸ ὄνομα, ὅτι με ἄξιον ἡγήσατο καὶ ἐγνώρισέν μοι τὰς ἁμαρτίας μου τὰς πρότερον. μετὰ δὲ τὸ ἐγερθῆναί με ἀπὸ τῆς προσευχῆς βλέπω ἀπέναντί μου τὴν πρεσβυτέραν ἣν καὶ πέρυσι ἑωράκειν, περιπατοῦσαν καὶ ἀναγινώσκουσαν βιβλαρίδιον. καὶ λέγει μοι· δύνῃ ταῦτα τοῖς ἐκλεκτοῖς τοῦ θεοῦ ἀναγγεῖλαι; λέγω αὐτῇ· κυρία, τοσαῦτα μνημονεῦσαι οὐ δύναμαι· δὸς δέ μοι τὸ βιβλίδιον ἵνα μεταγράψωμαι αὐτό. λάβε, φησίν, καὶ ἀποδώσεις μοι. ἔλαβον ἐγώ, καὶ εἴς τινα τόπον τοῦ ἀγροῦ ἀναχωρήσας μετεγραψάμην πάντα πρὸς γράμμα· οὐχ ηὕρισκον γὰρ τὰς συλλαβάς. τελέσαντος οὖν τὰ γράμματα τοῦ βιβλιδίου ἐξαίφνης ἡρπάγη μου ἐκ τῆς χειρὸς τὸ βιβλίδιον· ὑπὸ τίνος δὲ οὐκ εἶδον. Μετὰ δὲ δέκα καὶ πέντε ἡμέρας νηστεύσαντός μου καὶ πολλὰ ἐρωτήσαντος τὸν κύριον ἀπεκαλύφθη μοι ἡ γνῶσις τῆς γραφῆς.[30]

And I was going into the countryside at about the same time as the previous year, while walking along I remembered last year's vision, and again the spirit seized me and took me away to the same places as the previous year. So when I came to the place, I fell on my knees and began to pray to the Lord and glorify his name because he had found me worthy and had made me aware of my previous sins. When I got up from prayer, I saw before me the same elder lady that I had seen the previous year, walking and reading from a little book. She said to me: "Can you proclaim these things to God's elect?" I answered her: "Lady, I cannot remember so much, but give me the little book so I can copy it." "Take it," she said, "and return it to me." I took it to a certain place in the field and copied it all letter

---

30 Greek text in *Apostolic Fathers*, vol. 2 (Ehrman, LCL), 184 – 6.

by letter because I was having trouble separating the syllables. When I had completed the letters of the little book it was suddenly snatched out of my hand–by whom, I did not see. Fifteen days later, as I was fasting and greatly beseeching the Lord, the meaning of the writing was revealed to me (Vis. 2.1.1–2.2.1 [5.1–6.1]).³¹

A year has passed since the previous vision. Hermas again finds himself outside the city in the country and seized by the spirit and carried off. The seer marks the time and place of the direct contact with the otherworld, emphasizing the similarity of this situation to the last *horasis*. But here we have a new element, that of the βιβλαρίδιον/βιβλίδιον;³² a little book read by the same elderly lady that Hermas had seen the previous year. The woman walks and reads from the little book and asks Hermas if he is able to proclaim what is written in the book. The βιβλαρίδιον/βιβλίδιον contains a personal message to Hermas, a public message, and directions to him for public proclamation. Hermas is not able to understand what the little book contains, and thus, he painstakingly copies the book, letter by letter.

The passage emphasizes the close connection between proclamation and memory. Hermas does not feel confident of his ability to remember the contents of the little book, and so he asks to make a copy for himself. Upon finishing his transcription of the text, it is suddenly snatched out of Hermas's hands. It is only at that moment that an explanation of what was written in the little book is revealed to him in an unmediated experience of the otherworld. In addition to containing a message for the ones chosen by God (Vis. 2.1.3 [5.3]), there are connections between the little book and Hermas's personal life.

The text offers a snapshot of a difficult situation, according to which experience brings its own set of problems, since we only have a written text and no direct access to Hermas's experience in its "germinating" moment.³³ But at least,

---

31 Engl. transl. by Osiek, *The Shepherd of Hermas*, 52–53.
32 For this term, see Rev 10:2. See also Maria Lauretta Moioli, "Postille bibliologiche all'-'Apocalisse' di Giovanni," in *Annali della Facoltà di Lettere e Filosofia dell'Università degli Studi di Milano* 64/3 (2011): 281–9. See also Daniele Tripaldi, *Apocalisse di Giovanni. Introduzione, traduzione e commento*, Classici 24 (Rome: Carocci, 2012), esp. 151–2.
33 For a strong defense of the possibility of inferring experience from 'visionary' texts, see also Alan F. Segal, "Transcribing Experience," in *With Letters of Light. Studies in the Dead Sea Scrolls: Early Jewish Apocalypticism, Magic and Mysticism in Honor of Rachel Elior*, ed. Daphna V. Arbel and Andrei A. Orlov, Ekstasis 2 (Berlin: De Gruyter, 2011), 365–82. See also Christopher Rowland, Patricia Gibbons, Vicente Dobroruka, "Visionary Experience in Ancient Judaism and Christianity," in *Paradise Now: Essays on Early Jewish and Christian Mysticism*, ed. April D. DeConick, SymS 11 (Atlanta: Scholars Press, 2006), 41–56. See also Luca Arcari, *Vedere Dio. Le apocalissi giudaiche e protocristiane (sec. IV a.C.-sec. II d.C.)*, Frecce 293 (Rome: Carocci, 2020), esp. 61–95.

the Shepherd offers an example that purports to describe an experience of 'direct' contact with the otherworld, especially in relation to a psychotropic mechanism like that of reading/writing a book.

Hermas re-inscribes a reading/writing practice that enables his reincorporation of it in and for *his* present. Jewish and emergent Christian texts and authors between the 1st and the 2nd centuries deem that reading and writing practices have changed in that time, and attempt to re-adapt both precedents and novel practices of their day in accordance with their received materials of antiquity, thus contributing to the long series of careful adjustments that connect living practices to a distant past.[34] Hermas too emerges as a very 'prosumer'[35] that is balanced on a received past which is regimented into the service of a new group of people who is able to read and write. In so doing, Hermas shows also that the time of individual ritual reading, both symmetrical and porous, is the time of the text. Ancient practice definitely merges with Hermas's narration in a new form, i.e., a practice in which copying a little book derives. Here copying alludes to forms of both exegesis and re-adaptation of previous transmissions in and for new group situations.

What Hermas's description seems to say is that he has studied different texts, while reading and copying previous materials.[36] After a time of immersion, he suddenly experiences a form of re-visualization of what he has read and/or copied, which appears as an experience of 'direct' contact with the otherworld. This also explains why the subsequent visions in the text emerge as re-propositions of what the seer has previously experienced and narrated, in a constant cir-

---

[34] See Guy G. Stroumsa, *The Scriptural Universe of Ancient Christianity* (Cambridge: Harvard University Press, 2016).

[35] With this term, I allude here to the combination of *production* and *consumption*. Alvin Toffler (*The Third Wave* [New York: Bantam Books, 1980]) has described the term *prosumer* as the people who produce goods and services for their own consumption. Therefore, prosumption is the process in which prosumers produce their own goods and services. Some authors describe this concept as the combination of the producer and the consumer roles to *diminish* the role of the corporate producer, whereas others emphasize that they are the *coproducers* of the services. However, some sources in the literature define it as the combination of the words *professional* and *consumer*, describing prosumers as professional consumers demanding developed or high-performance services. See Edward Comor, "Contextualizing and Critiquing the Fantastic Prosumer: Power, Alienation and Hegemony," *Critical Sociology* 37 (2011): 309–27.

[36] Like in Rev 10:4: καὶ ὅτε ἐλάλησαν αἱ ἑπτὰ βρονταί, **ἔμελλον** γράφειν; on this topic, see Tripaldi, *Apocalisse di Giovanni*, esp. 151. A similar situation is presumed in 1QH 13.22–15.8. According to Angela Kim Harkins, *Reading with an "I" to the Heavens: Looking at the Qumran Hodayot through the Lens of Visionary Traditions*, Ekstasis 3 (Berlin: De Gruyter, 2012), esp. 190–203, one of the compositions in 1QH 13.22–15.8 is exegetically generated from a performative reading of a text in 1QH 11.

cularity of both images and arguments. This sheds light also on procedures according to which the text of Shepherd was composed and/or re-assembled. One could say that the little book disappears and re-appears as a new visionary account, namely, as Hermas's visionary account.

The distribution and consumption of reading and writing practices in the second century Roman Empire is emblematic of the emergence of what Smail calls "psychotropic economy."[37] Such practices were relatively widely consumed throughout the Roman world.[38] Seen from a social perspective, the consumption of reading and writing practices among emergent and economically ascendant groups was paralleled by a kind of enlargement of the traditional elites. Previously, reading and writing were consumed across the social spectrum exclusively among the traditional elite circles. In the second century an initial phase of the process of "reading mania"[39] started to appear, and such a process happened in parallel to a widely emerging new middle classes. Afterwards, sources from the following centuries describe this expansion by associating it with various experiences, like the rejection of reality and different forms of bodily immobility. In short, the emergence of such a process was strictly linked to that of the sacralisation of the book as a religious object, as it was viewed by many late-antique religious traditions.[40]

As emphasized by Smail,[41] an imagination excited by reading could be readily drawn to other solitary practices, including experiences reinterpreted as a mediated means of contact with the otherworld. Hermas's account seems to

---

37 Smail, *On Deep History and the Brain*, esp. 180–1.
38 See the seminal study by Harry Y. Gamble, *Books and Readers in the Early Church. A History of Early Christian Texts* (New Haven: Yale University Press, 1995).
39 Smail, *On Deep History and the Brain*, 181–2. What eigteenth-century German texts describe as a "reading mania" or "reading fever" (*Lesesucht, Lesefieber*, and *Lesewut*) is more or less similar to that growing reading abilities which are observable in second century Roman empire (despite the different cultural background): see H. Gregory Snyder, *Teachers and Texts in the Ancient World. Philosophers, Jews and Christians* (New York: Routledge, 2000); idem., *Christian Teachers in Second-Century Rome: Schools and Students in the Ancient City*, VCSup 159 (Leiden: Brill, 2020); see also some references in Heidi Wendt, *At the Temple Gates: The Religion of Freelance Experts in the Roman Empire* (Oxford: Oxford University Press, 2016).
40 See the study by Jan N. Bremmer, "From Books with Magic to Magical Books in Ancient Greece and Rome?" in *The Materiality of Magic*, ed. Dietrich Boschung and Jan N. Bremmer (Paderborn: Wilhelm Fink, 2015), 241–70. See also Luca Arcari, "P.Oxy. 1.5 and the Codex Sangermanensis as 'Visionary Living Texts': Visionary *habitus* and Processes of 'Textualization' and/or 'Scripturalization' in Late Antiquity," in *Lived Religion in the Ancient Mediterranean World. Approaching Religious Transformations from Archaeology, History and Classics*, ed. Valentino Gasparini et al. (Berlin: De Gruyter, 2020), 469–91.
41 Smail, *On Deep History and the Brain*, esp. 181–2.

cast light on an individual mind which flows in a new visionary narrative. In view of the fact that elites and religious agents had long been interested in the things and practices that alter the body chemistry of subjects and followers, it may not be a surprise that a recently manumitted slave like Hermas[42] comes to participate in this emerging market of reading and writing, in much the same way that other contemporary emerging cultural agents came to be licensed to read and write in and for new social actors.[43]

Concluding remarks

By way of conclusion, let me turn to the historical implications of the model I have been proposing in this essay. If culture is a biological phenomenon that takes shape in the form of neural networks and receptors, it is made possible by the plasticity of human neurophysiology. The second century Roman Empire, with its travelling and reading/writing practices and its growing array of consumer goods of these types, provides several opportunities to apply the emerging approach of neurohistory. The Shepherd depicts a cultural agent (i.e. Hermas) even more dependent on devices, practices, and rituals that shape or modulate brain-body chemistry, that of his own as well as those of his addressees. Paraphrasing what Smail has observed,[44] Hermas appears as a cultural agent who is fearful of the boredom that ensues when the body is not being continuously stimulated. He lives in an everyday cultural context that alters his moods and feelings on a regular basis, and he offers his readers yet another way to alter and regulate their moods and feelings.

Smail refers to the mood-altering practices, behaviours, and institutions generated by human culture as *psychotropic mechanisms*, i.e. mechanisms that have neurochemical effects that are not all that dissimilar from those produced by the drugs normally called psychotropic or psychoactive. It is often pointed out that Roman imperial society, like all human societies, was oriented around the deliv-

---

[42] Jörg Rüpke has described the sociological profile of Hermas as that of a second-century salt man, more concentrated on a figurative world characterized by the circumstances of his occupation. It is not by chance that "his ethical-theological message concentrates primarily on the problem of wealth, its economic basis, and the numerous dangers arising from it:" see Rüpke, *From Jupiter to Christ*, esp. 76–7. See also Emiliano R. Urciuoli, *Servire due padroni. Una genealogia dell'uomo politico cristiano (50–313 e.v.)* (Brescia: Morcelliana, 2018), 217–22.
[43] On the textual communities in the Roman Empire between the third and fifth centuries CE, see Rüpke, *Pantheon*, 158–82.
[44] See Smail, *On Deep History and the Brain*, esp. 157–8.

ery of status goods. Rituals, travels, new forms of life, reading and writing practices–all these institutions, actions, and commodities, and many more besides, had psychotropic effects. Hermas was immersed in such a psychotropic market and re-modulated it to meet the needs of his audience, and in so doing, recreated through his visionary text, a psychotropic mechanism that is drawn from his own cultural context. In such a view, Hermas emerges as an example on the possibilities of psychotropy. We need to acknowledge the crucial role that psychotropic mechanisms may have played in Hermas's ordinary life as well as their re-modulation as 'psychotropic generators' in Hermas's visionary account."[45]

Hermas's account is primarily a text. According to contemporary academic debate, experiences matter even more. Because they are now taken to be important forms of symbolic communication within societies, experiences have assumed a more central position in political and religious history, so thus the relationship of experiences to texts has also changed. Following Catherine Bell on rituals and texts,[46] experience is no longer imagined as the stereotyped activity of a script fixed by text, but as a form of individual expressive acting, for which the text can be understood to provide only architectural and spatial constraints. As such, texts may seem to be a kind of opaque mirror for the reconstruction of experiences.

The Shepherd offers a useful example for analyzing how Hermas acts through psychotropic experiences and re-modulates them. If psychotropic experiences matter in society, their literary re-modulations must matter in texts. The Shepherd does not constitute a hermetically sealed realm. It participates in the wider culture and society in which it was created. In that space, Hermas's account has a psychotropic dimension irrespective of the non-historical fictitious character in which these experiences are embedded. The Shepherd is inevitably part of a specific mode of re-modulating psychotropic experiences that we call religion.

---

45 Ibid., 163.
46 Catherine Bell, *Ritual Theory, Ritual Practice* (New York: Oxford University Press, 1992).

Angela Kim Harkins
Entering the Narrative World of Hermas's Visions

The following discussion of the Shepherd of Hermas is informed by interdisciplinary studies that apply insights from the cognitive science of visual perception and mental imaging to first-person narratives. The specific approach known as 'enactive reading' describes how the mental imaging of spaces and experiences in narrative resembles the constructive process of ordinary visual perception. We use this model to illustrate how the visualization of the first-person visionary reports attributed to the literary figure known as Hermas participates in the construction of further images and details. This constructive process is one in which the life experiences of the modern reader participate in the narrative logic of the ancient visions. While the apocalypse genre was relatively rare in antiquity, it is a significant one for understanding early Judaism and Christianity because it was a generative literary form that invited readers and hearers of subsequent generations to engage and interpret these texts in new ways, often producing further writings. This essay concludes with some thoughts about how emerging approaches such as enactive reading can enrich how we imagine the generative way the visualization of visions led to the production of other writings.

Immersion in a Narrative World

The integrative approaches that examine immersive reading experiences proceed from a bio-cultural understanding of religion that pushes for the reintegration of the mind and body, thereby overcoming the dualism that persists in the field of biblical studies.[1] The primary framework used for this research comes from the emerging field of cognitive literary theory, specifically enactive reading, which grows out of critical literary theory and studies of the cognitive science of embodied perception. Relevant insights from anthropology, the philosophy of mind, and religious studies will be used to investigate the immersive quality of religious narrative and the experience of 'realness' from narrative. These interdisciplinary methods will be used to construct a process of immersive reading as

---

1 Especially helpful is the work of Armin W. Geertz, "Brain, Body and Culture: A Biocultural Theory of Religion," *MTSR* 22 (2010): 304–21.

an embodied practice in which the knowledge and past experiences of the reader and hearer are brought to bear on the text that is being visualized. The enactive reading approach relies on descriptions of a character's awareness of having an extended body moving in space, known as *proprioception*, and a character's awareness of interior states like emotions or changes in the sympathetic nervous system that express themselves in the skin or viscera, known as *interoception*. These interoceptive displays include the blanching or reddening of the face that expresses anger or embarrassment, the blanching of the face or goosebumps that happens during fear, and bodily awareness of temperature, tickle, and sexual arousal. For scholars who study immersive narratives, fragments of a character's proprioception and interoception are the details that are extended in a reader's imagination to construct a narrative world that can feel 'real' and compelling.

According to Marco Caracciolo's description of enactive reading, a reader can become immersed in the narrative world as he or she reads and accumulates information about the world and how it operates.[2] Caracciolo writes:

> Engaging with stories is 'enactive' in the strong sense because it involves imaginatively enacting a non-actual set of situations and events: by coordinating with the sensemaking of the story producers, recipients bring forth a 'world' charged with significance. Narrative is, therefore, one of the means whereby human meaning-making can detach itself from the here and now, exploring possibilities that would be difficult or even impossible to consider in actuality.[3]

When considering enactivist models of reading, a reader's past experiences are used to fill in the gaps created from these partial bits of information.

For scholars who study the cognitive science of visual perception, it is clear that seeing an image is not experienced instantaneously in a coherent scene, like a snapshot all at once. This understanding differs strikingly from the popular conception of seeing that is depicted in the famous sketch by Ernst Mach in 1886. In that image, Mach draws the details of the room onto which he looks out from his own left eye. The room is sketched within a round frame, much like the view through a telescope, with the side contours of his nose visible in the sketch. Mach's image depicts visual perception as a coherent and fully integrated experience, like seeing a photograph. Instead, our mind is constructing

---

[2] Marco Caracciolo, "Narrative, Meaning, Interpretation: An Enactivist Approach," *Phenomenology and the Cognitive Sciences* 11 (2012): 367–84; see also Marco Caracciolo, *The Experientiality of Narrative: An Enactivist Approach* (Berlin: De Gruyter, 2014).

[3] Caracciolo, "Narrative, Meaning, Interpretation," 373–74.

the image from the partial bits of visual focal points. Cognitive literary theorist Merja Polvinen describes this phenomenon in the following way:

> The snapshot conception ... was overturned by twentieth-century research showing how visual perception, instead of registering a full picture of the space in view all at once, actually consists of fragmentary information gained from sequential focusing on various details through the eyes' saccadic movement. In addition, our visual accuracy is hounded by actual physical blind spots, change blindness or inattentional blindness . . . and visual experiences of things we do not strictly speaking see. As a result, the seamless, detailed visual field has been deemed an illusion—in the sense of it being a representation produced in our brains on the basis of the fragments provided by our eyes.[4]

In other words, the cognitive process of seeing a landscape is far more reconstructive than is often imagined. What we experience as a coherent image is an illusion that is constructed when our mind extends the specific focal points of attention based on our past experiences of what we know of the world and how it operates. Our mind fills in the visual gaps based on our previous experiences and knowledge. This accounts for the phenomenon of 'blindspots' or 'inattentional blindness'—namely, instances where we fail to see what is directly in front of our eyes simply because we were not focused on that detail. This phenomenon accounts for situations in which unknown changes to our routine surroundings may lead us to totally miss crucial details.[5] Enactive reading analyzes how readers take partial details of embodied perception provided by a narrative and then extend these fragments in their imaginations based on their own lived experiences of having an extended body in the actual world. A reader's experience of an unknown narrative landscape, what literary scholars call 'a possible world,' has been compared to the experience of groping your way through an unknown narrative world relying only on the fragmentary details provided by the narrative.[6] Familiar objects and movements in the text guide readers to fill in the gaps based on their past life experiences of moving and being in a physical world.

Empirical studies show that the process of imaginative reading in which gaps in the story are completed based on prior life experiences is different for

---

[4] Merja Polvinen, "Enactive Perception and Fictional Worlds," *The Cognitive Humanities: Embodied Mind in Literature and Culture*, ed. Jean Peter Garratt (London: Palgrave Macmillan, 2016), 19–34, here 27.
[5] Kevin O'Regan and Alvin Noë, "A Sensorimotor Account of Vision and Visual Consciousness," *Behavioral and Brain Sciences* 24 (2001): 939–1031, especially the authors' discussion of 'change blindness' and the related phenomenon of 'inattentional amnesia' on 954–55.
[6] Caracciolo, *The Experientiality of Narrative*, 95–96.

different types of readers. Cognitive literary theorist Andrew Elfenbein uses the language of 'specialist' and 'non-specialist' as a preliminary distinction between different types of readers.[7] In the context of Elfenbein's work, 'specialist' readers are scholars with academic training in nineteenth-century Romantic literature who have been formed to read selectively against the grain of a narrative in search of discipline-specific information. He distinguishes scholarly readers from the everyday ones he desires to understand: What do non-specialist readers find enjoyable about a story? What do they remember? What elements of narrative make a lasting impression on readers? Studies by Elfenbein and others who work in immersive narrative experiences note that readers must willingly suspend their disbelief as they read.[8]

In the case of the Shepherd, 'specialist' readers can be understood today as having increasingly diverse intersectional identities. The effects of the diversification of the academy in the twenty-first century and the increased awareness of intersectional identities highlight the range of positionalities of race, gender, and social class among contemporary scholars. These scholarly identities include women, people of color, individuals of different sexual orientation and sexual identities, and scholars of global and non-western backgrounds—and in many cases with no religious background.[9] Those in the academy today read with wide-ranging life experiences and seek to know more than just the history, theology, ecclesiology, or Christology that can be uncovered from an ancient text.

Allow me to return for a moment to Elfenbein's distinction between 'specialist' and 'non-specialist' readers. We know that the Shepherd was extremely popular among the late-antique readers at Oxyrhynchus, yet scholars from the twentieth century and earlier have not received the text in the same way.[10] Typical

---

[7] Andrew Elfenbein, *The Gist of Reading* (Stanford: Stanford University Press, 2018).

[8] Because cognitive literary theory can be transferred to empirical studies of a broad population sample, Elfenbein begins with these types of preliminary distinctions between specialist and non-specialist readers, but his scholarship extends beyond simple binary systems. Elfenbein's research has established him as a literary scholar of various alternative approaches, including gender and sexuality studies; Andrew Elfenbein, *Romantic Genius: The Prehistory of a Homosexual Role* (New York: Columbia University Press, 1999).

[9] See Patricia Hill Collins, *Intersectionality as Critical Social Theory* (Durham: Duke University Press, 2019).

[10] For the large number of manuscripts of the Shepherd in comparison with those that later became the canonical Gospels, see Malcolm Choat and Rachel Yeun-Collingridge, "The Egyptian Hermas: The Shepherd in Egypt before Constantine," in *Early Christian Manuscripts: Examples of Applied Method and Approach*, ed. by Thomas J. Kraus and Tobias Nicklas (Leiden: Brill, 2010), 191–212, esp. 196 and 201–204.

modern descriptions of the work include disdainful references to its literary style. Norbert Brox writes: "What had fascinated the ancients strikes him [the modern reader] as a series of banalities" ("Was die Alten fasziniert hat, wirkt auf ihn wie eine Abfolge von Banalitäten").[11] Cognitive literary approaches, like enactive reading, can help us to understand why modern scholarly responses to this ancient work stand in clear tension with the popular success that this book enjoyed among ancient readers. Modern readers who read the text with discipline-specific questions in mind are also enacting the text in their imaginations and filling in the narrative gaps with their own life experiences and expectations. The notable influence of postcolonial studies in ancient history and religion draws attention to the significant changes in both the demographics of the scholars who work in the academy and the different questions they bring to the study of ancient texts, changes that are due in part to the globalization of the academy.[12]

We turn now to two different ways enactive reading can be applied in the first part of the Shepherd of Hermas known as the Book of Visions. In the first example of the bathing Rhoda, we show how modern readers bring their own assumptions and knowledge about their modern western social experiences to the ancient narrative. This constructive process was surely different for ancient readers who similarly read the text in an enactive way. Fragmentary and partial details about a character's proprioception and interoception are crucial for understanding the enactive approach to reading. In the second example of Hermas's nighttime walk into the field, fragmentary details about his proprioception

---

[11] Norbert Brox, *Der Hirt des Hermas*, KAV 7 (Göttingen: Vandenhoeck & Ruprecht, 1991), 5. Theodor Zahn [*Der Hirt des Hermas* (Gotha: Friedrich Andreas Perthes, 1868)] describes Hermas's writing style as "a tiresome monotony from beginning to end" ("ist von Anfang bis zum Ende von einer ermüdenden Monotonie"), 486.

[12] The significant influence of postcolonialism in the study of ancient history and religion can be seen in the studies by Armin W. Geertz, "Global Perspectives on Methodology in the Study of Religion," *MTSR* 12 (2000): 49–73; Fernando F. Segovia, *Decolonizing Biblical Studies: A View from the Margins* (Maryknoll: Orbis, 2000); Saba Mahmood, *Politics of Piety: The Islamic Revival and the Feminist Subject* (Princeton: Princeton University Press, 2005, 2011); Paul J. Kosmin, *Time and its Adversaries in the Seleucid Empire* (Cambridge: Belknap Press, 2018); Greg Anderson, *The Realness of Things Past: Ancient Greece and Ontological History* (Oxford: Oxford University Press, 2018); Giovanni Bazzana, *Having the Spirit of Christ: Spirit Possession and Exorcism in the Early Christ Groups* (New Haven: Yale University Press, 2020); see too the changes in the social sciences in recent years, in George Steinmetz, *Sociology & Empire: The Imperial Entanglements of a Discipline* (Durham: Duke University Press, 2013) and Julian Go, *Postcolonial Thought and Social Theory* (Oxford: Oxford University Press, 2016). These changes have made us increasingly aware that the prior history of modern scholarship was characterized by scholars who lacked diversity with respect to race, class, and gender.

and interoception allow for a greater sense of immersion into the narrative world.

The Bathing Rhoda (Vis. 1.1.1–9 [1.1–9])

Our discussion of enactive reading shows how even modern readers respond to the proprioceptive and interoceptive details in the narrated scenes of the Visions, with the result of generating coherent scenarios that fit their modern context well.

> 1. Ὁ θρέψας με πέπρακέν με Ῥόδῃ τινὶ εἰς Ῥώμην. μετὰ πολλὰ ἔτη ταύτην ἀνεγνωρισάμην καὶ ἠρξάμην αὐτὴν ἀγαπᾶν ὡς ἀδελφήν. 2. μετὰ χρόνον τινὰ λουομένην εἰς τὸν ποταμὸν τὸν Τίβεριν εἶδον, καὶ ἐπέδωκα αὐτῇ τὴν χεῖρα καὶ ἐξήγαγον αὐτὴν ἐκ τοῦ ποταμοῦ. ταύτης οὖν ἰδὼν τὸ κάλλος διελογιζόμην ἐν τῇ καρδίᾳ μου λέγων· Μακάριος ἤμην εἰ τοιαύτην γυναῖκα εἶχον καὶ τῷ κάλλει καὶ τῷ τρόπῳ. μόνον τοῦτο ἐβουλευσάμην, ἕτερον δὲ οὐδέν.

> 1. The one who raised me sold me to a certain woman named Rhoda, in Rome. After many years, I regained her acquaintance and began to love her as a sister. 2. When some time had passed, I saw her bathing in the Tiber river; and I gave her my hand to help her out of the river. When I observed her beauty, I began reasoning in my heart, "I would be fortunate to have a wife of such beauty and character." This is all I had in mind, nothing else. (Vis. 1.1.1–2 [1.1–2])

The scene takes place at the Tiber River, one of the major waterways of Rome. The story of Hermas and Rhoda is an arresting scene that reuses a stock image from early Jewish and Roman writings: watching a beautiful woman as she bathes. Hermas has chosen to describe Rhoda's beauty indirectly, in a brief and very condensed way, far more fleeting than other descriptions, like that of the tower in Vis. 3 or the curious beast in Vis. 4. Hermas later has a vision of a woman in the heavens, who confronts him about his desire (ἐπιθυμία). It is widely held that the woman in the vision is Rhoda, because of the identification of her "as the one whom I had desired" (τὴν γυναῖκα ἐκείνην ἣν ἐπεθύμησα, Vis. 1.1.4 [1.4]), but I would suggest that the exchange with the heavenly Lady is intentionally ambiguous. The one in the vision is never called Rhoda, but only "Lady." This is true too for the visions of Lady Church that take place later. Hermas's use of the title befits his slavish subjectivity as well.

Hermas's excessive desire (ἐπιθυμία) in the form of sexual arousal is an example of his body's interoceptive experience, which he attempts to conceal from the heavenly Lady. While he denies it in line 2, his penitential act of kneeling to confess his sins just prior to his vision in line 3 suggests otherwise. As he sputters his defense, vigorously denying any lascivious thoughts, Hermas says, "Have

I not always regarded you as a goddess?" (οὐ πάντοτέ σε ὡς θεὰν ἡγησάμην, Vis. 1.1.7 [1.7]). The key passage appears in the following exchange:

4. προσευχομένου δέ μου ἠνοίγη ὁ οὐρανός, καὶ βλέπω τὴν γυναῖκα ἐκείνην ἣν ἐπεθύμησα ἀσπαζομένην με ἐκ τοῦ οὐρανοῦ, λέγουσαν· Ἑρμᾶ, χαῖρε. 5. βλέψας δὲ εἰς αὐτὴν λέγω αὐτῇ· Κυρία, τί σὺ ὧδε ποιεῖς; ἡ δὲ ἀπεκρίθη μοι· Ἀνελήμφθην ἵνα σου τὰς ἁμαρτίας ἐλέγξω πρὸς τὸν Κύριον. 6. λέγω αὐτῇ· Νῦν σύ μου ἔλεγχος εἶ; Οὔ, φησίν, ἀλλὰ ἄκουσον τὰ ῥήματα ἅ σοι μέλλω λέγειν. ὁ Θεὸς ὁ ἐν τοῖς οὐρανοῖς κατοικῶν καὶ κτίσας ἐκ τοῦ μὴ ὄντος τὰ ὄντα, καὶ πληθύνας καὶ αὐξήσας ἕνεκεν τῆς ἁγίας ἐκκλησίας αὐτοῦ, ὀργίζεταί σοι ὅτι ἥμαρτες εἰς ἐμέ. 7. ἀποκριθεὶς αὐτῇ λέγω· Εἰς σὲ ἥμαρτον; ποίῳ τρόπῳ; ἢ πότε σοι αἰσχρὸν ῥῆμα ἐλάλησα; **οὐ πάντοτέ σε ὡς θεὰν ἡγησάμην**; οὐ πάντοτέ σε ἐνετράπην ὡς ἀδελφήν; τί μου ἐνετράπην, ὦ γύναι, τὰ πονηρὰ ταῦτα καὶ ἀκάθαρτα.

While I was praying the sky opened up and I saw the woman I had desired, addressing me from heaven: "Hermas, greetings!" I looked at her and said, "Lady, what are you doing here?" 5. She replied to me, "I have been taken up to accuse you of your sins before the Lord." 6. I said to her, "So now are you accusing me?" "No," she said, "but listen to what I have to say to you. The God who dwells in heaven and who, for the sake of his holy church, created, increased, and multiplied that which exists out of that which does not exist, is angry at you for sinning against me." 7. I answered her: **Have I not always thought of you as a goddess?** Have I not always respected you as a sister? Why do you make such evil and foul accusations against me, O woman?" (emphasis mine)

In the next line, the Lady goes on to say knowingly that "an evil desire" (ἡ ἐπιθυμία τῆς πονηρίας) arose in Hermas's heart (1.1.8 [1.8]).

Hermas's reply to the heavenly Lady is defensive when he insists that he regarded her "as a goddess" (ὡς θεὰν, Vis. 1.1.7 [1.7]). Here, we might imagine that ancient readers associated the image of the beautiful bathing Rhoda with the goddess Venus. Depictions of Venus bathing are commonplace and linked closely to ancient Rome, the setting of the encounter. When Hermas speaks to the Lady, "the woman whom I had desired" (τὴν γυναῖκα ἐκείνην ἣν ἐπεθύμησα, Vis. 1.1.4 [1.4]), he directs his words to a vision in the heavens. Like a divine being, she somehow knows what is deep within Hermas's heart, despite his denials. Readers of the opening scene will notice that Rhoda was not bathing in a Roman bathhouse, but out in the open in a natural waterway, which fits well Hesiod's story about the birth of Venus.

As readers, we do not receive complete visual descriptions, but rather brief narrative details about characters, their bodies, and their encounters with its space as we "grope" our way through the narrative world. Ancient and modern readers have interpreted the opening scene of Rhoda bathing in the Tiber River very differently based on their lived experiences and cultural assumptions. Here, modern commentators often interpret the scene from an ethnocentric vantage-point when they remark on the presumed Christian identity of Rhoda, who is related to Hermas as a 'sister'. The praise of her moral character (Vis., 1.1.1–2 [1.1–2]) is understood by modern readers as a stark contradiction to the fact that she is bathing out in the open and allowing a man who is not her husband to assist her from the waters. The image of Rhoda bathing in the river is constructed from fragmentary details by many scholars as a middle-class Christian matron implausibly bathing out in a natural waterway. Martin Dibelius raises the question of whether or not a Roman matron who bathes in a public place in the Tiber and who allows a man to help her out of the water could really be regarded as morally exemplary.[13] Norbert Brox argues that a self-respecting woman simply would not do this.[14] In line with these assessments, Martin Leutzsch writes:

> Ein weiterer Widerspruch besteht Dibelius und Joly zufolge zwischen Rhodes von Hermas attestierter moralischer Höhe und ihrem faktischen Verhalten: Eine sittsame Frau bade nicht im Tiber und lasse sich nicht von einem Mann aus dem Wasser helfen.[15]
>
> According to Dibelius and Joly there is a further contradiction between Hermas's high esteem of her [as a Christian woman] and Rhoda's actual behavior: A decent woman does not bathe in the Tiber and does not allow herself to be helped by a man out of the water.

Graydon Snyder gestures to the implausibility of the scene when he writes in his commentary: "that a Roman matron would have been bathing openly in the Tiber is incredible."[16] Snyder's view is repeated in Antonius Hilhorst's more recent discussion of "Erotic Elements in the Shepherd of Hermas." He writes that "there is a historical improbability in a lady bathing in public."[17] Hilhorst goes on to say: "there was no need for a well-to-do lady to use a river" since, he reasons, wealthy villas and mansions would have had their own baths, and of course, public baths were available.[18] These modern assessments reflect the common perception that a Christian woman would not be seen bathing out in the open in the Tiber River.

---

[13] Martin Dibelius, *Der Hirt des Hermas* (Tübingen: J.C.B. Mohr, [P. Siebeck], 1923), 428; Dibelius cites Clement of Alexandria and Juvenal who strongly criticize women who are bathed by male slaves, but this is not the case with Hermas, since he comes upon Rhoda purely by chance.
[14] Brox, *Der Hirt des Hermas*, 77–78.
[15] Martin Leutzsch, *Die Wahrnehmung sozialer Wirklichkeit im „Hirten des Hermas"*, FRLANT 150 (Göttingen: Vandenhoeck & Ruprecht, 1989), 29.
[16] Graydon F. Snyder, *The Apostolic Fathers: A New Translation and Commentary. Volume 6: The Shepherd of Hermas* (London: Thomas Nelson & Sons, 1968), 28.
[17] Antonius Hilhorst, "Erotic Elements in the Shepherd of Hermas," in *Groningen Colloquia on the Novel IX*, ed. H. Hofmann and M. Zimmerman (Groningen: Egbert Forsten, 1998), 193–204, here 196.
[18] Hilhorst, "Erotic Elements in the Shepherd of Hermas," 196n8.

Hermas and Rhoda address one another as brother and sister, not as master and slave. As a result, she has long been understood by scholars as a Christ follower.[19] The enactive reading approach can help us to analyze the responses that modern scholars have had to certain scenes from Hermas's Visions. In the case of the opening scene of the bathing Rhoda, modern readers take the fragmentary details of the narrative and extend them in their imaginations with their own experiences shaped by modern western society, bringing their expectations of where a proper woman should or should not bathe. Brox, Leutzsch, Snyder, and Hilhorst reflect a common vantage point that is informed by modern middle-class expectations.

Using the enactive reading approach, how might we imagine ancient readers having constructed the fragmentary details of the bathing Rhoda, the woman whom Hermas desired? Perhaps they would have completed the image with the plentiful visual images of the beautiful bathing goddess Venus, who was closely connected with the city of Rome. The opening scene of the bathing woman fits well with the mythic origins of the birth of Venus, which Hesiod tells us occurred from the severed genitals of the god Uranus.[20] Depictions of the bathing goddess in various poses were placed prominently throughout the empire, serving as ubiquitous reminders of imperial Roman rule. Perhaps ancient readers would have turned to these images of the goddess when constructing a mental image from the partial details of Hermas's narration of the bathing Rhoda. Such a scenario may also make sense of Hermas's reference to the 'heavenly Lady' whom he had desired as "a goddess" (ὡς θεὰν).[21]

---

19 For a recent presentation of this language and the social expectations of these roles, see Marianne Bjelland Kartzow, *The Slave Metaphor and Gendered Enslavement in Early Christian Discourse: Double Trouble Embodied*, Routledge Studies in the Early Christian World (New York: Routledge Press, 2018). See also the recent discussion in which Emanuele Castelli argues that Rhoda was not a slave master but rather a slave who had been sold in Rome; see E. Castelli, "Gli esordi alternativi del *Pastore* di *Erma*," *Adamantius* 26 (2020): 551-75; idem, "Dati storici e aspetti romanzeschi nelle prime due *Visioni* del *Pastore* di *Erma*. Una riconsiderazione del problema alla luce di nuove scoperte testuali," *Augustinianum* 60 (2020); 321-40.
20 Hesiod, *Theogony*, §173.
21 Hilhorst notes that some mss attempt to smooth out the divine language here by reading "aunt" (θείαν) instead of "goddess" (θεαν). Hilhorst, "Erotic Elements in the Shepherd of Hermas," 200n21 where he references the discussion found in A. Hilgenfeld's review of O. Gerhardt and A. Harnack, Shepherd, *Zeitschrift für wissenschaftliche Theologie* 21 (1878): 123 – 33. Hilgenfeld writes, "Aber das θεὰν ist offenbar zu berichtigen in θείαν, Tante, wozu das folgende ἀδελφὴν gut stimmt" (126). Perhaps the reference to "aunt" may be understood as being analogous to a term of endearment. Even so, the more difficult reading of "goddess" is more likely to be the original reading; Dibelius writes that this reference to "goddess," along with other erot-

Hermas's Nighttime Walk in the Field (Vis. 3.1.4–5 [9.4–5])

Readers today might be confused by the peculiar scene just prior to the vision of the Tower in the Third Vision, which narrates in excruciating detail Hermas's nighttime journey into the field. In this passage, Hermas expresses his anxiety and fear as he awaits the Lady in the dark field:

> 4. ἐγενόμην οὖν, ἀδελφοί, εἰς τὸν ἀγρόν, καὶ συνεψήφισα τὰς ὥρας, καὶ ἦλθον εἰς τὸν τόπον ὅπου διεταξάμην αὐτῇ ἐλθεῖν, καὶ βλέπω συμψέλιον κείμενον ἐλεφάντινον, καὶ ἐπὶ τοῦ συμψελίου ἔκειτο κερβικάριον λινοῦν, καὶ ἐπάνω λέντιον ἐξηπλωμένον λινοῦν καρπάσιον. 5. ἰδὼν ταῦτα κείμενα καὶ μηδένα ὄντα ἐν τῷ τόπῳ ἔκθαμβος ἐγενόμην, καὶ ὡσεὶ τρόμος με ἔλαβεν, καὶ αἱ τρίχες μου ὀρθαί· καὶ ὡσεὶ φρίκη μοι προσῆλθεν, μόνου μου ὄντος. ἐν ἐμαυτῷ οὖν γενόμενος καὶ μνησθεὶς τῆς δόξης τοῦ θεοῦ καὶ λαβὼν θάρσος, θεὶς τὰ γόνατα ἐξωμολογούμην τῷ κυρίῳ πάλιν τὰς ἁμαρτίας μου ʿὡς καὶ πρότερον.

> 4. And so, brothers, I went into the field and counted the hours. I arrived at the place that I had directed her to come, and I saw an ivory couch set up. On the couch was placed a linen pillow, with a piece of fine linen cloth on top. 5. When I saw these things laid out with no one there, I was astounded and seized with trembling, and my hair stood on end—terrified, because I was alone. Then when I came to myself, I remembered the glory of God and took courage. I bowed my knees and confessed my sins again to the Lord, as I had done before. (Vis. 3.1.4–5 [9.4–5])

Painstaking details about Hermas's bodily movements are given to the reader as Hermas approaches the ivory couch, and then sits, and then is told to not sit but to move to another side of the couch.

> 8. καὶ μετὰ τὸ ἀναχωρῆσαι τοὺς νεανίσκους καὶ μόνων ἡμῶν γεγονότων λέγει μοι· Κάθισον ὧδε. λέγω αὐτῇ· Κυρία, ἄφες τοὺς πρεσβυτέρους πρῶτον καθίσαι. Ὃ σοι λέγω, φησίν, κάθισον. 9. θέλοντος οὖν μου καθίσαι εἰς τὰ δεξιὰ μέρη οὐκ εἴασέν με, ἀλλ᾽ ἐννεύει μοι τῇ χειρὶ ἵνα εἰς τὰ ἀριστερὰ μέρη καθίσω. διαλογιζομένου μου οὖν καὶ λυπουμένου ὅτι οὐκ εἴασέν με εἰς τὰ δεξιὰ μέρη καθίσαι, λέγει μοι· Λυπῇ, Ἑρμᾶ; ὁ εἰς τὰ δεξιὰ μέρη τόπος ἄλλων ἐστίν, τῶν ἤδη εὐαρεστηκότων τῷ θεῷ καὶ παθόντων εἴνεκα τοῦ ὀνόματος· σοὶ δὲ πολλὰ λείπει ἵνα μετ᾽ αὐτῶν καθίσῃς· ἀλλ᾽ ὡς ἐμμένεις τῇ ἁπλότητί σου, μεῖνον, καὶ καθιῇ μετ᾽ αὐτῶν, καὶ ὅσοι ἐὰν ἐργάσωνται τὰ ἐκείνων ἔργα καὶ ὑπενέγκωσιν ἃ καὶ ἐκεῖνοι ὑπήνεγκαν.

> 8. After the young men left and we were alone, she said to me, "Sit here." I said to her, "Lady, let the elders sit first." "Do what I tell you," she said. "Sit." 9. But then, when I wanted to sit on the right side, she did not let me, but signaled with her hand for me to sit on the left. As I was mulling this over and becoming upset that she did not allow me to sit on the right, she said to me, "Are you upset, Hermas? The place on the right is for others, who have

---

ic elements in the opening scene, is influenced by Greek literary sources that depict encounters between goddesses and humans; Dibelius, *Der Hirt des Hermas*, 429–30.

already pleased God and suffered on behalf of the name. Many things must happen to you before you can sit with them. But continue in your simplicity, as you are doing, and you will sit with them, as will everyone who does what they have done and endures what they have endured." (Vis. 3.1.8–9 [9.8–9])

In this curious passage about Hermas's nighttime encounter with the Lady in the field, we read Hermas's report of his awareness of movement (proprioception) and his emotional responses (interoception) to the unexpected objects that he stumbles upon in the field. These narrative fragments are instrumental in assisting the reader in entering the narrative space as a virtual reality. Hermas also narrates his meeting with the Lady who instructs him to sit down. Hermas takes a seat on the right and then is told to sit on the left. These kinesthetic details and Hermas's deep experience of embarrassment contribute to the immersive quality of the scene.

The nighttime encounter in the field takes place slowly. Hermas reports the events in a rambling and drawn out way. This recreates the first-hand experience of moving through the field and his confusion along the way. The events that take place there are described experientially from his vantage point. We gain important information about Hermas, namely that he falls "far short" of sitting on the right with the martyrs. This detail conveys that he was an ordinary figure, thus suggesting something about the implied reader of these visions. Later in Vision 3, the reader is told that Hermas is not able to see the Tower at first—he is only gradually able to apprehend it, but once he does, the Tower is dynamically described, allowing it to gain density and solidity.

The lengthy prelude to the Vision of the Tower describes Hermas engaged in locomotion and changing postures, viz., sitting and standing. Hermas's walk into the field effectively slows down the narrative, thus building anticipation and momentum towards the Tower Vision. We also read his report of what he sees and how he feels, which expresses the acquisition of knowledge gained by investigation. Hermas sees the couch and moves closer to inspect it, allowing the scene to resemble how we might also examine our own surroundings when we are in a new place. Such images could be experienced in the mind as egocentric episodes in which the first-person perspective of Hermas becomes the reader's guide to the landscape, one that he or she is expected to visualize in great detail.

Modern scholars frequently describe these details leading up to the Tower Vision as tedious and unnecessarily protracted. For example, scholars trained to examine discipline-specific questions about orthodox theology, genre, and history often read against the grain of the narrative, overlooking the very literary details that allow for an immersive experience of a narrative. Concrete language that narrates the kinesthetic movement and the interior emotional experiences of the characters are the crucial details needed for immersive readings. Modern commentators dismiss these narrative details in their pursuit of historical or theological information. Norbert Brox's negative assessment of the Shepherd is not unusual, and it does not differ much from that of Theodor Zahn's from nearly 125 years earlier.[22] Burnett H. Streeter's description of Hermas also disparages the character's unseemly behaviors and regards him negatively as "unheroic, a timid, fussy, kindly incompetent, middle-aged freedman, delightfully naïve, just a little vain of his prophetic gift, and with a wife and children decidedly out of hand."[23] Brox, Zahn, and Streeter sharply criticize the literary style of the Shepherd and illustrate how modern scholars disregard the very details that are crucial for immersive reading. Yet, this kind of modern response to the narrative can hardly account for the significant popularity the Shepherd enjoyed in antiquity, indicated by the fact that the number of manuscript copies of this work rival that of the canonical Gospels in the early centuries.[24]

These two examples illustrate how the peculiar narrative details in the Shepherd are misunderstood by twentieth-century scholars. Because they often examine the Shepherd with the hope of gathering further information about theological doctrines or the early history of Christ followers, they fail to consider how the literary style may have been experienced by ancient readers, who may have found the text appealing and entertaining as an immersive narrative. We might imagine ancient readers who willingly suspended their disbelief to immerse themselves in Hermas's world. They experienced the events through the first-person retellings by Hermas and responded emotionally with worry, fear, and confusion. These emotional responses are ways that the narrative can be said to cultivate predispositions that are preparatory for the reader's receptivity to the moral teachings in the work as a whole. In the case of Vision 3, the drawn-out literary style allows readers to experientially imagine Hermas's fatigued confusion in the field, leading them to anticipate and pay close attention to the instructions that Hermas receives. The readers' heightened receptivity to the teach-

---

[22] Brox, *Der Hirt des Hermas*, 5; Zahn, *Der Hirt des Hermas*, 486.
[23] Burnett Hillman Streeter, *The Primitive Church: Studied with Special Reference to the Origins of the Christian Ministry* (London: MacMillan and Co., Ltd., 1929), 203.
[24] Choat and Yuen-Collingridge, "The Egyptian *Hermas*," 191–97 and the review of manuscripts at 193–97; also, Thomas A. Wayment, *The Text of the New Testament Apocrypha (100–400 CE)* (London: Bloomsbury, 2013), 81–169, with select images of the mss on 286–390.

ings that Hermas receives can be understood to function strategically within the larger aim of the text as a popular catechetical work.[25]

Immersion in a Virtual World

Visions of otherworldly spaces and encounters with the strange beings who inhabit them produce social groups that anthropologist Tanya M. Luhrmann calls a paracosm, "a private-but-shared imagined world sufficiently rich in detail that people become engaged in the stories and can return to them again and again, exploring them from different angles, reliving different moments, recasting the scenes as if they were there, even adding new chapters to the story."[26] Here, this participation in the activities of the virtual world is described elsewhere as a 'fandom'—a term that recognizes the illusory nature of these virtual spaces and the deep personal investment in such spaces.[27] Empirical studies of these non-specialist readers show that they readily suspend their disbelief when reading narratives that describe fantastic experiences, thereby achieving an immersive experience of otherworldly realia.

Immersive experiences of non-specialist readers have been analyzed by empirical studies that point to the compelling and 'real' perceptions of the imagined worlds constructed by popular culture—those of fantasy novels like *Harry Potter* or *Lord of the Rings*, or of the virtual worlds of apocalyptic online role-playing games like *World of Warcraft*, *Ground Zero*, and *After the End*.[28] In her insightful analysis of apocalyptic themes in role-playing games, Rachel Wagner writes:

---

[25] Choat and Yuen-Collingridge ("The Egyptian *Hermas*," 201–204) discuss the work as an important catechetical text in the early centuries. Didymus the Blind refers to the work as ὁ βίβλος τῆς κατηχήσεως τῇ Ποιμένι, and Eusebius identifies it as an "indispensable" text for those who are in need of "elementary instruction". The relevant passage from Eusebius, *HistEccl*. 3.3 is: "Others, however, have judged it indispensable, especially to those in need of elementary instruction (ὑφ' ἑτέρων δὲ ἀναγκαιότατον οἷς μάλιστα δεῖ στοιχειώσεος εἰσαγωγικῆς, κέκριται)," trans. G. A. Williamson, revised by A. Louth (Harmondworth: Penguin Books, 1989), 66.
[26] Tanya Luhrmann, *How God Becomes Real: Kindling the Presence of Invisible Others* (Princeton: Princeton University Press, 2020), 27.
[27] Rachel Wagner, "A Sense of Presence: Mediating an American Apocalypse," *Religions* 12, 1 (2021): 1–11, here 2.
[28] The live-action role-playing games *Ground Zero* and *After the End* are discussed in Wagner, "A Sense of Presence," 6–7.

Both immersion and extractability are forms of media materialization in which things pass from the virtual to the physical, cultivating a sense of presence for the world beyond. Props—whether religious or secular—become a bridge between this world and another beyond. Props, relics, and sacred objects promise presence—a tangible link to a desirable world beyond. It is easy to see how fandom and religion similarly truck in both immersion and extractability, with special spaces that wrap around participants and hierophanic material objects that make otherworldly places feel immediately present. It is not much of a stretch to see how Orsi's observations about contemporary religious presence can then successfully be applied—in ways he did not anticipate—to the dark apocalyptic fandoms of American gun culture.[29]

The narrative worlds accessed through games or fantasy novels feel compelling and real "through the use of various objects and abilities". In the case of narratives about fantasy worlds or otherworldly realms, certain literary details are used that contribute to intensifying a reader's or gamer's experience of the narrative world. Such experiences can be immersive and feel 'real', even for modern, post-industrial people who willingly suspend their disbelief and allow themselves to become absorbed into a fantasy world.

We can use this observation to consider the following question: Do discipline-specific ways of reading ancient visions impede the ability of modern biblical scholars to understand them as compelling narratives that generated further experiences and writings among the people who read and heard them in antiquity? Does our scholarly training form us to overlook the very details that non-specialist readers see and to which they readily respond? What can we as scholars learn from the proliferation of apocalyptic groups in the modern period about how ancient readers read and responded to first-person reports of visionary experiences?

We know that ancient apocalypses could and did lead to the production of further writings on similar themes. An excellent example is the broad variety of 'para-Danielic' traditions and writings associated with the visions of Daniel.[30] Visions of the otherworld, like the further scene of paradise that appears in the Greek—but not the Syriac—text of Odes of Solomon 11, may also be thought

---

29 Wagner, "A Sense of Presence," 3.
30 See Lorenzo DiTommaso, *The Book of Daniel and the Apocryphal Daniel Literature*, SVTP 20 (Leiden: Brill, 2005). While the Greek additions to Daniel, viz., Prayer of Azariah and the Song of the Three Youths, Susanna and the Elders, and Bel and the Dragon, are well known, there is a sizeable body of apocalypses that extend the characters and scenes known from the biblical book of Daniel to new settings. Some of these apocryphal Daniel apocalypses locate the seer in new lands, Cyprus, Persia, Elam, a 'seven-hilled city', Crete, etc. and describe his encounters with different personalities, and his new visions; DiTommaso describes these in 87–224, with a bibliography in 316–508.

of as examples of texts that can be said to preserve some additional glimpse of the narrated world.³¹ While apocalypses are relatively rare as a genre, interdisciplinary approaches associated with cognitive literary theory that describe how narratives about otherworldly experiences were compelling can help us to think about the generative process of immersive reading. Did these immersive qualities of visionary narratives play some role in the further generation of visions by ancient Jewish and Christian readers? During immersive reading, a reader constructs and extends the fragmentary details found in visionary reports with his/her own knowledge and lived experience of the world. Can the constructive process of enactive reading help us to understand the phenomenon of pseudepigraphic writing, in which later authors continued to compose in the name of an ancient persona?

Immersion in Hermas's World

The narrative qualities of Hermas's experiences in the Visions, namely the protracted details about Hermas moving through his landscape and his interior experiences, function to contribute in a preparatory way to heighten receptivity to events that will take place, by cultivating states of curiosity, anticipation, and watchfulness. This includes the section that follows the Visions, namely the Mandates, to which we now turn.

It is well noted that the figure of Hermas completely disappears after the Visions. While the last mention of Hermas's name occurs in Vis 4.2.7 (23.7), his persona persists through Vis. 5. Again, the moment of encounter with the visionary interlocutor is accompanied by details that describe Hermas's interior state. We read in Vis. 5.4 (25.4):

> ἔτι λαλοῦντος αὐτοῦ ἠλλοιώθη ἡ ἰδέα αὐτοῦ, καὶ ἐπέγνων αὐτόν, ὅτι ἐκεῖνος ἦν ᾧ παρεδόθην, **καὶ εὐθὺς συνεχύθην, καὶ φόβος με ἔλαβεν, καὶ ὅλος συνεκόπην ἀπὸ τῆς λύπης**, ὅτι οὕτως αὐτῷ ἀπεκρίθην πονηρῶς καὶ ἀφρόνως.
>
> While he was still speaking, his appearance was changed, and I recognized him as the one to whom I was entrusted; **and immediately I was confused, and fear seized me, and I was completely afflicted with grief**, because I had answered him so wickedly and foolishly.

---

31 Angela Kim Harkins, "The Garden Space in *Odes of Solomon* 11 and the Reinvigoration of Memories about Paradise," in *Experiencing Presence in the Second Temple Period: Revised and Updated Essays*, Contributions to Biblical Exegesis and Theology 111 (Leuven: Peeters, 2022), 219–44.

The fifth Vision has been understood as an introduction to the Mandates. Within the second collection known as the Mandates, the reader is directly addressed by the speaker, allowing the reader to continue in the imagined role of Hermas, albeit in a more intense way than in the Visions. This happens through the shift from the first-person voice of the implied speaker, Hermas, to becoming the addressee of the Shepherd himself. Thus, while Hermas is never again named in the entirety of the work after Vis. 4.1.7 (22.7), the persona of Hermas persists as the reader shifts roles from the implied speaker, Hermas, in the Visions, to becoming a participant in the Mandates.[32]

The Re-actualization of Visionary Texts

Here I wish to engage the stimulating 2020 essay by Luca Arcari, which discusses intriguing additions to the text of Hermas's Mand. 11.9–10.[33] This is a papyrus scrap that is 12 x 11.4 cm in size and written in an informal uncial hand dated to approximately the III/IV centuries. Known as P.Oxy. I 5, II.8–16, the scrap contains an addition that appears to comment on the scene in a way that transforms the episode. In his discussion of Mand. 11, Arcari uses the term 'visionary *habitus*' to describe a process in which a received visionary text like the Shepherd can generate further visionary experiences in a process of 're-actualization'. Arcari uses the interdisciplinary theoretical model of Relevance Theory (RT), a branch of cognitive linguistics associated with the work of Deidre Wilson and Dan Sperber.[34]

In this overlap with Mand. 11.9–11 (43.9–11), there is additional material in P.Oxy. I 5 immediately after Mand. 11.9–10 (43.9–10). The larger literary context of this mandate is the passage on the process of inspiration, specifically the task

---

[32] See Angela Kim Harkins, *Reading with an "I" to the Heavens*, Ekstasis 3 (Berlin: De Gruyter, 2012), esp. 189–90; Christopher Rowland with Patricia Gibbons and Vicente Dobroruka, "Visionary Experience in Ancient Judaism and Christianity," in *Paradise Now*, ed. April D. DeConick, SymS 11 (Atlanta: SBL Press, 2006), 41–56.

[33] Luca Arcari, "P.Oxy. 1.5 and the Codex Sangermanensis as 'Visionary Living Texts': Visionary *habitus* and Processes of 'Textualization' and/or 'Scripturalization' in Late Antiquity," in *Lived Religion in the Ancient Mediterranean World: Approaching Religious Transformations from Archaeology, History and Classics*, ed. Valentino Gasparini et al. (Berlin: De Gruyter, 2020), 469–91.

[34] Arcari, "P.Oxy. 1.5 and the Codex Sangermanensis as 'Visionary Living Texts'," 471–73.

of distinguishing between a true prophet and a false prophet. The relevant passage from the Mandates is given for context:³⁵

Mand 11.9 (43.9) [ὅταν οὖν ἔλθῃ ὁ ἄνθρωπος ὁ ἔχων τὸ πνεῦμα τὸ θεῖον εἰς συναγωγὴν ἀνδρῶν δικαίων τῶν ἐχόντων πίστιν θείου πνεύματος, καὶ ἔντευξις γένηται πρὸς τὸν Θεὸν τῆς συναγωγῆς τῶν

ἀνδρῶν ἐκείνων, τότε ὁ ἄγγε-]
λος τοῦ πνεύματος τοῦ προφητ[ι]
κοῦ ὁ κείμενος ἐπ' αὐτῷ³⁶
π[ληροῖ τὸν ἄνθρωπο]ν, καὶ
(5) πληρωθεὶς ὁ ἄνθρωπος ἐκεῖνος τῷ πν(εύματ)ι τῷ ἁγίῳ λα
λεῖ καθὼς ὁ κ(ύριο)ς βούλεται.
οὕτως [οὖν] φανερὸν ἔστε τὸ
πν(εῦμ)α τῆς θεότητος. <u>τὸ γὰρ</u>
<u>(10) προφητικὸν πν(εῦμ)α τὸ σω-</u>
<u>μάτειόν ἐστιν τῆς προ-</u>
<u>φητικῆς τάξεως, ὃ ἔστιν</u>
<u>τὸ σῶμα τῆς σαρκὸς Ἰ(ησο)ῦ Χ(ριστο)ῦ</u>
<u>τὸ μιγὲν τῇ ἀνθρωπότη</u>
<u>τι διὰ Μαρίας. ὅτι δὲ</u>
<u>δόξῃ δεκτικόν ἐστιν</u>

the ang]el of the prophetic spirit which is appointed to him,
fi[lls the ma]n, and (5) being filled with the Holy Sp(iri)t, that man speaks, just as the Lord wills. In this way the Spirit of the deity will be obvious. For the
(10) spirit of prophecy is the foundation of the prophetic order, which is
the body of the flesh of Jesus Christ, which was mingled with human nature
(15) through Mary. That the glory is acceptable...

There are a few noteworthy points concerning this fragment. The first is that the P.Oxy. I 5 fragment is missing the words "to the multitude" (εἰς τὸ πλῆθος). The second and more interesting point is the significant addition in the P.Oxy. I 5 fragment: a mention of Jesus Christ and Mary by name—neither of whom ever appears in the Shepherd as we have received it. In this additional text, there

---

35 The Greek text that appears here is broken and formatted to show the line breaks. Cf., Manlio Simonetti's textus receptus ("Il Pastore di Erma," in *Seguendo Gesù. Testi cristiani delle origini*, vol. 2, edited by Emanuela Prinzivalli and Manlio Simonetti. Scrittori Greci e Latini. Fondazione Lorenzo Valla [Milan: Mondadori, 2015], 328) which reads: τότε ὁ ἄγγελος τοῦ πνεύματος τοῦ προφητικοῦ ὁ κείμενος ἐπ' αὐτῷ πληροῖ τὸν ἄνθρωπον, καὶ πληρωθεὶς ὁ ἄνθρωπος τῷ πνεύματι τῷ ἁγίῳ λαλεῖ εἰς τὸ πλῆθος, καθὼς ὁ Κύριος βούλεται. **10** οὕτως οὖν φανερὸν ἔσται τὸ πνεῦμα τῆς θεότητος. ὅση οὖν περὶ τοῦ πνεύματος τῆς θεότητος . . .
36 Cf. πρὸς αὐτὸν

is a description of the prophet's experience of the indwelling of the Holy Spirit that uses the language of mingling to describe the deep intersubjectivity within the prophet during inspiration. Here the ancient reader has incorporated his/her lived experience of revelation and knowledge of Christianity into the reading of Mand. 11.9–10 (43.9–10), thus transforming the text. The papyrus fragment P.Oxy. I 5 can be said to illustrate the further revelation that is generated when one experiences prophetic inspiration by the Holy Spirit.

Luca Arcari's discussion of P.Oxy. I 5 offers a model for conceptualizing the growth of texts over time. His study highlights the inadequacies of models for textual transmission that presume that changes in the text arise *strictly* from the usual scribal errors of parablepsis or homoioteleuton. Not all textual variants can be explained by Arcari's model of 'visionary *habitus*'. Even so, as a model of a re-actualization process, it moves helpfully toward raising the question that is often not asked, namely: how do texts grow over time and what are the conditions for the rise in variants? While some variant readings may be traced, of course, to mundane mechanical errors or confusions from the scribal processes, Arcari draws attention to a phenomenon by which reading can be productive and generative of new insights and experiences.[37] My study is similarly interested in this process by which reading generates new texts and experiences, but it has proposed a model based on a reader's immersion into a narrative world, a paracosm. Enactive reading and the deep imaginative engagement with the narrative world can alternatively account for this phenomenon of a 'living text', one in which the reader interacts with and transforms the text. In other words, immersive entry into a narrative world may play some role in the generation of texts, especially in writings that describe visionary experiences.

Conclusion

We have seen that non-specialist readers of literature about other worlds—fantasy literature—regularly suspend their disbelief in order to construct imaginary worlds or paracosms that 'feel real'. This phenomenon that regularly happens to non-specialist readers, even those today in our post-industrial, modern scien-

---

[37] Here, we are speaking of the false distinction between textual criticism and historical criticism, also known respectively by the arcane terms "Lower Criticism" and "Higher Criticism". See George J. Brooke, "The Qumran Scrolls and the Demise of the Distinction Between Higher and Lower Criticism," in *New Directions in Qumran Studies: Proceedings of the Bristol Colloquium on the Dead Sea Scrolls 8–10 September 2003*, ed. Jonathan G. Campbell, William John Lyons, and Lloyd K. Pietersen (London: T & T Clark International, 2005), 26–42, esp. 28–29.

tific world, can help us to understand how imaginary otherworldly spaces function compellingly in social systems that have this-worldly consequences. This observation can help specialist scholars appreciate the lasting power that ancient narratives about visions, viz., apocalypses, had on subsequent generations of readers.

Applying the enactive reading approach to Hermas's visions allows us to illuminate aspects of the text that are overlooked by historical-critical studies. The phenomenal experience of reading and hearing Hermas's visions does not depend on knowledge of any discipline-specific understanding of apocalypse, but on a broader understanding of how readers visualize and immerse themselves in the literary worlds found in the narrative. Descriptions of the speaker's proprioception and interoception are especially important in immersive readings of narrative. In the case of the Shepherd, the reader shifts from being the implied speaker in the visions (namely, Hermas) to being directly addressed by the Shepherd in the Mandates, effectively drawing the reader ever more personally into the text. The literary shift that takes place from the Visions to the Mandates cues a move in which the reader goes from experiencing the text from the perspective of Hermas, who narrates the visions in the first part of the Shepherd, to experiencing the text as a participant in a variety of scenes. This intensification happens in the Mandates as the words of the shepherd are directly addressed to the reader and hearer in second-person speech.

The manuscript evidence for the Shepherd points to its widespread popularity in the ancient world. This appeal among late antique readers, however, has neither been appreciated nor replicated in the modern academy. Cognitive literary approaches can highlight how modern scholars are trained to read ancient texts against the grain of the narrative and with a very different set of questions that do not allow for immersive experiences of the text. Academic training in reading against the grain for the sake of finding answers to specific exegetical, historical, or theological questions may create blind spots that prevent modern scholars from appreciating the experiential way Hermas's Visions invite readers to immerse themselves in his narrative world. Reading enactively as Caracciolo describes it can offer a way of understanding the many scenes in the Shepherd that previous scholars and commentators have judged to be inconsequential because of their tedious quality. Readers and hearers can be said to be guided to strategic immersive states that are preparatory for heightening receptivity to the ethical instruction found throughout the Book of Visions, Mandates, and Similitudes. Such insights into how the literary style of this popular work contributes to the overall program of moral formation of its readers and hearers can help us to understand it as an entertaining catechetical work and not just as a potential source for historical reconstruction of theological doctrines.

This exploratory look into the question of how Hermas's visions are experienced by readers relies on the model of enactive reading, which is informed by the understanding that visual perception is a highly constructive cognitive process. Readers regularly find fragmentary details about bizarre narrative worlds in apocalypses that they merge with their own memories or experiences of the lived world. This constructive process of creating a more complete narrative world offers us a model for thinking about the generative way apocalypses were actualized by subsequent readers who imagined the characters in these narratives as having new visionary encounters, like the one described in P.Oxy. I 5.[38]

---

[38] A shorter version of this essay was presented at the CISSR virtual meeting on October 2, 2021, and I am grateful for the feedback that I received at that time. A fuller discussion of these topics may be found in Angela Kim Harkins, *Re-reading the Visions in the Shepherd of Hermas*, Studies in Ancient Religion and Culture (Sheffield: Equinox, 2023).

Aldo Tagliabue
Experience through Narrative in the Shepherd of Hermas

Modern scholarship on the Shepherd of Hermas has largely addressed traditional disciplinary questions, including this text's relationship to apocalyptic literature,[1] and its contribution to the early development of a theology of both the church and Christian conversion.[2] This essay will offer a new approach to these two theological issues. In particular, it will argue that the first section of the Shepherd, the so-called Book of Visions, capitalizes on its narrative form and offers to the audience an experience of the church focused on both its human and divine temporalities. Following the scholarly consensus, I consider early followers of Jesus' religion as the likeliest (but not the only) audience of this text,[3] and I am open to Osiek's argument that the text of the Shepherd was as "a basis for oral proclamation";[4] as a result, my analysis takes both readers and listeners into account.[5]

---

[1] See e.g. Jens Schröter, "The Formation of the New Testament Canon and Christian Apocrypha," *The Oxford Handbook of Early Christian Apocrypha*, ed. Andrew F. Gregory et al., (Oxford: Oxford University Press, 2015), 167–84, 180: "The *Shepherd of Hermas* . . . also belongs to the apocalypses of early Christianity." For more bibliography on this issue, see Harry O. Maier, "Shepherd of Hermas," in *Oxford Research Bibliographies*, under "Genre."
[2] See Lage Pernveden, *The Concept of the Church in The Shepherd of Hermas* (Lund: Gleerup, 1966) and Mark Grundeken, *Community Building in the* Shepherd of Hermas: *A Critical Study of Some Key Aspects* (Leuven: Brill, 2015).
[3] For a survey of the early Christian reception of the Shepherd, see Bart D. Ehrman, "The *Shepherd of Hermas*," in the *Apostolic Fathers*, vol. 2 (Ehrman, LCL), 162–473, 169–70. Some scholars argue for a possible Jewish readership, e.g., Michael Holmes, *The Apostolic Fathers: Greek Texts and English Translations* (Grand Rapids, MI: Baker Academic, 2007), 442. However, on this issue, see the recent criticism by Grundeken, *Community*, 24–52. In light of recent comparative analysis between the Shepherd and other ekphrastic texts of the Imperial Era, it seems very likely that also non-Christian audiences were reading the Shepherd; on this point, see Aldo Tagliabue, "Learning from Allegorical Images in the *Book of Visions* of *The Shepherd of Hermas*," *Arethusa* 50 (2017): 221–55.
[4] Carolyn Osiek, *The Shepherd of Hermas: A Commentary*, Hermeneia (Minneapolis: Fortress Press, 1999), 15. See 13–16 for her full analysis of this matter.
[5] In light of the focus of my chapter, it would be appealing to argue that the Book of Visions was an originally independent section of the Shepherd, as it was first suggested by Campbell Bonner, *A Papyrus Codex of the Shepherd of Hermas (Similitudes 2–9) with a Fragment of the Mandates* (Ann Arbor: University of Michigan, 1934), 8–11. Since 1934, many other scholars embraced Campbell's view, see e.g. Robert Joly, *Hermas: Le Pasteur* (Paris: Cerf, 1958, 2011); Edith McEwan

The Book of Visions makes multiple mention of both the manifested and the spiritual churches, whose difference lies in their temporal dimension: while the former is quickly developing toward its fulfilment, the latter was born before the creation of the world and, therefore, lacks development. Throughout the text, the manifested church is made present through a focus on the rapid development in time of Hermas's life, one of its members, and on the ongoing construction of the tower which represents the church. At the end of Vision 3 the Lady Church stresses that the *eschatological fulfilment* of the manifested church is *imminent*:

> ἀσύνετε ἄνθρωπε, οὐχ ὁρᾷς τὸν πύργον ἔτι οἰκοδομούμενον; ὡς ἐὰν οὖν συντελεσθῇ ὁ πύργος οἰκοδομούμενος, ἔχει <u>τέλος</u>. ἀλλὰ <u>ταχὺ</u> ἐποικοδομηθήσεται.
>
> You fool! Do you not see that the tower is still under construction? Only when its construction is finished will <u>the end</u> arrive. But it will be built <u>quickly</u>. (Vis. 3.8.9 [16.9])[6]

Here τέλος ("the end") is used to express the end-time, the so-called *Parousia*, which "in primitive Christianity … referred to the triumphant return of Christ at the end of the age."[7] This end-time has some divine quality, but still participates in human sequentiality, inasmuch as Christ's final return was perceived as an event which was due to take place at the end of human history.

On the other hand, the spiritual church is mentioned in a dialogue between an angel and Hermas about the Lady Church's old age:

> Διατί οὖν πρεσβυτέρα; Ὅτι, φησίν, <u>πάντων πρώτη ἐκτίσθη</u>· διὰ τοῦτο πρεσβυτέρα, καὶ <u>διὰ ταύτην ὁ κόσμος κατηρτίσθη.</u>
>
> "Why then is she elderly?" "Because," he said, "<u>she was created first, before anything else</u>. This is way she is elderly, and <u>for her sake the world was created.</u>" (Vis. 2.4.1 [8.1])

Humphrey, *The Ladies and the Cities: Transformation and Apocalyptic Identity in Joseph and Aseneth, 4 Ezra, The Apocalypse and The Shepherd of Hermas* (Sheffield, England: Sheffield Academic Press, 1995), 126–29; Giovanni Bazzana, "'You Will Write Two Booklets and Send One to Clement and One to Grapte': Formal Features, Circulation, and Social Function of Ancient Apocalyptic Literature," in *Scribal Practices and Social Structures among Jesus Adherents: Essays in Honour of John S. Kloppenborg*, ed. William Arnal, BETL 285 (Leuven: Peeters, 2016), 43–70, esp. 58–59. And yet, the manuscript evidence discussed by Campbell is shaky and problematic, as recently discussed by Dan Batovici, "Two Notes on the Papyri of the Shepherd of Hermas," *Archiv für Papyrusforschung* 62 (2016): 384–95; see also Dan Batovici, *The Shepherd in Late Antiquity* (forthcoming). In light of this uncertainty, I will not commit my analysis to the status of the Book of Visions as an originally independent text.

6 Except where otherwise noted, both text and translation of the Book of Visions are taken from *Apostolic Fathers*, vol. 2 (Ehrman, LCL).

7 Richard Soulen and R. Kendall Soulen, *Handbook of Biblical Criticism*, 3rd ed. (Louisville: Westminster John Knox, 2001), 135.

Here the angel locates the church's origin as temporally prior to the creation of the world, therefore imputes to her an existence before human time, and, as a result, an image of divine timelessness.

While scholars have commented at great length on these theological statements,[8] they have paid little attention to the literary and narrative quality of the Book of Visions, with the exception of a few negative assessments of the inconsistencies of the text as a whole.[9] In 2011, however, Diane Lipsett began to subvert this scholarly trend with the following remarks:

> What kind of text, then, is *The Shepherd of Hermas?* Whether read with other literary apocalypses or other Apostolic Fathers, whether considered a resource for theology or for social history, *The Shepherd* presents itself as a narrative. The point, however obvious, is worth making. Unlike most of the Apostolic Fathers, Hermas is neither epistle nor tractate nor manual nor homily, but story.[10]

In my view, this quotation by Lipsett is the key to understanding the Shepherd of Hermas and its theological agenda, starting from the Book of Visions. Since "literary style and cognitive processes involved in reading ... contribute to the formation of the self and experiences of transformation,"[11] a focus on the literary and narrative quality of the Book of Visions brings with it the potential for uncovering a new aspect of the theology of this text, namely the religious experience it evokes.

Following the experiential approach of this volume, I wish to highlight a special aspect of this religious experience. After an introduction to my approach to narrative form, I argue that the Book of Visions introduces the audience to the experience of both the sequential and eschatological time characteristic of the manifested church, and of the timelessness proper to the spiritual church. In the conclusion, I discuss the application of this interpretation to the ancient audience of the Shepherd by setting this text within the literary context of the Imperial Era to which it belongs both chronologically (in light of its second-century

---

[8] See Pernveden, *Concept*, and Osiek, *The Shepherd of Hermas*.
[9] See Antonius Hilhorst, "Erotic Elements in *The Shepherd of Hermas*," *Groningen Colloquia on the Novel IX*, ed. H. Hofmann and M. Zimmerman (Groningen: Egbert Forsten, 1998), 193–204.
[10] B. Diane Lipsett, *Desiring Conversion: Hermas, Thecla, Aseneth* (Oxford: Oxford University Press, 2011), 27.
[11] Angela Kim Harkins, "Looking at the *Shepherd of Hermas* through the Experience of Lived Religion," in *Lived Religion in the Ancient Mediterranean World: Approaching Religious Transformations from Archaeology, History and Classics*, ed. Valentino Gasparini, Maik Patzelt, Rubina Raja, Anna-Katharina Rieger, Jörg Rüpke, Emiliano Urciuoli (Berlin: De Gruyter, 2020), 49–70, 51.

CE date) and formally (because in light of its narrative quality the Book of Visions contributes to contemporary discussion of *enargeia*).

A Phenomenological and Immersive Approach to Narrative

I approach narrative through the lens of Jonas Grethlein's phenomenological approach to narrative, the cognitive notion of immersion, and Joseph Frank's notion of spatial form.[12] According to Grethlein, lived human experience and narrative form share a number of structural similarities. Both develop in time and both have to deal with tensions which are predicated on a well-known past and unknown future. In real life, based on our experiences in the past, we direct our expectations towards the future, which can be fulfilled or disappointed. In narrative, experience and expectations belong to the characters and are introduced in the text mostly through the promotion of suspense, surprise, and curiosity.[13] Finally, this experience differs from the real world, because "the aesthetic distance, the 'as if' of fiction, is fundamental."[14]

On closer analysis, however, not every section of a narrative text allows the audience to experience human time, but only those sections which invite him or her to become immersed into the narrated world. As argued by Allan, de Jong and de Jonge, immersion "refers to the mental state of being absorbed in a virtual world such that one experiences it—to a certain extent—as if it were the actual world."[15] In Allan's view, immersive narratives display the following characteristics:[16]

---

[12] Jonas Grethlein, "The Narrative Reconfiguration of Time Beyond Ricœur," *Poetics Today* 31 (2010): 313–29 and Joseph Frank, "Spatial Form in Modern Literature: An Essay in Two Parts. Part 1," *The Sewanee Review* 53 (1945): 221–40.
[13] Grethlein, "The Narrative Reconfiguration of Time Beyond Ricœur," 313–29.
[14] Grethlein, "The Narrative Reconfiguration of Time Beyond Ricœur," 317.
[15] Rutger J. Allan, Irene J. F. de Jong, Casper C. de Jonge, "From *Enargeia* to Immersion: The Ancient Roots of a Modern Concept," *Style* 51 (2017): 34–51, 34. This contribution offers a detailed study of the notion of immersion in relationship to ancient Greek theory and literature, with the inclusion of relevant bibliography (e.g. Marie-Laure Ryan, *Narrative as Virtual Reality: Immersion and Interactivity in Literature and Electronic Media* [Baltimore, MD: Johns Hopkins University Press, 2001]).
[16] What follows is taken from Rutger J. Allan, "Herodotus and Thucydides: Distance and Immersion," in *Textual Strategies in Ancient War Narrative: Thermopylae, Cannae and Beyond*, ed. Lidewij van Gils, Irene J. F. de Jong and Caroline Kroon (Brill, Leiden: 2018), 131–54, 133–5, with minor variations.

(I) **Verisimilitude:** The text evokes a life-like (vivid) mental representation of persons, objects, actions and their setting. A life-like representation:
(a.) focuses on concrete, physical objects or agents and their motion
(b.) provides graphic sensory details
(c.) provides detailed spatial information
(d.) progresses at a relatively slow pace (*scene* narration: narration time approximates narrated time)
(e.) advances in chronological order (no flashbacks / flashforwards)

(II) **Perspective:** The text takes the perspective of (is focalized by) a character with whom the addressee may identify and feel empathy. Specific linguistic indications of this perspective shift are:
(a.) *proximal* ('here' and 'now') deixis (e.g. the use of the historical present)
(b.) imperfect aspect (to indicate an 'internal viewpoint')
(c.) character-oriented vocabulary

(III) **'Transparency' of the Text:** the artificiality of the text is concealed, the narrator remains invisible. More specifically, we will typically find
(a.) no metanarrative elements (e.g. narrator comments)
(b.) direct speech
(c.) no elements drawing attention to the conventionality of the textual (literary) genre.

(IV) **Interest and Emotional Involvement:** The theme of the text is of strong interest to the addressee. The text contains elements steering the addressee's emotional response The text is crucial to the main story line, creates *suspense*, and is serious rather than comic.

(V) **Principle of Minimal Departure:** the storyworld should not (or only minimally) depart from the "real world" as we know it. The story world should be internally consistent and subject to the main rules as "real life."

In approaching this typology, I further qualify Allan's notion of *verisimilitude* with the help of the theory of enactivism, which constitutes a recent branch of present-day embodiment theory.[17] According to cognitive scholars of the second

---

[17] A complete bibliography of research on embodiment is beyond the scope of this chapter. Fundamental books are Antonio R. Damasio, *The Feeling of What Happens: Body and Emotion in the Making of Consciousness* (New York: Harcourt Brace and Company, 1999); Alva Noë, *Action in Perception* (Cambridge, MA: MIT Press, 2004); Shaun Gallagher, *How the Body Shapes the Mind* (Oxford: Clarendon Press, 2005).

generation,[18] human perception does not primarily depend on the brain's processing of visual information as sensed through sight from a fixed standpoint (as in the traditional pictorialist view), but it is rather shaped by the interaction of body and mind, and is predicated on the inclusion of different senses and emotions. More precisely, according to the enactive view, human perception always takes place in the interaction with a given physical environment.[19]

This discovery has a significant impact on the study of the immersive quality of narrative. The pictorialist approach to perception has led to the established view that the narratives most conducive to immersion are those which provide the audience's brain with visual details to process.[20] Conversely, in light of enactive theory, immersive quality is rather ascribed to narratives that elicit an enactive experience of the narrated world. These narratives display the following *enactive features:*[21] bodily movements and simple actions (the narration of which generates an immediate understanding of what is going on in the narrated world), a 'just in time' representation of the world (individual features are presented when they play a role in the action), and affordances (the description of objects which focuses on potential ways of interacting with them). I argue in the next section that Vision 4 (22-24) lets the audience participate in the immersive narrative of Hermas's encounter with the beast, and, through it, lets him or her experience the human temporality of the manifested church.

By contrast, narrative sections that lack immersive quality have a different impact on the audience's experience. The presence in them of devices which alter the chronological order of the events or downplay their importance may produce the opposite effect of distancing the audience from experiencing human time. In the history of narratology, Frank has defined these devices as "spatial":[22] "Spatial form in its simplest sense designates the techniques by

---

[18] See Karen Kukkonen and Marco Caracciolo, "What is the 'Second Generation'?" *Style* 48 (2014): 261–74.
[19] See A. Noë, *Action in Perception*, idem, *Out of Our Heads: Why You Are Not Your Brain, and Other Lessons from the Biology of Consciousness* (New York: Hill and Wang, 2009).
[20] See Emily Troscianko, *Kafka's Cognitive Realism* (New York: Routledge, 2014), 54–64 on the literary history of pictorialism.
[21] The following list is a revised version of Jonas Grethlein and Luuk Huitink, "Homer's Vividness: An Enactive Approach," *JHS* 137 (2017): 67–91, 72–73. Cf. also Anežka Kuzmičová, "Presence in the Reading of Literary Narrative: A Case for Motor Enactment," *Semiotica* 189 (2012): 23–48.
[22] See Frank, "Spatial Form in Modern Literature: An Essay in Two Parts. Part 1," 221–40, esp. 225.

which novelists subvert the chronological sequence inherent in narrative."[23] Here, "spatial" does not refer to the space in which the protagonists move and act, but metaphorically to the reader's ability to grasp the story or parts of it more or less simultaneously in a way that undermines the chronological sequence. For the sake of clarity, however, I prefer to use the term "non-sequential." The list of non-sequential devices is long: it starts with the omission or underplaying of temporal markers,[24] but also includes retrospection, prolepses, analepses, repetitions and descriptions.[25]

As argued by Grethlein, the distancing effect of non-sequential form on the audience can assume further connotations in different kinds of texts. In Plutarch's *Lives*, for example, a loose temporal organization and the downplaying of temporal links between consecutive events invite the reader to experience the exemplary timeless quality of the protagonists rather than the suspenseful account of the narrated lives.[26] In the case of narratives focused on aspects of the divine, such as the Book of Visions, the combination of some of these devices can lead the audience to experience certain aspects of divine timelessness, and therefore, in our case, to gain a glimpse of the divine nature of the spiritual church.

The Audience's Experience of Both the Sequential and Eschatological Time of the Manifested Church

The Book of Visions contains a sequential account of Hermas's life and his conversion, from his initial acknowledgment of sin to his transformation into a stone, whereupon he becomes an active member of the church tower. By identi-

---

23 Jeffrey R. Smitten and Ann Daghistany, "Editors' Preface", in *Spatial Form in Narrative*, ed. Jeffrey R. Smitten and Ann Daghistany (Ithaca: Cornell University Press, 1981), 13–15.
24 As argued by Jeffrey R. Smitten ("Introduction: Spatial form and Narrative Theory," in *Spatial Form in Narrative*, ed. Jeffrey R. Smitten and Ann Daghistany [Ithaca: Cornell University Press, 1981], 15–34) "time can be eliminated from narrative (or at least severely attenuated) by the use of a very brief time period for the whole narrative, ... the removal of temporal indicators, and the scrambling of the time scheme" (25).
25 These two last spatial devices come from Jonas Grethlein, *Aesthetic Experiences and Classical Antiquity. The Content of Form in Narratives and Pictures* (Cambridge: Cambridge University Press, 2017), 62–65.
26 See Jonas Grethlein, *Experience and Teleology in Ancient Historiography* (Cambridge: Cambridge University Press, 2013), 117–21.

fication with this life, therefore, the reader and the listener of the Shepherd are invited to experience the sequential time of the manifested church. In this section, I will demonstrate this by focusing on Vision 4 (22-24), in which the narration of Hermas's encounter with the beast is conspicuous for its immersive quality and includes the mention of eschatological time. Vision 4 (22-24) begins:

> ἣν εἶδον, ἀδελφοί, μετὰ ἡμέρας εἴκοσι τῆς προτέρας ὁράσεως τῆς γενομένης, εἰς <u>τύπον τῆς θλίψεως τῆς ἐπερχομένης</u> …
>
> This is what I saw, brothers, twenty days after the earlier vision, as <u>a vivid sign of the coming affliction …</u> (Vis. 4.1.1 [22.1])

The "coming affliction" is a typical feature of the apocalyptic tradition, which is chronologically followed by the *Parousia*.[27] Here Hermas's comment suggests that the subsequent narrative will focus on a mysterious vivid sign—a τύπος, which anticipates both the eschatological affliction and the eschatological fulfilment of the manifested church.[28] After this passage, Hermas begins to narrate his encounter with the beast:

> καὶ προσέβην μικρόν, ἀδελφοί, καὶ <u>ἰδοὺ βλέπω</u> κονιορτὸν ὡς εἰς τὸν οὐρανόν, καὶ ἠρξάμην λέγειν ἐν ἐμαυτῷ· <u>μήποτε κτήνη ἔρχονται καὶ κονιορτὸν ἐγείρουσιν;</u> οὕτω δὲ ἦν ἀπ' ἐμοῦ ὡς ἀπὸ σταδίου. γινομένου μείζονος καὶ μείζονος κονιορτοῦ <u>ὑπενόησα εἶναί τι θεῖον</u>· μικρὸν ἐξέλαμψεν ὁ ἥλιος, καὶ <u>ἰδοὺ βλέπω</u> θηρίον μέγιστον <u>ὡσεὶ κῆτός τι</u>, καὶ ἐκ τοῦ στόματος αὐτοῦ ἀκρίδες πύριναι ἐξεπορεύοντο. ἦν δὲ τὸ θηρίον τῷ μήκει <u>ὡσεὶ</u> ποδῶν ρ', τὴν δὲ κεφαλὴν εἶχεν ὡσεὶ κεράμου. καὶ <u>ἠρξάμην κλαίειν</u> καὶ ἐρωτᾶν τὸν κύριον ἵνα με λυτρώσηται ἐξ αὐτοῦ. καὶ ἐπανεμνήσθην τοῦ ῥήματος οὗ ἀκηκόειν· μὴ διψυχήσεις, Ἑρμᾶ.
>
> I passed on a bit, brothers, and <u>look I see</u> a cloud of dust, reaching up to the sky. And I began saying to myself, "<u>Is that a herd of cattle coming, raising the dust?</u>" But it was still about two hundred yards away from me. And as the dust cloud grew larger and larger, <u>I realized that it was something divine</u>. The sun began to shine a bit and <u>suddenly I see</u> an enormous wild beast, <u>something like a sea monster</u>, with fiery locusts spewing from its mouth. The beast was <u>nearly</u> a hundred feet long, and its head looked like a ceramic jar. And <u>I began to weep</u> and ask the Lord to save me from it. Then I remembered the word I had heard: "Do not be of two minds, Hermas." (Vis. 4.1.5 – 7 [22.5 – 7] my trans.)

---

27 See Osiek, *The Shepherd of Hermas*, in loco for a survey of scholarly interpretations of θλίψις. I agree with Richard Bauckham's definition of θλίψις as "an impending persecution which he (Hermas) understands as part of a larger eschatological event" (R. Bauckham, "The Great Tribulation in the *Shepherd of Hermas*," *JTS* 25 [1974]: 27 – 40, 32).

28 τύπος ('type', 'figure' or 'model') is a term proper to early Christian exegesis, which is often used to characterise mimetic signs that have a prophetic reference (see Francis Young, *Biblical Exegesis and the Formation of Christian Culture* [Cambridge: Cambridge University Press, 1997], 232), as the beast of the Book of Visions does.

This passage has a distinctive immersive quality, and especially aligns with Allan's categories of *verisimilitude, interest* and *emotional involvement,* and *perspective*. This narration is chronological, proceeds with a slow motion, is focalized by Hermas, and includes his emotional responses to the beast.

As noted by Maier, the special use of tenses contributes to the *verisimilitude* of the narrative.[29] In particular, the double use of the historical present—βλέπω "I see"—stresses Hermas's closeness to the two main events of his experience, namely his vision of the cloud and the beast, and provides the reader with the illusion of being present at both, like Hermas was. This illusion is reinforced by the adverb ἰδού, "look," which conveys Hermas's surprise in front of both the cloud and the beast. Moreover, this passage is filled with character-oriented vocabulary, which reflects Hermas's perceptions. When facing the cloud, Hermas first thinks it is raised by a herd of cattle (Vis. 4.1.5 [22.5]), then by something divine (Vis. 4.1.6 [22.6]), and, finally, as he sees the beast, he tries to guess its identity and length—ὡσεὶ κῆτός τι ("something like a sea monster," Vis. 4.1.6 [22.6]) and τῷ μήκει ὡσεὶ ποδῶν ρ' ("nearly a hundred feet long," Vis. 4.1.7 [22.7]). Finally, Hermas's mention of the locusts (22.6) gives a sense of his frightening reaction which leads him to cry—καὶ ἠρξάμην κλαίειν ("I began to weep," Vis. 4.1.7 [22.7]). This passage's emphasis on Hermas's *perspective* is further stressed by his use of the indicative imperfect—ἦν and εἶχεν: in ancient Greek narratives, this tense is often used to present the described scene from an internal viewpoint.[30]

In light of this framework, I would define this passage as immersive. This observation likely affects the audience's experience of time. Hermas's narration highlights the tension between his recollected past (comprising of his earlier visions and God's past protection) and his changing expectations about how the coming danger will affect him. Through their immersion into this storyworld, therefore, the reader and the listener of the Shepherd are invited to experience the sequential development of Hermas's life.

This experiential effect extends to the last part of the narrative, in which this encounter between Hermas and the beast finally takes place:

ἐνδυσάμενος οὖν, ἀδελφοί, τὴν πίστιν τοῦ κυρίου καὶ μνησθεὶς ὧν ἐδίδαξέν με μεγαλείων, θαρσήσας εἰς τὸ θηρίον ἐμαυτὸν ἔδωκα. <u>οὕτω δὲ ἤρχετο τὸ θηρίον ῥοίζῳ</u>, ὥστε δύνασθαι αὐτὸ πόλιν λυμᾶναι. <u>ἔρχομαι</u> ἐγγὺς αὐτοῦ, καὶ τὸ τηλικοῦτο κῆτος <u>ἐκτείνει ἑαυτὸ χαμαὶ καὶ οὐδὲν εἰ μὴ τὴν γλῶσσαν προέβαλλεν</u>, καὶ ὅλως οὐκ ἐκινήθη <u>μέχρις ὅτε παρῆλθον</u>

---

29 See Harry O. Maier, "Making History with the *Shepherd of Hermas*," *Early Christianity* 10.4 (2019): 501–20.
30 See Allan's feature of *perspective* in his discussion of immersion, reported in Section 1 of this essay.

αὐτό· εἶχεν δὲ τὸ θηρίον ἐπὶ τῆς κεφαλῆς χρώματα τέσσερα· μέλαν, εἶτα πυροειδὲς καὶ αἱματῶδες, εἶτα χρυσοῦν, εἶτα λευκόν.

And so, putting on the faith of the Lord, brothers, and remembering the great things he had taught me, I courageously gave myself over to the beast. And so it came on with a roar, enough to lay waste a city. But when I approach it, the enormous sea monster stretches itself out on the ground and did nothing but stick out its tongue; otherwise it did not move at all until I had passed it by. And the beast had four colours on its head: black, fire- and blood-red, gold, and white. (Vis. 4.1.8–10 [22.8–10] my trans.)

This narration too is overtly immersive and, furthermore, is enactive: it advances in chronological order, in a slow motion; it mostly consists of a series of bodily movements and simple actions, and includes the sensorial detail of the beast's roar. Moreover, Hermas describes the monster through its stretching out on the ground and the use of its tongue, two affordances which allow Hermas to pass by it unharmed. Not only that, the fact that Hermas's action of passing by it is mentioned at the very end of the sentence keeps the account open and lets the audience experience, even for a short time, Hermas's suspense in front of his enemy. Finally, the delayed mention of colors is also enactive, because it is realistic that Hermas saw all of them only after passing the beast. Overall, this passage reinforces the audience's identification with Hermas's lived experience of sequential time.

Finally, at the very end of Vision 4, emphasis is placed on Hermas's and the audience's experience of the imminent arrival of the beast. After his encounter with the Lady Church appears, Hermas says:

ταῦτα εἴπασα ἀπῆλθεν καὶ οὐκ εἶδον ποίῳ τόπῳ ἀπῆλθεν· ψόφος γὰρ ἐγένετο· κἀγὼ ἐπεστράφην εἰς τὰ ὀπίσω φοβηθείς, δοκῶν ὅτι τὸ θηρίον ἔρχεται.

When she said these things she departed; but I did not see where she went. For there was a noise, and I turned around out of fear, thinking that the beast was coming. (Vis. 4.3.7 [24.7])

This passage contains a short enactive narrative, in which noise is combined with a reference to both Hermas's fear and his attempt to understand in space (by turning around) where both the Lady Church and the beast are. In this way, the imminent arrival of the beast is made experiential for the audience. Moreover, this brief narration constitutes the end of the Book of Visions and gives it an openness which contrasts with the expectation of closure that is proper to most narrative endings.[31] This contrast makes the imminent arrival of the

---

31 Cf. Osiek (*The Shepherd of Hermas*) who writes, "The ending is abrupt and unfinished, like the ending of the *Similitudes*" (97). This open ending would be even more remarkable, if the

beast even more experiential for the audience. Finally, the inclusion of the Lady Church in this narration suggests that, through the arrival of the beast, the reader and the listener of the Shepherd are invited to experience not only the imminent arrival of the eschatological affliction but also the oncoming eschatological fulfilment of the manifested church.

As both Angela Kim Harkins and I have shown in other contributions,[32] not only Vision 4 but also other sections of the Book of Visions display an immersive and enactive quality. A case in point is the passage at the beginning of Vision 3, where Hermas hears from the Lady that she will come at around eleven in the morning (Vis. 3.1.2 [9.2]), but he does not know the exact location of her appearance:

ἐγενόμην οὖν, ἀδελφοί, εἰς τὸν ἀγρόν, καὶ συνεψήφισα τὰς ὥρας, καὶ ἦλθον εἰς τὸν τόπον ὅπου διεταξάμην αὐτῇ ἐλθεῖν, καὶ βλέπω συμψέλιον κείμενον ἐλεφάντινον, καὶ ἐπὶ τοῦ συμψελίου ἔκειτο κερβικάριον λινοῦν, καὶ ἐπάνω λέντιον ἐξηπλωμένον λινοῦν καρπάσινον. ἰδὼν ταῦτα κείμενα καὶ μηδένα ὄντα ἐν τῷ τόπῳ ἔκθαμβος ἐγενόμην, καὶ ὡσεὶ τρόμος με ἔλαβεν, καὶ αἱ τρίχες μου ὀρθαί· καὶ ὡσεὶ φρίκη μοι προσῆλθεν, μόνου μου ὄντος·

And so, brothers, I went into the field and counted the hours. I arrived at the place that I had directed her to come, and I see an ivory couch set up. On the couch was placed a linen pillow, with a piece of fine linen cloth on top. When I saw these things laid out with no one there, I was astounded and seized with trembling, and my hair stood on end—terrified, because I was alone. (Vis. 3.1.4–5 [9.4–5] my trans.)

This brief narrative section contains some of Allan's immersive features, and also possesses an enactive dimension. This passage is focalized by Hermas, and readers are given access to his *perspective*—"I was astounded and seized with trembling ..." (Vis. 3.1.5 [9.5]). Moreover, this narration displays *verisimilitude*: it advances in chronological order and contains the same historical present as in Vision 4, βλέπω, "I see," which creates an illusion for the reader of being present at the narrated events. Furthermore, this *verisimilitude* is reinforced by the enactive quality of this narrative. The sentence "I went into the field ... I arrived at the place" (Vis. 3.1.4 [9.4]) narrates a series of bodily movements and simple ac-

---

Book of Visions were an originally independent text. On my decision not to advance this hypothesis, see n. 5.
32 Angela Kim Harkins, "Looking at the *Shepherd of Hermas*," and Aldo Tagliabue, "Experiencing the Church in the *Book of Visions* of the *Shepherd of Hermas*," in *Experience, Narrative, and Criticism in Ancient Greece: Under the Spell of Stories*, ed. Jonas Grethlein, Luuk Huitink and Aldo Tagliabue (Oxford: Oxford University Press, 2019), 104–24.

tions.³³ The couch is introduced with a focus on the pillow, an affordance that invites both Hermas and readers to imagine the experience of being seated there. As I have argued elsewhere, *perspective*, *verisimilitude*, and the other features listed by Allan characterize the whole of Hermas's account of his encounter with the Lady Church.³⁴ As a result, the audience is invited to an immersion in this narrative section in order to experience both the sequential time of the manifested church and the imminence of its fulfilment, which at the beginning of Vision 3 is impersonated by the long-awaited appearance of the Lady Church.

To conclude, the Book of Visions indeed has the goal of introducing its reader and listener to an experience of the development in time of the manifested church. Since Hermas is an active member of the church who is undergoing a conversion, and this character is offered for the audience's identification, the latter's experience consists of their participation in the former's life and conversion as well.

The Audience's Experience of the Timelessness of the Spiritual Church

Throughout the account of Hermas's visions, some devices interrupt its immersive quality and create a non-sequential pattern which is focused on the repeated appearance of the Lady Church. In the following section, I will argue that this pattern invites the reader and the listener to gain a different experience, one that is focused on the divine timelessness of the spiritual church.

Let us now consider Vision 2:

> Πορευομένου μου εἰς κώμας κατὰ τὸν καιρὸν ὃν καὶ πέρυσι, περιπατῶν ἀνεμνήσθην τῆς περυσινῆς ὁράσεως, καὶ πάλιν με αἴρει πνεῦμα καὶ ἀποφέρει εἰς τὸν αὐτὸν τόπον ὅπου καὶ πέρυσι. ἐλθὼν οὖν εἰς τὸν τόπον τιθῶ τὰ γόνατα καὶ ἠρξάμην προσεύχεσθαι τῷ κυρίῳ καὶ δοξάζειν αὐτοῦ τὸ ὄνομα, ὅτι με ἄξιον ἡγήσατο καὶ ἐγνώρισέν μοι τὰς ἁμαρτίας μου τὰς πρότερον. μετὰ δὲ τὸ ἐγερθῆναί με ἀπὸ τῆς προσευχῆς βλέπω ἀπέναντί μου τὴν πρεσβυτέραν ἣν καὶ πέρυσιν ἑωράκειν, περιπατοῦσαν καὶ ἀναγινώσκουσαν βιβλαρίδιον.

> I was traveling to the countryside at the same time as the previous year, and on the way I remembered the vision from the year before. And again a spirit takes me and bears me to the same place I have been then. And so, when I came to the place I bow my knees and began praying to the Lord and glorifying his name, because he considered me worthy

---

33 Cf. the rich analysis by Harkins, "Looking at the *Shepherd of Hermas*," who comments similarly on Hermas's "kinesthetic movement ... and his changing emotional state" (61).
34 See Tagliabue, *Experiencing*, 113–15.

and showed me my former sins. When I arose from prayer I see across from me the elderly woman I have seen the year before, walking and reading a little book. (Vis. 2.1.1–3 [5.1–3] my trans.)

On first examination, this passage displays some immersive and enactive features, such as the focalization by Hermas and the focus on his bodily movements and simple actions (e.g. "I bow my knees"). On a closer look, however, the underlined phrases challenge Allan's category of *verisimilitude*. Instead of offering a chronological account of his new vision, with sensory details and spatial information, here Hermas establishes a comparison between the current vision and the one from the preceding year, suggesting that the same past event, the appearance of the Lady Church, is happening again. Therefore, he combines analeptic references with an emphasis on repetition. Moreover, this narrative is characterized by its *lack* of specific temporal markers: the exact "when" of this new vision is not given, and, strikingly, this "when" is not even specified in the account of the vision that took place a year before.

μετὰ χρόνον τινὰ πορευομένου μου εἰς κώμας καὶ δοξάζοντος τὰς κτίσεις τοῦ θεοῦ, ὡς μεγάλαι καὶ ἐκπρεπεῖς καὶ δυναταί εἰσιν, περιπατῶν ἀφύπνωσα. καὶ πνεῦμά με ἔλαβεν καὶ ἀπήνεγκέν με δι' ἀνοδίας τινός, δι' ἧς ἄνθρωπος οὐκ ἐδύνατο ὁδεῦσαι.

When some time had passed, I was traveling to the countryside, glorifying the creations of God and thinking how great, remarkable, and powerful they are. On the way I fell asleep and a spirit took me and carried me through a certain deserted place that was impassable. (Vis. 1.1.3 [1.3])

This passage gives neither the date nor the time when the first vision took place. On the other hand, the intervention of a spirit is a motif that also appears in the beginning of Vision 2 and thereby reinforces the importance of analepses and repetition in that passage.

Overall, these devices downplay the immersive quality of the narrative and prevent the audience from immersing themselves in it. Rather, they draw attention to the repetition of the Lady Church's appearance.

Throughout the Book of Visions this repetition occurs at least three times, since the Lady Church appears four times in the text (cf. Vis. 1.2.2 [2.2], 2.1.3 [5.3], 3.1.2 [9.2] and 3.1.6 [9.6]) and is three times described in a similar way (see Vis. 1.2.2. [2.2], 2.1.3 [5.3] and 3.1.6 [9.6]). In noticing this repetition, the audience is invited to look at these individual episodes of the Book of Visions out of sequence, and to compare them with each other. By doing this, the audience may experience time not as sequential (as in the surrounding sections of the narrative) but in the form of a never-ending occurrence of the same event. This pattern likely conveys a sense of an invariance in time, which mirrors the lack of development and timelessness proper to the spiritual church. In summary, within the same account of Hermas' visions, the Book of Visions invites its reader and listener to experience not only the sequential and eschatological time of the manifested church through identification with Hermas, but also glimpses of the timelessness of the spiritual church.

Conclusion

After many decades in which the scholars of the Shepherd have raised traditional disciplinary questions around this text, the time has come to offer new approaches to it. Following the focus on lived religion which is adopted by this volume, this essay has used both a phenomenological narratology and cognitive approaches to immersion to argue that the Book of Visions offers its reader and listener an experience of both the sequential and eschatological time of the manifested church, and of the divine timelessness of the spiritual church. Through this rich experience, the theology of the Shepherd as focused on the church and Hermas's conversion is made experiential to the audience.

Like any other reader-oriented approach which is inspired by modern theories of narrative and cognition, this analysis raises a question about its application for the ancient readers and listeners of the Shepherd, which, as I mentioned in the Introduction, were likely to be the early followers of the Christ religion, with the inclusion of some non-Christian readers. In the limited space of this conclusion, I would like to suggest some ways in which this application can be regarded positively.

To begin with, as recently shown by Angela Kim Harkins, in the ancient world there was a lived experience of religion which did not presume ritual and ceremonial practices.[35] As a result, it is possible that the ancient audience could approach the Shepherd to gain a lived experience of religion. In addition, my identification of enactive quality within sections of the Book of Visions and its immersive effects gives a nod to the ancient notion of *enargeia* ("vividness") which is currently being studied widely across the world of Classics, and which in the ancient world became especially prominent in the Imperial Era, the time in which the Shepherd was written.[36]

---

[35] Angela Kim Harkins, "Looking at the *Shepherd of Hermas*."
[36] See Ruth Webb, *Ekphrasis, Imagination and Persuasion in Ancient Rhetorical Theory and Practice* (Farnham/Burlington: Ashgate, 2009), 87–106.

As recently argued by Luuk Huitink, "whilst acknowledging that *enargeia* is a multifaceted concept, recent classical scholarship holds that the term primarily refers to 'pictorial vividness', as brought about through the transference of picture-like internal representations from author to reader by means of detailed descriptions (*ekphrasis*)."[37] Despite this common trend, however, some classicists have more recently uncovered a new dimension of *enargeia* by construing it as a predecessor of the modern notion of immersion.[38]

Overall, the popularity of *enargeia* across ancient Greek and Roman literature – and especially during the Imperial Era—reinforces the likelihood that the reader and the listener of the Book of Visions could approach this text to gain an experience of both the sequential and the timeless aspects of the church. In future contributions, it would be helpful to explore whether the response to the Shepherd by the early Christian audience would be more similar or different from that of non-Christian readers. Moreover, subtle distinctions could concern the ancient Christian audience as well; the wealthy members of the early Christian communities would likely be more touched by the Lady Church's strong admonitions than the poor members; and the latter's experiences of the Book of Visions may therefore be different from the former's.

In 2011 Diane Lipsett said: "... *The Shepherd* presents itself as a narrative. The point, however obvious, is worth making."[39] I hope that this essay has begun to show the revolutionary and experiential value of this statement.

---

37 Luuk Huitink, "Enactivism, *Enargeia* and the Ancient Readerly Imagination," in *The Edinburgh History of Distributed Cognition*, ed. Miranda Anderson, David Cairns and Mark Sprevak, Vol. 1 (Edinburgh: Edinburgh University Press, 2019), 169–89, 170. For examples of this recent scholarship, see e.g. Graham Zanker, "*Enargeia* in the Ancient Criticism of Poetry," *Rheinisches Museum* 124 (1981): 297–311; Ann Vasaly, *Representations: Images of the World in Ciceronian Oratory* (Berkeley, CA: University of California Press, 1993); Webb, *Ekphrasis, Imagination and Persuasion in Ancient Rhetorical Theory and Practice*.
38 See Allan, de Jong, de Jonge, "From *Enargeia* to Immersion: The Ancient Roots of a Modern Concept."
39 Lipsett, *Conversion*, 27.

Jason Robert Combs
Shepherd of Hermas Vision 5 and the Christian Experience of Pagan Epiphany

When the eponymous shepherd of the Shepherd of Hermas first appears at the beginning of Vision 5 (Vis. 5.1–4 [25.1–4]), his presence is met with concern.[1] This "angel of repentance" (Vis. 5.7 [25.7]) is described at first as "a man glorious in appearance" who manifests himself "in shepherd form (σχήματι ποιμενικῷ), wearing a white goat skin, and carrying a sack on his shoulder and a staff in his hand" (5.1 [25.1]). He introduces himself to Hermas as follows: "I was sent by the holiest angel to dwell with you the rest of the days of your life" (5.2 [25.2]).[2] Despite the angel's glorious appearance and this introduction, Hermas expresses concern: "I thought that he was there to tempt me." His reply to the angel suggests that his concern is tied to the shepherd's identity: "Whoever are you? For I know to whom I have been entrusted" (Vis. 5.3 [25.3]).[3] That Hermas was worried by the "shepherd form" is confirmed when the angel alters his appearance: "While he was still speaking, his form changed (ἠλλοιώθη ἡ ἰδέα αὐτοῦ), and I recognized him since he was the very one to whom I was entrusted" (Vis. 5.4 [25.4]).[4] From the text of the Shepherd of Hermas alone it is not clear why the angelic being's original manifestation in the form of a shepherd would have caused Hermas to conclude that he was about to be tempted, or why the angel had to alter his shepherd-form in order for Hermas to recognize him. The logic of this narrative depends on something assumed, but not written.

---

[1] For the Greek text of Shepherd of Hermas, I rely on Martin Leutzsch, "Hirt des Hermas" in *Papiasfragmente. Hirt des Hermas. Eingeleitet, herausgegeben, übertragen und erläutert*, ed. Ulrich H.J. Körtner and Martin Leutzsch, Schriften des Urchristentums 3 (Darmstadt: Wissenschaftliche Buchgesellschaft, 1998), 105–497. Translations of Shepherd of Hermas are my own in consultation with the *Apostolic Fathers*, vol. 2 (Ehrman, LCL 25) and Michael W. Holmes, *The Apostolic Fathers: Greek Texts and English Translations*, 3rd ed. (Grand Rapids, MI: Baker, 2007).
[2] εἰσῆλθεν ἀνήρ τις ἔνδοξος τῇ ὄψει, σχήματι ποιμενικῷ, περικείμενος δέρμα [αἴγειον] λευκόν, καὶ πήραν ἔχων ἐπὶ τὸν ὦμον καὶ ῥάβδον εἰς τὴν χεῖρα. ... Ἀπεστάλην ἀπὸ τοῦ σεμνοτάτου ἀγγέλου, ἵνα μετὰ σοῦ οἰκήσω τὰς λοιπὰς ἡμέρας τῆς ζωῆς σου (Vis. 5.1–2 [25.1–2]).
[3] ἔδοξα ἐγὼ ὅτι πάρεστιν ἐκπειράζων με, καὶ λέγω αὐτῷ· Σὺ γὰρ τίς εἶ; ἐγὼ γάρ, φημί, γινώσκω ᾧ παρεδόθην (Vis. 5.3 [25.3]). On translating ἐκπειράζων as "temptation" rather than "test" see below.
[4] ἔτι λαλοῦντος αὐτοῦ ἠλλοιώθη ἡ ἰδέα αὐτοῦ, καὶ ἐπέγνων αὐτόν, ὅτι ἐκεῖνος ἦν ᾧ παρεδόθην (Vis. 5.4 [25.4]).

Early attempts to explain why Hermas anticipated temptation from the shepherd focused on ostensible literary parallels with hermetic literature, especially *Poimandres*.[5] Although arguments for literary dependence proved untenable, many scholars continued to assume that Hermas's alarm was caused by the shepherd-image's pagan associations, for instance, with the god Hermes.[6] This assumption is in part correct, even though direct literary comparisons are insufficient to account for Hermas's reaction. In order to make sense of the unwritten assumptions that lie behind the initial manifestation of the shepherd in Vision 5, it is necessary to read this passage in its cultural context. So far, scholars have failed to appreciate how well the narrative of Vision 5 reflects the way one might expect a Christian to react to the manifestation of an otherworldly shepherd given the cultural expectations surrounding dreams/visions and Christian responses to that culture.[7] In this essay, I will show how a culture that leads people

---

5 R. Reitzenstein argued for literary dependence of Shepherd of Hermas on *Poimandres*; see *Poimandres. Studien zur Griechisch-Ägyptischen und Frühchristlichen Literatur* (Leipzig: Teubner, 1904), 13, 33. For problems with assuming literary dependence, see the early critique by Gustave Bardy, "Le Pasteur d'Hermas et les Livres Hermétiques," *Revue Biblique* 8 (1911): 391–407; see also Carolyn Osiek, *Shepherd of Hermas: A Commentary*, Hermeneia (Minneapolis: Fortress Press, 1999), 100. Juan José Ayán Calvo also considers potential parallels to Hermetic literature, but does not draw a definitive conclusion; *Hermas: El Pastor*, Fuentes Patrísticas 6 (Madrid: Editorial Ciudad Nueva, 1995), 29, 117n134.

6 Martin Dibelius adapted Reitzenstein's argument (see above, n5) to argue for dependency on common themes from paganism as well as Judaism, instead of direct literary dependence: "Man wird nach alledem zwar Hermas und Hermes von demselben Epiphanie-Schema abhängig denken, aber nicht einen vom anderen"; see *Der Hirt des Hermas. Die apostolischen Väter*, Handbuch zum Neuen Testament 4 (Tübingen: Mohr-Siebeck, 1923), 492, 496; and Martin Dibelius, "Der Offenbarungsträger im 'Hirten' des Hermas," in *Botschaft und Geschichte. Gesammelte Aufsätze von Martin Dibelius*, ed. Günther Bornkamm (Tübingen: Mohr Siebeck, 1956), 80–93, here 85, 90–91. Robert Joly favors Dibelius's interpretation but notes problems in particular with Dibelius's lack of evidence for the angel transforming himself from a shepherd into the likeness of Hermas himself—a guardian angel as a divine twin; *Hermas, Le Pasteur. Introduction, texte, critique, traduction et notes*, Sources chrétiennes 53 (Paris: Cerf, 1958), 49–50, 142. Peter Lampe, in his social history of early Roman Christianity, suggests that Hermas's negative reaction to the shepherd shows how the author "anticipates the possible reaction of the reader" to the inclusion of "pagan motifs"; *From Paul to Valentinus: Christians at Rome in the First Two Centuries*, trans. M.D. Johnson (Minneapolis: Fortress Press, 2003 [org. 1989]), 228. Norbert Brox simply acknowledges that the text does not make it clear what kind of temptation Hermas fears or why the shepherd is originally unrecognizable; *Der Hirt des Hermas*, KAV 7 (Göttingen: Vandenhoeck & Ruprecht, 1991), 187; see also Leutzsch, "Hirt des Hermas," 440n556.

7 Translation of Greek and Latin terms into the English words "dream" or "vision" can cause confusion because these words do not reflect well all of the ancient or modern cultural assumptions associated with such phenomena. I prefer the combined "dream/vision" or simply "dream" to designate the broad category of phenomena that includes the human experience of an epiph-

to identify gods in dreams/visions based on the literary and artistic representations of those gods was reinterpreted by Christians to identify the manifestations of pagan gods as demonic temptations. I argue that Vision 5 gives narrative form to this early Christian polemic against pagan epiphanies. As such, Shepherd of Hermas reflects how some Christians experienced, or at least imagined that a Christian might experience, the problem of encountering pagan gods in dreams/visions.

Reading Dreams/Visions as Religious Experience

To study this text as religious experience, one need not assume that Hermas or the author accurately represents his own authentic experience.[8] Rather, the narrative represents something that readers in that time could have accepted as a plausible religious experience given the cultural expectations—expectations established in part through the various literary and artistic representations of dreams/visions extant in that period.[9] Additionally, to study this text as religious

---

any or manifestation of an otherworldly being in visible form. See J. S. Hanson, "Dreams and Visions in the Graeco-Roman World and Early Christianity," *ANRW* II/23.2:1395–427; and Gregor Weber, *Kaiser, Träume und Visionen in Prinzipat und Spätantike* (Stuttgart: F. Steiner, 2000), 33–34.

8 On the problems with presuming an unmediated religious-experience core within an ancient text, see Colleen Shantz, "Opening the Black Box: New Prospects for Analyzing Religious Experience," in *Experientia, Volume 2: Linking Text and Experience*, ed. Colleen Shantz and Rodney A. Werline (Atlanta: SBL Press, 2012), 1–15, here 3–4, 11; and Frances Flannery with Nicolae Roddy, Colleen Shantz, and Rodney A. Werline, "Introduction: Religious Experience, Past and Present," in *Experientia, Volume 1: Inquiry Into Religious Experience in Early Judaism and Christianity*, ed. Rodney Alan Werline, Frances Flannery, and Colleen Shantz (Atlanta: SBL, 2008), 1–10, here 5.

9 One need not go as far as Robin Lane Fox, who suggests that people in this period "kept nightly company with their gods," to acknowledge the abundance of epiphanies attested in the written and visual media of this period; *Pagans and Christians* (New York: Knopf, 1987), 165. On the increase in literary and artistic representations of gods manifesting themselves in dreams/visions around the period of Shepherd of Hermas, see Lane Fox, *Pagans and Christians*, 102–167; see also E. R. Dodds, *Pagan and Christian in an Age of Anxiety: Some Aspects of Religious Experience from Marcus Aurelius to Constantine* (Cambridge: Cambridge University Press, 2000 [org. 1965]), 37–68; and the response in John G. Gager, "Introduction: The Dodds Hypothesis," in *Pagan and Christian Anxiety: A Response to E.R. Dodds*, ed. Robert C. Smith and John Lounibos (Lanham, MD: University Press of America, 1984), 1–11. More recently, see William V. Harris, *Dreams and Experience in Classical Antiquity* (Cambridge, MA: Harvard University Press, 2009), 31–32, 215; n.b. that Harris has been credibly charged with serious accusations of sexual misconduct.

experience, one need not and should not disregard its textuality. What is available for study is not the unmediated experience of the dream/vision, but, borrowing Vincent Crapanzano's term (borrowed from Lacan), a "dream-text."[10] A dream-text may be inspired by an authentic dream-experience, but it is shaped by the cultural conventions of dream-narration and again by the literary conventions of its genre.[11] That is not to suggest that religious experience can be reduced to cultural patterns—dreams have the potential to flout prescribed cultural norms—or that it is possible to peel back the literary and cultural layers of a dream-text in order to reveal an authentic-experience core—experience does not exist prior to or apart from culture.[12] In studying a dream-text, therefore, we are examining an assemblage of literary genre, cultural norms, and personal/social (at very least authorial or readerly) experience.[13] To acknowledge this allows us to consider this dream-text from the Shepherd of Hermas within the broader context of its culture and the descriptions of religious experience from the time—without limiting ourselves by the constraints of literary dependence or literary genre alone.[14]

In what follows, I will begin with the Shepherd of Hermas, the dream-text itself, to show how the narrative distinguishes Hermas's reaction to the shepherd

---

[10] Vincent Crapanzano, "The Betwixt and Between of the Dream," in *Hundert Jahre "Die Traumdeutung." Kulturwissenschaftliche Perspektiven in der Traumforschung*, ed. Burkhard Schnepel (Köln: Koppe, 2001), 232–59, here 233, 250.

[11] Crapanzano, "Betwixt and Between of the Dream," 246. Similarly, Peter Burke has cautioned, "Historians need to bear constantly in mind the fact that they do not have access to the dream itself but at best to a written record, modified by the preconscious or conscious mind in the course of recollection and writing"; *Varieties of Cultural History* (Ithaca, NY: Cornell University Press, 1997), 28.

[12] *Pace* Lane Fox, *Pagans and Christians*, 381–395. On the problems with these extremes in past studies of religious experience, see Flannery, *et al.*, "Introduction," 2–5; and Shantz, "Opening the Black Box," 3–4, 7–8. On the problems with reducing religious experience to cultural patterns, see Shantz, "Opening the Black Box," 7; and on religious experience not existing prior to or apart from culture, see Flannery, *et al.*, "Introduction," 5n23.

[13] On the relationship between culture, experience, and text, see Shantz, "Opening the Black Box," 5; citing Pierre Bourdieu, *Outline of a Theory of Practice*, trans. Richard Nice (Cambridge: Cambridge University Press, 1977). See also Marc Augé, *The War of Dreams: Exercises in Ethno-Fiction* (Sterling, VA: Pluto Press, 1999). On the relationship between culture, experience, and text in the Shepherd of Hermas, see Angela Kim Harkins, "Looking at the Shepherd of Hermas through the experience of lived religion," in *Lived Religion in the Ancient Mediterranean World: Approaching Religious Transformations from Archaeology, History and Classics*, ed. Valentino Gasparini et al. (Berlin: De Gruyter, 2020), 49–70.

[14] That is to say, there are cultural currents that cross the boundaries of literary convention, and that literature both shapes and is shaped by these cultural currents.

from his reactions to other epiphanies. After demonstrating that Hermas initially presumes the shepherd is deceitful, I will explain how his reaction both corresponds with cultural expectations and deviates from those expectations in line with other Christian texts.

Hermas's Form of Address, Temptation, Other Manifestations, and Other Shepherds

There are at least four features within the text of Shepherd of Hermas that suggest Hermas perceived the initial manifestation of an otherworldly being in shepherd form not as a benevolent angel, but as a threat. These include, first, the form of address that Hermas uses to greet the otherworldly being; second, the use of the verb ἐκπειράζω to describe what Hermas expected from the otherworldly shepherd; third, Hermas's positive response to other manifestations; and, lastly, the negative role that a shepherd figure plays later in the Shepherd of Hermas.

The form of address that Hermas uses to greet otherworldly beings reflects his perception of them. When divine beings appear to Hermas and he recognizes them as divine beings, he addresses them as κυρία (e. g., Vis. 1.1.5 [1.5]; 1.2.2 [2.2]) or κύριε (e. g., Vis. 3.10.9 – 10 [18.9 – 10]; 3.11.4 [19.4]).[15] The first manifestation of the shepherd, however, is different. Hermas does not address the shepherd as κύριε, but as σύ; he asks: "Whoever are you?" (Σὺ γὰρ τίς εἶ – Vis. 5.3 [25.3]). As Mark Grundeken and Joseph Verheyden observe, "[This is] atypical, because Hermas normally uses *kyrie* or *kyria* when he speaks to a revelatory agent for the first time. [Σύ] is probably used to underline that Hermas does not immediately realize who the appearance is."[16] After the shepherd changes his form and is recognized by Hermas as benevolent (Vis. 5.4 [25.4]), Hermas addresses him again; this time he employs the epithet κύριε (Mand. 3.3 [28.3]). This change in form of address supports Grundeken and Verheyden's suggestion that originally Hermas did not recognize the otherworldly being in shepherd form.

Hermas's concern when the shepherd initially appears is also demonstrated by his use of the word ἐκπειράζω to describe the shepherd's presumed inten-

---

15 Mark R.C. Grundeken and Joseph Verheyden, "The Spirit before the Letter: Dreams and Visions as the Legitimization of the *Shepherd of Hermas* a Study of *Vision 5*" in *Dreams as Divine Communication in Christianity: From Hermas to Aquinas*, ed. Bart J. Koet (Leuven: Peeters, 2012), 23 – 56, here 46; see also n. 122 for a list of uses of κυρία and κύριε.
16 Grundeken and Verheyden, "The Spirit before the Letter," 46.

tions. Since Hermas's epiphanic encounters are primarily with benevolent angels, and this angel of repentance is eventually discovered to be benevolent, the word ἐκπειράζω in Vision 5.3 (25.3) has been translated by some as "test."[17] Yet this interpretation does not fully capture the concern originally expressed by Hermas within the text. Hermas makes it clear that he does not recognize the shepherd as the one to whom he has been entrusted (Vis. 5.3 [25.3]). Additionally, in the only other instances where the verb ἐκπειράζω appears in Shepherd of Hermas, it describes the temptations of the devil. In response to one of Hermas's later questions the shepherd responds: "After that great and holy calling, whoever sins—having been tempted (ἐκπειρασθείς) by the devil—has one (opportunity for) repentance" (Mand. 4.3.6 [31.6]).[18] The shepherd also warns Hermas: "So also the devil comes against all the servants of God in order to tempt (ἐκπειράζων) them" (Mand. 12.5.4 [48.4]).[19] Temptation (ἐκπειράζω) in both of these cases is the activity of the devil, never the act of a benevolent angel.[20]

The text of Shepherd of Hermas makes it clear that it is not otherworldly beings or epiphanies in general that concern Hermas, but the particular manifesta-

---

17 See Osiek, *Shepherd of Hermas*, 100; *Apostolic Fathers*, vol. 2 (Ehrman, LCL 25), 235; and Jonathan Lookadoo, *The Shepherd of Hermas: A Literary, Historical and Theological Handbook* (London: T&T Clark, 2021), 99. As evidence for reading ἐκπειράζω in Shepherd of Hermas as "test" instead of "temptation," Osiek points to four passages from the New Testament: Matt 4:7 par. Luke 4:12 (LXX Deut 6:16); Luke 10:25; 1 Cor 10:9. But Matt 4:7 and Luke 4:12 are Jesus's quotation of Deut 6:16 in the context of the Devil "tempting" Jesus, and 1Cor. 10:9 uses πειράζω, not ἐκπειράζω. Only Luke 4:12 provides a suitable example of ἐκπειράζω used as test. A better approach is to consider how the words ἐκπειράζω and πειράζω are used within the Shepherd of Hermas (see below). For additional support, Osiek cites Erik Peterson, "Kritische Analyse der fünften Vision des Hermas," in *Frühkirche, Judentum und Gnosis. Studien und Untersuchungen*, ed. Erik Peterson (Freiburg: Herder, 1959), 271–84, here 278n30; cited in Osiek, *Shepherd of Hermas*, 100n14. But Peterson argues that ἐκπειράζειν represents a temptation by one's "evil drive" as it relates to the Shepherd of Hermas's emphasis on two-ways: "Es ist eine Versuchung durch den bösen Trieb"; Peterson,"Kritische Analyse der fünften Vision des Hermas," 278n30. See also Grundeken and Verheyden, who compare the shepherd to the benevolent angel in Tobit 12:14; Grundeken and Verheyden, "The Spirit before the Letter," 42. Elsewhere, however, they write that Hermas's statement "carries the connotation of being put to the test by the devil"; see "The Spirit before the Letter," 45–6.
18 ἀλλὰ ἐγώ σοι λέγω, φησί, μετὰ τὴν κλῆσιν ἐκείνην τὴν μεγάλην καὶ σεμνὴν ἐάν τις ἐκπειρασθεὶς ὑπὸ τοῦ διαβόλου ἁμαρτήσῃ, μίαν μετάνοιαν ἔχει. (Herm. Mand. 4.3.6 [31.6]).
19 οὕτω καὶ ὁ διάβολος ἔρχεται ἐπὶ πάντας τοὺς δούλους τοῦ θεοῦ ἐκπειράζων αὐτούς. (Mand. 12.5.4 [48.4]).
20 The root of ἐκπειράζω, πειράζω, is used in Sim. 7.1 (66.1) and 8.1.7 (68.7) with the meaning "to test (someone)" and "to try or attempt (something)." ἐκπειράζω and πειράζω are not used synonymously in Shepherd of Hermas.

tion of an otherworldly shepherd. The reaction of Hermas to the shepherd is different than his reactions to other epiphanic images. In his first vision, Hermas sees a woman appear in the heavens who looks like Rhoda, his former master (Vis. 1.1.4 [1.4]). On another occasion, he sees an elderly woman in radiant clothes holding a book (Vis. 1.2.2 [2.2]) and later two men appear and lead her away to a white chair in the east (Vis. 1.4.3 [4.3]). Hermas sees that elderly woman on other occasions (Vis. 2.1.3 [5.3]; cf. 3.10.3–5 [18.3–5]) as well as a "most handsome young man" (Vis. 2.4.1 [8.1]; cf. 3.10.7 [18.7]). Yet, in each of these manifestations, Hermas never expresses fear of temptation or concern regarding the identities of these otherworldly beings.[21] Even in the instance when Hermas misidentifies the elderly woman as the sibyl, a pagan oracle, there is no concern regarding temptation (Vis. 2.4.1 [8.1]).[22] If, as some have argued, Hermas's initial reaction to the shepherd reflects concern with pagan associations in broad terms, one should expect a similar reaction to this "sibyl."[23]

---

21 Even in the situation when the elderly woman's physical appearance changes between manifestations, these manifestations do not cause alarm or mistrust, merely curiosity (see Vis. 3.10.3–5 [18.3–5] and the explanation in Vis. 3.11.1–3.13.4 [19.1–21.4]).

22 Most scholars agree that Hermas's misidentification of the old woman as the sibyl makes sense within the narrative given the description of her characteristics and function; for instance, Osiek lists: "great age, seated position, holding a book, revealing hidden secrets"; Osiek, *Shepherd of Hermas*, 58; see also Brox, *Der Hirt des Hermas*, 104–105; Dibelius, *Der Hirt des Hermas*, 451–52; and Leutzsch, "Hirt des Hermas," 401–402n210. Some would add to this list the mention of "Cumae" in Vis. 1.1.3 (1.3) and 2.1.1 (5.1) since Cumae is the seat of the famous Cumaean Sibyl. See Dibelius, "Der Offenbarungsträger im 'Hirten' des Hermas," 92; Dibelius, *Der Hirt des Hermas*, 452; Stanislas Giet, *Hermas et les pasteurs. Les trois auteurs du Pasteur d'Hermas* (Paris: Presses universitaires du France, 1963), 123, 284; Lampe, *From Paul to Valentinus*, 228; Graydon F. Snyder, *The Shepherd of Hermas*, The Apostolic Fathers: A New Translation and Commentary 6 (Camden, NJ: Thomas Nelson & Sons, 1968), 39. "Cumae" in Vis. 1.1.3 (1.3) and 2.1.1 (5.1), however, is a conjectural emendation—Greek MSS have κώμας—based on a presumed connection with the Cumaean Sibyl, but the emendation is not necessary; see Osiek, *Shepherd of Hermas*, 43; Lookadoo, *The Shepherd of Hermas*, 62–63; and Antonio Carlini, "Le passegiate di Erma verso Cuma (Su due luoghi controversi del *Pastore*)," in *Studi in onore di Edda Bresciani*, ed. S. F. Bondi et al. (Pisa: Giardini, 1986), 105–9.

23 Lampe makes this comparison between the sibyl and the shepherd explicit and argues that the author is attempting to avoid any accusation that Hermas evinces "pagan tendencies"; Lampe, *From Paul to Valentinus*, 228; but see Brox's critique of Lampe in Brox, *Der Hirt des Hermas*, 105. Similar to the early arguments about the shepherd and hermetic literature (see above, n5), some scholars originally argued that the early visions of Shepherd of Hermas are a Christianized edition of a text originally about the pagan sibyl; e.g., Daniel Völter, *Die Apostolischen Väter. Neu Untersucht. 1 Teil. Clemens, Hermas, Barnabas* (Leiden: Brill, 1904), 184–194. Others have argued that the author simply borrowed literary tropes familiar from descriptions of the sibyl in order to depict the visionary image of the Church; e.g., Dibelius, "Der Offenbarungsträger

Yet, despite the sibyl being a familiar pagan oracle, Hermas does not react negatively to her manifestations as he does when the shepherd first appears.[24] Whatever the explanation for his response to the sibyl, it is clear that Hermas's concern about temptation is specifically associated with the manifestation of a shepherd-figure and not with any other epiphanic-figure he encounters.

In the Shepherd of Hermas, the significance of the shepherd-form is ambiguous, if not potentially malevolent. In Similitude 6, the Angel of Repentance appears to Hermas in his home and instructs him not to doubt in the commandments of God (Sim. 6.1.1–3 [61.1–3]). He advises Hermas, and presumably all the penitent who read Shepherd of Hermas, to "cast aside the evil things (πονηρίας) of this age that wear you (pl.) down (ἐκτριβούσας)" (Sim. 6.1.4 [61.4]).[25] Then the angel takes Hermas to a field in order to illustrate precisely how evil things wear people down. When they arrive at the field, Hermas sees "a shepherd, a young man dressed in a saffron-colored suit of clothes; and he was feeding a large number of sheep" (Sim. 6.1.5–6 [61.5–6]).[26] The angel then informs Hermas, that this shepherd is an evil angel: "This is the angel of luxury and deceit. He wears down (ἐκτρίβει) the souls of the servants of God who are idle ..... deceiving them with evil (πονηραῖς) desires in which they are destroyed" (Sim. 6.2.1 [62.1]).[27] Whereas the Angel of Repentance had previously informed Hermas that the devil tempts all God's servants (Mand. 12.5.4 [48.4]), he now reveals that the "angel of deceit," who wears down the souls of God's serv-

---

im 'Hirten' des Hermas," 92; Dibelius, Der Hirt des Hermas, 452; and Peterson, "Beiträge zur Interpretation der Visionen im Pastor Hermae," 266–67.

24 Perhaps this can be explained by the fact that the sibyl had already been adopted by Jewish and Christian authors who produced their own sibylline oracles; see John J. Collins, "The Development of the Sibylline Tradition," ANRW II/20.1:421–59. Another possible explanation for Hermas's indifference to the sibyl-like manifestation when contrasted with his reaction to the shepherd is that the sibyl is not a common image assumed by pagan gods in epiphanies, whereas pagan gods do appear in the form of a shepherd; see below on the manifestation of pagan gods in the form of a shepherd.

25 οἱ οὖν μετανοοῦντες ἀποβάλλετε τὰς πονηρίας τοῦ αἰῶνος τούτου τὰς ἐκτριβούσας ὑμᾶς. (Sim. 6.1.4 [61.4]).

26 καὶ δεικνύει μοι ποιμένα νεανίσκον ἐνδεδυμένον σύνθεσιν ἱματίων, τῷ χρώματι κροκώδη. ἔβοσκε δὲ πρόβατα πολλὰ λίαν (Sim. 6.1.5–6 [61.5–6]).

27 Οὗτος, φησίν, ἐστὶν ἄγγελος τρυφῆς καὶ ἀπάτης. οὗτος οὖν ἐκτρίβει τὰς ψυχὰς τῶν δούλων τοῦ θεοῦ [τῶν κενῶν] καὶ καταστρέφει αὐτοὺς ἀπὸ τῆς ἀληθείας, ἀπατῶν αὐτοὺς ταῖς ἐπιθυμίαις ταῖς πονηραῖς, ἐν αἷς ἀπόλλυνται (Sim. 6.2.1 [62.1]). This shepherd of luxury is not explicitly called "evil." Yet he is engaged in "deceiving [his sheep] with evil desires" (Sim. 6.2.1 [62.1]) and he is contrasted with a shepherd who is explicitly identified as "righteous" (Sim. 6.3.2 [63.2]).

ants, appears in the form of a shepherd (Sim. 6.1.5–6.2.2 [61.5–62.2]).[28] This vision makes it clear that the manifestation of an otherworldly being in shepherd form is not a guarantee that such a being is benevolent.

Given the malevolent identity of the shepherd-figure in these later passages, it is understandable why Hermas would express concern regarding the unrecognized, though ultimately benevolent, "shepherd" who first appears to Hermas in Vision 5. Hermas's form of address to that shepherd and his description of the shepherd's supposed intentions as "temptation" make it clear that Hermas was concerned that this being was not a benevolent angel. This is especially clear when Hermas's initial response in Vision 5 is contrasted with Hermas's response to the other divine beings he encounters in his dreams/visions. What is not clear from the text alone, however, is why the manifestation of an otherworldly being in the form of a shepherd would, for Hermas or the author, suggest an impending temptation. Why does the manifestation of a glorious man in shepherd-form cause such concern? An answer is found only when this text is read in the context of Greco-Roman traditions regarding the shepherd-image and the identification of divine beings in epiphanies, as well as in the context of Christian responses to those traditions.

Shepherds as Pagan Gods and Heroes in Contemporaneous Art and Literature

The Shepherd of Hermas likely portrayed some of its "righteous angels" as shepherds because of their positive connotations within Christian and Jewish textual traditions. One can find God, Jesus, or angels described in metaphorical terms as shepherd-like in the Psalms, Isaiah, Wisdom of ben Sira, Enoch, Gospels such as Matthew and John, and in other Jewish and Christian writings.[29] Yet the image of

---

28 On the relationship between this shepherd's yellow/saffron suit and luxury, see Brox, *Der Hirt des Hermas*, 334. On the association of the shepherd image with luxury, see Jennifer Awes Freeman, "The Good Shepherd and the Enthroned Ruler: A Reconsideration of Imperial Iconography in the Early Church" in *The Art of Empire: Christian Art in Its Imperial Context*, ed. Lee M. Jefferson and Robin M. Jensen (Minneapolis: Fortress Press, 2015), 182. On the similar appearance of good and evil shepherds in Shepherd of Hermas, see Dibelius, *Der Hirt des Hermas*, 495–6.
29 For God, angels, and Jesus as shepherds, see Ps 23:1; Isa 40:10–11; Jer 31:10; Ezek 34:6–31; Sir 18:13b; 1 En 89.59–67; Matt 26:31–33; John 10:11, 14; Heb 13:20; 1 Pet 2:25; 5:4. The shepherd does not appear in Christian art until the beginning of the third century CE. On the introduction of the shepherd-image as Christ into Christian art, see Robin Margaret Jensen, *Understanding*

the shepherd was also popular in pagan art and literature. And for the author of Shepherd of Hermas, most likely living in Rome in the early- to mid-second century, it would have been nearly impossible to avoid the common literary and artistic associations of the shepherd-image with pagan heroes and deities.[30] Old traditions of the gods appearing in shepherd form continued to be told and retold. For instance, Ovid recounts the tale of Zeus appearing in the guise of a shepherd to engage in sexual intercourse with Mnemosyne (*Metam.* 6.114 ff). Ganymede, Zeus's cupbearer on Mount Olympus, was a shepherd according to Homer's *Iliad* (5.265 ff), and continued to be remembered as a shepherd in the Roman period, as in Apuleius's *Metamorphoses* (11.8). Plutarch, in his *Parallel Stories*, includes an account of Ares (Mars) appearing to women in the form of a shepherd in order to seduce them (*Mor.* 312 A, 314 E). Pausanias describes a sanctuary, statue, and festival dedicated to "Hermes with the Ram," all of which commemorated how the town of Tanagra to the north of Athens was saved from a plague by the god Hermes carrying a ram around the perimeter of the town. The festival featured a young man dressed as a shepherd carrying a ram through the streets, and the statue depicted Hermes in a similar fashion: dressed as a shepherd, carrying a ram (Pausanias, *Descr.* 9.22.2). In fact, Hermes, Apollo, and Orpheus were all recognizable in art, depicted in the form of a shepherd.[31] The popularity of the shepherd image in the time and location of the author of Shepherd of Hermas is further demonstrated by the fact that more than an hundred shepherd lamps—lamps with the image of a ram-carrying shepherd—were produced and distributed in central Italy by the late-second century CE.[32] And similar shepherd-images appear in mosaics and frescos throughout this period in Italy and the broader Roman empire.[33] For Christians living in or around Rome in the first half of the second century, their world was filled with visual cues associating the image of the shepherd with Roman religion and, in particular, with pagan gods and heroes. One should not assume that the metaphorical

---

Early Christian Art (New York: Routledge, 2000), 37–44; and Joan E. Taylor, *What did Jesus Look Like?* (London: Bloomsbury, 2018), 98–101. On the challenge of distinguishing between pagan and Christian images of the shepherd, see Paul Corby Finney, *The Invisible God: The Earliest Christians on Art* (Oxford: Oxford University Press, 1994), 125–132; and Jensen, *Understanding Early Christian Art*, 15–17. See also Thomas F. Mathews, *The Clash of Gods: A Reinterpretation of Early Christian Art* (Princeton: Princeton University Press, 1993).

30 On the date of Shepherd of Hermas, see Brox, *Der Hirt des Hermas*, 22–25; Leutzsch, "Hirt des Hermas" 135–37; and Osiek, *Shepherd of Hermas*, 18–20.

31 Nikolaus Himmelmann, *Über Hirten-Genre in der antiken Kunst*, Abhandlungen der Rheinisch-Westfälischen Akademie der Wissenschaften 65 (Opladen: Westdeutscher Verlag, 1980), 109–156.

32 Finney, *The Invisible God*, 116–131.

33 Himmelmann, *Über Hirten-Genre in der antiken Kunst*, 109–156.

shepherd language of Christian scripture would be sufficient to alter perception of the shepherd-image already in the second century. For a Christian living in Rome in this period, it would be impossible to disassociate completely the image of the shepherd from paganism and to appropriate it as a purely Christian image.[34] And, indeed, when Hermas first sees an otherworldly being in shepherd-form he expresses uncertainly about his identity and motivations. In the narrative of Shepherd of Hermas, however, the shepherd-image that Hermas encounters is not art, but epiphany.

Recognizing the Gods in Dreams/Visions

What does the image of gods as shepherds in mythology and art have to do with dreams/visions? There is little difference between identifying the statue of a shepherd as the god Hermes and recognizing an otherworldly shepherd in a dream/vision as Hermes. In fact, art and epiphanies are intimately connected. Studies of epiphanies in Greco-Roman antiquity have revealed what Verity Platt calls the "mutually reinforcing bond" between epiphany and representations of the gods:

> [W]ithin Greek culture, epiphany (by which I mean the manifestation of deities to mortals) inspired, and was in turn inspired by, practices of visual and literary representation, generating a mutually reinforcing bond that operated within both identifiably sacred contexts and the cultural imagination at large.[35]

The gods were identifiable as gods because they appeared extraordinarily tall, especially beautiful, pleasant smelling, or magnificently bright, and because

---

34 Shepherd of Hermas, with its diverse representation of shepherd figures, can be read as participating in a process of appropriation, or better, hybridization, as the author navigates the porous boundaries between Christianity and other Roman religions.
35 Verity Platt, *Facing the Gods: Epiphany and Representation in Graeco-Roman Art, Literature and Religion* (Cambridge: Cambridge University Press, 2011), 7; cf. Lane Fox, *Pagans and Christians*, 153; and Georgia Petridou, *Divine Epiphany in Greek Literature and Culture* (Oxford: Oxford University Press, 2015), 49. For a similar theory on the relationship between epiphany and visual representations in the modern world, see David Morgan, "Image, Art and Inspiration in Modern Apparitions," in *Looking Beyond: Visions, Dreams, and Insights in Medieval Art and History*, ed. Colum Hourihane; Index of Christian Art, Occasional Papers (Princeton: Index of Christian Art in association with Princeton University Press, 2010), 265–82.

they could transform their physical appearance.[36] When the otherworldly shepherd first appears to Hermas, he is described as "a man glorious in appearance" (Vis. 5.1 [25.1]). Yet such exalted characteristics did not aid in identifying the individual personality of a god—that is, whether the god who appeared was Athena or Aphrodite, Dionysus or Asclepius. Artistic and literary representations of the gods, however, could help to determine their identities. For instance, Aelius Aristides, in his *Sacred Tales*, describes recognizing Athena in a divine encounter based on his knowledge of literary and artistic representations of her. Aristides records the following experience as occurring in the summer of 165 CE:

> Athena appeared with her aegis and the beauty and magnitude and the whole form of the Athena of Phidias in Athens. There was also a scent from the aegis as sweet as could be, and it was like wax, and it too was marvelous in beauty and magnitude. She appeared to me alone, standing before me even from where I would behold her as fairly as possible. I also pointed her out to those present—they were two of my friends and my foster sister—and I cried out and I named her Athena, saying that she stood before me and spoke to me, and I pointed out the aegis. (*Or.* 48.41).[37]

When Aristides recorded this experience he could not remember all of the words that Athena had spoken to him. He did, however, recall that she spoke of Homer's *Odyssey:* "She reminded me of *The Odyssey* and said that these were not idle tales, but that this could be judged even by the present circumstances. It was necessary to persevere. I myself was indeed both Odysseus and Telemachus, and she must help me" (*Or.* 48.42). Aristides's familiarity with Athena from literary works influenced his identification of her—he recognized Athena's quotation of the *Odyssey* and saw that she bore the aegis familiar from myth. Aristides also suggests that he recognized Athena because her appearance matched the famous statue in Athens, crafted by Phidias: she appeared as "the whole form of the Athena of Phidias in Athens" (*Or.* 48.42).

Aristides was not the only person in this period to identify a god by appealing to art. In the novel *Daphnis and Chloe*, nymphs are identified by comparison with their statues: "The three Nymphs appeared to him, tall and beautiful ladies, semi-clothed and barefoot, with their hair unbound and looking like their stat-

---

36 For a summary of divine characteristics commonly featured in epiphanies, see H.S. Versnel, "What Did Ancient Man See when he Saw a God? Some Reflections on Greco-Roman Epiphany," in *Effigies Dei: Essays on the History of Religions*, ed. Dirk van der Plas (Leiden: Brill, 1987), 42–55.

37 *Or.* 48.40. Unless otherwise indicated, all translations of Aristides's *Orations* come from Charles A. Behr, *P. Aelius Aristides, The Complete Works: Volume II, Orationes XVII-LIII* (Leiden: Brill, 1981).

ues" (*Daph.* 2.23).[38] In Chariton's novel, *Callirhoe*, the role of art in recognizing a god is central to the plot. The protagonist, Callirhoe, is mistaken for the goddess Aphrodite because her appearance is similar to a statue in the local temple (*Chaer.* 2.3). In Plutarch's *Camillus* 6.1, the statue of Juno is itself the manifestation of the goddess. In Suetonius's *Life of Galba*, the identification motif is reversed. Rather than recognizing the god by comparison to a statue, Galba recognized the statue outside his door because it looked like the goddess who had appeared in his dream (*Galb.* 18.2). By the second century CE, visual representations of the gods were commonly associated with epiphanies in literature, and in cities throughout the empire visual representations of the gods were prevalent.[39]

Christians, like the author of Shepherd of Hermas, were part of this culture. Although Christians certainly could have rejected the dominant cultural norms—denied that the manifestations of pagan gods in the forms suggested by art and myth were real or meaningful—all extant evidence from this period suggests that Christians accepted these ideas.[40] The Shepherd of Hermas narrates the epiphany scene in Vision 5 as one would expect from reading Aelius Aristides and other Greco-Roman epiphany narratives from the time. The author describes the physical appearance of the otherworldly shepherd when he first appears to Hermas in a way that fits the cultural and literary trope of identifying otherworldly beings in dreams/visions by comparison to familiar images—"in shepherd form, wearing a white goat skin, and carrying a sack on his shoulder and a staff in his hand" (Vis. 5.1 [25.1]). Yet, rather than respond by naming the otherworldly shepherd based on recognition of his characteristics, Hermas responds with concern: "I thought that he was there to tempt me" (Vis. 5.3 [25.3]). Why? Christians did not simply adopt the dominant cultural trends, they reinterpreted them.

Christians and the Manifestations of Pagan Gods

One of the most common ways that early Christians contemporaneous with the author of the Shepherd of Hermas reinterpreted the cultural expectations sur-

---

[38] Longus, *Daphnis and Chloe* (Jeffrey Henderson, LCL).
[39] On the prevalence of artistic representation of the gods by the second century CE, see John R. Clarke, *Art in the Lives of Ordinary Romans: Visual Representation and Non-Elite Viewers in Italy, 100 B.C.–A.D. 315* (Berkeley: University of California Press, 2003), 73–94. For more on gods resembling their statues in epiphanies, see Harris, *Dreams and Experience in Classical Antiquity*, 61, 204; Platt, *Facing the Gods*, 258; and Petridou, *Divine Epiphany in Greek Literature and Culture*, 49–64.
[40] See the next section.

rounding the manifestations of otherworldly beings was to insist that the pagan gods who appear in dreams/visions were actually evil demons whose purpose was to tempt people.⁴¹ Christians adopted from Judaism the idea that the gods of pagans were actually evil spirits or evil demons.⁴² Then, beginning in the second century, Christians applied that belief to the culture surrounding dreams/visions. For instance, Justin Martyr, in his *First Apology* (c. 155 CE), identifies the gods of Greek and Roman mythology who engaged in immoral actions as evil demons and then writes: "In ancient times, wicked demons, in apparitions (ἐπιφανείας), committed adultery with women and seduced boys and made people see horrifying things" (*1 Apol.* 5.2).⁴³ Justin also warns his addressees in his own time that these same demons will try to prevent them from understanding the Christian message and that they will do so "through appearances in dreams" (δι' ὀνείρων ἐπιφανείας).

> For we warn you to take guard lest the demons whom we have previously accused deceive you and turn you aside from even encountering what we say and understanding it; for they strain to make you their slaves and servants; and sometimes through appearances in dreams [δι' ὀνείρων ἐπιφανείας], sometimes again through magical changes [διὰ μαγικῶν στροφῶν], they overpower those who do not strain in every way after their salvation. (*1 Apol.* 14.1).

---

41 Some important studies on dreams in antiquity have acknowledged that manifestations of pagan gods were a genuine concern for the apologists, but these studies did not address the issue of contemporaneous dreams—i.e., dreams that occur in the time of the apologist and even within the apologist's own community. See Lane Fox, *Pagans and Christians*, 137; Harris, *Dreams and Experience*, 69; Patricia Cox Miller, *Dreams in Late Antiquity: Studies in the Imagination of a Culture* (Princeton: Princeton University Press, 1994), 64.

42 E.g., Psalm 95:5 LXX; 1 Enoch 19:1; 99:7; 1 Cor 10:19–21. See Annette Yoshiko Reed, *Fallen Angels and the History of Judaism and Christianity: The Reception of Enochic Literature* (Cambridge: Cambridge University Press, 2005), 160–89; and Dale B. Martin, "When Did Angels Become Demons?" *JBL* 129 (2010): 657–77. For a description of a similar polemic against pagan gods within pagan philosophical literature, see Frederick E. Brenk, "In the Light of the Moon: Demonology in the Early Imperial Period," *ANRW* II 16.3:2068–2145; and Hubert Cancik, "Römische Dämonologie (Varro, Apuleius, Tertullian)" in *Die Dämonen (Demons). Die Dämonologie der israelitisch-jüdischen und frühchristlichen Literatur im Kontext ihrer Umwelt (The Demonology of Israelite-Jewish and Early Christian Literature in Context of their Environment)*, ed. Armin Lange, Hermann Lichtenberger, and K. F. Diethard Römheld (Tübingen: Mohr Siebeck, 2003), 447–60.

43 Unless otherwise indicated, all translations of Justin's *First Apology* come from Denis Minns and Paul Parvis, ed., *Justin, Philosopher and Martyr: Apologies*, Oxford Early Christian Texts (Oxford: Oxford University Press, 2009). Minns and Parvis note that "[t]he word ἐπιφάνεια, here translated 'apparitions,' was a standard term for manifestations of the gods in pagan religion"; Minns and Parvis, *Justin, Philosopher and Martyr*, 91n1.

Justin may also imply that demons will deceive people by altering their appearance. Justin says that demons will try to trick people "through magical changes" (διὰ μαγικῶν στροφῶν). Minns and Parvis suggest that this phrase, διὰ μαγικῶν στροφῶν, refers to "the demons assuming different shapes in their efforts to mislead."[44] Indeed, it was a common feature of ancient epiphany-narratives that gods could alter their appearance.[45] Yet, even if "magical changes" does not refer to the gods/demons metamorphic abilities, it is clear that Justin understands the manifestations of demons to be intimately linked with the representations of pagan gods in art. When Justin describes the statues of gods "whom human beings formed and set up in temples and called gods," he also explains that these statues "have the names and shapes of those wicked demons who were seen in apparitions" (1 Apol. 9.1).[46] For Justin, the images of the gods were inspired by the deceptive manifestations of evil demons, and demons continue to manifest themselves in the forms of those gods' images in order to lead people astray.

Tatian (c. 155–170 CE) likewise argues that the Greek gods are nothing more than evil demons in disguise, and that they manifest themselves in epiphanies. For instance, when Tatian explains that the gods must be evil demons because their actions are immoral, he includes epiphanies from familiar myths such as Zeus's seduction of Leda and abduction of Ganymedes (Or. Graec. 8–10). Tatian also describes incubation epiphanies occurring in his own time and suggests that evil demons continue to feign divinity by revealing themselves in the forms of pagan gods.

> Demons are like bandits, for just as bandits are in the habit of taking men prisoner and then releasing them to their families on payment, so too those supposed gods visit men's bodies, and then in dreams create an impression of their presence and order their victims to come forward in sight of all. When they have enjoyed the eulogies they fly away from the sick, terminate the disease they have contrived, and restore the men to their previous state. (Or. Graec. 18.3).[47]

Tatian argues that incubation epiphanies only seem to be effective because health results when the evil demons, who caused the illness, leave. People mis-

---

44 Minns and Parvis, *Justin, Philosopher and Martyr*, 111n6.
45 See Versnel, "What Did Ancient Man See when he Saw a God?," 42–55.
46 … ἀλλ' ἐκείνων τῶν φανέντων κακῶν δαιμόνιων καὶ ὀνόματα καὶ σχήματα ἔχειν; Justin, *1 Apol.* 9.1.
47 Unless otherwise indicated, all translations and Greek of Tatian are from Molly Whittaker, *Tatian: Oratio ad Graecos and Fragments*, Oxford Early Christian Texts (Oxford: Clarendon Press, 1982).

takenly believe that gods are healing them because demons, the "supposed gods" (οἱ νομιζόμενοι θεοί), produce "in dreams (δι' ὀνείρων) ... an impression of their presence."⁴⁸

The author and early readers of the Shepherd of Hermas would likely have been familiar with the culture surrounding the manifestations of pagan gods in dreams/visions as well as with this Christian polemic that reframed aspects of those cultural norms. Even before the second century, Jews and Christians associated pagan gods and their images with evil demons.⁴⁹ And, by the mid-second century, Christian apologists connected the manifestations of pagan gods in dreams/visions with demons.⁵⁰ Not one of these Christian authors debated the reality of pagan gods appearing in dreams/visions. They could not deny that cultural fact. Instead, they argued that behind that fact lurked evil demons. With Christians implicated in the broader Greco-Roman practice of identifying gods in dreams/visions based on their common literary and artistic depictions, we understand why the manifestation of an otherworldly being, a glorious man, in the form of a shepherd would have been perceived by Hermas as a temptation.⁵¹ For Christians in that period, demons appeared in the recognizable forms of pagan gods, forms such as the shepherd, in order to tempt people to worship false gods. The narrative of Vision 5 in Shepherd of Hermas fits the dominant cultural expectations as they were reinterpreted by Christians.

Conclusion

The unwritten assumptions behind the narrative of Shepherd of Hermas Vision 5 (25) make sense within the dominant culture of dreams/visions and the Christian response to that culture. For the author of Shepherd of Hermas, the dominant culture provided certain expectations for dream-texts, and most of the epiphanies in Shepherd of Hermas meet those expectations. Vision 5, however, diverges

---

48 *Or. Graec.* 18.3. Demons also deceive through "false appearances" (φαντασιῶν ἐξηπατήκασιν); Tatian, *Or. Graec.* 14.1; trans. mine.
49 See above, n42.
50 Much of this same polemic against pagan gods and their manifestations appears in the writings of other Christians from the second and third centuries; e.g., Athenagoras, *Leg.* 26–28; Tertullian, *Apol.* 22; *An.* 46.13, 47.1; Minucius Felix, *Oct.* 27.1, 4, 6, 8; Origen, *Cels.* 3.37; 7.6–7, 35; 8.43, 62.
51 On Hermas misidentifying the shepherd because of statues and myths, see Dibelius, "Der Offenbarungsträger im 'Hirten' des Hermas," 91. On problems with Dibelius's argument, see n6. For a similar argument regarding the sibyl in Shepherd of Hermas, see Peterson, "Beiträge zur Interpretation der Visionen im Pastor Hermae," 266–7.

in one significant way: when Hermas first sees the otherworldly shepherd he anticipates temptation and questions the shepherd's identity. The author does not explain why Hermas reacts in this way. Yet, given the dominant culture and the Christian response, he did not need to add details that would have been assumed by his readers. Even though Hermas's reaction represents a deviation from the dominant cultural expectations, it coheres with Christian apologists' polemic against that dominant culture. There are no precise literary parallels to Hermas's initial reaction to the shepherd in the extant Christian narratives from this period. Nevertheless, for a Christian familiar with the polemic against dreams/visions of pagan gods, Vision 5 represents in narrative form how one might expect a Christian to react to the manifestation of an otherworldly being who shares characteristics common to certain pagan deities. The fact that the otherworldly shepherd in Vision 5 turns out to be a benevolent angel does not detract from the narrative of Hermas's initial response in which he exhibits the reaction of a Christian encountering a pagan epiphany.

It is impossible to conclude definitively that Christians in the early second century experienced dreams/visions of pagan gods and interpreted that experience as a demonic temptation—all we have are texts. Yet text, in particular a dream-text, is an amalgamation of experience, culture, and literary features that cannot be teased apart.[52] Arguments in this essay have focused on literary and cultural evidence—literature and culture that necessarily give shape to and are shaped by experience. As a dream-text, Shepherd of Hermas Vision 5 necessarily reflects how some Christians experienced, or at least imagined that a Christian might experience, the problem of a pagan epiphany.[53]

---

[52] See above section, "Reading Dreams/Visions as Religious Experience."
[53] An earlier draft of this essay was presented at the SBL Annual Meeting, 2018, in Denver, CO, as part of the program unit, "Religious Experience in Antiquity," and I am grateful for the insights of our respondent, Harry O. Maier. I am also grateful for the helpful reviews of Shaily Shashikant Patel, Travis W. Proctor, Catherine Gines Taylor on previous drafts.

Brittany E. Wilson
God's Multiple Forms: Divine Fluidity in the Shepherd of Hermas

Scholars often use the term "fluid" or "polyvalent" to describe key aspects of the Shepherd of Hermas. Diane Lipsett, for instance, describes the narrative as having "a fluid pneumatology and christology," and Charles Gieschen likewise details the text's "fluid pneumatology."[1] Carolyn Osiek similarly speaks of the Shepherd's "polyvalent" symbols, and Philippe Henne characterizes the work's structure as a whole in terms of "allegorical polysemy."[2] In this essay, however, I argue that the term "fluidity," while applicable to the Shepherd's pneumatology, christology, imagery, narrative structure, and so forth, also extends to the ways in which the narrative portrays God and how Hermas (as the main human character) experiences God. In other words, I argue that Hermas experiences God in the Shepherd as a fluid entity who can become manifest in a variety of different, sometimes embodied, forms. In making this argument, I draw upon Benjamin Sommer's description of "divine fluidity" traditions in the Hebrew Bible, and I maintain that such traditions best account for the Shepherd's own—often ambiguous and seemingly contradictory—portrayals of the divine.[3] By focusing on divine fluidity, or the God of Israel's multiple—and at times embodied—manifestations, I hope to demonstrate that divine fluidity not only helps to explain some of the peculiarities of the text's multivalent images, but that it points to the text's inherently Jewish portrait of God.

By focusing on divine fluidity, I also hope to provide three main correctives to scholarship on the Shepherd of Hermas itself. First, a focus on divine fluidity situates scholarly treatments of the Shepherd's various heavenly beings within a

---

[1] B. Diane Lipsett, *Desiring Conversion: Hermas, Thecla, Aseneth* (New York: Oxford University Press, 2011), 44; Charles A. Gieschen, *Angelomorphic Christology: Antecedents and Early Evidence*, AGSU 42 (Leiden: Brill, 1998), esp. 224–25.
[2] Carolyn Osiek, *Shepherd of Hermas: A Commentary*, Hermeneia (Minneapolis: Fortress, 1999), e. g., 68; Philippe Henne, "La polysémie allégorique dans le *Pasteur* d'Hermas," ETL 65 (1989): 131–35.
[3] Indeed, scholars also frequently use words like "ambiguous" and "contradictory" to describe the Shepherd, and Osiek wisely cautions that trying to find consistency in the Shepherd will only cause frustration (e. g., *Shepherd of Hermas*, 119n6). I maintain, though, that these ambiguities and ostensible contradictions also support my point regarding how humans experience the divine according to the Shepherd. On Benjamin D. Sommer's discussion of divine fluidity, see *The Bodies of God and the World of Ancient Israel* (New York: Cambridge University Press, 2009).

wider framework—namely, the Shepherd's devotion to Israel's "Most High God." Many scholars look at the heavenly beings in the Shepherd in an atomistic fashion or focus on one or two of these beings and overlook the others. Moreover, while discussions of ecclesiology, pneumatology, angelology, and christology abound in scholarship on the Shepherd, discussions of God (or "theology") are strangely lacking.[4] This oversight is particularly perplexing given the sheer number of times that references to God emerge—references that far outweigh the mention of other characters, such as the Spirit or Jesus.[5] God is clearly an important character in the text, even if God never directly enters into the narrative (except, I argue, in a variety of mediated forms).

Second, a focus on divine fluidity complicates the tendency in scholarship to determine the precise relationship between the Shepherd's different mediator figures (such as angels, the Spirit, and Jesus) or to fit the Shepherd into a "binitarian" or trinitarian frame. Divine fluidity reminds us that there is a slippage among such figures and categories. It is difficult, for instance, to argue that the Shepherd has an "angelomorphic christology" as opposed to a "pneumatic christology" because Jesus overlaps with both angels and the Spirit, as we shall see.[6] It is also difficult to pigeonhole the Shepherd as binitarian or trinitar-

---

[4] This oversight is not a unique phenomenon when it comes to the study of early Christian texts. On the "curious neglect" of God in New Testament studies, for instance, see Larry W. Hurtado, *God in New Testament Theology*, Library of Biblical Theology (Nashville: Abingdon, 2010), 1–4. For an exception to this tendency in scholarship on the Shepherd of Hermas, see, for example, Harry Parkin, who argues that, in the Shepherd, "we have the recorded manifestations of an encounter between creature and Creator" ("The Numinous in 'The Shepherd,'" *CQ* 1 [1969]: 211–16, here 216).

[5] In the Shepherd as a whole, the term "spirit"/"Spirit" (πνεῦμα) appears over 100 times and "the Son" (υἱός) around 50 times. However, the term "God" (θεός) appears over 240 times and the term "Lord" (κύριος), as a reference to God, appears over 120 times. These statistics do not include textual variants, the Latin translations, nor the very end of the Shepherd (i.e., Sim. 9.30.3–10.4.5 [107.3–114.5]), which is not extant in the Greek manuscript tradition except for a few fragments. These statistics derive from the TLG, which relies on Whittaker's critical edition. Aside from concordance work, I rely elsewhere in this essay on the Greek text from *The Apostolic Fathers*, vol. 2 (Ehrman, LCL 25). At times, I also highlight Leutzsch's critical edition in Ulrich Körtner and Martin Leutzsch, *Papiasfragmente. Hirt des Hermas*, Schriften des Urchristentums 3 (Darmstadt: Wissenschaftliche Buchgesellschaft, 1998). All English translations are my own unless otherwise specified.

[6] Bogdan Gabriel Bucur, for instance, argues that the Son of God is the supreme "holy spirit" and critiques those (such as Charles Gieschen among others) who argue that the Spirit is "supreme" and that the Son is a manifestation of the Spirit (*Angelomorphic Pneumatology: Clement of Alexandria and Other Early Christian Witnesses*, VCS 95 [Leiden: Brill, 2009], esp. 121–23, 137–38; cf. Gieschen, *Angelomorphic Christology*, 222, 225). Even Bucur, however, concedes

ian since it is difficult to "rank" the Spirit's importance in relation to Jesus.[7] (Although, as Benjamin Sommer notes, later Christian trinitarian reflections are certainly consonant with depictions of divine fluidity.)[8]

Finally, a focus on divine fluidity blurs the boundaries between what is "real" and "symbolic" in the Shepherd of Hermas. Commentators frequently draw this distinction, and they do so for two main reasons: first, to differentiate Hermas's visionary experiences from his non-visionary experiences and second, to underscore that the text's image-rich (and often confusing!) statements concerning the divine should not be mistaken for metaphysical or doctrinal claims.[9] Yet while I agree that the Shepherd is a text concerned with neither metaphysics nor "doctrine," I am wary of relegating these images strictly to the symbolic realm, as though they are somehow not "real" or reflective of embodied experiences with the divine. For many ancients, visions were a key way to encounter the divine, and within the Shepherd itself, Hermas's visions include a variety of embodied encounters that involve cognitive, affective, and sensorial processes.[10] For our purposes, then, I will not consider the different forms in which the divine appear to be "mere" symbols. While many today speak of such forms (like God's "Name" or the "Lady Church") as symbols or personifications, many ancients likely conceived of and experienced these forms more in terms of concrete

---

that "the distinction is often blurred between the presence of the Son of God as supreme 'holy spirit' and that of the angelic 'spirits'" (*Angelomorphic Pneumatology*, 138).

7 Because Bucur argues that the Son "outranks" the Spirit, he maintains that the Shepherd displays a marked binitarian orientation: one that is concerned mostly with God and the Son of God (as the supreme holy spirit) (*Angelomorphic Pneumatology*, esp. 137–38).

8 As Sommer provocatively puts it, the Christian "belief in a God who has an earthly body as well as a Holy Spirit and a heavenly manifestation . . . is a perfectly Jewish one" (*Bodies of God*, 135).

9 See, for example, Osiek, *Shepherd of Hermas*, 35; cf. 93, 141.

10 Note, for instance, that visionary manifestations even touch Hermas at times, as when the Lady Church touches Hermas's breast (Vis. 1.4.2 [4.2]; cf. 3.1.6–7 [9.6–7]). Note also that, in at least two visions, Hermas is taken up and carried away (Vis. 1.1.3 [1.3]; 2.1.1 [5.1]), language that is more typical of physical transportation (e.g., Luke 24:[51b]; Acts 1:2, 9, 11; 8:39; 2 Cor 12:1–4; T. Ab. 8.2–3 recension B; cf. Ascen. Isa. 6.11–12). On the embodied nature of these visionary encounters, see the essays by Arcari, Harkins, and Tagliabue in this volume. In a similar vein, see Patricia Cox Miller, *Dreams in Late Antiquity: Studies in the Imagination of a Culture* (Princeton: Princeton University Press, 1994), 131–47. On how visions could function as one of the most direct ways in which to encounter the divine in the Greco-Roman world, see H. S. Versnel's classic essay, "What Did Ancient Man See When He Saw A God? Some Reflections on Greco-Roman Epiphany," in *Effigies Dei: Essays on the History of Religions*, ed. Dirk van der Plas (Leiden: Brill, 1987), 42–55, esp. 49–50.

realities.¹¹ Thus when the Shepherd explains, for example, that the Holy Spirit spoke with Hermas "in the form [ἐν μορφῇ] of the Church" (Sim. 9.1.1 [78.1]), I want to suggest that there is a "reality" to the Spirit becoming manifest in this form, at least in terms of Hermas's perceived experience.

To explore divine fluidity in the Shepherd of Hermas, this essay begins with a brief discussion of divine fluidity itself and how this fluidity blurs the boundaries between God and God's creation, as well as the human and divine. It then turns to the variety of ways in which the Shepherd depicts God becoming manifest, including divine attributes (such as God's "Name"), the Church, the Spirit, angels, and "the Son" (or Jesus). In this essay, I look across all three sections of the Shepherd (the Visions, the Mandates, and the Similitudes). I also assume the literary unity of the narrative (and will thus sometimes speak of the text's narrator), and I follow the consensus view that the Shepherd dates to around the early second century CE.¹² I conclude, then, that the Shepherd provides us a snapshot of how at least some early Christians incorporated Jewish representations of divine fluidity in their own depictions of the divine.

Divinity Fluidity: Boundary Blurring in the Shepherd of Hermas and Beyond

My language of God's fluidity, or multiple forms, will undoubtedly sound strange to many readers today. After all, how can God be "many" when God's "oneness" remains a key affirmation of Judaism and early Christianity? The Shema, for instance, famously announces that "the LORD is one" (depending on the translation at least),¹³ and in the Shepherd of Hermas, the Shepherd himself (as the text's primary agent of revelation from Vision 5 onward) affirms this classic formulation at the outset of the Mandates when he pronounces: "First of all, believe that God is one" (Mand. 1.1 [26.1]). Yet while articulations of God's "oneness" became increasingly common throughout the Second Temple period and beyond, these articulations were at the same time held in tandem with articulations of

---

11 For a critique of the modern tendency to dismiss divine attributes as personifications, see Gieschen, *Angelomorphic Christology*, esp. 36–45, 122.
12 On how the Shepherd presents itself as a narrative (and the implications of reading the Shepherd as a story), see Lipsett, *Desiring Conversion*, 27–28. For an overview of the Shepherd's literary unity and date, see Osiek, *Shepherd of Hermas*, 3–4, 8–10, 18–20.
13 This phrase from Deut 6:4 could just as easily be translated, *inter alia*, as: "The LORD is our God, the LORD alone."

God's ability to become manifest in different forms. During the Second Temple period, we see an explosion of interest in so-called intermediary figures, including divine attributes (such as God's Wisdom, Word, Power, Name, and Spirit), angels, and exalted humans (such as the patriarchs).[14] While some scholars have tried to argue that divine attributes are simply metaphors and that angels and exalted humans are independent agents that are wholly distinct from God, I agree with a growing number of scholars who argue that all of these intermediary figures point to a more inclusive understanding of monotheism during this time: one that upholds the supremacy of Israel's God, but still recognizes that the line between God and God's intermediary figures is often blurred in thought and practice.[15]

I furthermore hold that Hebrew Bible scholar Benjamin Sommer's language of "divine fluidity" also applies to this phenomenon. Sommer argues that the ancient Israelites (at least as reflected in the J and E strands of the Hebrew Bible) conceived of their God as having a "fluidity of divine selfhood" that could become manifest in multiple bodies (hence the title of Sommer's landmark book: *The Bodies of God and the World of Ancient Israel*). In these "fluidity" traditions, the deity is capable of existing at multiple sites at the same time, as opposed to the "anti-fluidity" traditions—i.e., the Priestly and Deuteronomic traditions—in which the deity is fixed and can only be at one place at a time. By describing depictions of the divine in terms of fluidity and anti-fluidity traditions, Sommer reframes the monotheism/polytheism binary by arguing that fluidity traditions are still "monotheistic."[16] That is to say, we do not see a development in ancient Israel from "polytheism" to "monotheism," for even the earlier J and E strands are "monotheistic." Sommer also maintains that fluidity traditions continue

---

14 Scholars classify intermediary figures in different ways; I have largely adapted the categories that Larry W. Hurtado provides in his book *One God, One Lord: Early Christian Devotion and Ancient Jewish Monotheism*, 2nd ed. (New York: Continuum, 1998).

15 For proponents of a more "inclusive" monotheism, see, e.g., Daniel Boyarin, *The Jewish Gospels: The Story of the Jewish Christ* (New York: New Press, 2012), 25–101; Crispin Fletcher-Louis, *Jesus Monotheism, Volume 1—Christological Origins: The Emerging Consensus and Beyond* (Eugene, OR: Cascade, 2015); Gieschen, *Angelomorphic Christology*; James F. McGrath, *The Only True God: Early Christian Monotheism in its Jewish Context* (Chicago: University of Illinois Press, 2009); Michael Peppard, *The Son of God in the Roman World: Divine Sonship in Its Social and Political Context* (Oxford: Oxford University Press, 2011). For proponents of a more "exclusive" monotheism, see, e.g., Hurtado *One God, One Lord*; Richard Bauckham, *Jesus and the God of Israel: God Crucified and Other Studies on the New Testament's Christology of Divine Identity* (Grand Rapids, MI: Eerdmans, 2008).

16 See esp. Sommer, *Bodies of God*, 145–74.

well beyond the Hebrew Bible itself and can be found in rabbinic literature and early Christian portrayals of the incarnation and Trinity.[17]

In line with this last point, I contend that divine fluidity traditions also continue in the portrayals of intermediary figures in the Second Temple period and its immediate aftermath.[18] During this time period, we find Jews evincing a distinctive devotion to their "Most High God," but still depicting this God in ways that overlap with intermediary figures. These figures are not independent gods, for they are still connected to Israel's singular God: they exert their own agency, yet also participate in God's divinity and activity; they are distinct from God, yet also somehow one with God. Discussing God in these terms was a common phenomenon in many Jewish circles, and we see this phenomenon continuing in many early Christian texts. In fact, for Christians, applying divine attributes to Jesus became a key way in which Christians tried to communicate Jesus' divinity and relationship with God.[19] Depicting Jesus in angelic (or angelomorphic) terms and as an exalted human (akin to the patriarchs and other exalted humans in Jewish tradition) also became a key way to communicate Jesus' special status. We should not be surprised, then, that the Shepherd makes similar moves, especially given its indebtedness to Jewish tradition. While the Shepherd never explicitly quotes from Jewish Scripture, its reliance on Jewish practices and scriptural texts is evident throughout, as scholars have long recognized.[20]

To be clear, even though I speak of God's ability to become manifest in different—including human—forms, it is important to recognize that the Shepherd still draws a distinction between God and God's creation. Throughout the Shepherd, God is the one who creates and who even creates *"out of nothing"* (e.g., "God ... created out of nothing the things that are" [Vis. 1.1.6 [1.6]; cf. Mand. 1.1 [26.1]), and references to God's creation abound.[21] Yet while there is a distinction in the text between Creator and creation (and thus creatures), this distinction is also blurred, especially with respect to how intermediary figures (or "crea-

---

[17] Sommer, *Bodies of God*, 124–43.
[18] For a more in-depth discussion of this point, see my chapter on divine fluidity in *The Embodied God: Seeing the Divine in Luke-Acts and the Early Church* (New York: Oxford University Press, 2021).
[19] On the depiction of Jesus in terms of intermediary figures more broadly, see, again, my discussion in *The Embodied God*. See also, e.g., Boyarin, *The Jewish Gospels*, 25–101; Fletcher-Louis, *Jesus Monotheism*; Gieschen, *Angelomorphic Christology*.
[20] See Osiek, *Shepherd of Hermas*, 24–28.
[21] On references to God as Creator and to God's creation, see Vis. 1.1.3, 6 [1.3, 6]; 1.3.4 [3.4]; 3.9.2 [17.2]; Mand. 7.5 [37.5]; 8.1 [38.1]; 9.3 [39.3]; 12.4.2 [47.2]; Sim. 4.4 [53.4]; 5.5.2 [58.2]; 9.1.8 [78.8]; 9.23.4 [100.4].

turely forms") such as angels and other anthropomorphic figures are portrayed. I will discuss this blurring in depth in the following section, but for the moment it is important to note that this blurring is consonant with depictions of intermediary figures more broadly. In a discussion of these figures, James McGrath—a proponent of "inclusive" monotheism—observes that the boundary between God and creation "may well have been more like a river than a wall . . . like a river that marks a country's border, the existence of a border, indeed its general location, may be clear, and nevertheless the edges of that border may be quite literally 'fluid'."[22] In a similar vein, Benjamin Sommer maintains that God's own perceived form is fluid: God can inhabit a body or many bodies at the same time, and it is this very fluidity that makes God and God's bodies "other."

Many Second Temple Jewish texts depict God in terms of "divine fluidity", but the Shepherd arguably describes this phenomenon itself when the narrator declares that God "contains all things but is alone uncontained" (Mand. 1.1 [26.1]). This idea is drawn from Hellenistic philosophy and would soon be adopted by other Christians, both "proto-orthodox"and "-heterodox" alike,[23] but within the narrative of the Shepherd itself, the idea is elsewhere connected with divine spirit possession. The same verb χωρέω ("contain") from Mand. 1.1 [26.1] appears later in the Shepherd in this concrete context when the narrator notes that a human "vessel" cannot "contain" (χωρεῖ) too many spirits but will overflow (Mand. 5.2.5 [34.5]).[24] Unlike these humans, the Shepherd suggests that God *can* contain different entities or forms, while at the same time being "uncontainable" (ἀχώρητος) (Mand. 1.1 [26.1]). Such language gestures toward what I am calling divine fluidity, or what others, such as Crispin Fletcher-Louis, call God's ability to "extend" God's self to include intermediary beings, without suffering a loss of divine being.[25]

Once again, while the Shepherd points to God's ability to "contain" all things or expand into different forms (including I would argue human forms), it is important to note that the Shepherd simultaneously affirms the distinction between

---

22 McGrath, *Only True God*, 13.
23 See, e. g., Aristides, *Apol.* 1; Gos. Truth 22.25; Eugnostos 73.6 – 8 // Wis. Jes. Chr. 9[6].1 – 3; Justin, *Dial.* 127; Theophilus, *Autol.* 1.5; 2.3; Augustine, *Conf.* 1.2; Osiek, *Shepherd of Hermas*, 103 – 104; William R. Schoedel, "Enclosing, Not Enclosed: The Early Christian Doctrine of God," in *Early Christian Literature and the Classical Intellectual Tradition: In Honorem Robert M. Grant*, ed. William R. Schoedel and Robert L. Wilken, ThH 53 (Paris: Beauchesne, 1980), 75 – 86.
24 See also the usage of the verb στενοχωρέω in relation to the Spirit, which can convey the sense of the Spirit being distressed or "pressed for room" (Mand. 5.1.3 [33.3]; 10.2.6 [41.6]; cf. 5.1.2 [33.2]).
25 Fletcher-Louis, *Jesus Monotheism*, 311.

the human and divine. "God is not like humans, who bear malice," the Shepherd tells Hermas, for God "is without malice and has compassion on his creation" (Mand. 9.3 [39.3]). The narrator's repeated references to human believers as God's "slaves"—an expression that appears nearly fifty times—especially captures this status differential.[26] At the same time, while the Shepherd is clear that God is the one who bestows the Spirit, the Shepherd is also clear that the Spirit (and other spirits and divine entities) dwell within a person. A person who claims prophetic inspiration is a "bearer of spirit" (πνευματοφόρος) (Mand. 11.16 [43.16]), and individual believers are intimately connected with the "Lady Church," who is herself intimately connected with "Lady Wisdom" (Sophia) and other divine forms (see discussion below). Overall, there is a fluidity between the human and divine, even as they are distinct.

Manifestations of the Divine: God's Different Forms in the Shepherd of Hermas

The remainder of this essay will now discuss the different forms in which the divine becomes manifest in the Shepherd of Hermas. To be clear, God is a distinct character in the Shepherd, and we largely learn about God through the discourse of other characters, such as the Lady Church and the Shepherd. These characters refer to God by applying a variety of different titles, including specifically Jewish ones, such as "the living God" (Vis. 2.3.2 [7.2]; 3.7.2 [15.2]; Sim. 6.2.2 [62.2]).[27] These characters also paint a portrait of *who* God is. For example, in addition to being the "one" Creator God, God is the one who has the power to provide healing from sins and who has authority over everything (Mand. 4.1.11 [29.11]; Sim. 7.4 [66.4];

---

26 Osiek notes that the term "slaves" typically appears in contexts of warning or as a challenge to a less-than-perfect church, whereas other terms for believers, such as "holy ones" or "chosen ones," usually occur in the Visions and in reference to the "ideal" church (*Shepherd of Hermas*, 47).

27 The epithet "living God" occurs frequently in Jewish idol polemic (e.g., Pss 115:4–8; 135:15–18; Isa 40:18–20; 44:9–20; 46:1–13; Jer 10:1–16; Hos 13:2–3; Hab 2:18–19). Note too that in Vis. 3.2.1 [10.1], martyrs sit to the right side of "the Holiness" (ἁγίασμα), a Jewish euphemism for the presence of God (cf. Mark 14:62) (Osiek, *Shepherd of Hermas*, 63). Of all God's epithets, "God" and "Lord" are the most frequent. In addition to these titles, we also find: "Father" (Vis. 3.9.10 [17.10]; Sim. 5.6.3–4 [59.3–4]; 9.12.2 [89.2]), "great King" (Vis. 3.9.8 [17.8]), "Master" (Vis. 2.2.4–5 [6.4–5]; 3.3.5 [11.5]; Sim. 1.9 [50.9]; cf. Sim. 5.2.1–11 [55.1–11]; 5.5.2 [58.2]; 9.26.4 [103.4]), "righteous Judge" (Sim. 6.3.6 [63.6]), and the word "divine"/"divinity" itself (θεότης: Mand. 10.1.4 [twice], 5, 6 [40.4 {twice}, 5, 6]; 11.5, 10 [twice], 14 [43.5, 10 {twice}, 14]); θεῖον: Vis. 4.1.6 [22.6]; Mand. 11.1–21 [43.1-21] passim).

8.11.3 [77.3]; 9.23.4 [100.4]); God is also the one who knows the human heart (Mand. 4.3.4 [31.4]; Sim. 7.5 [66.5]) and whose commandments must be obeyed (e.g., Vis. 3.5.3 [13.3]; Mand. 7.1, 4–5 [37.1, 4–5]; 12.5.1 [48.1]; Sim. 1.7 [50.7]; 6.2.2 [62.2]; 8.7.6 [73.6]). Overall, we find a God in the Shepherd who is consonant with the God of Jewish Scripture: a God who is in relationship with human beings, but who only rarely encounters humans "face-to-face."[28]

Yet while God, as in many other Jewish and Christian texts, never directly enters the narrative or engages with humans "face-to-face," I want to suggest that God does enter the narrative in different mediated forms. Indeed, Hermas (as the text's primary human recipient of divine revelation) does still encounter God, and he does so by encountering a number of distinct figures that intersect with God, as well as with one another. Such intersections are typical in depictions of intermediary figures in Jewish and early Christian texts, but they are especially apparent in the Shepherd. The Shepherd thus makes an especially fruitful case study in which to demonstrate this fluidity, for as Gieschen and others have rightly observed, there is an ambiguity to the narrator's depictions of the divine that characterizes the Shepherd as a whole. To assess this fluidity, I begin with divine attributes (especially God's Name) and the Church (and its members). I then move on to the Spirit and angelic figures, and I conclude with Jesus (or "the Son").

Divine Attributes

Divine attributes in the Shepherd do not occur in a univocal fashion. On the one hand, divine attributes function as descriptors of God's character and are not necessarily agents that act both independently and in tandem with God. In the Shepherd's opening vision, for instance, the Lady Church (as the primary revealer in Visions 1–4) refers to God's "invisible power," and she clarifies (with a series of datives of means) that God acts by means of God's wisdom, purpose, word, and foreknowledge, without suggesting that these descriptors have any agency themselves (Vis. 1.3.4 [3.4]).[29] Elsewhere in the Shepherd, however, divine

---

28 Moses is a famous exception to this rule (see, e.g., Deut 34:10; cf. 5:4–5). For other exceptions (such as Gen 32:30), see Wilson, *The Embodied God*, 63-65.
29 Note that the word "invisible" (as in God's "invisible power") only appears in the Latin, not the Greek (cf. Vis. 3.3.5 [11.5]). *Apostolic Fathers*, vol. 2 (Ehrman, LCL),182–83; Leutzsch, *Hirt des Hermas*, 152–53; Osiek, *Shepherd of Hermas*, 50. Note too that, in this same sentence, the Lady Church refers to God as "the God of powers [τῶν δυναμέων]." This suggests that the "powers" here are tangible realities and not only an "invisible" or unseen aspect of God since "powers"

attributes sometimes appear as semi-independent entities and actors who both receive and direct action (a tendency that some English translations capture by capitalizing these attributes).³⁰ God's "Name" in particular functions this way. The narrator depicts followers glorifying God's "Name," suffering on behalf of "the Name," and bearing "the Name" gladly.³¹ The Name also calls people (Sim. 8.1.1 [67.1]; 9.14.3 [91.3]; cf. 8.6.4 [72.4]; 9.17.4 [94.4]) and saves them ("you could not be saved by anything [or: anyone] except the great and glorious Name" [Vis. 4.2.4 (23.4)]).³² At one point, the narrator even specifies that the Name's own speech, or "word" (ῥῆμα), established the Church on a foundation (Vis. 3.3.5 [11.5]).³³ In all of these instances, divine attributes are portrayed in ways that exceed "personifications"; they instead are the direct objects of believers' actions or exert agency in a manner that coincides with God's own actions.

The Church and its Members

In contrast to divine attributes like God's "Name," it is easy to assume that the Shepherd portrays the Church solely as a non-divine entity. Whereas God's Name can be dismissed as being an aspect of God (and thus not having any distinct,

---

frequently refer to angels and other cosmic beings in the LXX and Second Temple Jewish literature (e. g., 3 Kgms 17:1; 18:15; Ps 23:10 LXX; Philo, *Conf.* 171–75; *Fug.* 94–105).

30 See, for instance, the translation by Michael W. Holmes: *The Apostolic Fathers: Greek Texts and English Translations*, ed. and rev. (Grand Rapids, MI: Baker, 1999). On how God's "Glory" (or God depending on how one translates it) created the world, see Mand. 12.4.2 (47.2). Bucur also suggests that the *Shepherd* depicts the Son as the Glory with the following parallel statements: ὤμοσεν γὰρ ὁ δεσπότης κατὰ τῆς δόξης αὐτοῦ (Vis. 2.2.5 [6.5]) // ὤμοσεν γὰρ κύριος κατὰ τοῦ υἱοῦ αὐτοῦ (Vis. 2.2.8 [6.8]) (*Angelomorphic Pneumatology*, 120–21n22).

31 On glorifying God's (or the Lord's) Name, see Vis. 2.1.2 (5.2); 3.4.3 (12.3); 4.1.3 (22.3); Sim. 9.18.5 (95.5). On suffering on behalf of the Name, see, e.g., Vis. 3.1.9 (9.9); 3.2.1 (10.1) [twice]; 3.5.2 (13.2); Sim. 9.28.6 (105.6). On gladly bearing the Name, see Sim. 8.10.3 (76.3). See also Sim. 6.2.3 (62.3); 8.6.[2], 4 (72.(2), 4]; 9.21.3 [98.3]. Note that many of these above references could arguably refer to Jesus, especially given the ambiguities in the manuscript tradition. (See Leutzsch's critical edition in particular.) Some witnesses make it clear that it is God's Name, whereas others lack a specific qualifier. See also the discussion below.

32 Note that there are translational and textual ambiguities with respect to the Name "calling." Depending on the witness (and/or the translation), Sim. 8.1.1 (67.1) refers to all those who are called in—or by—the Name of the Lord (Sim. 8.1.1 [67.1]), and Sim. 9.14.3 (91.3) refers to all those who called *upon* the Lord's Name or to all those called *by* (or: in) the Lord's Name. See Leutzsch, *Hirt des Hermas*, 280, 326–27.

33 Vis. 3.3.5 (11.5) reads: "the tower [i.e., the church] has been set on a foundation by the word of the all-powerful and glorious Name and is strengthened by the unseen power of the Master."

semi-independent agency), the Church can be dismissed as being wholly distinct from God (and thus not having any divine qualities). To be sure, the narrator is clear that the Church is a collective of human beings and not divine in the same sense as God.[34] Yet while the Church is distinct from the divine, the narrator also depicts the Church in ways that suggestively overlap with the divine. The Church, as noted earlier, overlaps with the divine attribute of God's "Wisdom," or Sophia, a female being who straddles the Creator/creation divide in many Second Temple texts.[35] Hermas, for instance, repeatedly addresses the female figure (i.e., "the Church") as "Lady" (κυρία), the feminine version of "Lord" (κύριος) and an epithet that recalls Sophia, or "Lady Wisdom." Like Lady Wisdom, the Lady Church speaks to Hermas as a mother instructing her children in virtue (esp. Vis. 3.9.1–10 [17.1–10]), a well-known wisdom motif and a role that Sophia herself adopts.[36] Like Lady Wisdom, the Lady Church is also pre-existent (Vis. 2.4.1 [8.1]; cf. Prov 8:22–31; Sir 24:9), and she has close ties with God's Spirit, whom we are later told speaks "in form of the Church" (Sim. 9.1.1 [78.1]). Furthermore, the very fact that the Church is to be "one body" (ἓν σῶμα) (Sim. 9.13.5, 7 [90.5, 7]; 9.17.5 [94.5]; 9.18.3–4 [95.3–4]) that is made of different members points to the Church's connection to the divine, for believers themselves can be inhabited by the divine. According to the Shepherd, "the Lord," "the angel," and "the spirit" all indwell in human beings, indicating that the division between the divine and the human is not as distinct as we may think.[37] Instead, the Church—in all its many, embodied forms—is one way in which God can become manifest, at least in part.

---

34 The Shepherd reiterates that the Church is a collective of human beings throughout. The different visual appearances and ages of the Lady Church reflect Hermas's own personal spiritual states (see esp. Vis. 3.11.1–3.13.4 [19.1–21.4]), and the non-human appearances of the Church signify a collective of different individuals and church members (tower/stones; willow tree/branches; twelve mountains/individual mountains). The Shepherd also distinguishes the Church from God, as when the narrator specifies that the Lady Church sits to the right of "the Holiness" alongside other followers who have suffered on behalf of the Name (Vis. 3.2.4 [10.4]; cf. 3.2.1 [10.1]). For an in-depth discussion of the Church, see Lage Pernveden, *The Concept of the Church in the Shepherd of Hermas* (Lund: CWK Gleerup, 1966).
35 See, e.g., Prov 8:22–31 LXX; Sir 24:2, 8–9; Wis 7:21–26; 8:3; 9:4, 10.
36 See, e.g., Prov 8:32; Wis 7:12; 8:7; Sir 4:11; 15:2; Luke 7:35, cited in Osiek, *Shepherd of Hermas*, 80n2.
37 See esp. Mand. 3.1 [28.1]; 5.1.2 [33.2]; 5.2.5 [34.5]; 6.2.2–3 [36.2–3]; 10.1.6 [40.6]; 10.2.5–6 [41.5–6]; 12.4.3, 5 [47.3, 5]; Sim. 5.4.3 [57.3]. Bucur, *Angelomorphic Pneumatology*, 125.

The Polymorphous Spirit

In the Second Temple period, God's Spirit became a prominent mode of God's presence, and in the Shepherd, the Spirit emerges as a key way in which God becomes manifest, surpassing even the central role that the Spirit plays in texts such as the book of Acts.[38] As Carolyn Osiek notes: "the Spirit of God is in *Hermas* the prevailing, polymorphous presence, personified to an unusual degree."[39] The Spirit's connection to God is evident through its epithets, such as "the Spirit of God" (Mand. 10.2.6 [41.6]) and "the Holy Spirit" (e.g., Sim. 5.6.5 [59.5]; 9.1.1 [78.1]), "holy" being a descriptor that designates one as belonging to God or reflecting God's own holiness (see, e.g., Vis. 3.2.1 [10.1]). The Spirit is also "preexistent" (τὸ προόν) and responsible for creating the entire creation (Sim. 5.6.5 [59.5]), a striking statement given the emphasis on God as Creator elsewhere. And while I would argue, contra Osiek, that the Shepherd's depiction of the Spirit exceeds that of "personification," the Spirit does certainly take on a range of embodied and anthropomorphic forms to an unusual degree. The Spirit, for instance, even evinces emotions, such as "grief" (λύπη) (Mand. 3.4 [28.4]; 10.2.1–6 [41.1–6]; 10.3.2 [42.2]), a characteristic that the Spirit shares with God and that situates both God and the Spirit as affective, anthropomorphic beings.[40]

In addition to being a key way in which God becomes manifest, the Spirit itself, as Osiek remarks, is a polymorphous presence. This polymorphic presence

---

38 On the increasingly important role of God's Spirit in the post-exilic period, see Nathan MacDonald, "The Spirit of Yнwн: An Overlooked Conceptualization of Divine Presence in the Persian Period," in *Divine Presence and Absence in Exilic and Post-Exilic Judaism*, ed. Nathan MacDonald and Izaak J. de Hulster, FAT 2/61 (Tübingen: Mohr Siebeck, 2013), 95–120. On the role of the Spirit in the Second Temple period, see John R. Levison, *The Spirit in First Century Judaism*, AGJU 29 (Leiden: Brill, 1997). On the role of the Spirit in the book of Acts, see Daniel Marguerat, "The Work of the Spirit," in *The First Christian Historian: Writing the "Acts of the Apostles"*, trans. Ken McKinney, Gregory J. Laughery, and Richard Bauckham, SNTSMS 121 (Cambridge: Cambridge University Press, 2002), 109–28.
39 Osiek, *Shepherd of Hermas*, 36.
40 Like the Spirit, God is also portrayed as an emotional being. For example, God's "compassion" (σπλάγχνον word group) is a frequent refrain in the Shepherd (Vis. 1.3.2 [3.2]; 2.2.8 [6.8]; 3.12.3 [20.3]; 4.2.3 [23.3]; Mand. 4.3.5 [31.5]; 9.2–3 [39.2–3]; Sim. 5.4.4 [57.4]; 5.7.4 [60.4]; 7.4 [66.4]; 8.6.1, 3 [72.1, 3]; 8.11.1 [77.1]; 9.14.3 [91.3]) (cf. Osiek, *Shepherd of Hermas*, 87n26). As with the Spirit, God's emotions are often elicited by humanity (so God for example can be "moved with compassion" when humans repent [Sim. 7.4 {66.4}]). For a helpful typology of divine anthropomorphism in biblical texts, which includes God's emotions and interaction with humans, see Anne K. Knafl, *Forming God: Divine Anthropomorphism in the Pentateuch* (Winona Lake, IN: Eisenbrauns, 2014), esp. 256–66.

in Mandate 11 when "the Holy Spirit" is connected to "a divine spirit" that inhabits a person.[41] Elsewhere we read that the Holy Spirit inhabits humans (Mand. 5.1.2 [33.2]; 5.2.5 [34.5]; Sim. 5.6.5 [59.5]), and Mandate 11—which focuses on spirit-inhabitation in relation to prophecy—specifically incorporates this same epithet (i.e., "Holy Spirit"; see Mand. 11.8, 9 [43.8, 9]).[42] But Mandate 11 also speaks of "a divine spirit" that is in opposition to "an earthly spirit" and that seems to be one among many spirits—albeit a spirit (unlike the earthly spirit) that "has the power of divinity" (Mand. 11.5 [43.5]).[43] It is not clear whether this divine spirit is the same as "the Holy Spirit" that we find elsewhere in the Shepherd, but this lack of clarity is precisely my point: the Shepherd speaks of "the Spirit"—or πνεῦμα—in a multiplicity of ways; indeed, the narrator even explains that the twelve virgins that Hermas saw in a vision are "holy spirits" (ἅγια πνεύματά) (Sim. 9.13.2 [90.2]), suggesting that "the Spirit" cannot be understood in solely singular terms.[44]

Just as the distinction between "the Spirit" and "spirits" is a fine one in the Shepherd, so is the distinction between "the Spirit" and angels. Bogdan Bucur, for example, notes that the language of "spirit" and "angel" is at times interchangeable in the Shepherd, especially in Mandates 5 and 6.[45] The parallelism is particularly notable at the level of shared vocabulary: the narrator speaks of "the spirit of righteousness" (Man 5.2.7 [34.7]) and "the angel of righteousness" (Mand. 6.2.3, 8–10 [36.3, 8–10]), and he applies the same descriptors (such as

---

[41] For an in-depth discussion of the eleventh mandate, see J. Reiling, *Hermas and Christian Prophecy: A Study of the Eleventh Mandate*, NovTSup 37 (Leiden: Brill, 1973).
[42] As in other instances, however, it is difficult to know whether this epithet is a reference to *the* Holy Spirit or whether it is a more general term for one of the many spirits that come from God and do God's work (i.e., "a holy spirit"). Clearer references to what we would call "the Holy Spirit" include, e.g., Mand. 5.2.5 (34.5); Sim. 5.6.5 (59.5); 9.1.1 (78.1). Yet Osiek cautions that, while Mand. 5.2.5 (34.5) seems to suggest a difference between the Holy Spirit and other good spirits, the attempt to distinguish one good spirit from another and from the "spirit of God" would have been beside the point during this time period when many Jews and Jewish-Christians believed in spirit possession. Osiek, *Shepherd of Hermas*, 33, 119.
[43] For the different ways that Mandate 11 refers to the "spirit" (i.e., the one in opposition to the earthly spirit, which can also dwell within humans), see Gieschen, *Angelomorphic Christology*, 218n11.
[44] Bucur, agreeing with John Christian Wilson, likewise maintains that the term "holy spirits" signifies a plural concept of the Holy Spirit. Bucur, *Angelomorphic Pneumatology*, 124; John Christian Wilson, *Towards a Reassessment of the Shepherd of Hermas: Its Date and Its Pneumatology* (Lewiston: Mellen, 1993), 154n129. For other references to multiple spirits in the *Shepherd*, see, e.g., Mand. 5.2.5 (34.5); 10.1.2 (40.2); Sim. 9.17.4 (94.4).
[45] Bucur, *Angelomorphic Pneumatology*, 118.

sensitive, meek, and tranquil) to the spirit and the angel.⁴⁶ As in Second Temple Jewish texts, the Shepherd speaks of the Spirit in terms of angels and vice versa (causing Bucur, for example, to speak of the Shepherd's "angelomorphic pneumatology").⁴⁷ The Shepherd, though, also speaks of the Spirit in terms of the Church and the Son. In Sim. 9.1.1 [78.1], the Shepherd famously "clarifies" for Hermas that "the Holy Spirit, which spoke with you in the form of the Church . . . that Spirit is the Son of God." In a somewhat tongue-in-cheek comment, Osiek dismisses taking this statement "with complete literalness," for such a "literal" reading would mean that the Spirit, the Church, and the Son were "all one and the same."⁴⁸ I want to suggest, though, that Osiek's "literal" reading is not so far off. These different entities are in fact somehow "one," while being at the same time distinct; the Shepherd's statement points to the Spirit's fluidity, as well as to the fluidity of the divine more broadly.

Angelic Figures

As with "the Spirit/spirits," God is also linked to angels (pneumatic or otherwise) in the Shepherd. On the one hand, angels are sometimes independent beings who are distinct from God and operate more as members of God's heavenly court. In Hermas's first three visions, for example, four, then six, young men appear who are later identified as holy angels who were created first of all and who participate in God's rule (Vis. 1.4.1–3 [4.1–3]; 3.1.6–8 [9.6–8]; 3.2.5–6 [10.5–6]; 3.4.1 [12.1]; Sim. 9.3.1–5 [80.1–5]; 9.6.1–2 [83.1–2]; cf. Sim. 5.5.3 [58.3]).⁴⁹ The

---

46 Indeed, the descriptors "sensitive"/"delicate" (τρυφερός), "meek"/"meekness" (πραότης/πραός), and "tranquil"/"tranquility" (ἡσυχία/ἡσύχιος) are applied to both the spirit (Mand. 5.1.3 [33.3]; 5.2.6 [34.6]) and the angel (Mand. 6.2.3 [36.3]). Bucur, *Angelomorphic Pneumatology*, 118. Contrast this argument with Wilson, who maintains that the angels are different from the spirits (*Towards a Reassessment of the Shepherd of Hermas*, 79). See also Bucur's critique (*Angelomorphic Pneumatology*, 118–19).
47 See also the Shepherd's reference to "the angel of the prophetic spirit" (Mand. 11.9 [43.9]). On the phenomenon of "angelic spirits" in the Second Temple period, see in particular the work of John R. Levison ("The Angelic Spirit in Early Judaism," SBLSP 34 [1995]: 464–93; idem, *The Spirit in First Century Judaism*, esp. 27–55, 229–35).
48 Osiek, *Shepherd of Hermas*, 35. Scholars respond to this confusing comment in a variety of ways. Bucur, for instance, argues that the Son of God is the main subject here, not the polymorphic Holy Spirit (i.e., the Son is the common referent; *Angelomorphic Pneumatology*, 121–23).
49 Note, though, that the six chief angels arguably look more like divine figures when they return in Similitude 9, for they are tall, glorious, and similar in appearance (Sim. 9.3.1 [80.1]). For an argument that these six angels, or "first created ones," represent an angelomorphic representation of the Holy Spirit, see Bucur, *Angelomorphic Pneumatology*, 136–38.

Shepherd himself is identified as the angel of "repentance", or "conversion" (Vis. 5.7 [25.7]; Mand. 12.4.7 [47.7]; 12.6.1 [49.1]; Sim. 9.1.1 [78.1]; 9.14.3 [91.3]; 9.23.5 [100.5]; 9.24.4 [101.4]; 9.31.3 [108.3]; 9.33.1 [110.1]).[50] He is an angel with a specific function (i.e., tending to the task of repentance), and he acts on behalf of God and another angel who sent him (see below).[51] Other individual angels who populate the pages of the Shepherd include angelic figures who interpret Hermas's visions for him (Vis. 2.4.1 [8.1]; 3.10.7–3.13.4 [18.7–21.4]), "the angel of wickedness" (Mand. 6.2.1–10 [36.1–10]), "the angel of luxury and deceit" (Sim. 6.2.1 [62.1]), "the angel of punishment" (Sim. 6.3.2 [63.2]; 7.1–2, 6 [66.1–2, 6]), and the numerous angels who help the six chief angels in the building of the tower (Vis. 3.2.5 [10.5]; 3.4.2 [12.2]; Sim. 9.3.1 [80.1]; cf. Sim. 5.5.3 [58.3]).

On the other hand, in contrast to these individual angels, other angels in the Shepherd intersect with God in more complex ways. Not only do angels overlap with spirits (both divine and demonic), but there are angelic figures who remain largely in the background of the Shepherd and who arguably all refer to the same supreme or "great angel." In the Visions, the Shepherd relates that he was sent by "the most revered angel" (Vis. 5.2 [25.2]), and in the Mandates, the Shepherd again mentions "the most revered angel," this time pronouncing that all who repent are justified, or "made righteous" (ἐδικαιώθησαν), by this angel (Mand. 5.1.7 [33.7]). Halvor Moxnes observes that the actions performed by this most revered angel are in fact actions typically reserved for God.[52] In Jewish Scripture, God is the one who sends angels, and in the Shepherd, God performs this action as well (including instances that specify that God sends the Shepherd).[53] God (and for Christians Jesus) is also typically the one to make human beings righteous (δι-

---

[50] On the translation of μετάνοια as "conversion," see Osiek, *Shepherd of Hermas*, 28–30.
[51] Note that depictions of the Shepherd (like the six chief angels) also sometimes overlap with divine figures. The Shepherd is glorious in appearance (Vis. 5.1 [25.1]), and his appearance, or "form," also transforms (Vis. 5.4 [25.1]; Mand. 12.4.1 [47.1]) in a manner akin to the Lady Church (Vis. 3.11.1–3.13.4 [19.1–21.4]) and other divine figures (see, e.g., Ovid's *Metamorphoses*). On Jesus's corporeal transformation in early Christian literature, see, e.g., Matt 17:2; Mark 9:2–3; Luke 9:29; Gos. Phil. 57:28–58:10; Acts John 90; Acts Pet. 21; Paul Foster, "Polymorphic Christology: Its Origins and Development in Early Christianity," *JTS* 58 (2007): 66–99.
[52] Halvor Moxnes, "God and His Angel in the Shepherd of Hermas," *ST* 28 (1974): 49–56.
[53] Thus while the "most revered angel" sends the Shepherd in Vis. 5.2 (25.2) (cf. Sim. 7.1, 5 [66.1, 5]; 9.1.3 [78.3]), the "Lord" (ὁ κύριος) sends the Shepherd in Sim. 8.6.3 (72.3) and 8.11.1 (77.1) (cf. Vis. 4.2.4 [23.4]; Mand. 4.2.1 [30.1]). In Mand. 12.6.1 (49.1), the passive ἀπεστάλην likewise suggests that God is the subject of the Shepherd's sending (i.e., this is an instance of a divine passive). Moxnes, "God and His Angel in the Shepherd of Hermas," 51–52. With these actions, Moxnes concludes that "ὁ κύριος and this angel seem to be interchangeable" (p. 52). See also Larry W. Hurtado on this point in *Lord Jesus Christ: Devotion to Jesus in Earliest Christianity* (Grand Rapids, MI: Eerdmans, 2003), here 604–605.

καιόω) (e.g., Rom 3:21–26, 30; 8:30, 33; 1 Cor 6:11; Gal 3:8), and in the Shepherd, God elsewhere performs this action (Vis. 3.9.1 [17.1]; cf. Sim. 5.7.1 [60.1]).[54] These shared actions between God and the revered angel lead Moxnes to conclude that this text draws from the *malak Yhwh*—or "the angel of the Lord"—tradition of the Hebrew Bible, a tradition in which the God of Israel encounters humans in theophanies in the form of an angel.[55] Moxnes writes: "it is difficult to distinguish between God and his angel. The angel is sharing in God's own work; he seems to have no activity apart from that. We seem to be nearer to the OT understanding of the 'malak Yahweh' more than to any specific angelic figure in later development of angelology."[56]

This same *malak Yhwh* also arguably appears in the Similitudes of the Shepherd, especially since the specific title "the angel of the Lord" likewise appears (Sim. 7.5 [66.5]; 8.1.2, 5 [67.2, 5]; 8.2.1 [68.1]). In the Similitudes, the angel who sends the Shepherd to Hermas is now called "the angel of the Lord" (Sim. 7.5 [66.5]), as well as "the glorious angel" (Sim. 7.1 [66.1]; 9.1.3 [78.3]; cf. 5.4.4 [57.4]).[57] In Similitude 8, the angel of the Lord who prunes and inspects the willow tree (i.e., the church) brings both of these descriptors together, for he is "the angel of the Lord" and also "glorious and very tall" (Sim. 8.1.2 [67.2]).[58] To be sure, later in Similitude 8, this particular angel in charge of the willow tree is identified as the archangel Michael (the Shepherd explains that "the great and glorious angel is Michael" [Sim. 8.3.3 {69.3}]). This later identification, however, does not necessarily mean that the angel in Similitude 8 (or the *malak Yhwh* in the text as a whole) is simply a member of God's heavenly court. For one, there is at times a blurriness between God and principal angels like Michael in Second Temple Jewish texts (and between Jesus and principal angels in early Christian texts).[59] Second, it may also be the case that the *malak Yhwh* himself (who appears elsewhere in the Shepherd) becomes manifest as the archangel Michael

---

[54] See also, e.g., Vis. 3.1.6 (9.6); Mand. 1.2 (26.2); 5.2.1 (34.1); 6.2.10 (36.10); 12.6.2 (49.2); Sim. 6.1.4 (61.4); Moxnes, "God and His Angel in the Shepherd of Hermas," 53. On other shared actions between the "great angel" and God, see Moxnes, "God and His Angel in the Shepherd of Hermas."

[55] On this tradition, see, e.g., Sommer, *Bodies of God*, 40–44.

[56] Moxnes, "God and His Angel in the Shepherd of Hermas," 55.

[57] Note that in Sim. 10.1.1 (111.1), the angel who sent the Shepherd to Hermas appears again (this time without any other descriptors). See discussion below.

[58] On how exceeding tallness, or supernatural height, is a descriptor often associated with divine beings, see, e.g., Ovid, *Fast.* 2.503–504; *Metam.* 9.268–270; Gos. Pet. 10:40; Hippolytus of Rome, *Haer.* 9.8.

[59] See especially Darrell D. Hannah, *Michael and Christ: Michael Traditions and Angel Christology in Early Christianity*, WUNT 2/109 (Tübingen: Mohr Siebeck, 1999).

in Similitude 8. The equation of the "great angel" with Michael is certainly not evident elsewhere in the narrative, and so they may be two different angels who directly overlap in Similitude 8 given their similar descriptors and functions. Third and finally, a number of interpreters argue that the angel in Similitude 8— and indeed the "great angel" in the text as a whole—is in fact the Son, Jesus. But before we explore this latter point in more detail, let us now turn to the Son: the final "form" in which God becomes manifest in the Shepherd.

The Son of God

Of course, Jesus—like the other characters surveyed thus far—is a distinct character in the Shepherd and a character that is also distinct from God. Jesus is repeatedly referred to as "the Son" or "the Son of God" throughout the narrative, and this "sonship" is articulated in relation to the character of God, who is the Son's (and the Spirit's!) "Father" (Sim. 5.6.3–4 [59.3–4]; 9.12.2 [89.2]; cf. the Spirit as God's "Son" in Similitude 5). The titles "Son" and "Son of God" are Jesus's primary epithets; the name "Jesus" itself never occurs in the Shepherd, and the title "Christ" only appears in a handful of manuscript variants.[60] Jesus's distinction from God emerges in particular during the extended parable of the vineyard in Similitude 5, where we find all three characters of God, Jesus, and the Spirit emerging as distinct entities. Indeed, it is because of this parable that many scholars label the Shepherd as having an "adoptionist" christology.[61] I am of the opinion, which I share with a growing number of scholars, that it is problematic to label the Shepherd as "adoptionist."[62] Not only is it problematic to import later Christological controversies and categories back onto this early second century text, but the Shepherd evinces no interest in providing "doctrine" or a systematic christology and the so-called "adoptionist" language of Similitude 5 itself is far too ambiguous to make a concrete claim either way (al-

---

60 Osiek, *Shepherd of Hermas*, 34.
61 "Adoptionistic" interpretations of Similitude 5 have persisted since the influential work of Adolf von Harnack (*History of Dogma*, 7 vols., trans. Neil Buchanan et al. [London: Williams & Norgate, 1896–99], 1:191–99).
62 Michael F. Bird, for example, concludes that it is better to speak of a christology of pre-existence and exaltation in the Shepherd rather than an "adoptionist" christology (*Jesus the Eternal Son: Answering Adoptionist Christology* [Grand Rapids, MI: Eerdmans, 2017], 107–112). See also, e.g., Bucur, *Angelomorphic Pneumatology*, 126–36; Hurtado, *Lord Jesus Christ*, 603–605; Peppard, *The Son of God in the Roman World*, 148–52.

though there is nothing to prohibit a later adoptionist re-reading!).[63] Regardless, the parable does demonstrate a triad of God, Spirit, and Son and indicates that each of these characters have distinct roles within the narrative world of the parable.[64]

But while Jesus is distinct from God in the Shepherd, Jesus also overlaps with God in a variety of different ways. Jesus's title "Lord" (κύριος) is one way in which this overlapping occurs. While the majority of references to "Lord" are references to God, a few specifically refer to Jesus and link Jesus to God. In Vis. 2.2.8 (6.8), for instance, we read: "For the Lord has sworn by his Son that those who have denied their Lord have been rejected from their life." Here the narrator differentiates between the Lord and the Son, but the second reference to "their Lord" appears to denote Jesus since the Son is the immediate antecedent (and indeed, some manuscripts read "Christ" or "Son" instead of "their Lord" here).[65] While the narrator's application of this title to Jesus should not be pushed too far since Hermas also addresses individual angels (such as the Shepherd) as "Lord" (and the Church as "Lady"), the narrator is clear that Jesus is a character who has "great authority and lordship" (Sim 5.6.1 [59.1]) and who is "Lord of the people, having received all authority from his Father" (Sim. 5.6.4 [59.4]).[66]

Another way that Jesus overlaps with God is through the divine attribute of God's "Name." In the Shepherd, as in other early Christian texts, the transference of this divine attribute to Jesus is striking, especially since Jesus's "Name," like God's "Name," has agency at times.[67] The import of Jesus's "Name" particularly emerges in Similitude 9—the most christologically-focused section of the Shep-

---

[63] It is striking, however, that later Christians refrain from labeling the Shepherd as "adoptionist" or condemning it as heretical. (On this point, see Bucur, *Angelomorphic Pneumatology*, 113–14, 134; Osiek, *Shepherd of Hermas*, 179–80; cf. Bird, *Jesus the Eternal Son*, 112n5; Hannah, *Michael and Christ*, 191–92.) Among modern scholars, the debate largely revolves around the explanation of the parable in Sim. 5.6.4b–7 (59.4b–7) and whether "flesh" here refers to Jesus or to the individual human in general. For an overview of this debate, see Osiek, *Shepherd of Hermas*, 179–81. See also Bucur, *Angelomorphic Pneumatology*, 126–36; Peppard, *The Son of God in the Roman World*, 148–52.
[64] Although note that Bucur, for example, argues that the "son" and "the slave" in the parable are two *aspects* of Christ, not two distinct characters (i.e., the Spirit and the Son) (*Angelomorphic Pneumatology*, 127).
[65] S reads "Christ"; L¹ reads "Son."
[66] Note that in Similitude 9, Jesus is "the lord" of the tower (Sim. 9.7.1 [84.1]), as well as its "master" (δεσπότης) (Sim. 9.5.7 [82.7]; 9.7.6 [84.6]; 9.9.4 [86.4]), which is yet another title for God (e.g., Vis. 3.3.5 [11.5]; Sim. 1.9 [50.9]).
[67] For a survey of "Name Christology" in the early church, see Charles A. Gieschen, "The Divine Name in Ante-Nicene Christology," *VC* 57 (2003): 115–58.

herd as a whole. Here we find a number of references to people bearing "the Name" and suffering on behalf of "the Name," recalling instances where people bear and suffer on behalf of God's Name.[68] Believers also preach "the Name of the Son of God" (Sim. 9.16.5 [93.5]) and come to know "the Name of the Son of God" (Sim. 9.16.7 [93.7]). Nations, moreover, are "called by the Name of the Son of God" (Sim. 9.17.4 [94.4]), and no one can enter the kingdom of God "unless they receive the Name of his Son" (Sim. 9.12.4 [89.4]; cf. Sim. 9.12.5, 8 [89.5, 8]; 9.13.2, 7 [90.2, 7]; 9.19.2 [96.2]).[69] Most striking of all is the following statement: "The Name of the Son of God is great and uncontained and supports the entire cosmos. If, therefore, all of creation is supported by the Son of God, what do you think of those who are called by him and who bear the Name of the Son of God and walk in his commandments?" (Sim. 9.14.5 [91.5]).[70] In this declaration, Jesus's Name sustains the very cosmos and is also "uncontained" (ἀχώρητος), an attribute otherwise only ascribed to God (Mand. 1.1 [26.1]) and that connects Jesus to God's own fluidity or "uncontainability."[71]

Jesus, as noted earlier, also has close links with God's Spirit, to the point where many scholars argue that the Shepherd has a "pneumatic christology."[72] The clearest evidence for this connection between Jesus and the Spirit occurs,

---

[68] On bearing "the Name" in Similitude 9, see 9.13.2, 3 (90.2, 3); 9.14.5, 6 (91.5, 6); 9.15.2 (92.2); 9.16.3 (93.3); 9.17.4 (94.4); 9.28.5 (105.5). (Cf. Sim. 9.13.3–5 [90.3–5]; 9.15.1–3 [92.1-3].) On suffering on behalf of "the Name" in Similitude 9, see Sim. 9.28.2, 3 (twice), 5 (105.2, 3 [twice], 5); cf. 9.21.3 (98.3); 9.28.6 (105.6). With these references, it is not always clear in the narrative and/or the manuscript tradition whether believers bear and suffer for God's Name or Jesus's Name, but this ambiguity is precisely my point. In some cases, either referent makes sense. Note, though, that historically speaking, declaring Jesus's name became a testing ground for Christians under persecution (cf. Osiek, *Shepherd of Hermas*, 56, 63, 71).
[69] Note again the ambiguity between God's Name and the Son's Name. For example, in Sim. 9.17.4 (94.4), A (Codex Athous) lacks "Son" and in Sim. 9.12.4 (89.4), A reads "his holy name" (Leutzsch, *Hirt des Hermas*, 322–23, 332–33). Note too the references that arguably refer to God's Name calling people (Sim. 8.1.1 [67.1]; 9.14.3 [91.3]).
[70] Because of this statement in particular, Gieschen concludes that "*Hermas* contains a very Jewish and highly developed theology of the Divine Name" (*Angelomorphic Christology*, 227). See also Gieschen, "The Divine Name in Ante-Nicene Christology," 152–53.
[71] Osiek (*Shepherd of Hermas*, 236) likewise observes that the terminology of being "uncontained" only applies to God and Jesus in the *Shepherd*. On this point, see also Sim. 9.2.1 (79.1); here Jesus is depicted as a rock that has the power "to contain" (χωρῆσαι) the entire cosmos.
[72] See, e.g., Norbert Brox, *Der Hirt des Hermas*, KAV 7 (Göttingen: Vandenhoeck & Ruprecht, 1991), 493–95; Gieschen, *Angelomorphic Christology*, 222–25; Wilson, *Towards a Reassessment of the Shepherd of Hermas*, 162–65. Like "adoptionist," the label of "pneumatic christology" or "spirit christology" also goes back to Harnack. See Harnack, *History of Dogma*, 1:191–99; Bucur, *Angelomorphic Pneumatology*, 130–31n52.

once again, in Similitude 9. Here we learn that the virgins who appeared to Hermas are "holy spirits" and are at the same time "powers of the Son of God" (Sim. 9.13.2 [90.2]), and we also learn that Hermas himself received the Son's "spirit" (Sim. 9.24.4 [101.4]).[73] However, Sim. 9.1.1 (78.1) is the clearest place where the confluence between the Spirit and the Son occurs. As noted earlier, the Shepherd at this point declares to Hermas: "I want to show you what the Holy Spirit, who spoke with you in the form of the Church, showed you; for that Spirit is the Son of God." In what Carolyn Osiek labels as one of the Shepherd's "most frustrating statements," there is a blurring of the distinction between the Spirit and the Son (not to mention the Church!).[74] Moreover, this blurring continues when the narrator later portrays the Son as being preexistent (a point that poses a problem for those who claim that the Shepherd is "adoptionist"). Like the Spirit (Sim. 5.6.5 [59.5]), and indeed the Church (Vis. 2.4.1 [8.1]), the Son exists before the rest of creation (Sim. 9.12.2 [89.2]). In his preexistent state, the Son himself is both a "counselor" to his Father in the act of creation and the one who also possibly creates since the narrator refers to "his [i.e., the Son's] creation" (Sim. 9.12.2 [89.2]).[75]

Finally, in addition to the Son's manifestations as God's Name and Spirit, the Son may also become manifest as the "great angel" or *malak Yhwh*. As noted earlier, scholars often argue that the "great angel" who appears throughout the Shepherd is Jesus.[76] They arrive at this conclusion largely because of the connections between the angel who inspects the willow branches in Similitude 8 and the "lord" (i.e., Jesus) who inspects the tower in Similitude 9. In Similitude 9, the lord of the tower is described as a tall, glorious man (Sim. 9.6.1 [83.1]; 9.7.1

---

[73] In Sim. 9.24.4 (101.4), A speaks of the Son's "seed" instead of "spirit."

[74] Osiek, *Shepherd of Hermas*, 35. As noted earlier in n. 48, Bucur maintains that the Son is the main referent here. For Bucur, the statement that the Spirit speaks in the form of the Church is primarily "symbolic," in that the Church is an adaptive manifestation of the Spirit/Son used to convey the divine presence to Hermas at an earlier stage of his spiritual ascent (*Angelomorphic Pneumatology*, 120–23).

[75] The role of being a "counselor" to God in the act of creation is a Wisdom motif; see Prov 8:22–31; Wis 9:9; Sir 24:10; Osiek, *Shepherd of Hermas*, 233. The role of straddling the Creator/creation divide is also a Wisdom motif (see earlier discussion).

[76] Martin Dibelius was an influential proponent of the position that the various angels in the Shepherd functioned christologically (*Die apostolischen Väter IV: Der Hirt des Hermas*, HNT [Tübingen: Mohr Siebeck, 1923], esp. 572–76). See also, e.g., Brox, *Hirt des Hermas*, 362–65, 490–92; Gieschen, *Angelomorphic Christology*, 220–25; Hannah, *Michael and Christ*, 187–88; Moxnes, "God and His Angel in the Shepherd of Hermas," 49–56. Contrast this position with, e.g., Pernveden, *The Concept of the Church in the Shepherd of Hermas*, 58–64. For an overview of this debate, see Osiek, *Shepherd of Hermas*, 34–35.

[84.1]; 9.12.8 [89.8]) and thus appears with the same descriptors as the angel in Similitude 8 (indeed, "the angel of the Lord" is "glorious and very tall" in Sim. 8.1.2 [67.2]; cf. 8.3.3 [69.3]).[77] The lord in Similitude 9 also performs the same role of inspecting members of the church, with the verb "to inspect" (κατανοεῖν) occurring in both Similitudes (Sim. 9.5.6–7 [82.6–7]; cf. 8.1.5 [67.5]), and he likewise delegates part of his authority to the Shepherd (Sim. 9.7.1–3 [84.1–3]; cf. 8.2.5 [68.5]).[78] Since the lord of the tower, or "glorious man," is explicitly called the Son of God (Sim. 9.12.8 [89.8]), this leads commentators to surmise that the angel who inspects the willow tree (and the great angel more broadly) is also the Son of God. Some scholars object that the angel in Similitude 8 could not possibly be the Son since the angel in Similitude 8 is Michael (Sim. 8.3.3 [69.3]). But as Darrell Hannah argues, identifying Jesus with a principal angel like Michael would not be out of the realm of possibility for early Christians, especially since the Son and Michael both perform similar roles in the narrative (see also Sim. 5.6.2–3 [59.2–3]; 8.3.2–3 [69.2–3]).[79] If we do identify the Son with Michael and/or the great angel more broadly, then it also means that the narrative as a whole ends on a Christological note, for the angel who sent the Shepherd to Hermas (i.e., the great angel) appears and delivers parting words in the final Similitude of the Shepherd (Sim. 10.1.1–10.4.4 [111.1–114.4]).[80] Though it is not always clear whether the Son is the "great angel" in the Shepherd as a whole, the text's suggestive overlapping of the Son's images and roles with the angel can certainly elicit the identification (and indeed has). There is an ambiguity in this overlapping, but the ambiguity is the very reason why at least some interpreters see the Son as a manifestation of God's angel: the *malak Yhwh* from Jewish Scripture.

---

[77] In Similitude 9, the glorious man is of supernatural stature, for he stands taller than the tower itself (Sim. 9.6.1 [83.1]). On how supernatural stature is used as an indicator of divinity, see the references listed earlier in n. 58. Of these references, note in particular Hippolytus of Rome, *Haer.* 9.8. Here the heretic Elchasai has a vision of the Son of God as an angel of great height (see, e.g., Osiek, *Shepherd of Hermas*, 28).

[78] Osiek, *Shepherd of Hermas*, 223. For a helpful comparison between the angel in Similitude 8 and the Son in Similitude 9, see Osiek, *Shepherd of Hermas*, 234–235n19; Pernveden, *Concept of the Church*, 63–64.

[79] Hannah, *Michael and Christ*, esp. 187–88. See also Hannah's discussion here of how both Michael and Christ dispense the Law according to Sim. 5.6.2–3 (59.2–3); 8.3.2–3 (69.2–3).

[80] The angel in Similitude 10, though not named, assumes a place of authority on a couch with the Shepherd standing at the angel's right hand (Sim. 10.1.1 [111.1]). This final divine/human encounter recalls Vision 3, wherein "the Holiness" has the place of authority on a couch and those of lesser importance sit to the right or left.

Conclusion

In this essay, I have argued that the Jewish tradition of divine fluidity best accounts for the ways in which God—and other divine beings—are portrayed in the Shepherd of Hermas. In this tradition, God primarily dwells in heaven (e.g., Vis. 1.1.6 [1.6]), yet can also become manifest on earth in visions and other concrete encounters. Indeed, God is "one" (e.g., Mand. 1.1 [26.1]), yet also encounters humans in a variety of different forms. Many of these forms are seen and experienced as anthropomorphic entities (both male and female), and some of these forms even inhabit humans themselves.[81] In this sense, the Shepherd portrays God as one who blurs the boundaries between Creator and creation and between the divine and the human. God is not the only one who creates, for the Spirit and the Son create too (Sim. 5.6.5 [59.5]; 9.12.2 [89.2]; cf. Mand. 12.4.2 [47.2]); God is not the only divine being, for humans and anthropomorphic entities can become manifestations of the divine. Because of this boundary blurring, the God of the Shepherd of Hermas emerges in a manner akin to the embodied God of many Jewish scriptural texts: an embodiment that, for the Shepherd, also cannot be separated from the embodied life of humans within the Church.[82]

---

[81] There are also, of course, a range of non-anthropomorphic ways in which the divine becomes manifest in the Shepherd. Although many of us today would probably not consider these manifestations to be "embodied," this was not always the case in the ancient world. See, for example, Matthew Thiessen, who draws from Sommer's discussion of God's "rock body" in Jewish Scripture and argues that Paul (among other early Christian authors) equates this rock with Jesus himself ("'The Rock was Christ': The Fluidity of Christ's Body in 1 Corinthians 10.4," *JSNT* 36 [2013]: 103–26). (In addition to 1 Cor 10:4, see also, e.g., Matt 21:42; Acts 4:11; Rom 9:33; 1 Pet 2:6–8; Justin, *Dial.* 113.) Note that the Shepherd makes a similar move with its identification of Jesus as a rock. After several references to this "rock" in Similitude 9, Hermas's question to the Shepherd in 9.12.1 (89.1) anticipates an anthropomorphic answer, for he asks not "what" is the rock, but "who" (τίς) (Osiek, *Shepherd of Hermas*, 233).

[82] As commentators often note, the Shepherd's portrayal of christology and so forth is ultimately in service to its emphasis on moral teaching and soteriology (e.g., Osiek, *Shepherd of Hermas*, 36). God's "body," then, I would argue, is expressly connected to the body of the church in the Shepherd.

* I would like to thank Bogdan Bucur and the participants of Duke's New Testament Colloquia for their feedback on this essay.

III Experiencing the Shepherd as Text

Marianne Bjelland Kartzow
The Former Slave Hermas, Lady Church and 'the Book'

Rethinking the Visions with Intersectionality and Book History

Recent studies of gender and book history have challenged the idea that writing, reading, and books were elite male domains. In the opening visions of the Shepherd of Hermas, we find an ongoing dialogue between a former male slave and an old female divine being in which book production and transmission, including activities such as reading, copying, memorizing and editing, are described. I am puzzled by the relationship between the old female figure, the Lady Church, and Hermas, and what role 'the book' plays, as artifact, container of meaning, symbolic tool, mediator, and means of power. Intersections of gender, age, and social status are central in order to rethink their complex relationship to each other and to the book. In this essay, I will map encounters between the Lady Church and Hermas in which 'the book' plays a role, but also discuss in what way the two characters represent exceptions or are commonplace to the ancient book culture.

Book production and circulation in antiquity were complex processes. Oral and written texts could overlap. Not only were male elites involved, women may have been scribes, and they appear as holders and readers of books.[1] In addition, slaves, both male and female, could play roles in book cultures.[2] With such perspectives, several elements of the opening visions of the Shepherd of Hermas are of great interest: the Lady Church is introduced as holding a book in her hands. She is confused with the Sibyl. She reads aloud for Hermas, but he struggles to memorize. He copies from her book, letter by letter. At one

---
[1] On women and book culture in the ancient world, see Sarit Kattan Gribetz, "Women as Readers of the Nag Hammadi Codices," *JECS* 26 (2018): 463–94. See also Kim Haines-Eitzen, "'Girls Trained in Beautiful Writing': Female Scribes in Roman Antiquity and Early Christianity," *JECS* 6 (1998): 629–46.
[2] Haines-Eitzen, "'Girls Trained in Beautiful Writing'," 641. For a discussion of various possible occupations for ancient slaves, see Jennifer A. Glancy, *Slavery in Early Christianity* (Oxford: Oxford University Press, 2002), 42–45.

point, she refers to an otherwise unknown book, a book known only by title.³ Hermas is also asked to send a copy of the book to Clement and a certain "Grapte," who "will admonish the widows and orphans," echoing an all-female book network. The book, as it were, plays a key role in the first two visions in complex and interesting ways. By paying attention to 'the book', I will explore details of the text most often overlooked by interpreters.

The Shepherd of Hermas is often characterized as an apocalypse, with a series of revelations made to Hermas. It records five visions experienced by Hermas, and it is named after the angel of repentance who appears in the fifth vision dressed as a shepherd. The Shepherd was probably written late 1st or mid-2nd century CE and seems to have had a great influence among early Christian groups.⁴ Some early Christian writers such as Irenaeus considered the Shepherd to be part of the Christian canon. In Codex Sinaiticus, the Shepherd, together with the Epistle of Barnabas, appears after Revelation. In the Codex Claromontanus, it is between the Acts of the Apostles and the Acts of Paul. According to Bart Ehrman, the Shepherd of Hermas was one of the most popular books of early Christianity. He argues: "Judged from the manuscript remains, it was copied and read more widely in the second and third centuries than any other non-canonical book, even more than many of the books that later came to be included in the New Testament."⁵ It had a canonical rank, at least temporarily.⁶ Harry O. Maier writes, "The Shepherd of Hermas was one of the most widely read and

---

3 See Marianne B. Kartzow, Liv Ingeborg Lied, and Esther Brownsmith, (eds.), *Books Known Only by Title*, a special themed issue of *Studies in Late Antiquity* 6 (2022): forthcoming.
4 Kirsopp Lake, ed., *The Shepherd of Hermas, The Martyrdom of Polycarp, The Epistle to Diognetus, The Apostolic Fathers*, vol. 2, LCL (London: William Heinemann; New York: G.P. Putnam's Sons, 1913), 3. For other introductory matters, see B. Diane Lipsett, *Desiring Conversion: Hermas, Thecla, Aseneth* (New York: Oxford University Press, 2011), 23–28. Carolyn Osiek, *Rich and Poor in the Shepherd of Hermas: An Exegetical-Social Investigation*, CBQMS 15 (Washington, DC: Catholic Biblical Association of America, 1983), 1–14. David Hellholm, *Das Visionenbuch des Hermas als Apokalypse. Formgeschichtliche und texttheoretische Studien zu einer literarischen Gattung*, ConBOT 1 (Lund: C. W. K. Gleerup, 1980).
5 Bart D. Ehrman, ed., *Epistle of Barnabas, Papias and Quadratus, Epistle to Diognetus, The Shepherd of Hermas*, vol. 2 of *The Apostolic Fathers* (Cambridge, MA: Harvard University Press, 2003), 162. All quotations of the Shepherd are taken from this edition.
6 Jörg Rüpke, "Fighting for Differences: Forms and Limits of Religious Individuality in the 'Shepherd of Hermas'," in *The Individual in the Religions of the Ancient Mediterranean*, ed. Jörg Rüpke (Oxford: Oxford Scholarship Online, 2013), 315–41, here 319. For a discussion of and criteria for Hermas's canonical status, see Dan Batovici, "The Shepherd of Hermas in Recent Scholarship on the Canon: A Review Article," *ASE* 34 (2017): 89–105, here 100–1.

geographically distributed writings of Christ religion in the pre-Constantinian period."[7]

The Shepherd is a long, loose, and repetitive narrative. Broadly speaking, it is divided into three parts: Book of Visions, Mandates, and Similitudes. It has been called the "jewel of non-canonical writings" and is often valued for its delightful and open-hearted character.[8] Most interpreters agree it is primarily concerned with *metanoia*, repentance or conversion, especially for believers who have been baptized.[9]

According to the opening scene, Hermas was raised as a slave by one owner and then sold to a woman at Rome named Rhoda: " Ὁ θρέψας με πέπρακέν με Ῥόδῃ τινὶ εἰς Ῥώμην" (Vis. 1.1.1 [1.1]). To present the protagonist or narrator as born and sold a slave is unique in early Christian literature. He was once a slave, but no clear description of his manumission is given.[10] According to Proctor, this background information contributes to the construction of Hermas as an idealized reader, scribe, and author of early Christianity.[11] Hermas probably became a freedman after staying with Rhoda, since he appears to have a wife and children, became a rich merchant, but lost his property.[12] Rhoda is also transfigured into a divine messenger later in the vision. Scholars discuss Hermas's vivid autobiography: how should one interpret the opening lines of the first vision; is the information authentic, a description of the author's own life experiences?[13] We do not have any information about who wrote the text, apart from the details

---

[7] Harry O. Maier, "Romans Watching Romans: Christ Religion in Close Urban Quarters and Neighbourhood Transformations," *Religion in the Roman Empire* 6 (2020): 106–21, here 110.
[8] Lipsett, *Desiring Conversion*, 23 and 19. See also Steve Young, "Being a Man: The Pursuit of Manliness in 'The Shepherd of Hermas'," *JECS* 2 (1994): 237–55, here 254.
[9] Lipsett, *Desiring Conversion*, 19–21. See also the introduction in Carolyn Osiek, *Rich and Poor in the Shepherd of Hermas*.
[10] See the discussion in Carolyn Osiek, *Shepherd of Hermas: A Commentary*, Hermeneia: A Critical and Historical Commentary on the Bible (Minneapolis: Fortress Press, 1999). See also Jonathan E. Soyars, *The Shepherd of Hermas and the Pauline Legacy* (Leiden: Brill, 2019).
[11] Travis W. Proctor, "Books, Scribes, and Cultures of Reading in the Shepherd of Hermas," *Journal of Ecclesiastical History* 72 (2021): 1–19.
[12] Frank L. Cross and E.A. Livingstone, eds., "Hermas," *ODCC*, 2nd ed. (Oxford: Oxford University Press, 2006).
[13] I discuss this so-called autobiographical data as it relates to the use of the slavery metaphor in the whole text in Marianne Bjelland Kartzow, *The Slave Metaphor and Gendered Enslavement in Early Christian Discourse: Double Trouble Embodied*, Routledge Studies in the Early Christian World (London: Routledge, 2018), 105–24. See also a similar connection made between the opening lines and one of the parables in Mary Ann Beavis, "The Parable of the Slave, Son, and Vineyard: An Early Christian Freedman's Narrative (Hermas Similitudes 5.2–11)," *CBQ* 80 (2018): 655–69.

in the narrative itself. Suggestions have been given that it comes from Rome, from a Jewish-Christian setting,[14] by an author with a limited level of education.[15] According to Joseph Verheyden, "Hermas did not receive any formal theological training, and has only a very limited acquaintance with theological reasoning and argumentation."[16] Still, he is portrayed as being able to read and copy, so he must have had at least some informal training. Perhaps the owners he had, including a woman, taught him the basics?[17] I take the personal information and writer profile to be part of the narrative frame, where the implied author presents himself as a former slave. I focus on the visions part in the beginning, but I do not discuss whether this part ever circulated as a separate part of the Shepherd.[18]

Book History and Intersectionality

Before mapping the various encounters with 'the book', I will briefly present the theoretical tools employed in this study. Recently, more attention has been directed to how insights from the discipline of book history can illuminate biblical studies, for example through the SBL Program Unit *Book History and Biblical Literature*, initiating "a theoretical and historical conversation about the culturally contingent concepts of text, authorship, readership, publication, and materiality."[19] The field of book history is concerned with all aspects of the book, such as the history of the creation, dissemination, and reception of script

---

[14] "It is a text of a Roman Jew," according to Rüpke, "Fighting for Differences," 320.
[15] See the discussion of Hermas's possible level of education, knowledge, and background in Soyars, *The Shepherd of Hermas and the Pauline Legacy*, 32.
[16] Joseph Verheyden, "The Shepherd of Hermas," *ExpTim* 117 (2006): 397–401, here 398.
[17] If Rhoda belonged to the upper socio-economic strata, she could be literate; see Jennifer A. Sheridan, "Not at a Loss for Words: The Economic Power of Literate Women in Late Antique Egypt," *Transactions of the American Philological Association* 128 (1974): 189–203, here 189.
[18] "Without doubt, the first four visions originally formed an independent text to which the later part refers," in Rüpke, "Fighting for Differences," 317. For a further discussion of the manuscript situation behind this discussion, see Dan Batovici, "Textual Revisions of the *Shepherd of Hermas* in Codex Sinaiticus," *ZAC* 18 (2014): 443–70; Dan Batovici, "Two Notes on the Papyri of the *Shepherd of Hermas*," *APF* 62 (2017): 385–95. For a recent discussion of the manuscript situation, see also Soyars, *The Shepherd of Hermas and the Pauline Legacy*, 4–8.
[19] See Daniel Picus' description of "Book History and Biblical Literatures" (paper presented at the Annual Meeting of the SBL, San Diego, CA, 2019), https://www.sbl-site.org/meetings/Congresses_ProgramUnits.aspx?MeetingId=35.

and printed materials.[20] The role the book plays in the Shepherd, including descriptions of the their dissemination and reception, will be used as an entry point to explore issues of authority, power relations, and social networks.

I will build on studies in which the role of women in scribal cultures of antiquity have been addressed. Since the Lady Church is the main character in charge of the book in the Visions, I will employ theories challenging the idea that book production and circulation were male elite phenomena.[21] In addition to this divine female figure, however, Hermas, a former male slave of a female owner, also takes part in book creation and dissemination. In order to engage the diversity of social categories and complex relationships as they appear in the Visions, I will employ theories of intersectionality. To understand the encounter in which 'the book' plays a central role, gender, sexuality, age, and social position must be taken into account. The central insight in the study of intersectionality is that various categories, such as gender, class, race, ethnicity, religion, age, ability, etc. mutually construct but also destabilize each other.[22] Gender is not stable when it intersects with status: a former male slave who was sexually attracted to his female owner was not necessarily a proper man.[23] Self-control and strength were vital to male identity construction, a possible challenge for a former slave.[24] A younger woman such as Rhoda represented a different kind of gender and sexual capital than an old one, such as the Lady Church. Accordingly, in order to understand the social environment of our ancient texts, we need to look at intersections and overlaps of categories and classification systems. To employ intersectional theories to rethink the complexity of hierarchy, identity and interrelatedness in early Christianity has pro-

---

20 For more on book history origins, see David Finkelstein and Alistair McCleery, "Theorizing the History of Books," in *An Introduction to Book History* (London/ New York: Routledge, 2005), 7–28.
21 Most people in the ancient world were illiterate, but with some interesting exceptions. A literate woman, accordingly, was a rarity. "Only among the upper socio-economic classes could one expect to find any women who could read and write," according to Sheridan, "Not at a Loss for Words," 189.
22 See Kimberle Crenshaw, "Demarginalizing the Intersection of Race and Sex: A Black Feminist Critique of Antidiscrimination Doctrine, Feminist Theory and Antiracist Politics," *The University of Chicago Legal Forum* 140 (1989): 139–67; Lena Gunnarsson, "Why We Keep Separating the 'Inseparable': Dialecticizing Intersectionality," *European Journal of Women's Studies* 24 (2017): 114–27.
23 I discuss this in Chapter 5 of Kartzow, *The Slave Metaphor and Gendered Enslavement in Early Christian Discourse*.
24 Jennifer A. Glancy, "Protocols of Masculinity in the Pastoral Epistles," in *New Testament Masculinities*, ed. Stephen D. Moore and Janice Capel Anderson, Semeia 45 (Atlanta: SBL Press, 2003), 235–64.

ven useful.²⁵ Intersectionality offers a nuanced and detailed heuristic tool that helps us better grasp the complex social web in which the Shepherd operates. This includes the way it constructs an encounter in which 'the book' plays a crucial role.²⁶

Mapping 'the book' as Mediator of Divine Revelation: Book Holding, Reading, Hearing, Memorizing, Copying, and Editing

What kind of discourses and practices related to books and book practices does the Shepherd describe? In this first part of the text, Hermas gets his visions from a divine female figure resembling Rhoda, the Lady Church, and different angels through three different media: oral, written, and visual.²⁷ I will highlight the role 'the book' plays as a revelation channel. In particular, it is in the dialogue between Hermas and the Lady Church where reading, writing, book production, and distribution are discussed. I will pay attention to three dimensions of book culture: first, I explore the role of 'the book' as a mediator for revelation; second, I briefly look at the phenomenon of *books known only by titles*; third, I reflect on how the book copied by Hermas is supposed to be circulated and made known.

---

25 Elisabeth Schüssler Fiorenza, "Introduction: Exploring the Intersections of Race, Gender, Status, and Ethnicity in Early Christian Studies," in *Prejudice and Christian Beginnings: Investigating Race, Gender and Ethnicity in Early Christian Studies*, ed. Laura Nasrallah and Elisabeth Schüssler Fiorenza (Minneapolis: Fortress Press, 2009), 1–23; Marianne Bjelland Kartzow, "Intersectional Studies," in *The Oxford Encyclopedia of the Bible and Gender Studies*, ed. Julia M. O'Brien (New York: Oxford University Press, 2014), 364–89.
26 Marianne Bjelland Kartzow, *Destabilizing the Margins: An Intersectional Approach to Early Christian Memory* (Eugene, OR: Pickwick Publications, 2012).
27 Aldo Tagliabue, "Learning from Allegorical Images in the *Book of Visions* of The Shepherd of Hermas," *Arethusa* 50 (2017): 221–55, here 227. See also Edith McEwan Humphrey, *The Ladies and the Cities: Transformation and Apocalyptic Identity in Joseph and Aseneth, 4 Ezra, the Apocalypse and the Shepherd of Hermas*, JSPSup 17 (Sheffield: Sheffield Academic Press, 1995), 139–41.

The Role of the Book and Book Creation

A book in her hands. The second divine female character in Hermas is introduced as sitting on a big, white chair, having a book in her hands (ἔχουσα βιβλίον εἰς τὰς χεῖρας [Vis. 1.2.2 (2.2)]). She is old and clothed in shining garments. She sits down alone and greets Hermas and asks why he is sad after his encounter with the divine version of Rhoda. Why is the Lady Church holding a book and what book is this supposed to be? The bible? At the time Hermas was written obviously no fixed collection of canonical books existed. The book in her hands is not primarily there as an instance of decorum or an arbitrary artefact, but as a symbol of power and truth, to construct her as an authoritative figure. We do not get any clear picture of which book she holds or the content of it when she is introduced.[28] In the overall story, however, several books (but not necessarily this book!) play important roles: she mentions "the books of life" (τὰς βίβλους τῆς ζωῆς [Vis. 1.3.2 (3.2)]) in which the members of Hermas's household will be recorded if they repent from sin.[29] Later, she asks if he wants her to read for him, a scene to be explored below. Then she walks and reads, edits and initiates circulation. She is doing many things with books, but not necessarily with this book. It becomes clear that 'the book' as a container of meaning, truth, and knowledge plays a central role in constructing her as a divine being. She has the revelations there in her hands. Her first appearance with 'the book' sets the stage for the whole encounter and the relationship between the two characters, the Lady Church and Hermas. This is a revelation dialogue in which the book plays a key role.

Reading, Hearing, and Remembering

The Divine Lady asks Hermas if he wants her to read for him (Vis. 1.3.3 [3.3]), presumably from the book she holds in her hands. He approves and hears great but also terrifying matters. The problem is, however, that when she reads, he is not able to remember everything. He only remembers the final words, a longer discourse about God's glory and creation. When she is finished reading, she rises and four young men take the chair (1.4.1 [4.1]). She calls Hermas over, touches

---

[28] "The book in her hand contains the coming revelation," according to Osiek, *Shepherd of Hermas*, 47. See also Lora Walsh, "The Lady as Elder in the *Shepherd of Hermas*," JECS 27 (2019): 517–47, here 518.
[29] Osiek, *Shepherd of Hermas*, 49.

his breast and says: "Did my reading please you?" (1.4.2 [4.2]).³⁰ He answers that the last part pleased him, while the first was difficult and hard. She offers him a brief explanation to what she has read, and then two men come to carry her away. Her last words to him are given cheerfully, although it is not entirely obvious how they will be interpreted: "Be a man, Hermas!" (1.4.3 [4.3]).³¹

In this scene, Hermas seems to fail in his own expectations of remembering. When she reads, he wants to hear and memorize all the details, but it is too difficult. He admits it to her, and then she gives an interpretation of what she has read. As we shall see later, because of this problem of remembering, an alternative solution is that he can borrow the book and copy it. Here we see how books as oral texts could be transmitted, in a vision from a divine being to the medium, although Hermas lacks the capacity to remember all her words. Elsewhere I have suggested that her cheerful last words to him about being a man have to do with the fact that Hermas, as a former slave, was lacking in masculinity, since he could not control his sexuality and his household.³² Perhaps this comment also plays with his missing masculine skills in remembering and understanding divine revelations? In an oral culture, to remember was a highly valued quality, not least when what was said should later be written down.³³ If Hermas lacks proper training and education, as among others Verheyden identifies,³⁴ this could be shameful for him.³⁵ As a former slave, his book competence was perhaps insufficient. Accordingly, it is hard for him to fill his male role in the book creation process, where he is expected to "be a man."³⁶

---

30 The touching here is of another kind than the potential touching of the bathing Rhoda, in Vis. 1.1.1 (1.1). The Lady church is both old and divine, making sexual tension less likely. See also Osiek, *Shepherd of Hermas*, 50.
31 The Lady Church says: Ἀνδρίζου, Ἑρμᾶ (1.4.3 [4.3]). Osiek writes that this is "a gender-specific term, not, however, limited to men" (ibid., 51).
32 Kartzow, *The Slave Metaphor and Gendered Enslavement in Early Christian Discourse*, 109–10. For further discussion on gender in Hermas, see Young, "Being a Man," and Lipsett's focused discussion on Hermas in *Desiring Conversion*, 19–53.
33 Jonathan A. Draper, "Practicing the Presence of God in John: Ritual Use of Scripture and the *Eidos Theou* in John 5:37," in *Orality, Literacy, and Colonialism in Antiquity*, ed. Jonathan A. Draper, Semeia 47 (Atlanta: SBL Press, 2004), 155–68; Richard A. Horsley, "Oral Tradition in New Testament Studies," *Oral Traditions* 18 (2003): 34–36.
34 Verheyden, "The Shepherd of Hermas," 398.
35 "Hermas is at least basically literate… though he has difficulties separating the letters into words, since ancient manuscripts did not leave space between words, but depended on the reader to interpret" (Osiek, *Shepherd of Hermas*, 52).
36 See discussion in Ulla Tervahauta, "A Just Man or Just a Man? The Ideal Man in the Visions of Hermas," *Patristica Nordica Annuaria* 35 (2020): 69–97.

Copying the Little Book

The story continues a year later when Hermas again meets the elderly woman (Vis. 2.1.3 [5.3]). This time she is presented as multitasking, as "walking and reading a little book" (περιπατοῦσαν καὶ ἀναγινώσκουσαν βιβλαρίδιον) in the fields. This unusual and probably rather impractical combination of activities presents her in a very different posture and place than the last time we saw her reading, when she was sitting on a big chair. Also, the term for book here is not the standard form of the noun used earlier, but the diminutive. Are we then to believe this is a new and different book or the same one she had in her hands in the opening scene?

This time, he is asked to announce her message to God's elect.[37] Hermas wants to but based on the experience with their last encounter, he says he cannot remember so many things. Then he suggests that she give him the book to make a copy (δὸς δέ μοι τὸ βιβλίδιον, ἵνα μεταγράψωμαι αὐτό [2.1.3 (5.3)]). The elderly woman approves, but says she wants it back afterward. The term μεταγράφω is most often translated as 'copy' or 'transcribe'. Copying helps Hermas to compensate for his poor memory. Hermas then goes to another part of the field, where he copies "it all, letter by letter, for I could not make out the syllables" (Vis. 2.1.4 [5.4]).[38] This probably gives a realistic picture of the struggles facing an ancient copyist, as explained in the footnote of Lake's translation: "Hermas no doubt means that it was written like most early manuscripts, in a continuous script with no divisions between the words."[39] After his task is completed, the book is taken out of his hands, but he does not know by whom. The woman said she wanted the book back, so this is probably her divine way to get back what was borrowed. After 15 days, Hermas receives an oral revelation that explains the meaning of what was written in the book.

---

37 Although not called a letter, it "contains a personal message to Hermas, a public message and directions to him for public proclamation," as argued in Osiek (ibid.).

38 . . . καὶ εἴς τινα τόπον τοῦ ἀγροῦ ἀναχωρήσας μετεγραψάμην πάντα πρὸς γράμμα· οὐχ ηὕρισκον γὰρ τὰς συλλαβάς.

39 See Kirsopp Lake, "Introduction," in *I Clement, II Clement, Ignatius, Polycarp, Didache, Barnabas, The Apostolic Fathers*, vol. 1, LCL (London: William Heinemann; New York: G.P. Putnam's Sons, 1913), 19.

Adding and Editing

The last encounter with the Lady Church I will discuss in this section, is a revelation Hermas gets in his house (2.4.2 [8.2]). She returns and asks if Hermas already has given the book to the presbyters. Notice that what had been described earlier as a 'little book' is characterized now as a 'book'. When Hermas says he has not sent the book yet, the Lady is relieved, since she has some more words for him to write down. Most of the book was copied, but then, something was to be added at the end, from an oral source. Again, this may give us some insight into the overlap between ancient oral and scribal culture.[40] Corrections and changes, additions, and comments in the margins could be added before a book was circulated. Written and oral source materials, and as we shall see, even imaginary books, were valuable.

Books Known Only by Titles

From where did Hermas receive his sources? Did the author come up with everything? Were parts of the story circulating orally? No other texts resembling the Shepherd as a possible source behind the text are known to us. There is one minor exception, however, noted by several interpreters as the only attributed quote in Hermas: he refers to something written in or by Eldad and Modat (Vis. 2.3.4 [7.4]).[41] Hermas is given the following advice, after a long section when he is exhorted to repentance to be saved and his family is accused of various sins:

> .... ἐρεῖς δὲ Μαξίμῳ· Ἰδοὺ θλῖψις ἔρχεται· ἐάν σοι δόκῃ πάλιν ἀρνεῖσθαι. Ἐγγὺς Κύριος τοῖς ἐπιστρεφομένοις, ὡς γέγραπται ἐν τῷ Ἐλδὰδ καὶ Μωδάτ, τοῖς προφητεύσασιν ἐν τῇ ἐρήμῳ τῷ λαῷ.

> ".... Say to Maximus, 'See, affliction is coming. If it seems right to you, make another denial.' The Lord is near to those who convert, as is written in the book of Eldad and Modat, who prophesied to the people in the wilderness." (Vis. 2.3.4 [7.4]).[42]

According to Ehrman in the later Loeb edition, this was an apocryphal book written in the names of the two prophets mentioned in Num 11:26, which no longer

---

40 Haines-Eitzen, "Girls Trained in Beautiful Writing."
41 Osiek, *Shepherd of Hermas*, 57, and Verheyden, "The Shepherd of Hermas," 401.
42 *Apostolic Fathers*, vol. 2 (Ehrman, LCL), 190–91.

survives.⁴³ Lake's edition from 1913, notes that this book is mentioned in the pseudo-Athanasian *Synopsis* and in the *Stichometry of Nicephorus* but is no longer extant. Perhaps it is also quoted in 2 Clem. 11.2.⁴⁴

What kind of book is this and what is the purpose of mentioning it here? Liv Ingeborg Lied and Matthew P. Monger discuss this phenomenon in ancient literature.⁴⁵ Several ancient sources mention books that for us do not exist. By mentioning this book, the Lady Church calls upon external literary authority and evidence. These two figures from the past, of whom we only know that they prophesized in the wilderness at the time of Moses, are supposed to have written something that can confirm the need to convert. This works to strengthen the argument; if it is also written elsewhere, by those prophets, it must be true and correct. So for Hermas, the one to whom this is addressed, and for the ancient audience, what Eldad and Modat had written becomes alive in the encounter. The fact that no manuscript of this book has survived leaves us with several options. Perhaps Hermas knew this book very well and recognized the Lady Church's arguments from his own reading or knew it through oral tradition.⁴⁶ Alternatively, as with many books known only by title, it has never existed except as an imagined book.⁴⁷ It is rather mentioned to construct a type of authority. Or, perhaps Hermas's bad memory troubled him again, and we can imagine him regretting his inability to recall the precise details of what he had just heard.

We know very little about potential sources for the Shepherd of Hermas. Of course, it is possible that The Book of Eldad and Modat was well known to ancient authors, written and copied many times, but became forgotten and lost to modern readers. But it is equally possible it only existed as an imagined

---

43 Ehrman, *Apostolic Fathers*, 191.
44 Kirsopp Lake, "Introduction," *Apostolic Fathers*, vol. 2 (LCL 23). See also Osiek, *Shepherd of Hermas*, 57, also 56n18.
45 See Liv Ingeborg Lied and Matthew P. Monger, "Lost Old Testament Pseudepigrapha Known Only by Title," in *Old Testament Pseudepigrapha: More Noncanonical Scriptures*, ed. Richard Bauckham and James R. Davila (Grand Rapids, MI: Eerdmans 2021), 173-89.
46 For a broader discussion of what Hermas might have read or not, heard discussed, or knew the content of, see several discussions in Soyars, *The Shepherd of Hermas and the Pauline Legacy*.
47 This phenomenon was studied in a research project in 2020–2021 led by Liv Ingeborg Lied and Marianne Bjelland Kartzow, "Books Known Only by Title: Exploring the Gendered Structures of First Millennium Imagined Libraries," at the Center for Advanced Study; see https://cas.oslo.no/research-groups/books-known-only-by-title-exploring-the-gendered-structures-of-first-millennium-imagined-libraries-article3333-827.html

book, serving primarily a rhetorical aim in this vision, giving stronger weight on the advice to Hermas's household to repent.[48]

Book Circulation and Intersectional Networks

The last point I will discuss in this part is the encounter where Hermas is told what to do with the book(s) after copying (2.4.3 [8.3]). Again, they are *small* books, like the ones that the Lady Church earlier was walking around in the fields reading:

> γράψεις οὖν δύο βιβλαρίδια καὶ πέμψεις ἓν Κλήμεντι καὶ ἓν Γραπτῇ. Πέμψει οὖν Κλήμης εἰς τὰς ἔξω πόλεις, ἐκείνῳ γὰρ ἐπιτέτραπται. Γραπτὴ δὲ νουθετήσει τὰς χήρας καὶ τοὺς ὀρφανούς. Σὺ δὲ ἀναγνώσῃ εἰς ταύτην τὴν πόλιν μετὰ τῶν πρεσβυτέρων τῶν προϊσταμένων τῆς ἐκκλησίας.
>
> And so, you will write two little books, sending one to Clement and the other to Grapte. Clement will send his to the foreign cities, for that is his commission. But Grapte will admonish the widows and orphans. And you will read yours in this city, with the presbyters who lead the church. (Vis. 2.4.3 [8.3])[49]

If we count these books, it is a bit unclear how many there are supposed to be: (1) Clement; (2) Grapte; (3) Hermas's copy, read with the elders, it seems that three books are needed. Three different places with three categories of people will be addressed and will hear this book read: those of the foreign cities, the group of widows and orphans, and the elders who lead the church in Rome.

The reference to the group of Grapte and the widows and orphans is noteworthy. Clement may be a known figure from Rome, but Grapte is otherwise unknown.[50] The two of them have been taken to be a couple, like Aquila and Prisca, but this suggestion builds more on normative gender expectations than textual evidence. Osiek calls this suggestion "unprovable but charming."[51] Grapte may rather resemble the widows mentioned in the Pastoral Epistles,

---

[48] A similar rhetorical device may be adduced from Col 4.16 in the reference to the letter of Paul from Laodicaea, which arguably helps to reinforce the authority of the narrative voice of Paul in a pseudonymous letter. See the discussion in Kartzow, "The Intersectional Power of 'the Book': The Shepherd of Hermas as Biblical Literature," In *From Text to Persuasion: Festschrift in Honour of Professor Lauri Thurén on the Occasion of His 60th birthday*, ed. Anssi Voitila, Niilo Lahti and Mikael Sundkvist, (Helsinki: Publications of the Finnish Exegetical Society, 2021), 173–89.
[49] *Apostolic Fathers*, vol. 2 (Ehrman, LCL), 192–93.
[50] Osiek, *Shepherd of Hermas*, 59.
[51] Osiek, *Shepherd of Hermas*, 59n11.

where old widows are given some kind of leadership role and are instructed to be enrolled in the widow's order.[52] Osiek argues that Grapte may have been like one of those older women who served younger women, as modelled in Titus 2:3–4, or like the female deacons 1 Tim 3:11. She also suggests Grapte may have been a freedwoman, based, among other things, on her name.[53] At the time in Rome, a woman like Grapte may have had a household church in her home, in which widows and orphans were welcomed. She is portrayed as a female church leader who received one of Hermas's books, who cared for other women and was able to read for them. We may see in these references the shape of an intersectional book network.

What is known as 'the book' started its journey with a divine Lady and was read and copied by a former male slave who once was sold to a woman named Rhoda. In this book circulation process, female characters are at both ends of the transmission line. If Grapte read it and widows heard it, the women in Vision 1–4 are presented as creators, transmitters, and receivers of books, by way of the freedman Hermas. An intersectional approach to book production and circulation offers an important insight by showing that book practices were not exclusive to elite males. Sheridan argues that literate women were a rarity in the ancient world, but in the Shepherd we find some very interesting exceptions made possible by a divine figure and a manumitted male slave.[54]

Before moving into the final discussion of the Lady Church in relation to intersecting patterns of literacy and revelation in the ancient world, I will sum up this mapping of what role 'the book' plays:
1. The Lady Church is introduced with a book in her hands;
2. She mentions the Book of Life as a safe place to be written for Hermas and his family;
3. She walks around reading from a little book and reads aloud for Hermas;
4. He struggles to memorize what she reads to him;
5. She asks if he wants to make a copy;
6. Later, when he thought he was finished, she wants to add more;
7. She mentions a "books known only by title" in her argumentation;
8. Books are to be sent to three groups of people at different places, including a woman named Grapte and the widows and orphans.

---

[52] Jouette M. Bassler, "The Widows' Tale: A Fresh Look at 1 Tim 5:3–16," *JBL* 103 (1984): 23–41. See also Marianne Bjelland Kartzow, "Female Gossipers and Their Reputation in the Pastoral Epistles," *Neot* 39 (2005): 255–72.
[53] This was a frequent name in Rome in the first four centuries of the common era, and a majority of the occurrences of the name refer to freedwomen; see Osiek, *Shepherd of Hermas*, 59.
[54] Sheridan, "Not at a Loss for Words," 189.

The Lady Church, the Sibyl, and Intersecting Structures of Literacy

In this final section, I will ask two interrelated questions: in what ways is the Lady Church unique to ancient book culture and early Christian discourse? How should we conceptualize Hermas's confusion of the Lady Church with the Sibyl?

As a character who mediates divine knowledge and wisdom, Lady Church has characteristics that make it complicated to categorize her. In what way is she presented in line with other early Christian female figures? Tagliabue suggests that "the appearance of a woman as the revelatory figure does not fit into this framework [of biblical literature] and is an innovation of the *BV*."[55] But is this really "a radical disjunction with tradition," as has been pointed out?[56] I will answer no and yes, but for different reasons, by building on insights from intersectionality and book history.

Tagliabue argues that the female personification of the Church was not widely known in the second century, but he finds possible relevant parallels in Eph 5:23 and Rev 19:7–8. He is uncertain if the writer knew any of these texts.[57] Whether they were known to him or not, I argue that identifying parallels between these female figures in the New Testament and the Lady Church can be challenged by intersectional critique. Lady Church is old and is never placed in a patriarchal household. In the NT texts that Tagliabue mentions, women are wives or wives-to-be: representing the church as subordinated wife (and mother), as presented in the household code of the Ephesians, signals a gender discourse. The Lady Church is connected to neither a husband nor children. Further, the reference to Revelation, in which the bride is presented to the lamb in a wedding setting, wearing shining clothes, is also a far-fetched parallel. The emphasis on radiant clothing perhaps constructs a bit of resemblance, but also this female figure is involved in a male-female pairing activity, in which female is subordinated to the male.[58] In these texts, masculine loyalty and house-

---

55 Tagliabue, "Learning from Allegorical Images," 231. See also Soyars, *The Shepherd of Hermas and the Pauline Legacy*, 32–50.
56 Quoted in Tagliabue, "Learning from Allegorical Images," 231n26. See also Osiek, *Shepherd of Hermas*, 16.
57 Tagliabue, "Learning from Allegorical Images," 231.
58 On pairing and hetero-gender, see Marianne Bjelland Kartzow, "The Complexity of Pairing: Reading Acts 16 with Plutarch's *Parallel Lives*," in *Engaging Early Christian History: Reading Acts*

hold regulations controlling the female are core values that are entirely absent in the portrait of the Lady Church. Female metaphors for the Church can be found in the New Testament, but the image of Lady Church in the Visions stands apart from these biblical references.[59] When comparing female figures, also when employed as church metaphors, we need to consider differences within the gender category such as age, marriage status, and/or family position.

The Old Lady is not like other female images of the Church we find in the the New Testament. She is an old woman whose restrictions neither are given by a household setting, nor is she expected to raise children or hold slaves. Instead, the image of her taps into a different biblical iconography where women seldom are found. As a prophetic character, the Lady Church resembles other biblical characters, sitting in her shining white chair. She is rather modelled after the angel described in the vision of Rev 20:1, with the key and not the book in his hand: "Then I saw an angel coming down from heaven, holding in his hand the key to the bottomless pit and a great chain." Or, like Jesus, who was transformed before the eyes of the disciples, as described in Mark 9:1–3: "Six days later, Jesus took with him Peter and James and John, and led them up a high mountain apart, by themselves. And he was transfigured before them, and his clothes became dazzling white, such as no one on earth could bleach them."[60] As an old divine figure, the Lady Church is not like a bride or a wife. She is a divine mediator, like an angel or Jesus himself. Her role vis-à-vis book creation and transmission, is crucial in authorizing and legitimating her divine position.

A dialogue in the Visions adds to the question of with whom the Lady Church can be compared (Vis. 2.4.1 [8.1]). "A very beautiful young man" approaches Hermas in a revelation and asks:

> Τὴν πρεσβυτέραν, παρ' ἧς ἔλαβες τὸ βιβλίδιον, τίνα δοκεῖς εἶναι; ἐγώ φημι· Τὴν Σίβυλλαν. Πλανᾶσαι, φησίν, οὐκ ἔστιν. Τίς οὖν ἐστίν; φημί. Ἡ Ἐκκλησία, φησίν. εἶπον αὐτῷ· Διατί οὖν πρεσβυτέρα; Ὅτι, φησίν, πάντων πρώτη ἐκτίσθη· διὰ τοῦτο πρεσβυτέρα, καὶ διὰ ταύτην ὁ κόσμος κατηρτίσθη.

> "The elderly woman from whom you received the little book—who do you think she is?" "The Sibyl," I replied. "You are wrong," he said; "it is not she." "Who then is it?" I asked. "The church," he said. I said to him, "Why then is she elderly?" "Because," he

---

in the Second Century, ed. Rubén R. Dupertuis and Todd Penner (Durham, England: Acumen Publishing, 2013), 123–39.
59 According to Verheyden, "The Shepherd of Hermas," 399–400, four different female figures are employed to illustrate the Church in the overall text: *kyria*, elder, virgin, and mother.
60 For a discussion of this and other biblical references, see Tagliabue, "Learning from Allegorical Images," 231.

said, "she was created first, before anything else. That is why she is elderly, and for her sake the world was created." (Vis. 2.4.1 [8.1])[61]

Osiek explains Hermas's confusion by pointing out how influential and popular the Sibyl was at the time of the writing. Sibylline oracles had been collected and institutionalized for several centuries in Rome. They were kept in the temple of Jupiter. It might have been a statue of the Sibyl in Rome in the period. Hellenistic Jewish sibylline oracles had already been produced for at least two centuries, soon to be joined by the Christian redactors. Osiek identifies Hermas as the first open reference to this popular figure among Christian authors.[62]

Several interpreters have pointed out the similarity with the Lady Church portrayed by the Shepherd with the Sibyl, such as old age, seated position, holding a book and revealing divine wisdom.[63] Tagliabue shows similarities between the Lady Church and ancient figurines: three Roman objects portray a woman with a scroll in her hands (*LIMC* 7, nos. 23–25), an iconographical image that he argues was probably meant to portray the so-called Sibylline Books consulted by the Romans at the time.[64] The point in the revelatory vision dialogue between Hermas and the very beautiful male angel, however, is to argue against the confusion of the Lady with the Sibyl. She is the Church, and she is old because she was the first to come into being, at the time of creation. So, although she may look like the Sibyl with the book in her hands, she is the Church. The portrait of her in the Shepherd, however, employs obvious characteristics from the Sibyl figure. The Shepherd takes over the image and constructs the Church with the book in her hands as the new Sibyl. She is old since she has been there since the time of creation. Her engagement with the book contributes to her construction as a figure of knowledge, wisdom, and authority and connects her to other women of the ancient world who were trained in reading and writing.

Although these women often were ridiculed, some sources illustrate that women in the ancient world could be literate.[65] In order to contextualize Eusebius's reference to a "girl trained in beautiful writing," Kim Haines-Eitzen presents an impressive overview of ancient sources in which female scribes appear.[66] She finds eleven Latin and two Greek inscriptions mentioning female

---

[61] *Apostolic Fathers*, vol. 2 (Ehrman, LCL), 190–91.
[62] Osiek, *Shepherd of Hermas*, 58.
[63] Tagliabue, "Learning from Allegorical Images," 231. See also Osiek, *Shepherd of Hermas*, 58.
[64] Tagliabue, "Learning from Allegorical Images," 232.
[65] Sheridan, "Not at a Loss for Words," 195.
[66] See Kim Haines-Eitzen, "'Girls Trained in Beautiful Writing'," 629–46.

scribes, four of them slave women. In addition, literary sources portray women with different roles in text production and preservation, including the infamous women of Juvenal, Satire 6, who, in addition to being accused of gossiping and adultery, also are blamed for reading and writing. Haines-Eitzen also discusses marble reliefs which depict women as writers. Additionally, she highlights the striking case of the mid-fifth century hagiographic account of Melania the Younger who "read the Old and New Testament three or four times a year. She copied them herself and furnished copies to the saints by her own hands."[67] Melania's reading and copying are employed to show her ascetic devotion. Also the vague, late tradition based on marginalia where Thecla should have had a hand in the writing of Codex Alexandrinus is of interest. Haines-Eitzen concludes her discussion by arguing that although women were less trained and educated than men, there is evidence that some had education and were trained to write. As scribes and copyists, they were engaged socially, culturally, and religiously, and took an active role in the (re)production and (re)creation of ancient texts.[68]

In a recent 2018 study called "Women as Readers of the Nag Hammadi Codices," Sarit Kattan Gribetz updates the evidence of women's literacy in antiquity and argues that new attention needs to be given to women as readers of the Coptic texts, in particular those from the monasteries in Upper Egypt.[69] She finds women behind, in, and in front of the text, and confirms that "Christian women participated in all aspects of textual transmission."[70]

In the light of this evidence, the Lady Church of the Visions is at the same time both exceptional and conventional. While it was rare for women to handle books, it was not unheard of. Other sources show that women in the ancient world could take part in the creation, transmission, and reception of books. Based on what she is doing with books, the Lady Church can be placed alongside other ancient literate women. With her old age, the book in her hands, her reading competence and book talk, no wonder she was confused with the Sibyl. She has more in common with her than with other female church images, such as a subordinated wife or the bride. The book facilitates the construction of her identity as a divine figure of authority, wisdom, and knowledge.

By highlighting the specific social profile of Hermas and other central characters in these book dialogues and practices, Proctor sees some potential for social mobility for slaves and other underprivileged people. He argues: "Through

---

[67] Haines-Eitzen, "'Girls Trained in Beautiful Writing'," 641.
[68] Haines-Eitzen, "'Girls Trained in Beautiful Writing'," 645–46.
[69] Gribetz, "Women as Readers of the Nag Hammadi Codices," 463–94.
[70] Gribetz, "Women as Readers of the Nag Hammadi Codices," 468.

its distinctive highlighting of the reading, copying, and auditing of texts, therefore, the Shepherd of Hermas provided a potential path towards social prestige and cultic influence for persons who typically resided at the margins of ancient Roman society."[71] In Hermas, we find several characters for whom active participation in book production and circulation seem to give possibilities for a different life and future.

Conclusion

This study has shown that the book plays a key role in the first two Visions of the Shepherd of Hermas. As an artefact, a book is in the hands of the Lady Church the very first time she is introduced. She and Hermas are engaged in an ongoing book-talk, and she mentions the Book of Life as a recommended place to be written for Hermas and his family. Further, the book is opened, and the content made known; she walks around reading, but Hermas struggles to remember everything. Books are also created and edited. Hermas gets the book and copies it, letter by letter, but later she wants him to add more material. In addition, she refers to a book known only by title. The transmission and reception of the copies of this book are also mentioned: books are to be sent to three groups of people at different places, including to a woman named Grapte and the widows and orphans.

The book is held, it is opened, read, heard, memorized, copied, removed in mysterious ways, edited, circulated, and finally received and probably read for groups. It is interpreted and given authority. The Visions show a full circle of ancient book production and circulation. The text gives a small glimpse into the required competence and potential challenges for those involved in these complex processes. The main character of this book story is a divine figure and the message of the book is God's revelation, which together add a heavenly dimension to the interaction. In addition, having a female figure and a manumitted slave playing the main parts in the story construct a complex intersecting web in which the book is placed.

Drawing on the image of the Sibyl, the Lady Church is introduced as a divine figure with a book in her hands. Unlike other female images of the church in early Christian literature, she is neither a wife nor a bride. In addition to her, the Visions mention two other women characters. The first is Rhoda who manumitted her slave, Hermas. If there ever existed such a socio-economic privileged

---

71 Proctor, "Books, Scribes, and Cultures of Reading in the Shepherd of Hermas," 19.

woman at Rome, she could have been literate. As part of her investment in her male slave, she could have given him some elementary training in reading and writing. If so, she can be added to those women in ancient sources said to have knowledge or reading and writing. Rhoda is also uplifted to be a divine figure, the first heavenly messenger whom Hermas meets. The second woman character (also named) is Grapte, who, like Rhoda, lives in Rome. She is the recipient of one of the books, probably an indication that she was supposed to read and interpret it, at least for the widows. If the suggestion that she may have been manumitted is correct, she can be listed among those female slaves who were trained in reading and writing. We have no further information concerning Rhoda and Grapte, but an intersectional analysis shows that it was not only men but women like them who could do things with books. All in all, Rhoda, the Lady Church, and Grapte represent very different women: Rhoda is presented as a slave owner, attractive in the eyes of Hermas as she is bathing in the river. The divine Lady is old and she can touch Hermas without any sexual connotations. Finally, Grapte is probably literate, possibly manumitted like Hermas, and has a group of widows and orphans with her. With intersectionality, it becomes clear that "female characters" connected to books in the Visions is a complex category. Gender intersects with age, sexuality, social status, and family position.

Also, slavery is intertwined with the book in the visions. First, Hermas had a slave background and was probably manumitted by Rhoda. From somewhere and by someone he was taught basics in reading and writing. Rhoda, who appears both as attractive woman and divine figure, is a slave owner. Perhaps she was literate and trained her slaves. Also, Grapte might have been a slave, of a male or female owner. If so, we not only find women in crucial stages in the process of book production, but also slaves and slave-owners potentially of both genders.

By reading the Visions with special attention to 'the book', a complex and intersecting network has been visible. Book creation, transmission and reception in the ancient world were processes in which a variety of people took part. 'The book' is a rich but complex resource, in its physical presence, as opened, or imagined. This study has shown that also male and female slaves, as well as different categories of women (slaves, slave-owners, old divine beings, and widows), could do things with books. Books worked to construct and distribute authority, wisdom, and knowledge, also in the hands of women and slaves.

Dan Batovici
Authority, Fragmentation, Dilution: Experiencing an Apocalyptic Text in Late Antiquity

If, as the contributions in this volume extensively show, the Shepherd is ripe for questions on the various types of experience it reflects, it is all the more fitting to ask: how was the book experienced by its early Christian readers? Unsurprisingly, there is no short-hand answer to this question, especially since the way we experience the book today hardly parallels its success with early and late-antique Christians. It is difficult to imagine many modern readers who read the book as an account of genuine revelation;[1] at the same time, virtually any graduate student undertaking research on the Shepherd will have heard at some point from other early Christianity scholars that their research question is interesting, but the book itself is *so* tedious. There is in fact a long-standing modern scholarly tradition of considering the book subpar as a literary work, as is occasionally documented in introductory sections of contributions on the Shepherd.[2]

Even when the author of the book is not judged against an imaginary classical or Pauline literary ideal, a comment such as that of Carolyn Osiek, according to whom the visions in the Mandates and Similitudes "are usually explained

---

[1] Although isolated, examples can be found. For instance, Roelof van Deemter addressed in 1929 the question of whether the Shepherd is an allegory or an apocalypse, and concludes that the book is intended as an apocalypse and not as a literary fictional construct and, even though allegory is heavily employed, the book is not to be regarded as a pure allegory but an account of Hermas's visionary experiences: "Aus dem bisher Gesagten wäre nur folgender Schluss zu ziehen: Es liegen keine Gründe vor, an dem Selbstzeugnis des Verfassers zu zweifeln. ... Wir müssen seine als visionäre Gottesoffenbarung auftretende Schrift als eine Apokalypse betrachten;" Roelof van Deemter, *Der Hirt des Hermas: Apokalypse oder Allegorie?* (Delft: W. D. Meinem, 1929), at 156.
[2] Examples of this view are collected by Travis W. Proctor, "Books, Scribes, and Cultures of Reading in the Shepherd of Hermas," *Journal of Ecclesiastical History* (June, 2021): 1–21, here 2. FirstView article, doi:10.1017/S0022046920002626; Edith McEwan Humphrey, *The Ladies and the Cities: Transformation and Apocalyptic in Joseph and Aseneth, 4 Ezra, the Apocalypse and The Shepherd of Hermas*, JSPSup 17 (Sheffield: Sheffield Academic Press, 1995), 119; B. Diane Wudel, "The Seduction of Self–Control: Hermas and the Problem of Desire," *Religion & Theology* 11 (2004): 39–49, at 39; and B. Diane Lipsett, *Desiring Conversion: Hermas, Thecla, Aseneth* (New York: Oxford University Press, 2011), 19.

by the revealer in prolonged and (to the modern reader) often boring detail,"[3] reflects a common view concerning the contents of the book. Moreover, J. Christian Wilson's suggestion that "its [the Shepherd's] far greater length than any canonical New Testament document may be the reason for its evolving out of the canon" is probably best understood as reflecting a modern reception of the book.

The sample of reception landmarks that we have for the Shepherd points in entirely different directions. Even though we might have to accept the fact that we do not have access to something as personal as the experience of an ancient person reading the book, we do have access nonetheless to bits and pieces that reflect a variety of ways in which the book was appropriated. We can, indeed, peek through the scarcity of the data and attempt to grasp how readers might have dealt with the text. To do this, we proceed in a cumulative manner, piecing together the clues that we have that add-up to an oddly kaleidoscopic picture of the uses of the Shepherd in late antiquity.

In a sense, before turning to the reception of the book, the obvious starting point is the fact that it famously describes how Hermas himself goes about handling a book that contains revealed material meant for the edification of the community, at the beginning and then at the end of Vision 2, an episode which is described by Kim Haines-Eitzen, that it is "the only passage that depicts copying in second-century Christian literature."[4] In Vis. 2.1.3–4 (5.3–4), following his prayer of thanks for being shown past and new visions, Hermas receives from the heavenly mediator—at this point still the elderly woman[5]—a little book (βιβλαρίδιον) for him to communicate its contents to the elect of God. Hermas asks for permission to copy it, which he does character by character (πρὸς γράμμα), apparently unable to work out the syllables on the spot. Then, in Vis. 2.4.1–3 (8.1–3), Hermas has another vision during his sleep where he learns that the elder woman is the Church (and not the Sibyl, his first guess), and who asks of him to copy more things and charges him with spreading the now completed message by sending copies out to Clement for the other churches and to Grapte for the widows and orphans.

---

[3] Carolyn Osiek, "The Genre and Function of the Shepherd of Hermas" in *Early Christian Apocalypticism: Genre and Social Setting*, ed. Adela Yarbro Collins, Semeia 14 (Decatur: SBL, 1979), 113–21, at 114.

[4] Kim Haines–Eitzen, *Guardians of Letters: Literacy, Power, and the Transmitters of Early Christian Literature* (Oxford: Oxford University Press, 2000), 22.

[5] On the shift in gender symbolism gradually eliminating maternal figures and feminine imagery across the successive recensions of the Shepherd, see Lora Walsh, "Lost in Revision: Gender Symbolism in *Vision* 3 and *Similitude* 9 of the *Shepherd of Hermas*," HTR 112 (2019): 467–90.

In relation to this, a recent article by Travis Proctor discusses how the Shepherd constructs a space where revelation is not only linked to texts but also to the very activity of copying and reading texts, within which Hermas is projected as an idealised reader, scribe, and auditor, building up in this way his role as a prophet.[6] Proctor also links the success of the Shepherd throughout its reception to the enhanced reading culture it envisages, suggesting that "it is possible ... that the text's promotion of its own copying and reading directly contributed to its wide dissemination."[7] This is not impossible, and it might potentially open a window into how early Christians read the book, but the difficulty for whomever will feel inclined to attempt verifying this hypothesis will be to link it to the data offered by the Shepherd's reception, and furthermore to weigh and distinguish this from other possible factors. In a sense, a similar attempt to link the reception of the book to its contents, put forth by Rachel Yuen-Collingridge and Malcolm Choat who explain the success of the Shepherd through the fact that it is an enhanced catechetical text,[8] is better grounded given that we do have several patristic testimonies that place the Shepherd in catechetical contexts, as the authors show. It may not be the only explanation, but it is certainly one that can be documented.

Several other proposals are available that seek to account for the reception of the Shepherd in late antiquity. To Phillipe Henne, it eventually became "le manuel de la vie chrétienne" in the West, while in the East "brutalement le *Pasteur* disparaît, sans doute victime de son succès initial."[9] To Norbert Brox, the available testimonies indicate that it had enough authority to have been a candidate for "kanonischen Rang," even though it was not a biblical book.[10] Carolyn Osiek considers that "the movement toward canonical rejection was steady, while retention for private reading remained."[11]

As such, a variety of possible reasons for the reception of the Shepherd have been put forward in recent scholarship in relation to the contents or outlook of

---

[6] Proctor, "Books, Scribes, and Cultures of Reading," 3–12.
[7] Proctor, "Books, Scribes, and Cultures of Reading," 16.
[8] Malcolm Choat and Rachel Yuen-Collingridge, "The Egyptian Hermas: The Shepherd in Egypt before Constantine," in *Early Christian Manuscripts: Examples of Applied Method and Approach*, ed. Thomas J. Kraus and Tobias Nicklas, TENTS 5 (Leiden/Boston: Brill, 2010), 191–212, at 203: "as Hermas has the mysteries of the world explained to him, so were they explained to the catechumens."
[9] Philippe Henne, "Canonicité du 'Pasteur' d'Hermas." *RThom* 90 (1990): 81–100, at 100.
[10] Brox, *Hirt*, 70.
[11] Carolyn Osiek, *The Shepherd of Hermas: A Commentary*, Hermeneia (Minneapolis: Fortress Press, 1999), 6.

the book: theology, apocalyptic character, paraenesis, repentance.¹² For instance, Christoph Markschies notes that "the extraordinary popularity of this book [...] can be explained easily with reference to the theme of repentance [...] and [to] the generally understandable level of the theology of the book." Here Markschies draws on Martin Dibelius, who, on the one hand in the conclusion to the introduction of his commentary considers the Shepherd to be "ein Denkmal des Alltagschristentums der kleinen Leute und breiten Schichten" and, on the other, that "Sein schriftstellerisches Ungeschick ist ebenso offenbar wie der untheologische Charakter seiner Frömmigkeit."¹³ The idea that the reception of the book is explained by its appeal to "everyday Christianity of small people and broad classes" is itself appealing, seemingly supported by its comparably "lesser" theology, although it does not serve well to account for the high view of the book in authors like Irenaeus, Clement of Alexandria, Origen, or Didymus the Blind.

A different explanation for the Shepherd's popularity in early Christianity is proposed by Bogdan Bucur,¹⁴ in response to the fairly common modern perplexity according to which "it is strange that this immensely popular document of the early church was never condemned for christological heresy."¹⁵ Bucur argues that the Shepherd shares in the older tradition that combines an angelomorphic pneumatology with a spirit Christology within a binitarian frame, a tradition which he also documents in Revelation, Justin Martyr and Clement of Alexandria.¹⁶ Irrespective of how peculiar or awkward this writing has seemed to modern scholarly interpretations,¹⁷ Bucur documents a central theological commonality

---

12 For the latter, a recent re-contextualisation of the Shepherd's understanding of repentance in the broader history of repentance in late antiquity is available in Alexis Torrance, *Repentance in Late Antiquity: Eastern Asceticism and the Framing of the Christian Life c.400 – 650 CE* (Oxford: Oxford University Press, 2013), esp. 71–74.
13 Christoph Markschies, *Christian Theology and Its Institutions in the Early Roman Empire: Prolegomena to a History of Early Christian Theology*, BMSSEC (Waco, TX: Baylor University Press / Tübingen: Mohr Siebeck, 2015), 216, and Martin Dibelius, *Der Hirt des Hermas*, Die apostolischen Väter 4 (Tübingen: Mohr Siebeck, 1923), respectively at 425 and 423.
14 Bogdan G. Bucur, *Angelomorphic Pneumatology: Clement of Alexandria and Other Early Christian Witnesses*, VCSup 95 (Leiden/Boston: Brill, 2009).
15 Osiek, *The Shepherd of Hermas*, 179–80.
16 Bucur, *Angelomorphic Pneumatology*, 113–38.
17 Indeed, it is not at all uncommon for modern readers to describe its prose as naive, dilettante and incompetent, or simply boring. Apart from Dibelius, *Der Hirt des Hermas*, 423, quoted in a previous note, see the examples gathered in Humphrey, *The Ladies and the Cities*, 119, and Lipsett, *Desiring Conversion*, 19.

between the Shepherd and other important products of early Christianity as a reasonable cause for its success and authority.

What such proposals ultimately indicate is that it is unlikely to reach a clear, single explanation for the reception of the Shepherd, or to grasp a simple understanding of how the book was experienced in Late Antiquity. Indeed, ancient authors seem to make use of the Shepherd in a variety of ways. It was considered a writing with revealed or inspired content (Clement of Alexandria, Origen) and employed at least in one instance in formulating the "canon of truth" (Irenaeus) even if likely secondary (Origen, and possibly Irenaeus). Importantly, the book was often used alongside writings that later were part of the biblical canon for theological reasoning (Irenaeus, Origen, Didymus of Alexandria), even as—again—it was deemed secondary (Eusebius of Caesarea, Athanasius of Alexandria). In fact, hesitation in its use is recorded early, beginning with Origen, before the Muratorian Fragment (however dated), Eusebius of Caesarea, and Athanasius. And, as mentioned, it was considered particularly useful for catechumens (Eusebius, Athanasius) and several witnesses suggest or imply that the book was read publicly in churches (the Muratorian Fragment, Eusebius, Athanasius of Alexandria, Jerome, Rufinus).

At the same time, the Shepherd is notoriously better preserved among the papyri than most biblical texts taken individually[18] and is included in Codex Sinaiticus, although the significance of this inclusion in such a biblical pandect remains unclear in the absence of explicit historical testimonies on the matter.[19] The entire Greek material reception of the Shepherd in early and late-antique Christianity is remarkable, yet the significance of this comparatively higher number of papyri is also unclear. Some may wish to see in this number an indication of authority, especially in conjunction with the inclusion in Codex Sinaiticus, relevant for the formation of the biblical canon,[20] though that is more than the

---

18 For an updated list of all Greek witnesses of the Shepherd see Paolo Cecconi, "1200 Years of Materialities and Editions of a Forbidden Text," in *Antike Texte und ihre Materialität. Alltägliche Präsenz, mediale Semantik, literarische Reflexion*, edited by Cornelia Ritter–Schmalz and Raphael Schwitter, Materiale Textkulturen 27 (Berlin: De Gruyter, 2019), 309–30.
19 For a survey of scholarly takes on the matter see Dan Batovici, "The Apostolic Fathers in Codex Sinaiticus and Alexandrinus," *Bib* 97 (2016): 581–605, esp. 582–84.
20 See, for instance, David Nielsen, "The Place of the *Shepherd of Hermas* in the Canon Debate," in *"Non–canonical" Religious Texts in Early Judaism and Early Christianity*, edited by Lee Martin McDonald and James H. Charlesworth, JCT 14 (London/New York: T&T Clark, 2012) 162–76; see also Daniel Stökl Ben Ezra, "Canonization—a Non–Linear Process? Observing the Process of Canonization through the Christian (and Jewish) Papyri from Egypt," *ZAC* 12 (2008): 229–50, at 213, suggests that "the strong attestation to at least *Hermas* among the papyri" may well indicate that its presence in Sinaiticus indicates canonical status. See also

papyri can indicate on their own. Indeed, as they stand, the papyri speak more to the use of the Shepherd and the context of this perusal, rather than the status of the book. To Roberts, the book's "popularity in provincial Egypt may give us a better insight into the character of the churches than anything else."[21] Epp rightly notes that "too much cannot be drawn from such comparative data, but it is clear by any measure available to us that the Shepherd of Hermas was very much a part of Christian literature in Oxyrhynchus at an early period."[22]

In the remainder of this contribution, however, I would like to address three virtually uncharted aspects of the material reception of the Shepherd. One has to do with the presence of the book in liturgical papyri, another mirrors its use in legal context with relevance to divorce regulations; the third aspect points to a pervasive phenomenon in the reception of the Shepherd wherein the book is employed in significant ways yet without preserving its identity as a distinct, book-shaped source.

Experiencing the Shepherd in Liturgical Texts

Bodl. Ms. Gr. liturg. c. 3 (P), better known as the Deir-Bala'izah Papyrus (P.Bala'izah), is reconstructed from several fragments and has been published several times as new fragments were connected to its text, the latest edition being that of van Haelst.[23] It preserves "a Greek anaphora, various prayers, and a

---

Markschies, *Christian Theology and Its Institutions*, 217, who, in his discussion of the Muratorian Fragment, considers the comparatively higher number of papyri a counter to the Fragment's "critical remarks" on the Shepherd, quoting then Dibelius, *Der Hirt des Hermas*, 419, according to which the Shepherd "ist bald an die Schwelle des Kanon und darüber hinaus gelangt."
21 Colin H. Roberts, *Manuscripts, Society and Belief in Early Christian Egypt: The Schweich Lectures 1997* (London: Oxford University Press, 1979), 26, preceded by: "The *Shepherd* was widely regarded as scripture at this time and remained a candidate for canonization; it was especially used for the instruction of catechumens," and at 63 he adds: "its popularity is evidence both of the continuing Jewish–Christian strain in Egypt and the link between Rome and Alexandria."
22 Eldon Jay Epp, in "The Oxyrhynchus New Testament Papyri: 'Not without honor except in their hometown'?, in his *Perspectives on New Testament Textual Criticism: Collected Essays, 1962–2004*, NovTSup 116 (Leiden: Brill, 2005), 743–803, at 757.
23 J. Van Haelst, "Une nouvelle reconstitution du Papyrus liturgique de Der-Balizeh," *ETL* 45 (1969): 444–55, which updates that of Colin H. Roberts and Bernard Capelle, *An Early Euchologium: The Der-Balizeh Papyrus Enlarged and Reedited*, Bibliothèque du Muséon 23 (Louvain: Muséon, 1949). See also Klaus Gamber, "Das Eucharistiegebet im Papyrus von Der-Balizeh und die Samstagabend–Agapen in Ägypten," *Ostkirchliche Studien* 7 (1958): 48–56. For a more recent discussion see Alistair C. Stewart, *Two Early Egyptian Liturgical Papyri: The Deir*

baptismal creed."[24] Although largely neglected as an artefact of the reception of the Shepherd, it incorporates a recognisable quotation from the book.

Indeed, lines 15–18 of what seems to be a liturgical prayer segment,[25] include a paraphrase of Mandate 1.1 (26.1), interpolated with further material (Ἰησοῦς Χριστός is mentioned, who is never mentioned by name in the Shepherd) and reset in a new context. The relevant part, regularised, reads: **ὁ θεὸς καὶ πατὴρ τοῦ κυρίου ἡμῶν Ἰησοῦ Χριστοῦ ὁ ποιήσας τὰ πάντα ἐξ οὐκ ὄντων καὶ εἰς τὸ εἶναι τὰ πάντα** [παραγαγὼν καὶ] **πάντα χωρῶν μόνος δὲ ἀχώρητος ὤν.**[26] Expectedly for a liturgical prayer, it is not introduced explicitly as a quotation, and it does not seem to be followed by an exposition explaining the reference. The text paralleled in the Shepherd is therefore incorporated without any indication that an earlier work is used. Although the various elements of this sequence have parallels in other texts,[27] the combination of them is peculiar to Mand. 1.1 (26.1) alone. It seems therefore clear that it is the Shepherd that is paraphrased here in a liturgical context, either directly or through an intermediary text.

There is another overlooked example: P.Monts.Roca inv. 126–178, better known as the Barcelona Papyrus, is a 52 leaves, one-quire, multiple-text papyrus codex that includes an important liturgical witness of late antiquity.[28] It is

---

Balyzeh Papyrus and the Barcelona Papyrus with Appendices Containing Comparative Material, Joint Liturgical Studies 70 (Norwich: Hymns Ancient and Modern, 2010), esp. 6–21.

24 Ágnes T. Mihálykó, *The Christian Liturgical Papyri: An Introduction*, STAC 114 (Tübingen: Mohr Siebeck, 2019), 110.

25 Mihálykó, *Christian Liturgical Papyri*, 175: "The ἄλλη of P. Bala'izah fol. I v. 11 originally indicated the function of the prayer, which probably coincided with the function of the previous prayer, presumably indicated in its title."

26 Cf. Mand. 1.1 (26.1): Πρῶτον πάντων πίστευσον ὅτι εἷς ἐστὶν ὁ θεός, ὁ τὰ πάντα κτίσας καὶ καταρτίσας, καὶ ποιήσας ἐκ τοῦ μὴ ὄντος εἰς τὸ εἶναι τὰ πάντα, καὶ πάντα χωρῶν, μόνος δὲ ἀχώρητος ὤν.

27 Graydon F. Snyder, *The Shepherd of Hermas*, The Apostolic Fathers 6 (London: Thomas Nelson & Sons, 1968), 63, signals several Jewish–Christian parallels: 2 Bar 48.8; Philo's *De specialibus legibus* 4.187; Rom 4:17; 2 Clement 1.8. Osiek, *The Shepherd of Hermas*, 103, also finds this to be "a familiar Hellenistic Jewish creedal formula," with further possible parallels for the creation out of nothing in 2 Macc 7:28, Wis 1:14, Philo's *De specialibus legibus* 2.225, *Vit. Mos.* 2.267. Further parallels are offered in Michael Zheltov, "The Anaphora and the Thanksgiving Prayer form the Barcelona Papyrus: An Underestimated Testimony of the Anaphoral History in the Fourth Century," *VC* 62 (2008): 467–504, 487 n. 65: Philo, *Quod deus sit immutabilis* 119, *De vita Mosis* 2. 267; Origen, *Commentarii in evangelium Joannis* 32.16.188; Athanasius of Alexandria, *De decretis Nicaenae Synodi* 18.3.

28 The best available edition is Zheltov, "The Anaphora and the Thanksgiving Prayer form the Barcelona Papyrus." For a previous edition see R. Roca-Puig, *Anàfora de Barcelona i altres*

usually dated to the fourth century,[29] and although it is considerably older than Deir-Bala'izah Papyrus, it is presented at this point because its parallel to the Shepherd is less clear and needs to be considered in relation to that papyrus.

The liturgical section of the codex is copied on the first seven leaves, 154b–157b,[30] and the parallel to the Shepherd appears on the first page,[31] in the 'creation narrative' part of the preface to the anaphora—the eucharistic prayer, here regularised:[32] Θεὲ παντοκράτωρ τοῦ κυρίου ἡμῶν Ἰησοῦ Χριστοῦ, **ὁ ποιήσας τὰ πάντα ἐκ τοῦ μὴ ὄντος εἰς τὸ εἶναι τὰ πάντα**· οὐρανούς, γῆν, θάλασσαν κτλ. Zheltov's translates this as: "[...] o Master, God Pantocrator of our Lord Jesus Christ, **who created all things from non-existence into being, all:** heaven and the earth, the sea [...]."[33] It is useful to visualise synoptically the parallels to Mand. 1.1 (26.1) in the two papyri, alongside the text established by Leutzsch:

Leutzsch (1998)	Bodl. Ms. Gr. liturg. c.3(P)	P.Monts.Roca 154b
Πρῶτον πάντων πίστευσον ὅτι εἷς ἐστιν ὁ θεός, ὁ τὰ πάντα κτίσας καὶ καταρτίσας, καὶ ποιήσας ἐκ τοῦ μὴ ὄντος εἰς τὸ εἶναι τὰ πάντα, καὶ πάντα χωρῶν μόνος δὲ ἀχώρητος ὤν.	ὁ θ(εό)ς ... ὁ ποιήσας τὰ πάντα [ἐ]ξ ο[ὐκ ὄν]τ[ω]ν καὶ εἰς 'τὸ' εἶναι τὰ πάντα [... καὶ π]άν[τα] χωρῶν, μόνο[ς] [δ]ὲ ἀχώρητο[ς] ὤν	θ(ε)ὲ ... ὁ ποιήσας τὰ πάντα ἐκ τοῦ μὴ ὄντος εἰς τὸ εἶναι, τὰ πάντα

---

pregàires. Missa del segle IV (Barcelona, 1994¹; 1996²; 1999³). Further discussion in Stewart, *Two Early Egyptian Liturgical Papyri*, 22–38.

29 The dating of this papyrus is proposed in a somewhat peculiar manner, suggesting that it is perhaps less secure: Zheltov, "The Anaphora and the Thanksgiving Prayer form the Barcelona Papyrus," 468n1: "My confidence in its dating is based not only on data from J. van Haelst's catalogue ... and R. Roca-Puig's book, but also on consultations with the leading papyrologists, including Bärbel Kramer and Paul Schubert, whom I thank gratefully."

30 See Zheltov, "The Anaphora and the Thanksgiving Prayer form the Barcelona Papyrus," where he writes, "The manuscript contains a few Latin texts as well as some Christian liturgical prayers in Greek, and a long Greek word–list" (468).

31 A black and white image reproduction is available in Roca–Puig, *Anàfora de Barcelona*, 127, and in colour on the front cover of the book.

32 The description of the contents of the liturgical section can be found in Zheltov, "The Anaphora and the Thanksgiving Prayer form the Barcelona Papyrus," 493.

33 Zheltov, "The Anaphora and the Thanksgiving Prayer form the Barcelona Papyrus," 486–87.

P.Monts.Roca 154b seems to parallel therefore one part of Mand. 1.1a (26.1a), namely θεός, ὁ [...] ποιήσας ἐκ τοῦ μὴ ὄντος εἰς τὸ εἶναι τὰ πάντα. Given that there are other possible parallels for this segment, it is not conclusively a use of the Shepherd. By contrast, Bodl. Ms. Gr. liturg. c. 3 (P) has enough elements in common with Mand. 1.1 (26.1) to be a positive identification.

But what is the relationship between the Deir-Bala'izah and the Barcelona papyrus with respect to the text of the Shepherd? The matter is clouded by the fact that, since Barcelona Papyrus is in fact a collection of various writings, including literary texts, it rather *reflects* a liturgical anaphora than being a liturgical papyrus used in liturgy.³⁴ Nevertheless, both contain liturgical texts that have the creation statement in the anaphora introductory prayer. Did the prayer have the Shepherd quotation to begin with? In that case, does the Barcelona Papyrus represent a tradition which is simplified in this regard, to the point that it rendered Mand. 1.1 (26.1) almost unrecognisable? Or, conversely, does the Deir-Bala'izah reflect a tradition which interpolated a simpler creation statement as the one in the Barcelona Papyrus—taken from any of the possible parallels—with the more developed formulation taken from Mand. 1.1 (26.1)? Both scenarios are interesting for the reception of the Shepherd in community contexts, however conceived.

There are indeed patristic authors who mention or imply that the book was read in churches. Eusebius of Caesarea reports that the Shepherd was not a received first-tier book but was judged by some useful for catechumens and was therefore read in churches (*Historia ecclesiastica* 3.3.6). Athanasius of Alexandria also describes the book as secondary and prescribes its use for instruction, specifically to be read to catechumens (*Festal Letter* 39.20). Jerome too reports that it is read publicly in some Greek churches (*De viris illustribus* 10: *apud quasdam Greciae Ecclesias etiam publice legitur*), while Rufinus places it among the books which are not canonical but nonetheless ecclesiastical and which the forefathers desired to be read in churches (*Exposition of the Creed* 38: *quae omnia legi quidem in ecclesiis uoluerunt*). Perhaps even the Muratorian Fragment, stating that the Shepherd should be read (*legi eum oportet*) but not publicly to the peo-

---

34 See Zheltov, "The Anaphora and the Thanksgiving Prayer form the Barcelona Papyrus," who writes, "It should be noted, however, that the codex from which the anaphora and thanksgiving prayer come was written not for liturgical but for some scholarly purposes and thereby could present not a full Eucharistic rite but just a portion of it" (497). On that same page, he goes on to say, "the anaphora contains several long citations from writings of the early Church fathers" indicative of "a deliberate work of some educated editor," and then adds: "A number of expression in the Anaphora finds parallels in the writings of Athanasius of Alexandria, so I cautiously suggest that this hypothetical editor could be Athanasius himself."

ple in the church neither among the prophets nor among the apostles, implies something of this sort, if read as a reaction. If it is simply a matter of categorization and not a reaction to a practice, it means that the Shepherd is to be disclosed, presumably read in public but neither as part of the prophets nor the apostles.

There is, however, a major difference between the patristic testimonies and that of the two liturgical papyri: if these authors mention the book as being read by name, the references to the Shepherd in the Deir-Bala'izah Papyrus or the Barcelona Papyrus are virtually unrecognizable as such. Therefore, the liturgical papyri testify to a more diluted use of the Shepherd, one in which its integrity as book is, as it were, lost. Perhaps we could extrapolate from this that the reading of the Shepherd was widespread enough that liturgical language could draw on it. This diluted usage could be construed as secondary to the one in which the book is obviously known by title and author but, as will be seen in the final part of this contribution, this points to a pervasive and in a sense more direct reception of the contents of the book. Before that, however, I would like to draw attention to an interesting reception landmark, wherein the Shepherd is perused in a legal context as proof text for civil matters, specifically for divorce regulation.

Divorce Regulation

Manuscript BnF Latin 3182 preserves an extract of Mandate 4 (29–32) of the Shepherd in the Palatina translation.[35] It is a large format parchment codex (245 × 400 mm) of 365 numbered pages, written in a two-column format by a Breton scribe named Maeloc, dated palaeographically to the 9th or the 10th century.[36] It contains a collection of ecclesiastical canons and synodal acts, normally referred to as the *Collectio canonum Fiscannensis*.

---

35 Christian Tornau and Paolo Cecconi, eds., *The Shepherd of Hermas in Latin: Critical Edition of the Oldest Translation Vulgata*, TU 173 (Berlin: De Gruyter, 2014), 9n40.
36 This is the date given in the description at https://archivesetmanuscrits.bnf.fr/ark:/12148/cc610287. Other authors give the dating "X^1," e.g. Ludwig Bieler, *The Irish Penitentials*, Scriptores latini Hiberniae 5 (Dublin: Institute for Advanced Studies, 1963), 12; "X^2," e.g., Michael M. Gorman, "Patristic and Pseudo–Patristic Citation in the *Collectio Hibernensis*," *Revue bénédictine* 121.1 (2011): 18–93, at 82; or, most recently, "X/XI," in Roy Flechner, ed., *The Hibernensis: A Study and Edition*, Book 1, Studies in Medieval and Early Modern Canon Law 17.1 (Washington, D.C.: Catholic University of America Press, 2019), 128*. I had the opportunity to conduct my own examination of the manuscript in January 2020.

The general title of Latin 3182, on page 1 in red ink, reads *Incipiunt uerba pauca tam de episcopo quam de presbitero aut de omnibus ecclesie gradibus et de regibus et de mundo et terra*. On page 19, there is the table of contents of a collection with its own dynamic of transmission, referred to as *Collectio canonum Hibernensis*. The title of the first section of the canons, *De episcopo capit(ula) xcxii*, starts on page 20. The Shepherd is copied in the part that precedes the *Collectio canonum Hibernensis*, yet the introductory 18 pages of the codex are themselves a composite document.[37] The first 12 pages contain a cluster of excerpts from Exodus, Leviticus, Numbers, and Deuteronomy, with occasionally interspersed titles in red ink (on p. 10, *incipit de libro deuteronomi*; on p. 11, *incipit de libro leuitico*). These excerpts form a coherent collection with its own history of transmission, edited in the modern period as the *Liber de lege Moysi*, and described as "an important witness to the significance of biblical law in the early medieval Irish Church, and the Irish jurists' approach to, and active dialogue with, the legal material of the Old Testament."[38] The *Liber de lege Moysi* in Latin 3182, however, differs in sequence from the edition quoted in the previous footnote and is incomplete, probably due to a loss of material, since the second column of text ends, at the bottom of page 12, in the middle of Lev 18:13: *Turpitudinem sororis matris tuae* [. . .].

The fragment from the Shepherd is copied in the second column of page 15 and the first column on page 16. It is preceded on page 13 by a chronological note on the ages of the world, a brief note on the bishop Narcissus of Jerusalem *qui fecit oleum de aqua*, and an excerpt from John Cassian, *Collatio* 20.8 (prefaced by *Incipiunt remissiones peccatorum quas sanctus in collatione sua Penuffius per sanctas construxit scripturas* in red ink) that continues on pages 14 and 15, and a second chronological note on the ages of the world at the top of the second column.

An excerpt on marriage from Mandate 4—conflating in fact 4.1.4–8 (29.4–8)[39] and 4.4.1–2 (32.1–2)—begins in the middle of the column, after the title, *incipit de libro hermas*, in red ink, and the introductory formula, *dixit autem hermas ad pastorem angelum*. These excerpts are 'legalistic' in nature, since in the former the Shepherd explains to Hermas what rules the husband

---

[37] See the description of contents in Flechner, *The Hibernensis* 1, 129*–131*.
[38] Sven Meeder, "The *Liber ex lege Moysi*: Notes and Text," *Journal of Medieval Latin* 19 (2009): 173–218, at 173.
[39] The first part of the quotation also appears in Cambridge, Corpus Christi College, MS 265, on pp. 61–62, as mentioned by Tornau and Cecconi, *The Shepherd of Hermas in Latin*, 9n40. Images of the manuscript are available online at https://parker.stanford.edu/parker/catalog/nh277tk2537.

should follow in cases in which the wife is found in adultery: he can no longer live with her when he learns of this, lest he becomes responsible for her sin. He must divorce her, yet not marry another, on the chance that the wife might repent, in which case he must take her back. He then adds that this procedure applies to both husband and wife. Similarly, in Mand. 4.4.1–2 (32.1–2), the Shepherd explains that the widower or widow can remarry, even though remaining single gains for oneself *magnam gloriam apud Deum*.

The excerpt from the Shepherd is followed by a series of biblical quotations: Matt 19:9, 1 Cor 7:10–11 and 39–40, Num 30:3–10 (the latter ending on the following page). The quotation from Matt 19:9, introduced by *in euangelio mathei dominus noster iesus christus ait*, is also a rule on remarrying, just as the quotations from 1 Corinthians, introduced by *Paulus ait*, give rules on divorce and taking a repenting spouse back, respectively on whether a widow should remarry or remain alone. The slightly longer excerpt from Numbers, introduced by *item in libris legis*, develops further on these themes. As such, the cluster of excerpts from the Shepherd, Matthew, 1 Corinthians, and Numbers[40] continues the "legalistic" character of the *Liber de lege Moysi* in the first part of the introduction, and their succession seems to suggest that the scriptural quotations are brought in to confirm or develop the extracts from Mand. 4.1 (29) and 4.4 (32).[41]

To briefly conclude, BnF Latin 3182 is a peculiar landmark in the Latin reception of the Shepherd where it is used in a canonical law collection as proof-text for marital issues, in close connection with biblical texts. In as much as Meeder's assessment of the significance of the *Liber de lege Moysi* quoted above is correct, the same is true for this cluster of texts on marriage: indeed, BnF Latin 3182 is also "an important witness to … the Irish jurists' approach to, and active dialogue with, the legal material of" the Shepherd, specifically, in conjunction with Matthew, 1 Corinthians, and Numbers.[42]

---

[40] Flechner, *The Hibernensis* 1, 129* lists it as follows: "pp. 15–17: Excerpts on divorce from the Shepherd of Hermas, … Matthew, Paul, and Mosaic Law." He further lists witnesses that include this cluster in similar collections: at 127*: Orleans, Bibliothèque municipale, 221 (192), on pp. 19–20; and at 136*, and London, British Library, Cotton Otho E XIII, on fol. 10r–10v.

[41] This section is followed on pages 17–18 by *Virtutes quas Dominus dominica die fecit*, an apocryphon containing a letter written in heaven by Jesus about Sundays, known as *Carta Dominica*, 'The Sunday Letter.' On this document, see Clare A. Lees, "The 'Sunday Letter' and the 'Sunday Lists,'" *Anglo-Saxon England* 14 (1985): 129–51.

[42] The initial quotation, specifically with regard to the Old Testament, is in Meeder, "The *Liber ex lege Moysi*," 173.

Fragmentation, Dilution, Misattribution

The Deir-Bala'izah Papyrus and the Barcelona Papyrus briefly presented above already offered examples of the Shepherd being used without any indication of it being the source. This type of reception, where the identity of the source as a distinct book is virtually lost, could be seen as instances where the Shepherd is too fragmentary and diluted to be anything other than secondary. Nevertheless, the liturgical context makes them relevant for considering the reception history of the Shepherd in late antiquity, irrespective of whether the users would have recognised it or not as such. This fragmented and diluted usage complements that mentioned by patristic authors according to which the book was read in churches, as well as the named references to the book in late antique literature. What is more, it points to a pervasive type of reception of the Shepherd where its contents are freely and creatively used. It is then profitable to look briefly at such instances as a whole, where the book is employed in significant ways, yet without any evidence of an identity as a distinct, book-shaped source.

To begin with, there are two other papyri that contain quotation from the Shepherd embedded in other texts, P.Oxy. I 5 and P.Mich. inv. 6427r. The former is a fragmentary papyrus, dated to the late third, early fourth century,[43] possibly a remnant of a codex leaf. It opens abruptly with a modified quotation from Mand. 11.9–10 [43.9–10], the angel "of the prophetic spirit which lies upon that person fills him; and being filled with the holy spirit, this person speaks as the Lords wills. In this way the spirit of the divine nature will be manifest,"[44] and continues with considerations on what the nature of the prophetic spirit is. However, since the beginning is missing it is not clear whether this was initially a named reference or not. P.Mich. inv. 6427r on the other hand is a papyrus sheet that has on the horizontal fibre side a prayer, a petition to God that incorporates a quotation from Isa 40:16 and Mand. 1.1 (26.1), dated palaeographically to the fourth century.[45] The nature of the quotation is not entirely clear since the Shepherd is not mentioned in the available text in any way, and the textual overlap is

---

[43] Eric G. Turner, *The Typology of the Early Codex* (Philadelphia: University of Pennsylvania Press, 1977), 131.
[44] For a recent discussion of how this quotation is modified in this papyrus see Luca Arcari, "P.Oxy. 1.5 and the Codex Sangermanensis as 'Visionary Living Texts': Visionary *habitus* and Processes of 'Textualization' and/or 'Scripturalization' in Late Antiquity," in *Lived Religion in the Ancient Mediterranean World: Approaching Religious Transformations from Archaeology, History, and Classics*, ed. Valentino Gasparini et al. (Berlin: De Gruyter, 2020), 469–91.
[45] Martin Gronewald, "Ein liturgischer Papyrus: Gebet und Ode 8: P. Mich. Inv. 6427," *ZPE* 14 (1974): 193–200.

limited, as only one of the four statements that compose Mand. 1.1 (26.1) is present, that about the incomprehensibility of God. If this is indeed a reference to Mand. 1.1 (26.1), it would be the same passage as that referenced in the two liturgical papyri, the Deir-Bala'izah Papyrus and the Barcelona Papyrus. Together, the four non-continuous papyri are witnesses to how the contents of the Shepherd informed prayer, prophetic, and liturgical language presumably in Egypt from the late third through the sixth centuries.

However, such a fragmentary and diluted usage starts considerably earlier. Irenaeus already quotes from the Shepherd without mentioning its name to the point that it is not necessarily clear whether he knows it as a book or just the one reference that he regularly employs.[46] Incidentally, Irenaeus uses in various ways the very same passage from the Shepherd found on the two liturgical papyri and the prayer in the Michigan papyrus: the monotheist statements in the first part of Mand. 1.1 (26.1). On the one hand, at least in one instance Irenaeus quotes this as coming from a book (in *Adv. haer.* 4.20.2 where it is introduced by καλῶς οὖν ἡ γραφὴ ἡ λέγουσα, "well has it the writing/scripture that says") and on the other not mentioning its name can be explained through Irenaeus' quotation habits.[47] Irenaeus, however, also uses the same quotation in his formulation of the canon of truth in *Epideixis* 4 and perhaps in *Adv. haer.* 1.21.1.[48] Since in these two instances no hint is given that the author is quoting from a different writing, Irenaeus' unsuspecting reader might not have detected the reference to the Shepherd, but it remains significant for study of its reception history that the latter had informed the language of Irenaeus' canon of truth and of his readers.

In a different patristic example toward the other end of late antiquity, Antiochus of Mar Saba, a seventh century monk at this monastery, wrote his *Pandect* as a collection of biblical and patristic excerpts on spiritual life for monastic use.[49] It includes a series of extensive excerpts from the Mandates and Similitudes which are paraphrased but still partially relevant for text-critical

---

[46] On the various scholarly takes see D. Jeffrey Bingham, "Senses of Scripture in the Second Century: Irenaeus, Scripture, and Noncanonical Christian Texts," *JR* 97 (2017): 26–55, esp. 35–45.

[47] On the latter point see Dan Batovici, "Hermas' authority in Irenaeus' works: a reassessment," *Augustinianum* 55.1 (2015): 5–31, at 18.

[48] On this overlooked usage see Batovici, "Hermas' authority in Irenaeus," 26–30.

[49] See Yannis Papadogiannakis, "An Education through Gnomic Wisdom: The Pandect of Antiochus as Bibliotheksersatz," in *Education and Religion in Late Antique Christianity: Reflections, Social Contexts and Genres,* ed. Peter Gemeinhard, Lieve Van Hoof and Peter Van Nuffelen (London/New York: Routledge, 2016), 61–72.

matters as they supply occasionally the Greek text where it has not survived in direct witnesses.[50] The fact that, much like Pseudo-Athanasius' Διδασκαλίαι πρὸς Ἀντίοχον in the previous century, Antiochus quotes freely and copiously from the Shepherd without mentioning the source, leads Carolyn Osiek, for instance, to note that there were still Greek copies of the text in Egypt and Palestine from which these authors "could plagiarize it [the Shepherd] repeatedly without feeling the need to acknowledge sources, perhaps indicating a serious decline in use."[51] Whether or not this indicates decline in use, Antiochus of Mar Saba offers an example where the Shepherd, even anonymously, informs collections meant for monastic life.

In a sense, given that the comparatively high number of Greek papyri of the Shepherd are also highly fragmentary,[52] there may be cause to question whether all the papyri we count as continuous papyri of this book are remnants of codices of the book as we know it today or excerpts of the book that were initially clearly stated as such (as opposed to tacit quotations embedded in other works). P.Oxy. LXIX 4705, for instance, is a small papyrus fragment considered to be an opisthograph roll, i.e. a repurposed papyrus roll, on the back of which (the vertical fiber side) a section from Vis. 1.1.8–9 [1.8–9] was copied in the third century. However, its size—a mere 8 × 8 cm—makes it less clear whether this was a roll that contained the whole book, a section or an excerpt clearly attributed to Hermas, or an anonymized excerpt copied for its apocalyptic content without knowledge of the book it originally belonged to, or similarly a quotation tacitly included in other works as in the non-continuous papyri or the works of Pseudo-Athanasius and Antiochus of Mar Saba. The same goes for instance for P.Mich. 2.2.130, an 8.7 × 12.1 cm fragment of a papyrus opisthograph roll where sections of Mand. 2 (27) and 3 (28) are preserved on the vertical fiber side.

Perhaps this question could be extended even to the smallest of the papyrus codex fragments, where not enough context has survived to establish beyond doubt that it was part of a copy of the Shepherd clearly stated as such, and to

---

50 The list of relevant passages is given in Molly Whittaker (ed.), *Der Hirt des Hermas*, Die apostolischen Väter 1 (Berlin: Akademie-Verlag, 1967), xix.
51 Osiek, *The Shepherd of Hermas*, 6.
52 About half of the Shepherd papyri were notoriously found in the rubbish heaps at Oxyrhynchus, which would explain their fragmentary state. Indeed, the two more consistent codices do not come from Oxyrhynchus finds: the provenance of P.Mich. 2.2.129 is Theadelphia and that of P. Bodmer 38 is normally simply listed as 'Egypt.' However, the eleven remaining continuous papyri seemingly coming from places other than Oxyrhynchus (Hermopolis, Fayyum, or more generally Egypt) are also very fragmentary.

rule out the possibility that it was in fact part of an extended anonymous or misattributed quotation. The oldest papyri of the Shepherd, P.Iand. I 4 of the 2nd c., P.Oxy. L 3528 of the 2/3rd century, or P.Oxy. XV 1828 of the 3rd for instance, as well as P.Berl. Sarischouli 9 (=BKT 9.163) of the 6th century at the other end, would allow such a question. It is merely a common assumption in the field that a papyrus fragment with the same text running on both sides comes from a codex of the same writing, but other scenarios remain possible, including the possibility that sections of a writing are copied, read, and preserved without indication or knowledge of the source book. To the best of my knowledge, the only manuscript from late antiquity, either Greek or Coptic, that preserves the title of the book—ΠΟΙΜΗΝ—is Codex Sinaiticus.[53] We just assume that in all cases the book would have been recognizable in the initial codex before segmentation, but it is not inconceivable that parts of the Shepherd might have circulated bearing no clear paratextual feature to signal its identity.

For instance, Campbell Bonner's proposal based on his reconstruction P.Mich 2.2.129 according to which Vis. 1–5 (1–25) had initially circulated separately from the rest of the book prefaced by Vision 5,[54] is well known in the scholarship on the Shepherd, and works on the assumption that this manuscript originally preserved in some way the identity of the book, or of this particular recension of the book. Despite some reservations,[55] Bonner's proposal proved remarkably successful in subsequent scholarship,[56] virtually in absence of scrutiny. I have offered elsewhere the argument, which I will not rehearse here, that Bonner's reconstruction of of P.Mich 2.2.129 involves two conjectural moves away from the actual state of the codex, and is not supported by the data in

---

[53] The matter is complicated by the fact that no Greek witness preserves the end of the book and therefore there is no extant colophon from Late Antiquity.
[54] Campbell Bonner, *A Papyrus Codex of the Shepherd of Hermas (Similitudes 2–9), with a Fragment of the Mandates* (Ann Arbor: University of Michigan Press, 1934). Bonner published in advance a description and important variant readings in C. Bonner, "A Papyrus Codex of the Shepherd of Hermas," *HTR* 18.2 (1925): 115–27.
[55] Kurt Aland and Hans-Udo Rosenbaum, *Repertorium der griechischen christlichen Papyri*, vol. 2. Kirchenväter-Papyri, Part 1. Beschreibungen, PTS 42 (Berlin: De Gruyter, 1995), lxxxix–xciv; Leutzsch in U.H.J. Körtner and M. Leutzsch (eds.), *Papiasfragmente. Hirt des Hermas* (Darmstadt: Wissensch. Buchgesell., 1998), 130; Mark Grundeken, *Community Building in the Shepherd of Hermas: A Critical Study of Some Key Aspects*, VCSup 131 (Leiden: Brill, 2015), 15.
[56] For more recent examples see Cecconi, "1200 Years of a Forbidden Text," 318; Jonathan E. Soyars, *The Shepherd of Hermas and the Pauline Legacy*, NovTSupp 176 (Leiden: Brill, 2019), 10; Arcari, "P.Oxy. 1.5 and the Codex Sangermanensis as 'Visionary Living Texts'," 481–82.

any of the Greek, Latin, or Coptic transmissions.[57] The general point was that, while it is entirely possible—and likely!—that smaller or larger parts of the Shepherd circulated separately, the divide after Vision 4, however obvious from the narrative point of view, is not supported by any positive evidence among our manuscripts, irrespective of how impressive the scholarly reception of Bonner's proposal is.[58]

To offer an example from a very interesting recent contribution, Paolo Cecconi offers a table with all known Greek witnesses of the book (save the Barcelona Papyrus), each being categorized in the fifth tab according to contents. These include the categories (alongside 'the whole Shepherd' and 'Fragments of the Visions,' 'of the Commandments, 'of the Parables') "Revelation of the Church" for Visions 1–4 (1–24) and "Revelation of the Shepherd" for the rest of the book starting with Vision 5 (25)—the title of the table being 'Editions of the Shepherd.'[59] What I would call into question is not the possibility that parts of the Shepherd circulated separately—this is in fact very likely,[60] as with any other lengthy text—but the overly exact division after Vision 4.3 (24) as well as the presumed identity of the two recensions in the transmission of the book. As a matter of fact, the designations "Revelation of the Church" and "Revelation of the Shepherd" appear nowhere in the manuscript tradition; they are entirely scholarly projections based on an ingenious but nonetheless speculative reconstruction. While appealing, their use effectively excludes the possibility that other, differently delimited excerpts were in circulation, as well as the possibility that these excerpts were circulated without any information that they belonged to a book named ΠΟΙΜΗΝ.

Yet we see at least one example of the latter situation in the Georgian translation, which is misattributed to Ephrem the Syrian in the only available witness, codex H-622 of the Georgian National Centre of Manuscripts, tentatively dated to the 9th–10th century. Bernard Outtier, who identified the book in H-622 and who is preparing a critical edition, also showed that the Georgian translation was made

---

57 Dan Batovici, "Two Notes on the Papyri of the Shepherd of Hermas and Its Egyptian Transmission," *APF* 62 (2016): 384–395; idem, "Dating, Split-Transmission Theory, and the Latin Reception of the Shepherd of Hermas," *Jahrbuch für Antike und Christentum* 60 (2017 [2018]): 83–90; and "Some Observations on the Coptic Reception of the Shepherd of Hermas," *Comparative Oriental Manuscript Studies Bulletin* 3 (2017): 81–96.
58 As will be seen below, the exception seems to be the Georgian translation, but that case seems to imply that the identity of the book in the exemplar was not self-evident; and, of course, its relevance for an early Egyptian transmission is limited.
59 Cecconi, "1200 Years of a Forbidden Text," 314–15, with the categories explained at the top of 314.
60 E. g. Choat and Yuen-Collingridge, "The Egyptian Hermas," 196.

from an Arabic translation rather than directly from the Greek.⁶¹ In order to misattribute a writing, one needs to lack previous knowledge of it *and* to lack (or miss) a clear title in the manuscript. It seems that the Arabic or Georgian translator indeed had access to an exemplar that did not preserve the title of the book in any clear manner. Moreover, the fact that the writing is attributed to Ephrem not only in the title but also within the text (i.e., the lines of the character Hermas are attributed to Ephrem, e.g. "and saint Ephrem said," etc.), could be linked to the fact that in the Greek, Hermas (the name) is not mentioned beyond Vision 4.1.7 (22.7); thus suggesting that the Arabic or Georgian translator did not have access to Vis. 1–4 (1–24). Indeed, the Georgian text begins with Vision 5 and includes all twelve Mandates. It would seem very likely therefore that the translator had access to a manuscript that contained only a section of the Shepherd (however extensive) and no mention of its title, namely a witness that did not have the paratextual features that preserve the identity of the book.⁶²

Finally, before concluding, one last example of reception where the identity of the book is lost is offered by the isolated quotation in the Armenian catena on the Catholic Epistles. The Armenian quotation has a correspondent in the Greek catena, as published by Cramer, where the inscription clearly mentions the source: Ἐκ τοῦ Ποιμένος ἐντολη θ', "from the Shepherd, Mandate 9."⁶³ The excerpt from Mand. 9.1–3 [39.1–3] is adduced to explain Jas 1:8. The inscription is also preserved in the Armenian catena. However, (ἐκ τοῦ) Ποιμένος is transliterated as a proper name "(of father) Pimen," rather than translated: Պիմէնի Հաւր յիննէրորդ պատուիրանացն, "From the ninth commandment

---

61 Bernard Outtier, "La version géorgienne du Pasteur d'Hermas," *Revue des études géorgiennes et caucasiennes* 6–7 (1990–1991): 211–15, esp. 212–13, where he also notes that the hypothesis that the whole H-622 could have been translated from an Arabic source has been verified for other texts in the codex, for which the Arabic model exists at Sinai.
62 A somewhat similar situation can be found in Greek in the thirteen-century florilegium, now split in two manuscripts, Athos Lavra K 96 and Paris BnF gr. 1143, where extracts from Similitudes alone are introduced (in Lavra K 96) as coming "from the Apocalypse of St. Germanos" (ἐκ τῆς ἀποκαλύψεως τοῦ ἁγίου Γερμανοῦ), for which see Michele Bandini, "Un nuovo frammento greco del *Pastore* di Erma," *Revue d'Histoire des Texts* 30 (2000): 109–22, at 110. Bandini edited in this article the fragments in Athos Lavra K 96 which, as noted in Jonathon Lookadoo, *The Shepherd of Hermas: A Literary, Historical, and Theological Handbook* (London: T&T Clark, 2021), 22n19, are not yet used in the current critical editions of the Shepherd; the excerpts in BnF gr. 1143 were already published by Eurydice Lappa-Zizicas, "Cinq fragments du *Pasteur* d'Hermas dans un manuscrit de la Bibliothèque nationale de Paris," *Recherches de science religieuse* 53 (1965): 251–56. I owe thanks to Chance Bonnar for drawing my attention by the means of a Twitter post to the misattribution in Athos Lavra K 96.
63 John A. Cramer, ed., *Catenae Græcorum Partum in Novum Testamentum, tomus 8: In Epistolas Catholicas et Apocalypsin* (Oxford: The University Press, 1844), 4.

of Father Pimen."⁶⁴ It seems that the Armenian translator neither recognized the Shepherd from the contents in the excerpt nor the book title in the Greek catena inscription.

Concluding Remarks

To conclude, the data we have from late antiquity suggest that the Shepherd of Hermas was read in a kaleidoscopic manner, as a collection of discrete, often isolated ways of appropriation. Various patristic authors considered it inspired in some ways, or an account of genuine revelation and prophecy. Many authors used it freely (explicitly or not) with biblical books in theological contexts to formulate articles of faith (e.g. Origen, in the *prefatio* of *De principiis*), canons of truth (Irenaeus), or in collections meant to inform monastic life. Most authors who are explicit about the secondary position of the Shepherd in relation to the New Testament, rather than rejecting the book entirely, prescribe that it should in fact be read (Eusebius, Athanasius, the Muratorian Fragment); some of these, along with other authors, find it useful in the instruction of catechumens, and a few testimonies suggest that it was sometimes read in churches.

The late antique manuscript witnesses also reflect the free usage of the book with biblical texts, in prophetical contexts, and copied in what we would otherwise describe as biblical manuscripts (Codex Sinaiticus). Excerpts from the book were used as exegesis for biblical texts (catena on James), as a proof text for civil matters, or as a source for liturgical language. Finally, the sheer variety of ways and contexts in which the Shepherd is excerpted, copied, and repurposed without preserving the identity of the source as a book (both in patristic literature and in manuscripts) raises the question of whether it is a help or a hinderance to project postulated recensions of the fragmentary papyri (or even the common assumption that they reflect the book as we know it) in trying to understand the work's use and transmission.

---

64 Text in Charles Renoux, ed., *La chaîne arménienne sur les Épîtres Catholiques. I. La chaîne sur l'Épître de Jacques*, Patrologia Orientalis 43.1, No. 193 (Turnhout: Brepols, 1985), 76, who tacitly corrects the title in his translation to "Du neuvième précepte du Pasteur." I thank Anahit Avagyan for drawing my attention to this.

Bibliography

Ahmed, Sara. "Happy Objects." Pages 29–51 in *The Affect Theory Reader*. Edited by Gregory J. Seigworth and Melissa Gregg. Durham, NC: Duke University Press, 2010.
Aland, Kurt, and Hans–Udo Rosenbaum. *Repertorium der griechischen christlichen Papyri*, vol. 2: Kirchenväter–Papyri, Part 1: Beschreibungen. PTS 42. Berlin: De Gruyter, 1995.
Allan, Rutger J., Irene J. F. de Jong and Casper C. de Jonge. "From *Enargeia* to Immersion: The Ancient Roots of a Modern Concept." *Style* 51 (2017): 34–51.
Allan, Rutger J. "Herodotus and Thucydides: Distance and Immersion." Pages 131–54 in *Textual Strategies in Ancient War Narrative: Thermopylae, Cannae and Beyond*. Edited by Lidewij van Gils, Irene J.F. de Jong and Caroline Kroon. Brill, Leiden: 2018.
Anderson, Greg. *The Realness of Things Past: Ancient Greece and Ontological History*. Oxford: Oxford University Press, 2018.
Arcari, Luca. "P.Oxy. 1.5 and the Codex Sangermanensis as 'Visionary Living Texts': Visionary *habitus* and Processes of 'Textualization' and/or 'Scripturalization' in Late Antiquity." Pages 469–91 in *Lived Religion in the Ancient Mediterranean World. Approaching Religious Transformations from Archaeology, History and Classics*. Edited by Valentino Gasparini, Maik Patzelt, Rubina Raja, Anna–Katharina Rieger, Jörg Rüpke and Emiliano R. Urciuoli. Berlin: De Gruyter, 2020.
Arcari, Luca. *Vedere Dio. Le apocalissi giudaiche e protocristiane (sec. IV a.C.–sec. II d.C.)*. Frecce 293. Rome: Carocci, 2020.
Argarate, Pablo. "The Holy Spirit in Prin I. 3." Pages 25–48 in *Origeniana Nona: Origen and the Religious Practice of his Time*. Edited by György Heidl and Róbert Somos. Leuven: Peeters, 2009.
Ashton, John. *The Religion of Paul the Apostle*. New Haven, CT: Yale University Press, 2000.
Aune, David E. "Mastery of the Passions: Philo, 4 Maccabees and Earliest Christianity." Pages 125–58 in *Hellenization Revisited: Shaping a Christian Response within the Greco-Roman World*. Edited by Wendy E. Helleman. Lanham, MD: University Press of America, 1994.
Augé, Marc. *The War of Dreams: Exercises in Ethno-Fiction*. Sterling, VA: Pluto Press, 1999.
Aune, David E. *Prophecy in Early Christianity and in the Ancient Mediterranean*. Grand Rapids, MI: Eerdmans, 1983.
Austin, John L. *How to Do Things with Words*. Edited by J. O. Urmson. Cambridge: Harvard University Press, 1962.
Avrahami, Yael. *The Senses of Scripture*. Sheffield: T&T Clark, 2012.
Ayán Calvo, Juan José. *Hermas. El Pastor*. Fuentes Patrísticas 6. Madrid: Editorial Ciudad Nueva, 1995.
Bacigalupo, Ana M. *Thunder Shaman: Making History with Mapuche Spirits in Chile and Patagonia*. Austin: University of Texas Press, 2016.
Bakhtin, Mikhail M. "The Problem of Speech Genres." Pages 60–102 in *Speech Genres and Other Late Essays*. Translated by Vern W. McGee. Edited by Caryl Emerson and Michael Holquist. Austin: University of Texas Press, 1986.
Bandini, Michele. "Un nuovo frammento greco del *Pastore* di Erma." *Revue d'Histoire des Textes* 30 (2000): 109–22.

Bardy, Gustave. "Le Pasteur d'Hermas et les Livres Hermétiques." *Revue Biblique* 8 (1911): 391–407.
Baskin, Judith R. "Origen on Balaam: The Dilemma of the Unworthy Prophet." *VC* 37 (1983): 22–35.
Bassler, Jouette M. "The Widows' Tale: A Fresh Look at 1 Tim 5:3–16." *JBL* 103 (1984): 23–41.
Batovici, Dan. "Textual Revisions of the *Shepherd of Hermas* in Codex Sinaiticus." *ZAC* 18 (2014): 443–70.
Batovici, Dan. "Hermas' Authority in Irenaeus' Works: A Reassessment." *Augustinianum* 55.1 (2015): 5–31.
Batovici, Dan. "Two Notes on the Papyri of the *Shepherd of Hermas* and Its Egyptian Transmission." *APF* 62.2 (2016): 384–95.
Batovici, Dan. "The Apostolic Fathers in Codex Sinaiticus and Alexandrinus." *Bib* 97.4 (2016): 581–605.
Batovici, Dan. "The Shepherd of Hermas in Recent Scholarship on the Canon: A Review Article." *ASE* 34 (2017): 89–105.
Batovici, Dan. "Some Observations on the Coptic Reception of the *Shepherd of Hermas*." *Comparative Oriental Manuscript Studies Bulletin* 3.2 (2017): 81–96.
Batovici, Dan. "Dating, Split-Transmission Theory, and the Latin Reception of the *Shepherd of Hermas*." *Jahrbuch für Antike und Christentum* 60 (2017 [2018]): 83–90.
Batovici, Dan. *The Shepherd in Late Antiquity*. Piscataway, NJ: Gorgias Press, forthcoming.
Bauckham, Richard. "The Great Tribulation in the *Shepherd of Hermas*." *JTS* 25 (1974): 27–40.
Bauckham, Richard. *Jesus and the God of Israel: God Crucified and Other Studies on the New Testament's Christology of Divine Identity*. Grand Rapids, MI: Eerdmans, 2008.
Bazzana, Giovanni B. "'Il corpo della carne di Gesù Cristo' (P. Oxy. I.5). Conflitti ecclesiologici nel cristianesimo del II secolo." *Adamantius* 10 (2004): 100–122.
Bazzana, Giovanni. "'You Will Write Two Booklets and Send One to Clement and One to Grapte': Formal Features, Circulation, and Social Function of Ancient Apocalyptic Literature." Pages 43–70 in *Scribal Practices and Social Structures among Jesus Adherents: Essays in Honour of John S. Kloppenborg*. Edited by William Arnal. BETL 285. Leuven: Peeters, 2016.
Bazzana, Giovanni B. *Having the Spirit of Christ: Spirit Possession and Exorcism in the Early Christ Groups*. New Haven: Yale University Press, 2020.
Beavis, Mary Ann. "The Parable of the Slave, Son, and Vineyard: An Early Christian Freedman's Narrative (Hermas *Similitudes* 5.2–11)." *CBQ* 80 (2018): 655–69.
Bell, Catherine. *Ritual Theory, Ritual Practice*. New York: Oxford University Press, 1992.
Bennett, Jane. *Vibrant Matter: A Political Ecology of Things*. Durham: Duke University Press, 2010.
Berchman, Robert M. "Arcana mundi between Balaam and Hecate: prophecy, divination, and magic in later Platonism." *SBLSP* 28 (1989): 107–83.
Betts, Eleanor, ed. *Senses of the Empire: Multisensory Approaches to Roman Culture*. New York: Routledge, 2017.
Bieler, Ludwig. *The Irish Penitentials*. Scriptores latini Hiberniae 5. Dublin: Institute for Advanced Studies, 1963.
Bingham, D. Jeffrey. "Senses of Scripture in the Second Century: Irenaeus, Scripture, and Noncanonical Christian Texts." *JR* 97 (2017): 26–55.

Bird, Michael F. *Jesus the Eternal Son: Answering Adoptionist Christology*. Grand Rapids, MI: Eerdmans, 2017.
Boddy, Janice. *Wombs and Alien Spirits: Women, Men, and the Zâr Cults of Northern Sudan*. Madison, WI: University of Wisconsin Press, 1989.
Boddy, Janice. "Spirit Possession Revisited: Beyond Instrumentality." *ARA* 23 (1994): 407–34.
Bucur, Bogdan G. "Scholarship on the Old Testament Roots of Trinitarian Theology: Blind Spots and Blurred Vision." Pages 29-49 in *The Bible and Early Trinitarian Theology*. Edited by Christopher Beeley and Mark Weedman. Washington, DC: CUA Press, 2018.
Bonner, Campbell. *A Papyrus Codex of the Shepherd of Hermas (Similitudes 2–9) with a Fragment of the Mandates*. Ann Arbor: University of Michigan, 1934.
Bonner, Campbell. "A Papyrus Codex of the Shepherd of Hermas," *HTR* 18 (1925): 115–27.
Bourdieu, Pierre. *Outline of a Theory of Practice*. Translated by Richard Nice. Cambridge: Cambridge University Press, 1977.
Bourguignon, Erika. *Religion, Altered States of Consciousness, and Social Change*. Columbus: Ohio State University Press, 1973.
Boyarin, Daniel. *The Jewish Gospels: The Story of the Jewish Christ*. New York: New Press, 2012.
Bradley, Keith. "Animalizing the Slave: The Truth of Fiction." *Journal of Roman Studies* 90 (2000): 110–25.
Bremmer, Jan N. "From Books with Magic to Magical Books in Ancient Greece and Rome?" Pages 241–70 in *The Materiality of Magic*. Edited by Dietrich Boschung and Jan N. Bremmer. Paderborn: Wilhelm Fink, 2015.
Brenk, Frederick E. "In the Light of the Moon: Demonology in the Early Imperial Period." Pages 2068–2145 in *Aufstieg und Niedergang der römischen Welt*. Vol. 2. Edited by Hildegard Temporini and Wolfgang Haase. Berlin: Walter De Gruyter, 1972.
Brooke, George J. "The Qumran Scrolls and the Demise of the Distinction Between Higher and Lower Criticism." Pages 26–42 in *New Directions in Qumran Studies: Proceedings of the Bristol Colloquium on the Dead Sea Scrolls 8–10 September 2003*. Edited by Jonathan G. Campbell, William John Lyons, and Lloyd K. Pietersen. London: T & T Clark International, 2005.
Brown, Peter. *The Making of Late Antiquity*. Cambridge: Harvard University Press, 1976.
Brown, Peter. *The Body and Society: Men, Women, and Sexual Renunciation in Early Christianity*. New York: Columbia University Press, 2008.
Brown, William P. *The Seven Pillars of Creation: The Bible, Science, and the Ecology of Wonder*. Oxford: Oxford University Press, 2010.
Brox, Norbert. *Der Hirt des Hermas*. KAV 7. Göttingen: Vandenhoeck & Ruprecht, 1991.
Bucur, Bogdan Gabriel. *Angelomorphic Pneumatology: Clement of Alexandria and Other Early Christian Witnesses*. VCSup 95. Leiden: Brill, 2009.
Bucar, Bogdan G., "Scholarship on The Old Testament Roots of Trinitarian Theology: Blind Spots and Blurred Vision." Pages 29–49 in *The Bible and Early Trinitarian Theology*. Edited by Christopher Beeley and Mark Weedmand. Washington, DC: CUA Press, 2018.
Bucur, Bogdan Gabriel. "The Son of God and the Angelomorphic Holy Spirit: A Rereading of the Shepherd's Christology." *ZNW* 98 (2007): 121–43.
Buell, Denise K. "The Microbes and Pneuma That Therefore I Am." Pages 63–87 in *Divinanimality: Animal Theory, Creaturely Theology*. Edited by Stephen D. Moore. New York, NY: Fordham University, 2014.

Burke, Peter. *Varieties of Cultural History.* Ithaca, NY: Cornell University Press, 1997.
Burkert, Walter. "Epiphanies and Signs of Power: Minoan Suggestions and Comparative Evidence." *Illinois Classical Studies* 29 (2004): 1–23. Reprinted as pages 156–76 in *Kleine Schriften VI: Mythica, ritualia, religiosa 3: Kulte und Feste.* Edited by E. Krummen. Göttingen: Vandenhoeck & Ruprecht, 2011.
Burman, Jeremy T. "Bringing the Brain into History: Behind Hunt's and Smail's Appeals to Neurohistory." Pages 64–82 in *Psychology and History. Interdisciplinary Explorations.* Edited by Cristian Tileagă and Jovan Byford. Cambridge: Cambridge University Press, 2014.
Cairns, Douglas. "A Short History of Shudders." Pages 85–107 in *Unveiling Emotions II— Emotions in Greece and Rome: Texts, Images, Material Culture.* Edited by Angelos Chaniotis and Pierre Ducrey. HABES 55. Stuttgart: Franz Steiner Verlag, 2013.
Cancik, Hubert. "Römische Dämonologie (Varro, Apuleius, Tertullian)." Pages 447–60 in *Die Dämonen (Demons). Die Dämonologie der israelitisch–jüdischen und frühchristlichen Literatur im Kontext ihrer Umwelt (The Demonology of Israelite–Jewish and Early Christian Literature in Context of their Environment).* Edited by Armin Lange, Hermann Lichtenberger, and K.F. Diethard Römheld. Tübingen: Mohr Siebeck, 2003.
Caracciolo, Marco. "Narrative, Meaning, Interpretation: An Enactivist Approach." *Phenomenology and the Cognitive Sciences* 11 (2012): 367–84.
Caracciolo, Marco. *The Experientiality of Narrative: An Enactivist Approach.* Berlin: De Gruyter, 2014.
Carlini, Antonio. "P. Michigan 130 (inv. 44–H) e il problema dell'unicità di redazione del Pastore di Erma." *La parola del passato* 208 (1983): 29–37.
Carlini, Antonio. "Le passaggiate di Erma verso Cuma (su due luoghi controversi del Pastore)." Pages 105–9 in *Studi in onore di Edda Bresciani.* Edited by S. F. Bondì, S. Pernigotti, F. Serra, A. Vivian. Pisa: Giardini, 1985.
Carlini, Antonio. "Testimone e testo. Il problema della datazione di PIand I 4 e il Pastore di Erma." *SCO* 42 (1992): 17–30.
Castelli, Emanuele. "Gli esordi alternativi del *Pastore* di *Erma.*" *Adamantius* 26 (2020): 551-75.
Castelli, Emanuele. "Dati storici e aspetti romanzeschi nelle prime due *Visioni* del *Pastore* di Erma. Una riconsiderazione del problema alla luce di nuove scoperte testuali." *Augustinianum* 60 (2020): 321-40.
Castelli, Elizabeth A. *Martyrdom and Memory: Early Christian Culture Making.* New York: Columbia University Press, 2004.
Cecconi, Paolo. "1200 Years of Materialities and Editions of a Forbidden Text." Pages 309–30 in *Antike Texte und ihre Materialität. Alltägliche Präsenz, mediale Semantik, literarische Reflexion.* Edited by Cornelia Ritter–Schmalz and Raphael Schwitter. Materiale Textkulturen 27; Berlin: De Gruyter, 2019.
Chadwick, Henry. Review of *Der Hirt des Hermas,* by Norbert Brox. *Journal of Ecclesiastical History* 47 (1996): 119.
Chadwick, Henry. "Philosophical Tradition and the Self." In *Late Antiquity: A Guide to the Postclassical World,* edited by G.W. Bowersock, Peter Brown, and Oleg Grabar. Cambridge: Belknap Press of Harvard University Press, 1999.
Charles, Ronald. *The Silencing of Slaves in Early Jewish and Christian Texts.* Routledge Studies in the Early Christian World. New York: Routledge, 2019.

Chartier, Roger. "Reading and Reading Practices." Pages 399–404 in vol 3 of *Encyclopedia of the Enlightenment*. Edited by Alan C. Kors. 4 vols. Oxford: Oxford University Press, 2003.
Chin, Catherine. "Who is the Ascetic Exegete? Angels, Enchantments, and Transformative Food in Origen's Homilies on Joshua." Pages 203–18 in *Asceticism and Exegesis in Early Christianity: The Reception of New Testament Texts in Ancient Ascetic Discourses*. Edited by Hans Ulrich Weidemann. Göttingen: Vandenhoeck & Ruprecht, 2013.
Choat, Malcolm and Rachel Yuen-Collingridge. "The Egyptian Hermas: The Shepherd in Egypt before Constantine." Pages 191–212 in *Early Christian Manuscripts: Examples of Applied Method and Approach*, edited by Thomas J. Kraus and Tobias Nicklas. Leiden: Brill, 2010.
Clarke, John R. *Art in the Lives of Ordinary Romans: Visual Representation and Non-Elite Viewers in Italy, 100 B.C.–A.D. 315*. Berkeley: University of California Press, 2003.
Cioffi, Robert L. "Travel in the Roman World." *Oxford Handbook Online*, 2016. DOI: 10.1093/oxfordhb/9780199935390.013.110 (*l.a.* 02/03/2020).
Clark, Kenneth W. "The Sins of Hermas." Pages 102–19 in *Early Christian Origins: Studies in Honor of H. R. Willoughby*. Edited by A. Wikgren. Chicago: Quadrangle Books, 1961.
Cobb, L. Stephanie. *Dying to be Men: Gender and Language in Early Christian Martyr Texts*. New York: Columbia University Press, 2008.
Coblentz Bautch, Kelley. "Spatiality and Apocalyptic Literature." *Hebrew Bible and Ancient Israel* 3 (2016): 273–88.
Coleborne, William. "A Linguistic Approach to the Problem of Structure and Composition of the Shepherd of Hermas." *Colloquium* 3 (1967): 133–42.
Collins, John J. "The Development of the Sibylline Tradition." Pages 421–59 in *Aufstieg und Niedergang der römischen Welt*. Edited by Hildegard Temporini and Wolfgang Haase. Berlin: De Gruyter, 1972.
Comor, Edward. "Contextualizing and Critiquing the Fantastic Prosumer: Power, Alienation and Hegemony." *Critical Sociology* 37.3 (2011): 309–27.
Conway, Colleen. "Gender and Divine Relativity in Philo of Alexandria." *JSJ* 34 (2003): 471–91.
Cramer, J.A., ed. *Catenae græcorum patrum in Novum Testamentum, tomus 8. In Epistolas Catholicas et Apocalypsin*. Oxford: The University Press, 1844.
Crapanzano, Vincent. "The Betwixt and Between of the Dream." Pages 232–59 in *Hundert Jahre "Die Traumdeutung". Kulturwissenschaftliche Perspektiven in der Traumforschung*. Edited by Burkhard Schnepel. Köln: Koppe, 2001.
Crenshaw, Kimberle. "Demarginalizing the Intersection of Race and Sex: A Black Feminist Critique of Antidiscrimination Doctrine, Feminist Theory, and Antiracist Politics." *The University of Chicago Legal Forum* 140 (1989): 139–67.
Crislip, Andrew. "The Shepherd of Hermas and Early Christian Emotional Formation." *Studia Patristica* 9 (2017): 231–40.
Cross, Frank L., and E.A. Livingstone, eds. "Hermas." *Oxford Dictionary of the Christian Church*, 2nd ed. Oxford: Oxford University Press, 2006.
Damasio, Antonio R. *The Feeling of What Happens: Body and Emotion in the Making of Consciousness*. New York, San Diego and London: Harcourt Brace and Company, 1999.
Daniélou, Jean. *The Theology of Jewish Christianity*. London: Darton, Longman & Todd, 1964.
Deemter, Roelof van. *Der Hirt des Hermas. Apokalypse oder Allegorie?* Delft: W.D. Meinem, 1929.
Deissmann, Adolf. *Die Neutestamentliche Formel "in Christo Jesu"*. Marburg: Elwert, 1892.

DeLanda, Manuel. *Assemblage Theory*. Edinburgh: Edinburgh University Press, 2016.
Deleuze, Gilles, and Félix Guatarri. *A Thousand Plateaus: Capitalism and Schizophrenia*. Translated by Brian Massumi. Minneapolis: University of Minnesota Press, 1987.
Deleuze, Gilles. *Spinoza: Practical Philosophy*. San Francisco: City Lights Books, 1988F.
Dibelius, Martin. *Die apostolischen Väter IV. Der Hirt des Hermas*. HNT. Tübingen: Mohr Siebeck, 1923.
Dibelius, Martin. "Der Offenbarungsträger im 'Hirten' des Hermas." Pages 80–93 in *Botschaft und Geschichte. Gesammelte Aufsätze von Martin Dibelius*. Edited by Günther Bornkamm. Tübingen: Mohr Siebeck, 1956.
DiTommaso, Lorenzo. *The Book of Daniel and the Apocryphal Daniel Literature*. SVTP 20. Leiden: Brill, 2005.
Dodds, Eric Robertson. *The Greeks and the Irrational*. Boston: Beacon Press, 1957.
Dodds, Eric Robertson. *Pagan and Christian in an Age of Anxiety: Some Aspects of Religious Experience from Marcus Aurelius to Constantine*. Cambridge: Cambridge University Press, 2000.
Drake, Susanna. *Slandering the Jew: Sexuality and Difference in Early Christian Texts*. Philadelphia: University of Pennsylvania Press, 2013.
Draper, Jonathan A. "Practicing the Presence of God in John: Ritual use of Scripture and the *Eidos Theou* in John 5:37." In *Orality, Literacy, and Colonialism in Antiquity*. Edited by Jonathan A. Draper. Semeia Studies 1–6. Atlanta: SBL Press, 2004.
Dunning, Benjamin H. *Aliens and Sojourners: Self as Other in Early Christianity*. Philadelphia: University of Pennsylvania Press, 2009.
Ehrman, Bart D., ed. and trans. *Epistle of Barnabas, Papias, and Quadratus, Epistle to Diognetus, The Shepherd of Hermas*. Vol. 2 of *The Apostolic Fathers*. LCL 25. Cambridge, MA: Harvard University Press, 2003.
Elfenbein, Andrew. *The Gist of Reading*. Stanford: Stanford University Press, 2018.
Enenkel, Karl A. E., and Walter Melion, eds. *Meditation–Refashioning the Self: Theory and Practice in Late Medieval*. Leiden: Brill, 2010.
Epp, Eldon Jay. "The Oxyrhynchus New Testament Papyri: 'Not without honor except in their hometown'?" Pages 743–803 in his *Perspectives on New Testament Textual Criticism: Collected Essays, 1962–2004*. NovTSup 116. Leiden/Boston: Brill, 2005.
Espírito Santo, Diana. "Imagination, Sensation, and the Education of Attention among Cuban Spirit Mediums." *Ethnos* 77 (2012): 252–71.
Eyl, Jennifer. *Signs, Wonders, and Gifts: Divination in the Letters of Paul*. New York: Oxford University Press, 2019.
Finkelstein, David, and Alistair McCleery. "Theorizing the History of Books." Pages 7–28 in *An Introduction to Book History*. Edited by David Finkelstein and Alistair McCleery. London, New York: Routledge, 2005.
Finney, Paul Corby. *The Invisible God: The Earliest Christians on Art*. Oxford: Oxford University Press, 1994.
Flannery, Frances, Nicolae Roddy, Colleen Shantz, and Rodney A. Werline. "Introduction: Religious Experience, Past and Present." Pages 1–10 in *Experientia, Volume 1: Inquiry Into Religious Experience in Early Judaism and Christianity*. Edited by Rodney Alan Werline, Frances Flannery, and Colleen Shantz. Atlanta: SBL Press, 2008.

Flechner, Roy, ed. *The Hibernensis: A Study and Edition*, Book 1. Studies in Medieval and Early Modern Canon Law 17.1. Washington DC: Catholic University of America Press, 2019.

Fletcher-Louis, Crispin. *Jesus Monotheism, Volume 1—Christological Origins: The Emerging Consensus and Beyond*. Eugene, OR: Cascade, 2015.

Foster, Paul. "Polymorphic Christology: Its Origins and Development in Early Christianity." *JTS* 58 (2007): 66–99.

Foucault, Michel. *The Use of Pleasure*. Vol 2 of *The History of Sexuality*. Translated by Robert Hurley. New York: Vintage Books, 1990.

Fox, Robin Lane. *Pagans and Christians*. London: Penguin, 2006.

Frank, Joseph. "Spatial Form in Modern Literature: An Essay in Two Parts. Part 1." *The Sewanee Review* 53.2 (1945): 221–40.

Freeman, Jennifer Awes. "The Good Shepherd and the Enthroned Ruler: A Reconsideration of Imperial Iconography in the Early Church." Page 182 in *The Art of Empire: Christian Art in Its Imperial Context*. Edited by Lee M. Jefferson and Robin M. Jensen. Minneapolis: Fortress Press, 2015.

Gager, John G. "Introduction: The Dodds Hypothesis." Pages 1–11 in *Pagan and Christian Anxiety: A Response to E.R. Dodds*. Edited by Robert C. Smith and John Lounibos. Lanham, MD: University Press of America, 1984.

Gallagher, Shaun. *How the Body Shapes the Mind*. Oxford: Clarendon Press, 2005.

Galli, Marco. "Pilgrimage as Elite *Habitus*: Educated Pilgrims in Sacred Landscape During the Second Sophistic." Pages 253–90 in *Pilgrimage in Graeco-Roman and Early Christian Antiquity: Seeing the Gods*. Edited by Jaś Elsner and Ian Rutherford. Oxford: Oxford University Press, 2005

Gamber, K. "Das Eucharistiegebet im Papyrus von Der-Balizeh und die Samstagabend-Agapen in Ägypten." *Ostkirchliche Studien* 7 (1958): 48–56.

Gamble, Harry Y. *Books and Readers in the Early Church. A History of Early Christian Texts*. New Haven: Yale University Press, 1995.

Gatens, Moira, and Genevieve Lloyd. *Collective Imaginings: Spinoza, Past and Present*. London: Routledge, 1999.

Geertz, Armin W. "Global Perspectives on Methodology in the Study of Religion." *MTSR* 12 (2000): 49–73.

Geertz, Armin W. "Brain, Body and Culture: A Biocultural Theory of Religion." *MTSR* 22 (2010): 304–21.

Gemünden, Petra von. *Affekt und Glaube. Studien zur historischen Psychologie des Frühjudentums und Urchristentums*. NTOA 73. Göttingen: Vandenhoeck & Ruprecht, 2009.

Gieschen, Charles A. "The Divine Name in Ante-Nicene Christology." *VC* 57 (2003): 115–58.

Gieschen, Charles A. *Angelomorphic Christology: Antecedents and Early Evidence*. AGSU 42. Leiden: Brill, 1998.

Giet, Stanislas. *Hermas et les Pasteurs. Les trois auteurs du Pasteur d'Hermas*. Paris: Presses universitaires du France, 1963.

Gill, Christopher. *The Structured Self in Hellenistic and Roman Thought*. Oxford: Oxford University Press, 2006.

Gilmour, Calum. "Religious Vascillation and Indecision: Doublemindedness as the Opposite of Faith: A Study of *Dispychos* and Its Cognates in the *Shepherd of Hermas* and Other Early Christian Literature." *Prudentia* 16 (1984): 13–42.

Glancy, Jennifer A. *Slavery in Early Christianity.* Oxford: Oxford University Press, 2002.

Glancy, Jennifer A. "Protocols of Masculinity in the Pastoral Epistles." Pages 235–64 in *New Testament Masculinities*. Edited by Stephen D. Moore and Janice Capel Anderson. Semeia 45. Atlanta SBL Press, 2003.

Gleason, Maud W. *Making Men: Sophists and Self-Presentation in Ancient Rome.* Princeton: Princeton University Press, 1995.

Go, Julian. *Postcolonial Thought and Social Theory.* Oxford: Oxford University Press, 2016.

Goldingay, Sarah. "To Perform Possession and to Be Possessed in Performance: The Actor, the Medium, and the Other." Pages 205–22 in *Spirit Possession and Trance: New Interdisciplinary Perspectives*. Edited by Bettina E. Schmidt and Lucy Huskinson. London: Continuum, 2010.

Goodman, Martin. "The Pilgrimage Economy of Jerusalem in the Second Temple Period." Pages 59–67 in his *Judaism in the Roman World: Collected Essays*. AJEC 66. Leiden: Brill, 2007.

Gorman, Michael M. "Patristic and Pseudo-Patristic Citation in the *Collectio Hibernensis*." *Revue bénédictine* 121 (2011): 18–93.

Gregory, Andrew. "Disturbing Trajectories: *1 Clement*, the *Shepherd of Hermas*, and the Development of Early Roman Christianity." Pages 142–66 in *Rome in the Bible and the Early Church*. Edited by Peter Oakes. Carlisle: Paternoster, 2002.

Grethlein, Jonas. "The Narrative Reconfiguration of Time Beyond Ricœur." *Poetics Today* 31 (2010): 313–29.

Grethlein, Jonas. *Experience and Teleology in Ancient Historiography.* Cambridge: Cambridge University Press, 2013.

Grethlein, Jonas. *Aesthetic Experiences and Classical Antiquity. The Content of Form in Narratives and Pictures.* Cambridge: Cambridge University Press, 2017.

Grethlein, Jonas and Luuk Huitink. "Homer's Vividness: An Enactive Approach." *JHS* 137 (2017): 67–91.

Gribetz, Sarit Kattan. "Women as Readers of the Nag Hammadi Codices." *JECS* 26 (2018): 463–94.

Gronewald, M. "Ein liturgischer Papyrus: Gebet und Ode 8. P. Mich. Inv. 6427." *ZPE* 14 (1974): 193–200.

Grundeken, Mark. *Community Building in the Shepherd of Hermas: A Critical Study of Some Key Aspects.* VCSup 131. Leiden: Brill, 2015.

Grundeken, Mark, and Joseph Verheyden. "The Spirit before the Letter: Dreams and Visions as the Legitimization of the *Shepherd of Hermas* a Study of *Vision 5*." Pages 23–56 in *Dreams as Divine Communication in Christianity: From Hermas to Aquinas*. Edited by Bart J. Koet. Leuven: Peeters Publishers, 2012.

Gunnarsson, Lena. "Why We Keep Separating the 'Inseparable': Dialecticizing Intersectionality." *European Journal of Women's Studies* 24 (2017): 114–27.

Hadot, Pierre. *Philosophy as a Way of Life: Spiritual Exercises from Socrates to Foucault.* Translated by Michael Chase. Oxford: Blackwell, 1995.

Haelst, J. Van. "Une nouvelle reconstitution du Papyrus liturgique de Der-Balizeh." *ETL* 45 (1969): 444–55.

Haines-Eitzen, Kim. "'Girls Trained in Beautiful Writing': Female Scribes in Roman Antiquity and Early Christianity." *JECS* 6 (1998): 629–46.

Haines-Eitzen, Kim. *Guardians of Letters: Literacy, Power, and the Transmitters of Early Christian Literature*. Oxford University Press, 2000.

Hallett, Judith and Marilyn B. Skinner, ed. *Roman Sexualities*. Princeton: Princeton University Press, 1997.

Hannah, Darrell D. *Michael and Christ: Michael Traditions and Angel Christology in Early Christianity*. WUNT 2/109. Tübingen: Mohr Siebeck, 1999.

Hanson, John S. "Dreams and Visions in the Graeco-Roman World and Early Christianity." Pages 1395–427 in *Aufstieg und Niedergang der römischen Welt*. Edited by Hildegard Temporini and Wolfgang Haase. Berlin: Walter De Gruyter, 1972.

Harkins, Angela Kim. *Reading with an "I" to the Heavens: Looking at the Qumran Hodayot through the Lens of Visionary Traditions*. Ekstasis 3. Berlin, Boston: De Gruyter, 2012.

Harkins, Angela Kim. "The Pro-Social Role of Grief in Ezra's Penitential Prayer." *BibInt* 24 (2016): 466–91.

Harkins, Angela Kim. "Experiencing the Journey: Spaces in the *Book of Visions* of the *Shepherd of Hermas*." Unpublished paper presented to the Boston Area Patristics Group, Harvard Divinity School, January 2019.

Harkins, Angela Kim. "Looking at the *Shepherd of Hermas* through the Experience of Lived Religion." Pages 49–70 in *Lived Religion in the Ancient Mediterranean World: Approaching Religious Transformations from Archaeology, History and Classics*. Edited by Valentino Gasparini, Maik Patzelt, Rubina Raja, Anna-Katharina Rieger, Jörg Rüpke, and Emiliano Urciuoli. Berlin: De Gruyter, 2020.

Harkins, Angela Kim. *Experiencing Presence in the Second Temple Period: Revised and Updated Essays*. Contributions to Biblical Exegesis and Theology 111. Leuven: Peeters, 2022.

Harkins, Angela Kim. "Immersing Oneself in the Narrative World of Second Temple Apocalyptic Visions." In *Re-imagining Apocalypticism: Apocalypses, Apocalyptic Literature, and the Dead Sea Scrolls*. Edited by Lorenzo DiTommaso and Matthew J. Goff. SBLEJL. Atlanta: SBL Press, 2022.

Harkins, Angela Kim. *Re-reading the Visions in the Shepherd of Hermas*. Studies in Ancient Religion & Culture. Sheffield: Equinox Press, 2023.

Harnack, Adolf von. *History of Dogma*. Translated by Neil Buchanan *et al.* 7 vols. London: Williams & Norgate, 1896–99.

Harris, James Rendel. "Hermas in Arcadia." *Journal of the Society of Biblical Literature and Exegesis* 7 (1887): 69–83.

Harris, James Rendel. *Hermas in Arcadia and Other Essays*. Cambridge: Cambridge University Press, 1896.

Harris, William V. *Dreams and Experience in Classical Antiquity*. Cambridge, MA: Harvard University Press, 2009.

Haxby, Mikael. "The First Apocalypse of James: Martyrdom and Sexual Difference." Ph.D. diss., Harvard University, 2013.

Heine, Ronald E. *The Montanist Oracles and Testimonia*. Leuven: Peeters, 1989.

Hellholm, David. *Das Visionenbuch des Hermas als Apokalypse. Formgeschichtliche und texttheoretische Studien zu einer literarischen Gattung*. ConBOT 1. Lund: C.W.K. Gleeup, 1980.

Henne, Philippe. "La polysémie allégorique dans le *Pasteur* d'Hermas." *ETL* 65 (1989): 131–35.
Henne, Philippe. "Canonicité du 'Pasteur' d'Hermas." *RThom* 90 (1990): 81–100.
Henne, Philippe. "La pénitence dans le *Pasteur* d'Hermas." *Revue Biblique* 98 (1991): 358–97.
Henne, Philippe. *L'Unité du Pasteur. Tradition et Rédaction*. Paris: J. Gabalda, 1992.
Hilgenfeld, A. Review of O. Gerhardt and A. Harnack, Shepherd, *Zeitschrift für wissenschaftliche Theologie* 21 (1878): 123–33.
Hilhorst, Antonius. "Erotic Elements in *The Shepherd of Hermas*." Pages 193–204 in *Groningen Colloquia on the Novel IX*. Edited by H. Hofmann and M. Zimmerman. Groningen: Egbert Forsten, 1998.
Himmelmann, Nikolaus. *Über Hirten-Genre in der antiken Kunst*. Abhandlungen der Rheinisch–Westfälischen Akademie der Wissenschaften 65. Opladen: Westdeutscher Verlag, 1980.
Holmes, Michael. *The Apostolic Fathers: Greek Texts and English Translations*. Grand Rapids, MI: Baker Academic, 2007.
Holmes, Peter. *Ante-Nicene Fathers. Vol. 3: Latin Christianity: Its Founder, Tertullian; I. Apologetic; II. Anti-Marcion; III. Ethics*, repr. ed. Grand Rapids, MI: Eerdmans, 1986.
Horsley, Richard A. "Oral Traditions in New Testament Studies." *Oral Traditions* 18 (2003): 34–36.
Huitink, Luuk. "Enactivism, *Enargeia* and the Ancient Readerly Imagination." Pages 169–89 in vol. 1 of *The Edinburgh History of Distributed Cognition*. Edited by Miranda Anderson, David Cairns and Mark Sprevak. Edinburgh: Edinburgh University Press, 2019.
Humphrey, Edith McEwan. *The Ladies and the Cities: Transformation and Apocalyptic Identity in Joseph and Aseneth, 4 Ezra, the Apocalypse and The Shepherd of Hermas*. JSPSup 17. Sheffield, England: Sheffield Academic Press, 1995.
Hurtado, Larry W. *One God, One Lord: Early Christian Devotion and Ancient Jewish Monotheism*. 2nd ed. New York: Continuum, 1998.
Hurtado, Larry W. *Lord Jesus Christ: Devotion to Jesus in Earliest Christianity*. Grand Rapids, MI: Eerdmans, 2003.
Hurtado, Larry W. *God in New Testament Theology*. Library of Biblical Theology. Nashville: Abingdon, 2010.
Hylen, Susan E. *Women in the New Testament World*. New York: Oxford University Press, 2019.
Irwin, Eleanor. "The Invention of Virginity on Olympus." Pages 13–23 in *Virginity Revisited: Configurations of the Unpossessed Body*. Edited by Bonnie MacLachlan and Judith Fletcher. Toronto: University of Toronto Press, 2007.
Jensen, Robin Margaret. *Understanding Early Christian Art*. New York: Routledge, 2000.
Joerstad, Mari. *The Hebrew Bible and Environmental Ethics: Humans, Nonhumans, and the Living Landscape*. Cambridge: Cambridge University Press 2019.
Johnson, Luke T. *Brother of Jesus, Friend of God: Studies in the Letter of James*. Grand Rapids, MI: Eerdmans, 2004.
Johnson, Paul C. "Toward an Atlantic Genealogy of 'Spirit Possession'." Pages 23–45 in *Spirited Things: The Work of "Possession" in Afro-Atlantic Religions*. Edited by Paul C. Johnson. Chicago: University of Chicago, 2014.
Johnston, Sarah Iles. "The Divine Experience: Delphi and Dodona." Pages 33–75 in *Ancient Greek Divination*. Edited by Sarah Iles Johnston. Oxford: Wiley Blackwell, 2008.

Joly, Robert. "Philologie et psychanalyse. C. G. Jung et le 'Pasteur' d'Hermas." *L'Antiquité classique* 22 (1953): 422–28.
Joly, Robert. *Hermas: Le Pasteur*. Paris: Cerf, 1958, 1968.
Jung, Carl Gustav. *Mysterium Coniunctionis: An Inquiry into the Separation and Synthesis of Psychic Opposites in Alchemy*. Volume 14 of *The Collected Works of C.G. Jung*, edited by Gerhard Adler et al. Princeton: Princeton University Press, 2014.
Jung, Carl Gustav. *Psychological Types*. Volume 6 of *The Collected Works of C.G. Jung*, edited by Gerhard Adler et al. Princeton: Princeton University Press, 2014.
Kartzow, Marianne Bjelland. "Female Gossipers and Their Reputation in the Pastoral Epistles." *Neot* 39 (2005): 255–72.
Kartzow, Marianne Bjelland. *Destabilizing the Margins: An Intersectional Approach to Early Christian Memory*. Eugene, OR: Pickwick Publications, 2012.
Kartzow, Marianne Bjelland. "The Complexity of Pairing: Reading Acts 16 with Plutarch's *Parallel Lives*." Pages 123–39 in *Engaging Early Christian History: Reading Acts in the Second Century*. Edited by Rubén R. Dupertuis and Todd Penner. Durham, England: Acumen Publishing, 2013.
Kartzow, Marianne Bjelland. "Intersectional Studies." Pages 364–89 in *The Oxford Encyclopedia of the Bible and Gender Studies*. Edited by Julia M. O'Brien. New York: Oxford University Press, 2014.
Kartzow, Marianne Bjelland. *The Slave Metaphor and Gendered Enslavement in Early Christian Discourse: Double Trouble Embodied*. Routledge Studies in the Early Christian World. New York: Routledge, 2018.
Kartzow, Marianne Bjelland. "The Intersectional Power of 'the Book': The Shepherd of Hermas as Biblical Literature." Pages 173-89 in *A Festschrift for Lauri Thurén*. Edited by Anssi Voitila, Niilo Lahti, and Mikael Sundkvist. Helsinki: Publications of the Finnish Exegetical Society, 2021.
Kartzow, Marianne Bjelland, Liv Ingeborg Lied, and Esther Brownsmith, eds. *Books Known Only by Title*. Special Issue under contract with *Studies in Late Antiquity*, forthcoming.
Kelley, Nicole. "Philosophy as Training for Death: Reading the Ancient Christian Martyr Acts as Spiritual Exercises." *Church History* 75 (2006): 723–47.
King, Daniel. *Experiencing Pain in Imperial Greek Culture*. Oxford Classical Monographs. Oxford: Oxford University Press, 2018.
King, Daniel. "Galen and Grief: The Construction of Grief in Galen's Clinical Work." Pages 251–73 in *Unveiling Emotions II: Emotions in Greece and Rome: Texts, Images, Material Culture*. Edited by Angelos Chaniotis and Pierre Ducrey. HABES 55. Stuttgart: Franz Steiner Verlag, 2013.
King, Karen. "Martyrdom and its Discontents in the Tchacos Codex." Pages 23–42 in *Codex Judas Papers: Proceedings of the International Congress on the Tchacos Codex held at Rice University, Houston, Texas, March 13–16, 2008*, edited by April D. DeConick. Boston: Brill, 2010.
Knafl, Anne K. *Forming God: Divine Anthropomorphism in the Pentateuch*. Winona Lake, IN: Eisenbrauns, 2014.
Knust, Jennifer Wright. *Abandoned to Lust: Sexual Slander and Ancient Christianity*. New York: Columbia University Press, 2006.

Koenen, Ludwig. "The Ptolemaic King as a Religious Figure." Pages 25–115 in *Images and Ideologies: Self-Definition in the Hellenistic World*. Edited by Anthony Bulloch, Erich S. Gruen, A. A. Long and Andrew Stewart. Berkeley: University of California Press, 1993.

Körtner, Ulrich H.J., and Martin Leutzsch, ed. *Papiasfragmente. Hirt des Hermas*. Schriften des Urchristentums 3. Darmstadt: Wissenschaftliche Buchgesellschaft, 1998.

Kosmin, Paul J. *Time and its Adversaries in the Seleucid Empire*. Cambridge: Belknap Press, 2018.

Kostrosits, Maia. *Rethinking Early Christian Identity: Affect, Violence, and Belonging*. Minneapolis: Fortress, 2015.

Kugel, James L. ed. *Poetry and Prophecy: The Beginnings of a Literary Tradition*. Ithaca: Cornell University Press, 1990.

Kukkonen, Karen and Marco Caracciolo. "What is the 'Second Generation'?" *Style* 48 (2014): 261–74.

Kuzmičová, Anežka. "Presence in the Reading of Literary Narrative: A Case for Motor Enactment." *Semiotica* 189 (2012): 23–48.

Lambek, Michael. "From Disease to Discourse: Remarks on the Conceptualization of Trance and Spirit Possession." Pages 36–61 in *Altered States of Consciousness and Mental Health: A Cross-Cultural Perspective*. Edited by Colleen A. Ward. London: Sage, 1989.

Lambek, Michael. "Rheumatic Irony: Questions of Agency and Self-Deception as Refracted Through the Art of Living with Spirits." Pages 40–59 in *Illness and Irony: On the Ambiguity of Suffering in Culture*. Edited by Michael Lambek and Paul Antze. New York: Berghahn, 2004.

Lambek, Michael. "How to Make Up One's Mind: Reason, Passion, and Ethics in Spirit Possession." *University of Toronto Quarterly* 79 (2010): 720–41.

Lambek, Michael. "The Continuous and Discontinuous Person: Two Dimensions of Ethical Life." *JRAI* 19 (2013): 837–58.

Lambek, Michael. "Afterword," Pages 261–62 in *Spirited Things: The Work of "Possession" in Afro-Atlantic Religions*. Edited by Paul C. Johnson. Chicago: University of Chicago, 2014.

Lampe, Peter. *From Paul to Valentinus: Christians at Rome in the First Two Centuries*. Translated by M.D. Johnson. Minneapolis: Fortress Press, 2003.

Lappa-Zizicas, Eurydice. "Cinq fragments du *Pasteur* d'Hermas dans un manuscript de la Bibliothèque nationale de Paris." *Recherches de science religieuse* 53 (1965): 251–56.

Latour, Bruno. *Reassembling the Social: An Introduction to Actor Network Theory*. Clarendon Lectures in Management Studies. Oxford: Oxford University Press, 2007.

Leutzsch, Martin. *Die Wahrnehmung sozialer Wirklichkeit im „Hirten des Hermas"*. FRLANT 150. Göttingen: Vandenhoeck & Ruprecht, 1989.

Levison, John R. "The Debut of the Divine Spirit in Josephus' Antiquities." *HTR* 87 (1994): 123–38.

Levison, John R. "The Angelic Spirit in Early Judaism." *SBLSP* 34 (1995): 464–93.

Levison, John R. "The Prophetic Spirit as an Angel According to Philo." *HTR* 88 (1995): 189–207.

Levison, John R. *The Spirit in First Century Judaism*. AGJU 29. Leiden: Brill, 1997.

Levison, John R. *Of Two Minds: Ecstasy and Inspired Interpretation in the New Testament World*. North Richland Hills: Bible Press, 1999.

Levison, John R. *Filled with the Spirit*. Grand Rapids, MI: Eerdmans, 2009.

Levison, John R. *Inspired: The Holy Spirit and the Mind of Faith*. Grand Rapids, MI: Eerdmans, 2013.
Lewis, Ioan M. *Ecstatic Religion. A Study of Shamanism and Spirit Possession*. 3rd ed. London: Routledge 2003.
Lied, Liv Ingeborg, and Matthew P. Monger. "Lost Old Testament Pseudepigrapha Known Only by Title." In *Old Testament Pseudepigrapha: More Noncanonical Scriptures*. Edited by Richard Bauckham and James R. Davila. Grand Rapids, MI: Eerdmans, forthcoming.
Lied, Liv Ingeborg, and Marianne Bjelland Kartzow. "Books Known Only by Title: Exploring the Gendered Structures of First Millennium Imagined Libraries." Center for Advanced Study. https://cas.oslo.no/research-groups/books-known-only-by-title-exploring-the-gendered-structures-of-first-millennium-imagined-libraries-article3333-827.html.
Lincicum, David. "The Paratextual Invention of the Term 'Apostolic Fathers'." *JTS* 66 (2015): 139–48.
Lipsett, B. Diane. *Desiring Conversion: Hermas, Thecla, Aseneth*. New York: Oxford University Press, 2011.
Loader, William. *Philo, Josephus, and the Testaments on Sexuality*. Grand Rapids, MI: Eerdmans, 2011.
Long, Anthony A. *From Epicurus to Epictetus: Studies in Hellenistic and Roman Philosophy*. Oxford: Clarendon Press, 2006.
Lookadoo, Jonathan. *The Shepherd of Hermas: A Literary, Historical and Theological Handbook*. London: T&T Clark, 2021.
Luhrmann, Tanya. *How God Becomes Real: Kindling the Presence of Invisible Others*. Princeton: Princeton University Press, 2020.
MacDonald, Nathan. "The Spirit of YHWH: An Overlooked Conceptualization of Divine Presence in the Persian Period." Pages 95–120 in *Divine Presence and Absence in Exilic and Post-Exilic Judaism*. Edited by Nathan MacDonald and Izaak J. de Hulster. FAT 2/61. Tübingen: Mohr Siebeck, 2013.
Mahmood, Saba. "Feminist Theory, Embodiment, and the Docile Agent: Some Reflections on the Egyptian Islamic Revival." *Cultural Anthropology* 16 (2001): 202–36.
Mahmood, Saba. *Politics of Piety: The Islamic Revival and the Feminist Subject*. Princeton: Princeton University Press, 2005, 2011.
Maier, Harry O. *The Social Setting of the Ministry as Reflected in the Writings of Hermas, Clement and Ignatius*. Waterloo, ON: Wilfrid Laurier Press, 1991.
Maier, Harry O. *Apocalypse Recalled: The Book of Revelation after Christendom*. Minneapolis: Fortress, 2002.
Maier, Harry O. "The Politics of the Silent Bishop: Silence and Persuasion in Ignatius of Antioch." *JTS* 55 (2004): 503–19.
Maier, Harry O. "From Material Place to Imagined Space: Emergent Christian Community as Thirdspace in the *Shepherd of Hermas*." Pages 66–89 in *Christian Communities in the Second Century: Between Ideal and Reality*. Edited by Joseph Verheyden and Mark Grundeken. Tübingen: Mohr Siebeck, 2015.
Maier, Harry O. "Genre" in "Shepherd of Hermas." *Oxford Bibliographies: Biblical Studies*. Oxford: Oxford University Press, 2017. DOI: 10.1093/OBO/9780195393361-0230.
Maier, Harry O. "Making History with the *Shepherd of Hermas*." *Early Christianity* 10 (2019): 501–20.

Maier, Harry O. "Romans Watching Romans: Jesus Religion in Close Urban Quarters and Neighbourhood Transformations" *Journal of Religion in the Roman Empire* 6 (2020): 106–21.

Marguerat, Daniel. "The Work of the Spirit." Pages 109–28 in *The First Christian Historian: Writing the "Acts of the Apostles"*. Translated by Ken McKinney, Gregory J. Laughery, and Richard Bauckham. SNTSMS 121. Cambridge: Cambridge University Press, 2002.

Markschies, Christoph. *Christian Theology and Its Institutions in the Early Roman Empire: Prolegomena to a History of Early Christian Theology*. BMSSEC. Waco, TX: Baylor University Press / Tübingen: Mohr Siebeck, 2015.

Martens, Peter W. "Revisiting the Allegory/Typology Distinction: The Case of Origen." *JECS* 16 (2008): 283–96.

Martens, Peter W. *Origen and Scripture: The Contours of the Exegetical Life*. Oxford: Oxford University Press, 2014.

Martin, Dale. *The Corinthian Body*. New Haven: Yale University Press, 1995.

Martin, Dale. *Inventing Superstition: From the Hippocratics to the Christians*. Cambridge: Harvard University Press, 2004.

Martin, Dale B. "When Did Angels Become Demons?" *JBL* 129 (2010): 657–77.

Martin, Luther H. *Deep History, Secular Theory. Historical and Scientific Studies of Religion*. Religion and Reason 54. Berlin: De Gruyter, 2014.

Marx, Karl. *Scritti sull'alienazione. Per la critica della società capitalistica*. Edited by Marcello Musto. Donzelli: Rome, 2018.

Masquelier, Adeline. "From Hostage to Host: Confessions of a Spirit Medium in Niger," *Ethos* 30 (2002): 49–76.

Massumi, Brian. *Parables for the Virtual: Movement, Affect, Sensation. Post-Contemporary Interventions*. Durham: Duke University Press, 2002.

Mathews, Thomas F. *The Clash of Gods: A Reinterpretation of Early Christian Art*. Princeton: Princeton University Press, 1993.

Matory, James Lorand. "Government by Seduction: History and Tropes of 'Mounting' in the Oyo-Yoruba." Pages 58–85 in *Modernity and Its Malcontents: Ritual and Power in Postcolonial Africa*. Edited by Jean Comaroff and John L. Comaroff. Chicago: University of Chicago Press, 1993.

Maurer, Christian. "σκευή." *TDNT* 7: 1039.

McGrath, James F. *The Only True God: Early Christian Monotheism in its Jewish Context*. Chicago: University of Illinois Press, 2009.

Meeder, Sven. "The *Liber ex lege Moysi*: Notes and Text." *Journal of Medieval Latin* 19 (2009): 173–218.

Meeks, Wayne. *The Origins of Christian Morality: The First Two Centuries*. New Haven: Yale University Press, 1993.

Mihálykó, Ágnes T. *The Christian Liturgical Papyri: An Introduction*. STAC 114. Tübingen: Mohr Siebeck, 2019.

Miller, Patricia Cox. "'A Dubious Twilight': Reflections on Dreams in Patristic Literature." *Church History* 55 (1986): 133.

Miller, Patricia Cox. *Dreams in Late Antiquity: Studies in the Imagination of a Culture*. Princeton: Princeton University Press, 1994.

Mitchell, Margaret M. *Paul and the Rhetoric of Reconciliation: An Exegetical Investigation of the Language and Composition of 1 Corinthians*. Tübingen: Mohr–Siebeck, 1991.

Moberly, R.W.L. *Prophecy and Discernment*. Cambridge: Cambridge University Press, 2006.
Moioli, Maria Lauretta. "Postille bibliologiche all'"Apocalisse' di Giovanni." *Annali della Facoltà di Lettere e Filosofia dell'Università degli Studi di Milano* 64/3 (2011): 281–9.
Moore, Stephen D. and Janice Capel Anderson, "Taking It Like A Man: Masculinity in 4 Maccabees." *JBL* 117 (1998): 249–73.
Morgan, David. "Image, Art and Inspiration in Modern Apparitions." Pages 265–82 in *Looking Beyond: Visions, Dreams, and Insights in Medieval Art and History*. Edited by Colum Hourihane. Index of Christian Art, Occasional Papers. Princeton: Index of Christian Art in association with Princeton University Press, 2010.
Morgan-Wynne, John E. "The 'Delicacy' of the Spirit in the *Shepherd of Hermas* and in Tertullian." *Studia Patristica* 21 (1989): 154–57.
Mount, Christopher. "1 Corinthians 11:3–16: Spirit Possession and Authority in a Non-Pauline Interpolation." *JBL* 124 (2005): 313–40.
Moxnes, Halvor. "Asceticism and Christian Identity in Antiquity: A Dialogue with Foucault and Paul." *JSNT* 26 (2003): 3–29.
Moxnes, Halvor. "God and His Angel in the Shepherd of Hermas." *ST* 28 (1974): 49–56.
Nielsen, David. "The Place of the *Shepherd of Hermas* in the Canon Debate." Pages 162–176 in *'Non-canonical' Religious Texts in Early Judaism and Early Christianity*. Edited by L. M. McDonald and J. H. Charlesworth. JCT 14. London: T&T Clark, 2012.
Noë, Alva. *Action in Perception*. Cambridge, MA.: MIT Press, 2004.
Noë, Alva. *Out of Our Heads: Why You Are Not Your Brain, and Other Lessons from the Biology of Consciousness*. New York: Hill and Wang, 2009.
Norelli, Enrico. "Due viaggi di Erma: verso villaggi o verso Cuma?" *Adamantius* 26 (2020): 537-50.
North, Helen. *Sophrosyne: Self-Knowledge and Self-Restraint in Greek Literature*. Ithaca: Cornell University Press, 1966.
Nürnberger, Anna. *Zweifelskonzepte im Frühchristentum. Dispychia und Oligopistia im Rahmen menschlicher Dissonanz- und Einheitsvorstellungen in der Antike*. Göttingen: Vandenhoeck & Ruprecht, 2019.
Nussbaum, Martha. "The Stoics on the Extirpation of the Passions." *Apeiron* 20 (1987): 122–77.
O'Hagan, Angelo P. *Material Recreation in the Apostolic Fathers*. TU 100. Berlin: Akademie Verlag, 1968.
O'Regan, Kevin and Alvin Noë. "A Sensorimotore Account of Vision and Visual Consciousness." *Behavioral and Brain Sciences* 24 (2001): 939–1031.
Osiek, Carolyn. "The Genre and Function of the Shepherd of Hermas." Pages 113–21 in *Early Christian Apocalypticism: Genre and Social Setting*. Edited by Adela Yarbro Collins. Semeia 14. Decatur: SBL Press, 1979.
Osiek, Carolyn. *Rich and Poor in the Shepherd of Hermas: An Exegetical-Social Investigation*. CBQMS 15. Washington, DC: Catholic Biblical Association of America, 1983.
Osiek, Carolyn. "The Oral World of Early Christianity in Rome: The Case of Hermas." Pages 151–74 in *Judaism and Christianity in First-Century Rome*. Edited by Karl P. Donfried and Peter Richardson. Grand Rapids, MI: Eerdmans, 1998.
Osiek, Carolyn. *The Shepherd of Hermas: A Commentary*. Hermeneia. Minneapolis: Fortress Press, 1999.

Outtier, Bernard. "La version géorgienne du Pasteur d'Hermas." *Revue des études géorgiennes et caucasiennes* 6–7 (1990–1991): 211–15.

Padel, Ruth. *In and Out of the Mind: Greek Images of the Tragic Self.* Princeton: Princeton University Press, 1992.

Papadogiannakis, Yannis. "An Education through Gnomic Wisdom: The Pandect of Antiochus as Bibliotheksersatz." Pages 61–72 in *Education and Religion in Late Antique Christianity: Reflections, Social Contexts and Genres.* Edited by Peter Gemeinhard, Lieve Van Hoof and Peter Van Nuffelen. New York: Routledge, 2016.

Paramelle, Joseph. and Pierre Adnès. "Hermas (Pasteur D'), 2ᵉ siècle." Pages 316–34 in *Dictionnaire de spiritualité. Ascétique et mystique. Doctrine et histoire,* vol.7. Edited by A. Derville et al. Paris: Beauchesne, 1969.

Parkin, Harry. "The Numinous in 'The Shepherd'." *CQ* 1 (1969): 211–16.

Peppard, Michael. *The Son of God in the Roman World: Divine Sonship in Its Social and Political Context.* Oxford: Oxford University Press, 2011.

Pernveden, Lage. *The Concept of the Church in the Shepherd of Hermas.* Lund: CWK Gleerup, 1966.

Peterson, Erik. "Kritische Analyse der V. Vision des Hermas." *Historisches Jahrbuch* 77 (1958), 362–69.

Peterson, Erik. "Kritische Analyse Der Fünften Vision des Hermas." Pages 271–84 in *Frühkirche, Judentum und Gnosis. Studien und Untersuchungen.* Edited by Erik Peterson. Freiburg: Herder, 1959.

Petrey, Sandy. *Speech Acts and Literary Theory.* New York: Routledge, 1990.

Petridou, Georgia. *Divine Epiphany in Greek Literature and Culture.* Oxford: Oxford University Press, 2015.

Petsalis-Diomidis, Alexia. "The Body in Space: Visual Dynamics in Graeco-Roman Healing Pilgrimage." Pages 183–218 in *Pilgrimage in Graeco-Roman and Early Christian Antiquity: Seeing the Gods.* Edited by Jaś Elsner and Ian Rutherford. Oxford: Oxford University Press, 2005.

Picus, Daniel. "Book History and Biblical Literatures." Paper presented at the Annual Meeting of the SBL. San Diego, CA, 2019. https://www.sbl-site.org/meetings/Congresses_ProgramUnits.aspx?MeetingId=35

Platt, Verity. *Facing the Gods: Epiphany and Representation in Graeco-Roman Art, Literature, and Religion.* Cambridge: Cambridge University Press, 2011.

Ploeg, Ghislaine van der. *The Impact of the Roman Empire on the Cult of Asclepius.* Impact of Empire 30. Leiden: Brill, 2018.

Polvinen, Merja. "Enactive Perception and Fictional Worlds." Pages 19–34 in *The Cognitive Humanities: Embodied Mind in Literature and Culture.* Edited by Jean Peter Garratt. London: Palgrave Macmillan, 2016.

Proctor, Travis W. "Books, Scribes, and Cultures of Reading in the Shepherd of Hermas." *Journal of Ecclesiastical History* 72 (2021): 1–19.

Reddy, William M. *The Navigation of Feeling. A Framework for the History of Emotions.* Cambridge: Cambridge University Press, 2008.

Reed, Annette Yoshiko. *Fallen Angels and the History of Judaism and Christianity: The Reception of Enochic Literature.* Cambridge: Cambridge University Press, 2005.

Reiling, Jannes. *Hermas and Christian Prophecy: A Study of the Eleventh Mandate.* NovTSup 37. Leiden: Brill, 1973.

Reitzenstein, Richard. *Poimandres: Studien zur Griechisch–Ägyptischen und Frühchristlichen Literatur.* Leipzig: Teubner, 1904.
Renoux, Charles, ed. *La chaîne arménienne sur les Épîtres catholiques. I. La chaîne sur l'Épître de Jacques.* Patrologia Orientalis 43.1, No. 193. Turnhout: Brepols, 1985.
Roberts, C.H. *Manuscripts, Society and Belief in Early Christian Egypt: The Schweich Lectures 1997.* London: Oxford University Press, 1979.
Roberts, C.H., and B. Capelle. *An Early Euchologium: The Der–Balizeh Papyrus Enlarged and Reedited.* Bibliothèque du Muséon 23. Louvain: Muséon, 1949.
Roca–Puig, R. *Anàfora de Barcelona i altres pregàires. Missa del segle IV.* Barcelona, 1994^1; 1996^2; 1999^3.
Rosen, Ralph M. and Ineke Sluiter. *Andreia: Studies in Manliness and Courage in Classical Antiquity.* Leiden: Brill, 2003.
Rosen–Zvi, Ishay. *Demonic Desires: Yetzer Hara and the Problem of Evil in Late Antiquity.* Philadelphia: University of Pennsylvania Press, 2011.
Rothschild, Clare K. *New Essays on the Apostolic Fathers.* WUNT 375. Tübingen: Mohr-Siebeck 2017.
Rowland, Christopher, Patricia Gibbons and Vicente Dobroruka. "Visionary Experience in Ancient Judaism and Christianity." Pages 41–56 in *Paradise Now: Essays on Early Jewish and Christian Mysticism.* Edited by April D. DeConick. SymS 11. Atlanta: SBL Press, 2006.
Rüpke, Jörg. "Fighting for Differences: Forms and Limits of Religious Individuality in the 'Shepherd of Hermas'." Pages 315–40 in *The Individual in the Religions of the Ancient Mediterranean.* Edited by Jörg Rüpke. Oxford: Oxford University Press, 2013.
Rüpke, Jörg. *From Jupiter to Christ. On the History of Religion in the Roman Imperial Period.* Oxford: Oxford University Press, 2014.
Rüpke, Jörg. *Pantheon. A New History of the Roman Religion.* Translated by David M. B. Richardson. Princeton: Princeton University Press, 2018.
Ryan, Marie–Laure. *Narrative as Virtual Reality: Immersion and Interactivity in Literature and Electronic Media.* Baltimore, MD: Johns Hopkins University Press, 2001.
Safrai, Samuel. *Relations between the Diaspora and the Land of Israel.* Pages 184–215 in *The Jewish People in the First Century: Historical Geography, Political History, Social, Cultural and Religious Life and Institutions.* Edited by Samuel Safrai, Menahem Stern, David Flusser and Willem C. van Unnik. CRINT 1/1. Assen: Van Gorcum, 1974.
Scheck, Thomas P., and Christopher A. Hall. *Homilies on Numbers.* Downers Grove: IVP Press, 2013.
Schmid, Wolfgang P. "Eine frühchristliche Arkadienvorstellung." Pages 510–18 in *Ausgewählte philologische Schriften.* Edited by Harmut Erbse and Jochem Küppers. Berlin: De Gruyter, 1984.
Schmidt, Ernst A. "Arkadien. Abendland und Antike." *Antike und Abendland* 21 (1975): 36–57.
Schoedel, William R. "Enclosing, Not Enclosed: The Early Christian Doctrine of God." Pages 75–86 in *Early Christian Literature and the Classical Intellectual Tradition: In Honorem Robert M. Grant.* Edited by William R. Schoedel and Robert L. Wilken. ThH 53. Paris: Beauchesne, 1980.
Schröter, Jens. "The Formation of the New Testament Canon and Christian Apocrypha." Pages 167–84 in *The Oxford Handbook of Early Christian Apocrypha.* Edited by Andrew F. Gregory *et al.* Oxford: Oxford University Press, 2015.

Schüssler Fiorenza, Elisabeth. "Introduction: Exploring the Intersections of Race, Gender, Status, and Ethnicity in Early Christian Studies." Pages 1–23 in *Prejudice and Christian Beginnings: Investigating Race, Gender, and Ethnicity in Early Christian Studies*. Edited by Laura Nasrallah and Elisabeth Schüssler Fiorenza. Minneapolis: Fortress Press, 2009.

Seddon, Keith. *Epictetus's Handbook and the Tablet of Cebes: Guides to Stoic Living*. London; New York: Routledge, 2005.

Segal, Alan F. "Transcribing Experience." Pages 365–82 in *With Letters of Light. Studies in the Dead Sea Scrolls: Early Jewish Apocalypticism, Magic and Mysticism in Honor of Rachel Elior*. Edited by Daphna V. Arbel and Andrei A. Orlov. Ekstasis 2. Berlin: De Gruyter, 2011.

Segovia, Fernando F. *Decolonizing Biblical Studies: A View from the Margins*. Maryknoll: Orbis, 2000.

Seigworth, Gregory J., and Melissa Gregg. "An Inventory of Shimmers." Pages 1–28 in *The Affect Theory Reader*. Edited by Gregory J. Seigworth and Melissa Gregg. Durham, NC: Duke University Press, 2010.

Seitz, Oscar J.F. "Relationship of the *Shepherd* of Hermas to the Epistle of James." *JBL* 63 (1944): 131–40.

Seitz, Oscar J.F. "Antecedents and Signification of the Term δίψυχος." *JBL* 66 (1947): 211–19.

Seitz, Oscar J.F. "Afterthoughts on the term δίψυχος." *NTS* 4 (1958): 327–34.

Shantz, Colleen. "Opening the Black Box: New Prospects for Analyzing Religious Experience." Pages 1–15 in *Experientia, Volume 2: Linking Text and Experience*. Edited by Colleen Shantz and Rodney A. Werline. Atlanta: SBL Press, 2012.

Shaw, Brent. "Body / Power / Identity: Passions of the Martyrs." *JECS* 4 (1996): 269–312.

Sheridan, Jennifer A. "Not at a Loss for Words: The Economic Power of Literate Women in Late Antique Egypt." *Transactions of the American Philological Association* 128 (1998): 189–203.

Shryock, Andrew, Daniel L. Smail, and Timothy Earle, ed. *Deep History: The Architecture of Past and Present*. Berkeley: University of California Press, 2011.

Simonetti, Manlio. "Il Pastore di Erma." in *Seguendo Gesù. Testi cristiani delle origini, vol. 2*. Edited by Emanuela Prinzivalli and Manlio Simonetti. Scrittori Greci e Latini. Fondazione Lorenzo Valla. Milan: Mondadori, 2015.

Sluhovsky, Moshe. *Believe Not Every Spirit. Possession, Mysticism, and Discernment in Early Modern Catholicism*. Chicago: University of Chicago, 2007.

Smail, Daniel L. *On Deep History and the Brain*. Berkeley: University of California Press, 2008.

Smail, Daniel L. "Psychotropy and the Patterns of Power in Human History." Pages 43–8 in *Environment, Culture, and the Brain: New Explorations in Neurohistory*. Edited by Edmund Russell. *Rachel Carson Center Perspectives* 6 (2012): 43–48.

Smith, Fredrick M. *The Self Possessed: Deity and Spirit Possession in South Asian Literature and Civilization*. New York City: Columbia University Press, 2006.

Smith, Jonathan Z. "Re: Corinthians." Pages 17–33 in *Redescribing Paul and the Corinthians*. Edited by Ron Cameron and Merrill P. Miller. ECL 5. Atlanta: SBL Press, 2011.

Smitten, Jeffrey R. and Ann Daghistany, ed. *Spatial Form in Narrative*. Ithaca: Cornell University Press, 1981.

Snell, Bruno. "Arkadien, die Entdeckung einer geistigen Landschaft." *Antike und Abendland* 1 (1945): 26–4.

Snyder, Graydon F. *The Shepherd of Hermas*. The Apostolic Fathers 6. London: Thomas Nelson & Sons, 1968.
Snyder, Harlow Gregory. *Teachers and Texts in the Ancient World. Philosophers, Jews and Christians*. New York: Routledge, 2000.
Snyder, Harlow Gregory. *Christian Teachers in Second-Century Rome: Schools and Students in the Ancient City*. VCSup 159. Leiden: Brill, 2020.
Sommer, Benjamin D. *The Bodies of God and the World of Ancient Israel*. New York: Cambridge University Press, 2009.
Sorabji, Richard. *Emotion and Peace of Mind: From Stoic Agitation to Christian Temptation*. The Gifford Lectures. Oxford University Press, 2000.
Soulen, Richard and R. Kendall Soulen. *Handbook of Biblical Criticism*. 3rd edition. Louisville: Westminster John Knox, 2001.
Soyars, Jonathan E. *The Shepherd of Hermas and the Pauline Legacy*. NovTSupp 176. Leiden: Brill, 2019.
Spinoza, Benedictus (Baruch). "On the Origins and Nature of the Emotions." Pages 93–156 in *Ethics*, Part 3. Edited by Matthew J. Kisner. Cambridge: Cambridge University Press, 2018.
Steinmetz, George (ed.). *Sociology & Empire: The Imperial Entanglements of a Discipline*. Durham: Duke University Press, 2013.
Stewart, Alistair C. *Two Early Egyptian Liturgical Papyri: The Deir Balyzeh Papyrus and the Barcelona Papyrus with Appendices Containing Comparative Material*. Joint Liturgical Studies 70. Norwich: Hymns Ancient and Modern, 2010.
Stökl Ben Ezra, D. "Canonization—A Non-Linear Process? Observing the Process of Canonization through the Christian (and Jewish) Papyri from Egypt." *ZAC* 12 (2008): 229–50.
Strathern, Marilyn. *The Gender of the Gift: Problems with Women and Problems with Society in Melanesia*. Berkeley: University of California Press, 1988.
Streeter, Burnett Hillman. *The Primitive Church: Studied with Special Reference to the Origins of the Christian Ministry*. London: MacMillan and Co., Ltd., 1929.
Stroumsa, Guy G. *The Scriptural Universe of Ancient Christianity*. Cambridge: Harvard University Press, 2016.
Ström, Åke von. *Der Hirt des Hermas. Allegorie oder Wirklichkeit?* Arbeiten und Mitteilungen aus dem neutestamentalichen Seminar zu Uppsala. Leipzig: A. Lorenz, 1936.
Sturman Sax, William, Johannes Quack, and Jan Weinhold, ed. *The Problem of Ritual Efficacy*. Edited by. Oxford: Oxford University Press, 2010.
Tagliabue, Aldo. "Learning from Allegorical Images in the *Book of Visions* of the *Shepherd of Hermas*." *Arethusa* 50 (2017): 221–55.
Tagliabue, Aldo. "Experiencing the Church in the *Book of Visions* of the *Shepherd of Hermas*." Pages 104–24 in *Experience, Narrative, and Criticism in Ancient Greece: Under the Spell of Stories*. Edited by Jonas Grethlein, Luuk Huitink and Aldo Tagliabue. Oxford: Oxford University Press, 2019.
Taylor, Charles. *A Secular Age*. Cambridge, MA: Harvard University Press, 2007.
Taylor, Joan E. *What did Jesus Look Like?* London: Bloomsbury, 2018.
Tervahauta, Ulla "A Just Man or Just a Man? The Ideal Man in the Visions of Hermas." *Patristica Nordica Annuaria* 35 (2020): 69–97.

Thiessen, Matthew. "'The Rock was Christ': The Fluidity of Christ's Body in 1 Corinthians 10.4." *JSNT* 36 (2013): 103–26.
Thompson, David and J. Arthur Baird. *A Critical Concordance to the Shepherd of Hermas.* Wooster, OH: Biblical Research Associates, Inc., 1998.
Tibbs, Clint. *Religious Experience of the Pneuma: Communication with the Spirit World in 1 Corinthians 12 and 14.* WUNT 2/230. Tübingen: Mohr Siebeck, 2007.
Toffler, Alvin. *The Third Wave.* New York: Bantam Books, 1980.
Tomkins, Silvan S. *Affect Imagery Consciousness: The Complete Edition.* New York: Springer, 2008.
Torjesen, Karen Jo. *Hermeneutical Procedure and Theological Method in Origen's Exegesis.* Berlin: De Gruyter, 1986.
Tornau, C., and P. Cecconi, ed. *The Shepherd of Hermas in Latin: Critical Edition of the Oldest Translation Vulgata.* TU 173. Berlin: De Gruyter, 2014.
Torrance, Alexis. *Repentance in Late Antiquity: Eastern Asceticism and the Framing of the Christian Life c.400–650 CE.* Oxford: Oxford University Press, 2013.
Tripaldi, Daniele. *Apocalisse di Giovanni. Introduzione, traduzione e commento.* Classici 24. Rome: Carocci, 2012.
Troscianko, Emily. *Kafka's Cognitive Realism.* New York; London: Routledge, 2014.
Tugwell, Simon. *The Apostolic Fathers.* London: Geoffrey Chapman, 1989.
Turner, E.G. *The Typology of the Early Codex.* Philadelphia: University of Pennsylvania Press, 1977.
Upson-Saia, Kristi, Carly Daniel-Hughes and Alicia J. Batten, ed. *Dressing Judeans and Christians in Antiquity.* Farnham: Ashgate 2014.
Urciuoli, Emiliano R. *Servire due padroni. Una genealogia dell'uomo politico cristiano (50–313 e.v.).* Brescia: Morcelliana, 2018.
Uro, Risto. *Ritual and Christian Beginnings: A Socio-Cognitive Analysis.* Oxford: Oxford University Press, 2016.
Ussher, Robert G. *The Characters of Theophrastus.* London: MacMillian & Co, 1960.
Vasaly, Ann. *Representations: Images of the World in Ciceronian Oratory.* Berkeley, CA: University of California Press, 1993.
Verheyden, Joseph. "The Shepherd of Hermas." *ExpTim* 117 (2006): 397–401.
Versnel, H. S. "What Did Ancient Man See When He Saw A God? Some Reflections on Greco-Roman Epiphany." Pages 42–55 in *Effigies Dei: Essays on the History of Religions.* Edited by Dirk van der Plas. Leiden: Brill, 1987.
Vliet, Jacques van der. "Spirit and Prophecy in the Epistula Iacobi Apocrypha (NHC I,2)." *VC* 44 (1990): 25–53.
Völter, Daniel. *Die apostolischen Väter. Neu Untersucht. I. Teil. Clemens, Hermas, Barnabas.* Leiden: Brill, 1904.
Wagner, Rachel. "A Sense of Presence: Mediating an American Apocalypse." *Religions* 12, no. 1 (2021): 1–11, https://doi.org/10.3390/rel12010059.
Walsh, Lora. "The Lady as Elder in the Shepherd of Hermas." *JECS* 27 (2019): 517–47.
Walsh, Lora. "Lost in Revision: Gender Symbolism in *Vision* 3 and *Similitude* 9 of the *Shepherd of Hermas*." *HTR* 112 (2019): 467–90.
Wayment, Thomas A. *The Text of the New Testament Apocrypha (100–400 CE).* London: Bloomsbury, 2013.

Webb, Ruth. *Ekphrasis, Imagination and Persuasion in Ancient Rhetorical Theory and Practice*. Farnham / Burlington: Ashgate, 2009.
Weber, Gregor. *Kaiser, Träume und Visionen in Prinzipat und Spätantike*. Stuttgart: F. Steiner, 2000.
Wendt, Heidi. *At the Temple Gates: The Religion of Freelance Experts in the Roman Empire*. Oxford: Oxford University Press, 2016.
Whitman, Jon. *Allegory: The Dynamics of an Ancient and Medieval Technique*. Cambridge MA: Harvard University Press, 1987.
Whitmarsh, Tim. *Ancient Greek Literature*. Malden, MA: Polity Press, 2004.
Whittaker, Molly, ed. *Der Hirt des Hermas*. Die apostolischen Väter 1. Berlin: Akademie-Verlag, 1967.
Wilson, Brittany E. *Unmanly Men: Refigurations of Masculinity in Luke–Acts*. New York: Oxford University Press, 2015.
Wilson, Brittany E. *The Embodied God: Seeing the Divine in Luke–Acts and the Early Church*. New York: Oxford University Press, 2021.
Wilson, John Christian. *Towards a Reassessment of the Shepherd of Hermas: Its Date and Its Pneumatology*. Lewiston: Mellen, 1993.
Wilson, Walter T. *The Sentences of Sextus*. Atlanta: SBL Press, 2012.
Wirtz, Kristina. *Ritual, Discourse, and Community in Cuban Santería: Speaking a Sacred World*. Gainesville, FL: University of Florida Press, 2007.
Wudel, B. Diane. "The Seduction of Self-Control: Hermas and the Problem of Desire," *Religion & Theology* 11 (2004): 39–49.
Young, Francis. *Biblical Exegesis and the Formation of Christian Culture*. Cambridge: Cambridge University Press, 1997.
Young, Steve. "Being a Man: The Pursuit of Manliness in *The Shepherd of Hermas*." *JECS* 2:3 (1994): 237–55.
Zahn, Theodor. *Der Hirt des Hermas*. Gotha: Friedrich Andreas Perthes, 1868.
Zanker, Graham. "*Enargeia* in the Ancient Criticism of Poetry." *Rheinisches Museum* 124 (1981): 297–311.
Zheltov, Michael. "The Anaphora and the Thanksgiving Prayer form the Barcelona Papyrus: An Underestimated Testimony of the Anaphoral History in the Fourth Century." *VC* 62 (2008): 467–504.

List of Contributors

Luca Arcari is Associate Professor of History of Christianity at the University of Naples Federico II. His research interests lie mainly in the field of Jewish and proto-Christian visionary texts. Prominent among his publications are the monographs, *"Una donna avvolta nel sole…" (Apoc 12,1). Le raffigurazioni femminili nell'Apocalisse di Giovanni alla luce della letteratura apocalittica giudaica*, (Edizioni Messaggero, 2008); *Visioni del figlio dell'uomo nel Libro delle Parabole e nell'Apocalisse*, ANT 19 (Morcelliana, 2012), and the editor of the work, *Beyond Conflicts*, STAC 103 (Mohr Siebeck, 2013). His most recent publication is the monograph *Vedere Dio. Le apocalissi giudaiche e protocristiane (sec. IV a.C.-sec. II d.C.)*, Frecce 291 (Carocci, 2020).

Dan Batovici is a Research Associate at KU Leuven and UCLouvain, having received his PhD from the former in 2015. He has published broadly on early Christian manuscripts and patristic exegesis. Currently he is working on the reception of the so-called 'Apostolic Fathers' and their own pseudepigrapha in ancient translations. He is the author of *The Shepherd of Hermas in Late Antiquity* (2022) and *Parabiblical Papyri: Secondary Spaces and the Reception of Early Christian Literature* (2022).

Giovanni B. Bazzana is Professor of New Testament at Harvard Divinity School. His research focuses chiefly on the critical study of the early Christ movement in the context of Second Temple Judaism and of ancient Mediterranean history, religions, and material cultures. His most recent book, *Having the Spirit of Christ: Spirit Possession and Exorcism in the Early Christ Groups* (Yale University Press, 2020) shows how possession, besides being a harmful event that should be exorcized, can also have a positive role. Often it helps individuals and groups to reflect on and reshape their identity, to plan their moral actions, and to remember in a most vivid way their past. When read in light of these materials, ancient documents reveal the religious, cultural, and social meaning that the experience of possession had for the early Christ groups

Jung H. Choi, ThD (Harvard University) is Senior Director of Wesleyan Formation Initiatives, Co-Director of the Asian House of Studies, and a consulting faculty member at Duke Divinity School, Durham, North Carolina. Her academic interests lie in prophecy in both the ancient Mediterranean and contemporary world concerning race, gender, and power. Choi is currently working on a monograph on discourse on prophecy, scriptural practices, and the cultivation of the self in early Christianity.

Jason Robert Combs is an Assistant Professor of Ancient Scripture at Brigham Young University in Provo, UT (USA). He holds Masters degrees in Biblical Studies from Yale Divinity School and in Classics from Columbia University, as well as a Ph.D. in early Christianity from the University of North Carolina at Chapel Hill. Combs has published several academic articles on the literary and cultural contexts of canonical and apocryphal gospels, as well as the textual transmission of gospels. He is currently finishing his monograph on the development of Christian discourse surrounding dreams and visions in the second and third centuries CE.

Angela Kim Harkins (co-editor) is an Associate Professor of New Testament at Boston College (USA). From 2014–2016 Harkins was a Marie Curie International Incoming Fellow at the University of Birmingham (England), and a Fulbright award at Hebrew University in 1997–1998. Her work on visions and the lived experience of religion covers a wide range of Jewish and Christian writings from the Second Temple period. Harkins is the author of *Reading with an "I" to the Heavens: Looking at the Qumran Hodayot through the Lens of Visionary Traditions* (De Gruyter, 2012), *Experiencing Presence in the Second Temple Period* (Peeters, 2022), and more than three dozen articles and essays. She is the co-editor of five edited volumes on Second Temple texts and traditions, including *Selected Studies on Deuterocanonical Prayers* (Peeters, 2021). Her monograph, *Re-reading the Visions in the Shepherd of Hermas* (Equinox, 2023) applies enactive reading to the Book of Visions and asks why some modern scholars have not found the Shepherd as entertaining and appealing as ancient readers!

Marianne Bjelland Kartzow is Professor of New Testament Studies at the University of Oslo, Norway. She is the co-chair of the international research project at the Center for Advanced study called "Books known Only by Title: Exploring the Gendered Structures of the First Millennium Imagined Library" convening in 2020–2022 (https://cas.oslo.no/research-groups). In addition to several articles and edited volumes, she is the author of three monographs: *Gossip and Gender: Othering of Speech in the Pastoral Epistles* (De Gruyter, 2009); *Destabilizing the Margins: An Intersectional Approach to Early Christian Memory* (Wipf and Stock, 2012); and *The Slave Metaphor and Gendered Enslavement in Early Christian Discourse: Double Trouble Embodied* (Routledge, 2018). Kartzow is also the editor of the volume, *The Ambiguous Figure of the Neighbor in Jewish, Christian and Islamic Texts and Receptions* (Routledge, 2022).

B. Diane Lipsett is an Associate Professor of Religion and co-director of Health Humanities at Salem College in Winston-Salem, North Carolina. She is the author of *Desiring Conversion: Hermas, Thecla, Aseneth* (Oxford University Press, 2011) and the co-editor with Phyllis Trible of *Faith and Feminism: Ecumenical Essays* (Westminster John Knox Press, 2014). A scholar of first and second-century Christian texts, Lipsett has particular interests in gender and conversion, in disability, health and healing, and in religion and migration.

Harry O. Maier (co-editor) is Professor of New Testament and Early Christian Studies at the Vancouver School of Theology, Canada where he teaches and researches on the unceded territories of the Musqueam, Squamish, and Tsleil-Waututh Nations. He is also a Fellow of the Max Weber Center for Advanced Cultural and Social Studies at the University of Erfurt, Germany where he works on the DFG funded project, "Religion and Urbanity Reciprocal Formations." He publishes widely on the social history of early Christ religion. Recent books include, *New Testament Christianity in the Roman World* (Oxford University Press, 2018), *Picturing Paul in Empire: Imperial Image, Text, and Persuasion in Colossians, Ephesians, and the Pastoral Epistles* (T&T Clark/Bloomsbury, 2013), and, co-edited with Katharina Waldner, *Desiring Martyrs: Locating Martyrs in Space and Time* (De Gruyter, 2021).

Aldo Tagliabue is an Assistant Professor at the University of Notre Dame. In 2011 he earned a joint PhD in Classics at the University of Padua (Italy) and Swansea (UK). After working in Lampeter (UK) and Heidelberg (Germany), in 2017 Aldo joined the Department of Classics at Notre Dame. His first research focus is on the ancient novel, and in 2017 he published a book on *Xenophon's Ephesian Story* with Barkhuis. His second research focus is on the experiential representation of the divine in both Pagan and Christian texts written in the Imperial era.

Brittany E. Wilson is Associate Professor of New Testament at Duke University Divinity School. She is the author of *The Embodied God: Seeing the Divine in Luke-Acts and the Early Church* (Oxford University Press, 2021) and *Unmanly Men: Refigurations of Masculinity in Luke-Acts* (Oxford University Press, 2015). Her research interests focus on questions related to embodiment, Christology, and visuality in the New Testament, as well as the relationship between early Christianity and Judaism.

Index of Subjects

actor network 77f., 78f., 81–83, 88, 91, 96, 156
adoptionist christology 187
adventus 109
Aelius Aristides 164f.
affect theory 1, 3, 69, 73–78, 81–92, 95–97, 102f., 145
andreia 58, 59, 71
angel 88, 95, 153, 158, 160, 186, 191, 196
anthropology 1, 10f., 24, 27f., 31, 73, 95, 97, 117, 129
Apollo 35, 46f., 162
apologists 166, 168f., 192
Apuleius 162, 166
Arcadia 80, 83, 89, 93, 108
art 23f., 110, 161–165, 167
Asclepius 110, 164
assemblage 77, 78–84, 88, 91, 97
Athena 164
autobiography 83, 107, 197
autotropy 106

Balaam 32, 45, 50–56
bathing 79, 83, 106, 121–125, 202, 213
binary 17, 19, 26, 82, 120, 175
blindspot 119
book 4f., 32, 40, 45, 50f., 59, 63f., 75, 77, 79, 85f., 107, 111–114, 121, 129f., 135, 137–141, 143f., 146–151, 159, 175, 182, 195–213, 215–224, 227–233
buffered self 10, 15, 21, 78

catechetical/catechumens ix, 44, 129, 135, 217, 219, 220, 223, 233
Celsus 45
Church 3–5, 9, 31, 33, 43f., 57–59, 63–73, 75, 79, 82, 104, 114, 123, 128, 137–139, 142–144, 147f., 150f., 159, 161, 174, 176, 178–181, 184, 186, 188, 190–192, 206–212, 216, 218–220, 223–225, 227, 231, 233
Cicero 41
cognicentric 24

cognitive literary theory 1, 117, 119f., 131
colonization 10, 17f., 121
control 2, 21, 23f., 28f., 31f., 34, 37–40, 44–50, 53, 55f., 59f., 70, 82, 105, 199, 202, 215
cross-cultural(ly) 17, 18, 21, 28, 97

demon 23, 60, 166–168
devil 27, 35f., 69, 80, 158, 160
satan 17
desire 17–24, 33–36, 38–40, 50, 52, 57f., 60, 64, 67, 70, 79, 81, 85, 87–89, 93, 95f., 120, 122f., 160, 215
dipsychos 64, 24, 27, 33, 35, 64, 82f., 94f., 97, 144, 252
dividual 3, 73, 78, 92, 96
divination 2, 13, 20, 26, 29, 33–35, 37, 41–43, 46, 48, 50
divine fluidity 5, 171–177, 192
divine revelation 43, 89, 179, 200, 202
divinity 49, 85, 167, 174, 176, 178, 183, 191
divorce regulation 220, 224
double-mindedness 24, 27f., 34, 40, 64, 82f., 86, 94, 97, 105
dream 32f., 41, 66f., 79f., 154–157, 161, 163, 165–169, 173
dream-text 4, 156, 168f.

ekphrasis 85f., 150f.
Eldad and Modat 43, 204f.
emotion 1, 15f., 40, 48, 66, 70, 74f., 77, 82f., 85–88, 90, 102, 107, 115, 118, 141f., 182
enactivism 2, 4, 117–119, 121f., 125, 131, 134–136, 141f., 151
enargeia 140, 150–151,
enkrateia 2, 39, 45, 56, 58, 59–60, 71,
Enochic literature 94, 166
Epictetus 34, 40
epiphanies 4, 75, 110, 155, 157f., 160f., 163–165, 166, 167f.

epithumia 34f., 22, 36, 39f., 43–45, 64, 122–123, 160
eschatology 138–139, 140–148, 150
ethnography 11f., 16f., 20, 23, 25, 28

fasting 2, 41–44, 112
fear 22, 40, 71, 75f., 102, 118, 126, 128, 131, 146, 154, 159

Galen 14, 75f.
garrulousness 57, 60–62
gender 5, 32, 53, 56–59, 62, 69, 71, 95, 120f., 195, 199f., 202, 206, 208f., 213, 216
God 5, 9, 19, 21f., 26–29, 31, 33f., 36f., 42–48, 51–55, 58, 60, 65f., 76, 87, 93–95, 106, 109, 111f., 123, 125–127, 129, 145, 149, 154, 158, 160–165, 167, 171–192, 201–203, 212, 216, 222, 227f.
goddess 123, 125f., 165
gods 41, 110, 155, 160–169, 176
Grapte 59, 138, 196, 206f., 212f., 216

habitus 110
happy objects 3, 73, 84, 86, 90–92
Hermes 89, 154, 162f.
hilaros 36f., 77f., 82f., 88, 89–92, 94

Iamblichus 41–43
images 22, 24, 31, 37, 49, 67f., 75, 110, 114, 117, 125, 127f., 137, 151, 159, 162, 165, 167f., 171, 173, 191, 200, 208–212, 225
immersion 4, 113, 117f., 120, 122, 128–131, 134f., 140, 142, 145, 148, 150f.
incubation 167
interoception 118, 121f., 127, 135
intersectionality 5, 120, 195, 198–200, 208, 213

Justin Martyr 166, 218

Lady 5, 59, 111f., 122–127, 138, 146–149, 151, 173, 178f., 181, 185, 188, 195, 199–202, 204–213
literacy 62f., 202, 207f., 211, 216
liturgy 220–224, 228

loss of consciousness 28
lupē 40, 75, 76f., 77f., 82f., 86, 87, 94, 131, 182

manuscript fragment 5, 20f., 41f., 108f., 118f., 120f., 127, 128, 133f., 135, 137, 138f., 167, 172, 180, 187, 196, 203, 215, 219f., 223, 224, 225, 227, 229–233
masculinity 2f., 52f., 53, 57, 58–60, 62, 70, 71, 199, 202, 208
medical 14–16, 20, 75f.
mental imaging 4, 117
metanoia 3, 57, 50f., 59, 68f., 82f., 71f., 197
misattribution 227, 232
modernity 10f., 15–17, 20f., 24, 78, 92f., 95, 97, 121, 125
monotheism 5, 175–177
Montanism 34
moral 10, 12–14, 17, 20f., 24f., 32, 39f., 43, 46f., 54f., 59f., 64–66, 69f., 80, 97, 124, 128, 135, 192

name 16, 45, 50, 54, 58f., 74f., 82, 87f., 94, 111, 127, 131, 133, 148, 167, 173–175, 179–181, 187–190, 204, 207, 221, 224, 228, 232
narrative 4, 45, 50, 57, 59, 63, 69, 71–73, 78, 80f., 85f., 94, 111, 115, 117–123, 125, 127–131, 134–137, 139f., 142–151, 153–156, 159, 163, 165, 167–169, 171f., 174, 177, 179, 187–189, 191, 197f., 206, 222, 231
negotiation 12f., 20, 24–29, 110
neurohistory 28, 101–116

oracle 27, 32, 34f., 41–43, 46–49, 159f., 210
oracular 2, 13, 26, 28
orality 3, 63, 202
Origen 2, 32, 45–56, 168, 218f., 221, 233
Orpheus 162
Ovid 162, 185f.
Oxyrhynchus 33, 114, 120, 132–134, 136, 220, 227, 229f.

papyri 31, 138, 198, 219f., 222, 227–231, 233
paracosm 129, 134
partibility 81, 92, 94–96
passive 31–32, 37, 38, 43, 45, 64
Pausanias 162
performance 25–27, 31, 57, 63, 109, 113
phenomenological approach 140
phrikē 75, 76f., 147
Plutarch 43, 47f., 61f., 66, 70, 143, 162, 165, 208
pneumatology 19, 171–173, 180f., 183f., 187–190, 218
Poimandres 154
porosity 2, 3, 16, 43, 70, 71, 78, 95, 97
possession 2, 9–14, 16–21, 24–29, 31, 33, 35–37, 42, 49, 53, 80, 92, 94, 96, 121, 177, 183
prayer 2, 31, 41, 44, 70f., 90, 104, 111, 130, 149, 216, 220–223, 227f.
preexistence 181, 187f.,
profectio 109
prophecy 2f., 13, 26–28, 31–56, 61, 64, 66, 69, 133f., 183, 204f., 217, 224, 233
proprioception 118, 121, 127, 135
prosumers 113
psychology 2, 13–15, 18, 22, 29, 79f., 94, 97, 101
psychotropy 101–104, 107, 111, 116
Pythia 35, 46–51, 53, 56

re-actualization 132, 134
reading 3–5, 14, 25, 29, 31, 44f., 53, 55–57, 63, 66, 77, 85, 94, 97, 102–104, 108, 111, 113–116, 118–121, 125, 129f., 132, 134–137, 139, 142, 149, 155, 158, 165, 169, 174, 184, 188, 195, 197, 200–203, 205–208, 210–213, 215–217, 224, 230
realness 93, 117, 121
reception 2, 5, 42, 51, 137, 166, 198f., 211–213, 216–221, 223f., 226–228, 231f.
religious experience 1, 9–12, 20, 25, 29, 104f., 111, 139, 155f., 169
repentance 67, 69, 71, 79, 88f., 97, 158, 185, 197, 204, 218

repetition 52, 63f., 143, 149
revelation 29, 38, 58f., 63, 66–68, 71, 73, 76, 78–81, 83, 85–87, 91, 93, 104, 134, 174, 196, 200f., 203f., 207–209, 212, 215, 217f., 231, 233
Rhoda 59, 79f., 106–108, 121–125, 159, 197–202, 207, 212f.
ritual 2f., 12f., 17, 25–27, 41–43, 102–105, 109f., 113, 115f., 150, 202
Rome 9f., 31, 58, 63, 75, 106f., 112, 114, 122f., 125, 154, 162f., 186, 191, 197f., 206f., 210, 213, 220

sacrifice 42
self 1–3, 15f., 20, 22, 24f., 31f., 38f., 43–45, 49, 51f., 55, 57–62, 64–66, 70f., 73, 81–83, 92, 95–97, 101f., 107f., 110, 122, 124, 135, 137, 139, 144, 177, 199, 215, 219, 231
self-restraint 2, 57f., 62, 69–71
Shepherd-form 153, 160f., 163
Sibyl 159f., 168, 195, 208–212, 216
slavery 3, 5, 10, 17, 19, 21, 23–25, 29, 37, 43, 58, 65, 67, 80, 107–110, 115, 124f., 166, 178, 188, 195, 197–199, 202, 207, 209, 211–213
son 9, 17, 19, 29, 37, 44f., 58, 60, 66, 73, 82f., 90, 94, 124, 133, 137f., 158f., 161f., 172–177, 179f., 184–192, 196f., 203, 209, 217, 221f., 226
spatiality 3, 73, 80, 81, 83, 84, 85, 95, 96, 110f., 118f., 123, 127, 129, 135, 140, 142, 143, 146, 149, 217
speech 3, 33, 53, 57, 60–67, 70f., 135, 141, 180
spirit 2, 9–21, 23–29, 31–49, 51–54, 56, 58, 65, 70f., 80, 92–94, 104, 106, 109, 111f., 121, 133f., 148f., 157f., 166, 172–175, 177–179, 181–185, 187–190, 192, 218, 227
statue 162–165, 167f., 210
sticky objects 84–88
Stoic 14, 20, 34, 39f., 66
Suetonius 165

Tatian 167f.
teletropy 106

temptation   66, 153–155, 157–161, 168 f.
Tertullian   36, 41, 104, 166, 168
tower   3, 58 f., 67 f., 70, 73, 80 f., 83, 85, 88–96, 122, 126 f., 138, 143, 180 f., 185, 188, 190 f.
transmission   1, 5, 104 f., 113, 134, 195, 200, 207, 209, 211–213, 225, 231, 233
travel   108–110, 116

Venus   123, 125
vessel   15–17, 21, 31, 36–39, 44 f., 53, 62, 177
virgins   59, 80, 90–92, 183, 190
virtual reality   127, 140
virtue   2 f., 19, 31, 39, 43–47, 49–51, 54–59, 61, 66, 69, 81, 181
vision   1–5, 12, 26, 32 f., 39–41, 44, 48–50, 55, 57 f., 60, 63, 66–68, 70–73, 75, 78 f., 81, 83–93, 96, 101, 103–117, 119, 121–123, 125–132, 134–140, 142–151, 153–161, 163, 165 f., 168 f., 173 f., 178 f., 183–185, 191 f., 195–200, 202, 206 f., 209–213, 215 f., 227, 230–232
visionary habitus   4, 33, 114, 132, 134, 227

wealth   80, 83, 95 f., 115
widows and orphans   59, 96, 196, 206 f., 212 f., 216
wisdom   45, 54, 61, 161, 175, 178 f., 181, 190, 208, 210 f., 213, 228
worthy   37, 43–47, 50–52, 58–60, 70, 111, 148
writing practices   113–116

Ancient Text Index

Hebrew Bible/ Septuagint/ Old Testament

Genesis
– 32:30   179
Leviticus
– 18:13   225
Numbers
– 11:26   204
– 11:29   43
– 22–24   50
– 22   52
– 23:16   51
– 24:1–3   54
– 30:3–10   226
Deuteronomy
– 5:4–5   179
– 6:4   174
– 6:16 LXX   158
– 34:10   179
3 Kingdoms
– 3 Kgdms 17:1   180
– 18:15   180
– Isaiah   161
– 40:10–11   161
– 40:16   227
– 40:18–20   178
– 44:9–20   178
– 46:1–13   178
– 55:12   93
Jeremiah
– 10:1–16   178
– 31:10   161
Ezekiel
– 34:6–31   161
Daniel   130
Hosea
– 13:2–3   178
Habakkuk
– 2:18–19   178
Psalms   161
– 23:1   161
– 23:10 LXX   180
– 95:5 LXX   166
– 115:4–8   178
– 135:15–18   178
Proverbs
– 8:22–31 LXX   181, 190
– 8:32   181

Deuterocanon / Apocrypha

Additions to Daniel
Prayer of Azariah   130
Song of the Three Youths   130
Susannah and the Elders   130
Bel and the Dragon   130
2 Macc
– 7:28   221
4 Macc   59, 60, 69
Sirach/ Wisdom of ben Sira   161
– Sir 4:11   181
– 15:2   181
– 18:13b   161
– 20:8a   61
– 20:24   60
– 24:2   181
– 24:8–9   181
– 24:9   181
– 24:10   190
Tobit
– Tob 12:14   158
Wisdom of Solomon
– Wis 1:14   221
– 7:12   181
– 7:21–26   181
– 8:3   181
– 8:7   181
– 9:4   181
– 9:9   190
– 9:10   181

Dead Sea Scrolls and Pseudepigrapha

Ascension of Isaiah
– Ascen. Isa. 6.11–12 173
2 Baruch
– 2 Bar. 29.1–8 93
– 48.8   221
1 Enoch   161
– 1 En. 19:1 166
– 24–36 93
– 60:15–22 94
– 61:10 94
– 80:1–8 94
– 82:4–20 94
– 85–90 94
– 89:59–67 161
– 99:7   166
2 Enoch
– 2 En. 4:1–2 94
– 19:1–6 94

4 Ezra
– 3:4–36 66
– 4:1–25 66
– 4:13–21 93
– 4:26–5:12 66
– 5:13   66
Book of Jubilees
– Jub. 2:2 93
1QHodayot/Thanksgiving Hymns
– 1QH 11   113
– 13.22–15.8 113
Odes of Solomon
– Odes Sol. 11 130, 131
Sibylline Oracles 160
– Sib. Or. 5.514–530 93
Testament of Abraham
– T. Ab. 8.2–3 [recension B] 173

Other Jewish Literature

Josephus
– *Antiquitates judaicae*
  – *Ant.* 4.118 53
  – 4.119   53
  – 4.121   53
Philo
– *De cherubim*
  – *Cher.* 32 53
  – 32–3   52
De confusion linguarum
  – *Conf.* 171–75 180
Quod deus sit immutabilis

– *Deus* 119 221
De fuga et inventione
  – *Fug.* 94–105 180
De vita Mosis
  – *Mos.* 1.273–74 52
  – 2.267   221
De somniis
  – *Somn.* 2.275 61
De specialibus legibus
  – *Spec.* 2.225 221
  – 4.187   221

Rabbinic Literature

B.Shabbbat 92a 39
B.Nedarim 38a 39

Book of Balaam 50

New Testament

Matthew   161
– 4:7   158
– 12:29   17

– 17:2   185
– 19:9   226
– 21:42   192

– 26:31–33 161
Mark
  – 3:27 17
  – 9:1–3 209
  – 9:2–3 185
  – 14:62 178
Luke
  – 4:12 158
  – 7:35 181
  – 9:29 185
  – 10:25 158
  – 11:21–22 17
  – 24:51b 173
John 14, 161
  – 5:37 202
  – 10:11, 14 161
Acts 182, 196
  – 1:2 173
  – 1:9 173
  – 1:11 173
  – 4:11 192
  – 8:39 173
  – 16 208
Romans
  – Rom 1:3–4 25
  – 3:21–26 186
  – 3:30 186
  – 4:17 221
  – 8:9–11 25
  – 8:30 186
  – 8:33 186
  – 9:33 192
  – 16:14 32
Corinthians 11
  – 1 Corinthians 29
  – 6:11 186
  – 6:12–20 25
  – 7:10–11 226
  – 7:39–40 226
  – 10:4 192

– 10:9 158
– 10:19–21 166
– 11:3–16 18
– 12 29
– 12–14 13, 26, 28
– 12:3 29
– 14 29
– 15:45 25
2 Corinthians
  – 3:17 25
  – 4:7–15 25
  – 12:1–4 173
Galatians
  – 2:19–20 25
  – 3:8 186
  – 3:27 18
Ephesians
  – 5:23 208
Colossians
  – 4:16 206
1 Timothy
  – 3:11 207
  – 5:3–16 207
Titus
  – 2:3–4 207
Hebrews
  – 13:20 161
James 24, 60, 233
  – 1:8 232
1 Peter
  – 2:6–8 192
  – 2:25 161
  – 5:4 161
Revelation 196, 218
  – 1:9 110
  – 10:2 112
  – 10:4 113
  – 12:16 93
  – 19:7–8 208
  – 20:1 209

Apostolic Fathers

Epistle of Barnabas 196
1 Clement
  – 30:3 60

2 Clement
  – 1.8 221
  – 11.2 205

Shepherd of Hermas

Book of Visions (Vis.) 12, 39, 121, 135, 137, 138, 139, 140, 143, 144, 148, 149, 150, 151, 174, 197, 198, 199, 200, 212, 213, 230
- 1.1–4.3 (1–24) 3, 4, 207, 231, 232
- 1.1.1–9 (1.1–9) 122
- 1.1.1–4 (1.1–4) 106
- 1.1.1–2 (1.1–2) 122, 124
- 1.1.1 (1.1) 197, 202
- 1.1.3–1.2.2 (1.3–2.2) 37
- 1.1.3 (1.3) 108, 149, 159, 173, 176
- 1.1.4 (1.4) 122, 123, 159
- 1.1.5 (1.5) 157
- 1.1.6 (1.6) 176, 192
- 1.1.7 (1.7) 123
- 1.1.8–9 (1.8–9) 229
- 1.1.8 (1.8) 58, 80, 86, 123
- 1.2.1 (2.1) 75, 108
- 1.2.2 (2.2) 149, 157, 159, 201
- 1.2.4 (2.4) 60
- 1.3.1 (3.1) 58
- 1.3.1–2 (3.1–2) 86
- 1.3.2 (3.2) 64, 182, 201
- 1.3.3–4 (3.3–4) 63
- 1.3.3 (3.3) 201
- 1.3.4 (3.4) 176, 179
- 1.4.1–3 (4.1–3) 184
- 1.4.1 (4.1) 201
- 1.4.2 (4.2) 173, 202
- 1.4.3 (4.3) 2, 58, 69, 159, 202
- 2 (5.1–8.3) 3
- 2.1.1 (5.1) 159, 173
- 2.1.1–2 (5.1–2) 109, 110
- 2.1.1–3 (5.1–3) 149
- 2.1.1–2.2.1 (5.1–6.1) 111, 112
- 2.1.2 (5.2) 180
- 2.1.3–4 (5.3–4) 63, 216
- 2.1.3 (5.3) 112, 149, 159, 203
- 2.1.4 (5.4) 203
- 2.2 (6.1) ix
- 2.2.1 (6.1) 41, 44
- 2.2.2 (6.2) 58
- 2.2.2–3 (6.2–3) 86
- 2.2.3 (6.3) 62, 64
- 2.2.4–5 (6.4–5) 178
- 2.2.5 (6.5) 69, 180
- 2.2.8 (6.8) 180, 182, 188
- 2.3.1 (7.1) 86
- 2.3.2 (7.2) 178
- 2.3.4 (7.4) 43, 204
- 2.4.1–3 (8.1–3) 216
- 2.4.1 (8.1) 138, 159, 181, 185, 190, 209, 210
- 2.4.2 (8.2) 204
- 2.4.3 (8.3) 59, 63, 206
- 3.1–3.13 (9.1–21.4) 4, 58, 67, 73, 78, 88, 216
- 3.1.1 (9.1) 110
- 3.1.2 (9.2) 41, 44, 147, 149
- 3.1.3 (9.3) 86
- 3.1.4 (9.4) 86, 147
- 3.1.4–5 (9.4–5) 126, 147
- 3.1.5 (9.5) 75, 76, 147
- 3.1.6 (9.6) 86, 149, 186
- 3.1.6–7 (9.6–7) 173
- 3.1.6–8 (9.6–8) 184
- 3.1.8–9 (9.8–9) 126
- 3.1.9 (9.9) 87, 180
- 3.2.1 (10.1) 178, 180, 181, 182
- 3.2.4 (10.4) 181
- 3.2.4–9 (10.4–9) 67
- 3.2.5 (10.5) 185
- 3.2.5–6 (10.5–6) 184
- 3.3.1 (11.1) 67
- 3.3.1–2 (11.1–2) 67
- 3.3.2 (11.2) 63
- 3.3.4 (11.4) 86
- 3.3.5 (11.5) 67, 178, 179, 180, 188
- 3.4.1 (12.1) 184
- 3.4.2 (12.2) 185
- 3.4.3 (12.3) 180
- 3.5.2 (13.2) 180
- 3.5.3 (13.3) 179
- 3.6.5 (14.5) 67, 80
- 3.7.2 (15.2) 178
- 3.7.5 (15.5) 67, 89
- 3.8.1 (16.1) 63
- 3.8.4 (16.4) 58
- 3.8.9 (16.9) 67, 89, 138
- 3.8.11 (16.11) 64, 67

– 3.9.1–10 (17.1–10) 181
– 3.9.1–2 (17.1–2) 110
– 3.9.1 (17.1) 186
– 3.9.2 (17.2) 176
– 3.9.8 (17.8) 178
– 3.9.10 (17.10) 178
– 3.10.3–5 (18.3–5) 159
– 3.10.6 (18.6) 41, 44
– 3.10.7–3.13.4 (18.7–21.4) 185
– 3.10.7 (18.7) 159
– 3.10.9 (18.9) 86
– 3.10.9–10 (18.9–10) 157
– 3.11.1–3.13.4 (19.1–21.4) 159, 181
– 3.11.1–3.13.4 (19.1–21.4) 185
– 3.11.4 (19.4) 157
– 3.12.2 (20.2) 58, 94
– 3.12.3 (20.3) 182
– 3.13.4 (21.4) 67
– 4 (22.1–24.7) 4, 79, 142, 144, 231
– 4.1.1–3 (22.1–3) 110
– 4.1.1 (22.1) 144
– 4.1.2–3 (22.2–3) 109
– 4.1.3 (22.3) 67, 180
– 4.1.4 (22.4) 86
– 4.1.5 (22.5) 145
– 4.1.5–7 (22.5–7) 144
– 4.1.6 (22.6) 145, 145, 178
– 4.1.7 (22.7) 132, 145, 232
– 4.1.8 (22.8) 94
– 4.1.8–10 (22.8–10) 146
– 4.2.3 (23.3) 182
– 4.2.4 (23.4) 180, 185
– 4.2.7 (23.7) 131
– 4.3 (24) 231
– 4.3.7 (24.7) 146
– 5 (25.1–7) 4, 154, 155, 157, 161, 165, 168, 169, 174, 231, 232
– 5.1 (25.1) 110, 153, 164, 165, 185
– 5.1–4 (25.1–4) 153
– 5.1–2 (25.1–2) 153
– 5.2 (25.2) 153, 185
– 5.3 (25.3) 153, 157, 158, 165
– 5.4 (25.4) 131, 153, 157, 185
– 5.5–7 (25.5–7) 63
– 5.7 (25.7) 153, 185
Mandates (Mand.) 12, 13, 17, 21, 27, 37, 39, 132, 135, 174, 197, 215, 228, 232

– 1.1 (26.1) 174, 176, 177, 189, 192, 221, 222, 223, 227, 228
– 1.2 (26.2) 94, 186
– 2 (27) 229
– 2.2 (27.2) 60
– 2.7 (27.7) 86
– 3 (28) 65, 229
– 3.1 (28.1) 60, 181
– 3.1–3 (28.1–2) 81
– 3.3 (28.3) 157
– 3.3–4 (28.3–4) 65
– 3.4 (28.4) 182
– 3.5 (28.5) 65, 80, 86
– 4 (29–32) 224
– 4.1 (29) 226
– 4.1.3 (29.3) 58
– 4.1.4–8 (29.4–8) 225
– 4.1.11 (29.11) 178
– 4.2.1 (30.1) 94, 185
– 4.2.2–3 (30.2–3) 69
– 4.3.4 (31.4) 179
– 4.3.5 (31.5) 182
– 4.3.6 (31.6) 69, 158
– 4.4 (32) 226
– 4.4.1–2 (32.1–2) 225, 226
– 5 (33–34) 14, 15, 17, 18, 20, 21, 22, 26, 36, 183
– 5.1.1–5.2.8 (33–34) 35
– 5.1.1–4 (33.1–4) 36
– 5.1.2 (33.2) 17, 177, 181, 183
– 5.1.3 (33.3) 36, 177, 184
– 5.1.7 (33.7) 86, 185
– 5.2.1 (34.1) 21, 186
– 5.2.2 (34.2) 36, 37, 80
– 5.2.2–4 (34.2–4) 81
– 5.2.4–5 (34.4–5) 15
– 5.2.5 (34.5) 177, 181, 183
– 5.2.5–6 (34.5–6) 39
– 5.2.5–8 (34.5–8) 81, 82
– 5.2.6 (34.6) 37, 184
– 5.2.7 (34.7) 183
– 5.2.8 (34.8) 22, 94
– 6 (35–36) 19, 20, 22, 23, 26, 183
– 6.1–2 (35–36) 40
– 6.1.5 (35.5) 40
– 6.2.1–10 (36.1–10) 185
– 6.2.2–3 (36.2–3) 181

- 6.2.3-4 (36.3-4) 19
- 6.2.3 (36.3) 183, 184
- 6.2.5 (36.5) 39, 95
- 6.2.6 (36.6) 21
- 6.2.7-8 (36.7-8) 23
- 6.2.8-10 (36.8-10) 183
- 6.2.10 (36.10) 186
- 7.1 (37.1) 179
- 7.4-5 (37.4-5) 179
- 7.5 (37.5) 86, 176
- 7.7 (37.7) 86
- 8.1 (38.1) 71, 176
- 8.1.5 (38.5) 39
- 8.3-5 (38.3-5) 60
- 8.10 (38.10) 38
- 9-11 (39-43) 40
- 9 (39) 232
- 9.1-3 (39.1-3) 232
- 9.1 (39.1) 86
- 9.2-3 (39.2-3) 182
- 9.3 (39.3) 176, 178
- 9.7 (39.7) 94
- 10.1.2 (40.2) 65, 183
- 10.1.4 (40.4) 80, 95, 178
- 10.1.5 (40.5) 178
- 10.1.6 (40.6) 178, 181
- 10.2 (41.2) 40, 76, 82
- 10.2.1 (41.1) 65
- 10.2.1-6 (41.1-6) 182
- 10.2.5-6 (41.5-6) 181
- 10.2.6 (41.6) 177, 182
- 10.3.2 (42.2) 182
- 11 (43) 13, 25, 26, 28, 29, 31, 32, 35, 36, 39, 64, 132, 183
- 11.1-21 (43.1-21) 178
- 11.2 (43.2) 33, 34
- 11.2-21 (43.2-21) 82
- 11.3 (43.3) 27, 35
- 11.4 (43.4) 27, 35
- 11.5 (43.5) 33, 34, 178, 183
- 11.6 (43.6) 35
- 11.7b-8 (43.7b-8) 38
- 11.8 (43.8) 27, 33, 38, 39, 183
- 11.9 (43.9) 26, 28, 35, 58, 133, 183, 184
- 11.9-11 (43.9-11) 132
- 11.9-10 (43.9-10) 132, 134, 227
- 11.10 (43.10) 178
- 11.12 (43.12) 28, 62
- 11.13 (43.13) 37, 58
- 11.14 (43.14) 58, 178
- 11.15 (43.15) 37
- 11.16 (43.16) 178
- 12 (44-49) 17, 18, 21, 22, 39, 65
- 12.1-2 (44-45) 40
- 12.1.1-2 (44.1-2) 18
- 12.1.2 (44.2) 21, 94
- 12.2.4 (45.4) 22, 23, 94
- 12.2.5 (45.5) 23
- 12.4.1-2 (47.1-2) 65
- 12.4.1 (47.1) 185
- 12.4.2 (47.2) 86, 176, 180, 192
- 12.4.3 (47.3) 181
- 12.4.5 (47.5) 181
- 12.4.7 (47.7) 185
- 12.5.1 (48.1) 179
- 12.5.4 (48.4) 158, 160
- 12.6.1 (49.1) 185
- 12.6.2 (49.2) 186

Similitudes (Sim.) 12, 39, 135, 146, 174, 197, 215, 228, 232
- 1.4 (50.4) 80
- 1.6 (50.6) 81
- 1.7 (50.7) 179
- 1.8 (50.8) 95
- 1.9 (50.9) 178, 188
- 2-9 (51-110) 230
- 2.1-9 (51.1-9) 81
- 3-4 (52-53) 81, 87
- 3.1-3 (52.1-3) 87
- 4.1-3 (53.1-3) 87
- 4.2 (53.2) 87
- 4.4 (53.4) 176
- 4.5 (53.5) 80, 86, 95
- 5 (54-60) 58, 70, 187
- 5.2.1-11 (55.1-11) 178
- 5.3 (56.1) ix
- 5.4.1-2 (57.1-2) 70
- 5.4.3 (57.3) 70, 181
- 5.4.4 (57.4) 182, 186
- 5.5.1 (58.1) 64, 70
- 5.5.2 (58.2) 176, 178
- 5.5.3 (58.3) 184, 185
- 5.6.1 (59.1) 188
- 5.6.2-3 (59.2-3) 191

- 5.6.3–4 (59.3–4) 178, 187
- 5.6.4b–7 (59.4b–7) 188
- 5.6.4 (59.4) 188
- 5.6.5–6 (59.5–6) 37
- 5.6.5 (59.5) 182, 183, 190, 192
- 5.6.6 (59.6) 58
- 5.7.1 (60.1) 186
- 5.7.4 (60.4) 182
- 6.1–6.5 (61–65) 87, 160
- 6.1.1–3 (61.1–3) 160
- 6.1.2 (61.2) 86, 94
- 6.1.4 (61.4) 160, 186
- 6.1.5–6 (61.5–6) 160
- 6.1.5–6.2.2 (61.4–62.2) 4, 161
- 6.2.1 (62.1) 160, 185
- 6.2.2 (62.2) 178, 179
- 6.2.3 (62.3) 180
- 6.2.5 (62.5) 87
- 6.2.7 (62.7) 87
- 6.3.1 (63.1) 87
- 6.3.2 (63.2) 160, 185
- 6.3.4 (63.4) 87
- 6.3.6 (63.6) 178
- 7.1–2 (66.1–2) 185
- 7.1 (66.1) 94, 158, 185, 186
- 7.2 (66.2) 58
- 7.4 (66.4) 178, 182
- 7.5 (66.5) 179, 185, 186
- 7.6 (66.6) 185
- 8 (67–77) 81, 187, 190, 191
- 8.1–11 (67–77) 87
- 8.1.1 (67.1) 88, 180, 189
- 8.1.2 (67.2) 88, 186, 191
- 8.1.5 (67.5) 186, 191
- 8.1.7 (68.7) 158
- 8.1.16 (67.16) 88
- 8.1.18 (67.18) 88
- 8.2.1–4 (68.1–4) 88
- 8.2.1 (68.1) 186
- 8.2.3 (68.3) 94
- 8.2.5 (68.5) 191
- 8.2.6–9 (68.6–9) 88
- 8.2.9 (68.9) 88
- 8.3.2–3 (69.2–3) 191
- 8.3.3 (69.3) 186, 191
- 8.6.1 (72.1) 182
- 8.6.2 (72.2) 180
- 8.6.3 (72.3) 182, 185
- 8.6.4 (72.4) 180
- 8.7.6 (73.6) 179
- 8.8.1 (74.1) 80
- 8.10.3 (76.3) 180
- 8.11.1 (77.1) 182, 185
- 8.11.3 (77.3) 179
- 9 (78–110) 58, 59, 73, 78, 88, 184, 188, 190, 191, 192, 216
- 9.1.1 (78.1) 174, 181, 182, 183, 184, 185, 190
- 9.1.2 (78.2) 70
- 9.1.3 (78.3) 71, 185, 186
- 9.1.4 (78.4) 83, 108
- 9.1.4–10 (78.4–10) 89
- 9.1.8 (78.8) 90, 176
- 9.1.10 (78.10) 90
- 9.2.1 (79.1) 189
- 9.2.4 (79.4) 82, 90
- 9.2.5 (79.5) 59
- 9.3.1–8 (80.1–8) 91
- 9.3.1–5 (80.1–5) 184
- 9.3.1–2 (80.1–2) 89
- 9.3.1 (80.1) 91, 184, 185
- 9.3.2 (80.2) 91
- 9.3.4–5 (80.4–5) 91
- 9.5.1–2 (82.1–2) 89
- 9.5–9 (82–86) 68
- 9.5.6–7 (82.6–7) 191
- 9.5.7 (82.7) 188
- 9.6.1–2 (83.1–2) 184
- 9.6.1 (83.1) 85, 90, 190, 191
- 9.6.2 (83.2) 91
- 9.6.3 (83.3) 91
- 9.6–9 (83–86) 81
- 9.7 (84) 68
- 9.7.1–3 (84.1–3) 191
- 9.7.1 (84.1) 188, 190
- 9.7.6 (84.6) 188
- 9.7–9 (84–86) 68
- 9.8–9.9 (85–87) 92
- 9.8.3–9.9.4 (85.3–86.4) 90
- 9.9.4 (86.4) 188
- 9.9.5 (86.5) 82, 90
- 9.9.6 (86.6) 90
- 9.9.7 (86.7) 68, 91
- 9.10.1 (87.1) 90, 91, 92

- 9.10.3 (87.3) 90
- 9.10.7 (87.7) 90
- 9.11.3 (88.3) 94
- 9.11.4 (88.4) 92
- 9.11.5 (88.5) 90, 92
- 9.11.8 (88.8) 90
- 9.12.1 (89.1) 192
- 9.12.2 (89.2) 178, 187, 190, 192
- 9.12.4 (89.4) 189
- 9.12.5 (89.5) 189
- 9.12.8 (89.8) 189, 191
- 9.13.2–7 (90.2–7) 82
- 9.13.2 (90.2) 94, 183, 189, 190
- 9.13.3–5 (90.3–5) 189
- 9.13.3 (90.3) 94, 189
- 9.13.5 (90.5) 94, 181
- 9.13.7 (90.7) 94, 181, 189
- 9.13.8 (90.8) 82, 94
- 9.14.3 (91.3) 180, 182, 185, 189
- 9.14.5 (91.5) 189
- 9.14.6 (91.6) 189
- 9.15.1–3 (92.1–3) 189
- 9.15.2 (92.2) 94, 189
- 9.15.3 (92.3) 94
- 9.15.4 (92.4) 58
- 9.16.1–5 (93.1–5) 82
- 9.16–31 (93–108) 81
- 9.16.3 (93.3) 60, 189
- 9.16.5 (93.5) 189
- 9.16.7 (93.7) 189
- 9.17.2 (94.2) 89
- 9.17.4 (94.4) 180, 183, 189
- 9.17.5 (94.5) 181
- 9.18.3–4 (95.3–4) 181
- 9.18.5 (95.5) 180
- 9.19 (96) 89
- 9.19.1–3 (96.1–3) 89
- 9.19.2 (96.2) 189
- 9.20 (97) 89
- 9.20.1 (97.1) 82, 95
- 9.20.1–2 (97.1–2) 80
- 9.20.4 (97.4) 89
- 9.21.3 (98.3) 180, 189
- 9.21.4 (98.4) 89
- 9.22 (99) 89
- 9.23 (100) 89
- 9.23.4 (100.4) 176, 179
- 9.23.5 (100.5) 185
- 9.24.1 (101.1) 89
- 9.24.4 (101.4) 185, 190
- 9.26.1 (103.1) 89
- 9.26.4 (103.4) 178
- 9.26.6 (103.6) 89
- 9.28.2 (105.2) 189
- 9.28.3 (105.3) 189
- 9.28.5 (105.5) 189
- 9.28.6 (105.6) 180, 189
- 9.30.3–10.4.5 (107.3–114.5) 172
- 9.31.3 (108.3) 185
- 9.32.3–4 (109.3–4) 94
- 9.33.1 (110.1) 89, 185
- 10 (111–114) 77, 191
- 10.1.1–10.4.4 (111.1–114.4) 191
- 10.1.1 (111.1) 63, 186, 191
- 10.4.1–5 (114.1–5) 94
- 10.4.1 (114.1) 58, 69, 71
- 10.4.4 (114.4) 89

New Testament Apocrypha and Pseudepigrapha

Acts John
 – 90   185
Acts of Paul 196
Acts Peter
 – 21   185
Carta Dominica 226
 – Gospel of Peter
 – Gos. Pet. 10:40 186

Nag Hammadi and Gnostic

Gospel of Truth
 – Gos. Truth 22.25 177

Gospel of Philip
 – Gos. Phil. 57:28–58:10 185

First Apocalypse of James 44
Epistula Iacobi Apocrypha 31

Nag Hammadi Codices 211
Tchacos Codex 44

Classical and Ancient Christian Writings

Aelius Aristides
- *Orations* 164
  - 48.40   164
  - 48.41   164
  - 48.42   164
Apol. 1   177
Apuleius
- *Metamorphoses* 11.8 162
Athanagoras
- *Leg.* 26–28 168
Athanasius
- *De decretis Nicaenae Synodi*
  - 18.3   221
- *Festal Letter*
  - 39.20   223
Augustine
- *Conf.* 1.2 177
Chariton
- *Chaer.* 2.3 165
Cicero
  - *de Divinatione* 1.29.60 41
  - *de Divinatione* 2.58.119 41
Clement of Alexandria 218, 219
- *Strom* 12.2 59
Corpus Hermeticum
- *Poimandres* 154
Epictetus   40
- *Enchiridion* 34
Eugnostos
  - 73.6–8 177
  - //Wis. Jes. Chr. 9[6].1–3 177
Eusebius
- *Hist. eccl.*
  - 3.3   129
  - 3.3.6   223
Hesiod
- *Theogany*
  - 173   125
Hippolytus of Rome
  - *Haer.* 9.8 186, 191

Homer
- *Illiad*
  - 5.265 ff 162
Iamblichus
  - *Myst.* 3.11 42
Irenaeus
- *Adv. haer.*
  - 1.21.1   228
  - 4.20.2   228
- *Epideixis*
  - 4   228
Jerome
- *De viris illustribus* 10 223
John Cassian
- *Collatio* 20.8 225
Justin Martyr 218
- *1 Apol.*
  - 5.2   166
  - 9.1   167
  - 14.1   166
- *Dial.*
  - 113   192
  - 127   177
Juvenal
- *Satire* 6   211
Longus
- *Daph.* 2.23 165
Marcus Aurelius
  - *Meditations*
  - II.17   66
  - III.4, 7   66
  - IV.45   66
  - V.30   66
  - IX.35   66
Minucius Felix
  - *Oct.* 27.1, 4, 6, 8 168
Origen   219
- *de Principiis* 47, 233
  - 3   51
  - 3.2   32
  - 3.3   51

- *Contra Celsum*
  - *Cels.* 2.51 46
  - 3.37   168
  - 4.95   46
  - 5.42   46
  - 7   32, 45, 47, 51, 55, 56
  - 7.3   46, 48, 49
  - 7.3.25   47
  - 7.4   49
  - 7.6–7   168
  - 7.7   46, 47
  - 7.10   47, 55
  - 7.18   47
  - 7.35   168
  - 8.43   168
  - 8.62   168
- *Hom. Num.* 32, 50, 51, 53
  - 8   32
  - 14–17   32, 45, 53, 55, 56
  - 14–19   54
  - 14.3.2   52
  - 14.4.1   54
  - 15.2.2   51
  - 17.3.1   54
  - 17.3.5   54
  - 17.4.4   54, 55
  - 27   54
- *Hom. Josh.* 50
- *Hom. Jer.* 14.5 55
- *Commentary on John*
  - 32.16.188 221
- *Commentary on Romans* 46
  - 10.31   32
Ovid
  - *Fast.*
  - 2.503–504 186
  - *Metam.*
  - 6.114ff 162
  - 9.268–270 186
Pausanias
  - *Descr.* 9.22.2 162
Philostratus
  - *Vit. Apoll.* iii. 42 43
Plutarch
  - *Camillus*
  - *Cam.* 6.1 165
  - *De sera numinis vindicta*

- *Sera* 566c 43
- *De defectu oraculorum, Moralia* 47
  - *Def. orac.* 405 C 48
  - 413e–432b 43
  - 437 D   47, 48
- *De genio Socratis*
  - *Gen. Socr.* 588d–e 43
  - 589b–c 43
- *Parallela minora, Moralia*
  - 312 A   162
  - 314 E   162
- *De garrulitate, Moralia*
  - 507–508.11 62
  - 17, 510E 61
  - 19, 511E 61
  - 23, 514E–F 61
- *Quomodo quis suos in virtute sentiat profectus, Moralia* 66, 70
- *Vitae*   143, 208
Pollux
- *Onomasticon* 1.15 36
Pseudo-Athanasius 205
Rufinus
- *Commentarius in symbolum apostolorum*
  - *Symb.* 38 223
Seneca
- *De ira*
  - *Ira* 3.36.1–3 66
- *De tranquillitate animi*
  - *Tranq.* 2.215–37 66
Sentences of Sextus
  - 158–159 60
  - 165a–b, f 60
Stichometry of Nicephorus 205
Suetonius
  - *Galba*   165
  - *Galb.* 18.2 165
Tatian
- *Oratio ad Graecos*
  - *Or. Graec.* 8–10 167
  - 14.1   168
  - 18.3   167, 168
Tertullian
- *De anima*
  - *An.* 9.4 104
  - 46.13   168
  - 47.1   168

- *Apologeticus*
  - *Apol.* 22 168
- *De exhortation castitatis*
  - *Exh. cast.* 10:5 41
Theophilus
- *Ad Autolycum*
  - *Autol.* 1.5 177
  - 2.3   177

Theophrastus
- *Characteres*
  - Char. 3 61
  - 3.1–2 61
  - 3.7   61
  - 7   61
  - 7.1   61
  - 7.5–9 61

Manuscripts and Miscellaneous Texts

Athos Lavra K 96 232
Barcelona Papyrus 221, 222, 223, 224, 227, 228, 231
BnF Latin 3182 (Palatina) 224, 225, 226
P.Berl. Sarischouli 9 (=BKT 9.163) 230
P.Bodmer 38 229
Codex H-622 231
Codex Alexandrinus 211, 219
Codex Athous 189
Codex Sangermanensis 33, 114, 132, 230
Codex Sinaiticus 196, 198, 219, 230, 233
Codex Claromontanus 196
Deir-Bala'izah Papyrus 220, 221, 222, 223, 224, 227, 228
Liber ex lege Moysi 225, 226
Muratorian Fragment 219, 220, 223, 233
MS 265 225
P.I and I 4 230
P.Mich. 130 13
P.Mich. 2.2.129 229, 230
P.Mich. 2.2.130 229
P.Mich. Inv. 6427r 227
P.Oxy. I 5 33, 114, 132, 133, 134, 136, 227, 230
P.Oxy. L 3528 230
P.Oxy. XV 1828 230
P.Oxy. LXIX 4705 229
Pandect of Antiochus of Mar Saba 228
Paris BnF gr. 1143 232
translatio Latina vetus 108
translatio Latina palatina 108, 224

www.ingramcontent.com/pod-product-compliance
Lightning Source LLC
Chambersburg PA
CBHW020224170426
43201CB00007B/311